CW00400338

1 MONTH OF
FREE
READING

at

www.ForgottenBooks.com

By purchasing this book you are eligible for one month membership to ForgottenBooks.com, giving you unlimited access to our entire collection of over 1,000,000 titles via our web site and mobile apps.

To claim your free month visit:

www.forgottenbooks.com/free611267

* Offer is valid for 45 days from date of purchase. Terms and conditions apply.

ISBN 978-0-428-97447-3
PIBN 10611267

This book is a reproduction of an important historical work. Forgotten Books uses
state-of-the-art technology to digitally reconstruct the work, preserving the original format
whilst repairing imperfections present in the aged copy. In rare cases, an imperfection in
the original, such as a blemish or missing page, may be replicated in our edition. We do,
however, repair the vast majority of imperfections successfully; any imperfections that
remain are intentionally left to preserve the state of such historical works.

Forgotten Books is a registered trademark of FB &c Ltd.
Copyright © 2018 FB &c Ltd.
FB &c Ltd, Dalton House, 60 Windsor Avenue, London, SW19 2RR.
Company number 08720141. Registered in England and Wales.

For support please visit www.forgottenbooks.com

THE

Old and New Testament

Student.

WILLIAM R. HARPER, Ph. D., Editor.

VOLUME XI.

July to December, 1890.

WITH

PORTRAIT OF PROF. WILLIS J. BEECHER, D. D.

THE STUDENT PUBLISHING COMPANY,
336 Asylum Street, Hartford, Conn.
London Agency: Trübner & Co., 57 and 59 Ludgate Hill.

37082

TABLE OF CONTENTS.

JULY.

AUGUST.

SEPTEMBER.

OCTOBER.

NOVEMBER.

DECEMBER.

Prof. WILLIS J. BEECHER, D. D., of Auburn..

THE

Old and New Testament Student

VOL. XI.   JULY, 1890.   NO. 1.

THE list of special articles announced elsewhere to be published in the present volume of the STUDENT presents a
series of subjects connected with biblical study which cannot
fail to interest all earnest and broad-minded students. It is
amazing, if one but stops to think of it, how many fields of
investigation border closely upon the Bible; or, putting it
from another point of view, into how many fields of investigation the student of the Bible must penetrate. What with old
questions which need reconsideration, and new questions
which, all the time, are springing up, the interest continues
and deepens. We feel that we have provided for the table of
our constituency during the coming months substantials and
delicacies which, while satisfying and gratifying every taste,
will prove nourishing to all.

THERE are some men whom every one likes; their teachings
are appreciated and enjoyed not only by those who accept
them, but also by those who hold opinions differing from
them. It is the spirit of the man which exerts this influence.
This spirit is one of openness and frankness; it betokens a
manliness of the true sort. There is an honesty, a candor
which demand respect. All this is seen in the working of
the man's mind, in the influence it exerts upon others. It is
refreshing; it is stimulating. Such a man is really a rarity.
Open-minded, ready to receive, and yet not led away by
every new form of thought; liberal, appreciative, and yet

conservative in respect to all essential truths; with the historical sense thoroughly trained, with a literary taste well cultivated, with a love for truth which regulates and controls every thought,—this man is Willis J. Beecher, with whom the readers of the STUDENT have been familiar from the very beginning of its history, and of whom they will be pleased to read the accurate and sympathetic statement of his colleague, Professor Riggs.

A YEAR ago, it sometimes seems like a decade, the question of the plan of organization of the " Institute of Sacred Literature" was under consideration. There was much uncertainty in the minds of all in reference to the wisest course of action. A multitude of details must be agreed upon and systematized. It was not known whether the co-operation of those desired could be secured. In the minds of some there was serious doubt whether the plan, after all, was feasible. Within a single year the whole situation has changed. The details have been arranged, published, and are in successful operation. The heartiest assistance has been rendered by the leading men of every denomination. From hundreds of instructors and ministers has come the testimony, " This is just the organization we have needed for a long time." Fifteen men known in every section of the county as broad, aggressive and scholarly workers, have taken hold with a zeal and a determination which will certainly secure success. For some months two directorships of the fifteen remained unfilled. These vacancies are now filled, the Rev. Arthur Brooks, of New York City, and the Right Rev. Henry C. Potter, D. D., Bishop of New York, having accepted the positions. All the departments of study are organized. The Summer Schools of the Institute have opened most auspiciously. Every month the outlook broadens. Additional directors will, it is believed, be appointed, in order that the Board may include representatives of the South, of the Far West, and of Canada. Plans for the efficient organization of every state are being consummated. Friends are multiplying; possibilities increasing. What the

result of another year's development will be no one can forecast.   It is a great work, a glorious work.

———

THE frank and strong utterances of the participants in the
"Symposium" on expository preaching which readers of the
STUDENT have observed and doubtless enjoyed, are now
crowned by the last word which is spoken by Dr. Wm. M.
Taylor, a prince among expository preachers.   The experiences of these men and their advice growing out of this
experience ought to be carefully pondered by many clergymen.   The effect of their words will not be lost.   Many
congregations will enjoy the fruit in the beginnings of successful expository work on the part of their preachers.   Much
interest has already been manifested in the "symposium"
and suggestions as well as experiences have come unsolicited
from readers.   One of these contributions which adds names
of weight to those who have already expressed themselves on
the subject is as follows:

"The importance of expository preaching was urged upon
the attention of the students of Union Seminary by Dr. Wm.
Adams, who said once, 'Young gentlemen, do not forever
give your people crumbs of the bread of life, but now and
then give them a good generous slice.'   When one of his
pupils explained to his church the blessedness of believers as
shown in the eight beatitudes, a hearer said to him 'you
gave us a good slice of the bread of life to-day and it was
well buttered.'   Dr. R. D. Hitchcock, that noble preacher,
said that the salvation of a young clergyman depended on
his study of the Bible.   'Every young man,' he remarked,
'has about material enough for a hundred sermons; when
that is gone he must repeat, or move on, unless he studies.   I
advise you to have one-half of your sermons expository of
some book or character.'"

———

THE average man has no interest in the past, and very
little if any in the future, having ears, eyes and thought only
for the present.   It is the task of the historical scholar to

show him that in the past were grown the ideas and movements which appear in the present and will have their influence also upon the future. This is often a thankless task and
must look for its reward in the enjoyment and the benefit
which lie in the elucidation of truth and the grasp which such
study gives upon the course and destiny of humanity. There
are certain lines of work in which the historical scholar and
the student of the Bible are co-laborers. In the fundamental
purpose just stated in its relation to history in general, the student of the Bible finds his most important work. To follow
down the course of the biblical ideas as they enter and permeate the life of men—to discover for us the influence of the
biblical life upon the subsequent history of humanity and to
demonstrate before the eyes of the present how much we owe
to that sacred past—this is one of the highest and most salutary achievements of the historical student of the Scriptures.
But his labors too, are often disregarded and he must again
and again remind men of the dependence of this age with its
methods of thought and its standards of truth and life upon
the life and thought of the Bible.

It has been well said by a recent writer that many movements of our time indicate a way of looking at life and its
problems which would never have been possible but for the
Old Testament with its law and its history of the chosen people. It is this portion of the Bible, too much neglected by
men, which has entered into the very essence of our civilization. It is readily granted that our debt to the Founder of
Christianity is overwhelmingly great. It is not so clearly
understood that the Old Testament not only made Christianity, in a very real sense, possible, gave it a standing place
from which to move the world—but has, also, independently,
been taken up into the world's life, baptized with the spirit
of the Gospel, and sent forth on its mission of proclaiming
the ethical ideal of man and the strong imperative of duty.
What does not man to-day owe to the Old Testament? One
must remember also that for centuries the Jew has steadily
held to his heart this volume and found, even in what we
must regard as a narrow literalism, life and light in its pages.
Let us be generous; nay, let us be honest, and acknowledge

that there is much to be said in favor of the words of this same writer, who declares: "Thus it is that while ready and willing to acknowledge all it owes to the art and philosophy of Greece and what little it owes to Rome, people too readily forget that nearly all that is precious in the moral aspects of our gradually developing civilization, the ever increasing respect for human life and the feeling of human brotherhood, not only originated in the code of Sinai, but have been preserved through the ages by Jewish piety, and often at the cost of Jewish martyrdom."

THE secret of success in anything is concentration. Especially is this true in study. Of no department of study is it more true than of the Bible. There is no book or class of books in the study of which less concentration of effort has been practised than the Bible. This deficiency is seen (1) in the failure to give *consecutive time* to its study; for who is there that gives week after week, or month after month, of close, continuous study to its mastery? Not the Sunday-school pupil, for a few minutes a week is the most which he devotes to it, the result being not much greater than if it were a few seconds rather than a few minutes. Not the Sunday-school teacher, for he finds it difficult to secure even two hours for study, and this is too frequently broken into fragments, or spent in an effort to learn how to teach something which he has not learned, and which he does not know. Not the college student, even in colleges where the Bible is taught, for it is but one of half a dozen of subjects, taken up once or twice a week, with time between each exercise for the effect of the preceding exercise to have been utterly dissipated. Not the theological student, whose case is virtually that of the college student. Not the minister, for his time is occupied, so far as he makes use of the Bible, in an effort to adjust it to the great ideas which, with herculean effort, he has brought forth from within himself; and if he makes use of the original languages, as possibly one in a hundred, or one in a thousand does, perhaps ten minutes each morning are devoted to it. The deficiency is seen moreover (2) in the failure to employ a *consecutive method* of study. *Verses* are studied as if the particular verse under consideration were a diamond, and all that preceded and followed it were but common clay. One reads three or four chapters in Isaiah, forgetful that these are but part of a whole, the comprehension of which in its entirety is, after all, the great thing to be desired.

It cannot be denied that the faculty of concentration is one difficult to acquire; some never obtain it. It is also true that the opportunity to concentrate is hard to find, even by those who may have the ability. But, no matter how difficult it may be, it is, of all things, the essential thing. If the same amount of time now given to the Bible by the average Sunday-school pupil or teacher, on fifty-two Sundays, could be condensed within *ten*, the result would be five times as great. If the college or divinity student who attends two exercises a *week* in a given subject for thirty weeks, could have them one a day for ten weeks, or two a day for five weeks, he would accomplish twice or three times as much. The same thing will be found true in every line of work. The bane of modern education is the dissipation of effort resulting from a lack of appreciation of this fundamental principle.

AMERICAN OLD TESTAMENT SCHOLARS:
WILLIS JUDSON BEECHER.

By Rev. Professor J. S. RIGGS,

Auburn Theological Seminary, Auburn, N. Y.

Prof. Willis Judson Beecher, D. D., was born April 29th, 1838, in the little town of Hampden, on the Western Reserve, in Ohio, when his father was there settled as the pastor of a Home Mission Church. The family came originally from New Haven, Conn., and the same indomitable energy which had marked the father's struggles for an education doubtless led him to undertake the arduous duties of the home missionary of those days. The account we have before us tells how, in addition to all mission duties, he gradually rendered habitable the little unfurnished house which he had bought, adding room to room largely by the labor of his own hands. Amid such humble but stimulating and ennobling surroundings began Prof. Beecher's life. His father's energy certainly reappears in him; and it began to manifest itself very early, for at the age of three little Willis read English without even having been known to learn to read, and when only nine years old, he was poring over Rollin's Ancient History, Josephus, Calmet's Dictionary and the Encyclopedia of Religious Knowledge. He could have been fully ready to enter Yale College at the age of twelve, but wise counsels prevailed, and his growing absorption in books was for a time prevented by interest in other things. Twice before this alteration in his son's course, his father had changed his field of labor, going first to Ellsworth, Litchfield County, Conn., where he remained five years, and then to Central New York. Declining health here warned him against the strenuous labors of the pulpit, and he purchased a farm in Vernon Centre. To the care of this all the forces of the family were called, and for a time the cause of theological education ran an imminent risk of losing one of its strongest helpers, for the ambition to be a farmer gained in attractiveness despite the genuinely hard work which it forced upon the boys. "I became convinced that agriculture is the bed rock of the social system, and inclined to devote my life to its glorious pursuits." This was not, however, the father's desire for his son, and at the age of sixteen pressure was brought to bear upon him to renew his preparation for college. It is of interest to note that something of the old ease in study had gone when books were taken up again, but the steady habit of hard, earnest, careful work had been but strengthened, so that we are not surprised to read that he graduated from Hamilton College in 1858 as the Valedictorian of the class, and with the highest prize in the classics. Among his associates in college were Drs. Herrick Johnson, A. T. Pierson, J. H. Hall, J. A. Paine, Judge G. J. Wallace, and others who have made their mark. The same year of his graduation his father died. For three years after leaving college he was a teacher in Whitestone Seminary, near Utica, and thence he went to Auburn to take his course in theology. The same quiet, thoughtful studiousness that had marked his life in college was again very evident in his course in the seminary, and gave a forecast of what his life would be. Upon graduation from the seminary, he became a pastor at Ovid, N. Y., where he remained only two years, accepting a call at the end of that time to become Professor of Moral Science and Belles Letters in Knox College, Galesburg, Ill. He was also for two years a pastor in Galesburg, whence in 1869 he was called back to Auburn to take the Professorship of Hebrew Language and Literature in the Theological Seminary. Despite the fact that there is in this recital no account of fellowships and foreign study, so common now as part of a preparation for a professorship, there is yet that happy combination of the teacher's experience with that of the pastor, which works toward the highest efficiency in the peculiar work of a theological seminary—contact with men as well as books; a study of minds as well as thoughts—these have all through been working together toward results now so strong and helpful in Professor Beecher's life and influence. It has been the custom for the incumbent of the Hebrew Chair in Auburn Seminary upon beginning his work to contribute some

literary offering to the Board of Publication. Dr. Beecher
sent them his first book, "Father Tompkins and His
Bibles," a little work full of interest and instruction, and
written in a careful, lucid style, characteristic of his pen.
Indeed, this was by no means the beginning of his literary
activity outside of merely professional work. As far back as
the time when he was in college he had written various newspaper articles, and in the three years following his college
course he published essays in the local papers in Waterville,
Vernon, Fredonia and Utica. Student as he is, in the best
senses of the word, Dr. Beecher has nevertheless had a keen
and watchful interest in all the social, political and religious
problems of the day. From the time he left college he has
been in touch with all the important movements of the day,
and sought for a clear, well-defined judgment regarding them.
These judgments he has given to the world in our leading
religious journals and reviews. They are characterized by a
noteworthy clearness in style, sobriety and conclusiveness in
statement. Such are, e. g., his articles—"Is Total Abstinence True Temperance?" in the *Presbyterian Review*, April,
1882; "The New Total Abstinence Creed," *Forum*, 1886; "A
Few Thoughts on New Departures," a pamphlet published in
1884. So busy has he been in this way, that could all his
publications of a general character be brought together, they
would make a good-sized volume. One of Dr. Beecher's
notable traits—fidelity to duty in any society or organization
of which he is a member—has also brought him a vast amount
of extra work. Reports, records, special papers, addresses—
these would go a long way toward another volume—and yet
we have not entered upon the record of his distinctive work as
a professor. Here he has been indefatigable. Beside his
constant contributions of careful book reviews to the *Presbyterian Review*, the *Bibliotheca Sacra*, the *Andover Review*, and the
Presbyterian and Reformed Review, he has had a part in the
leading articles of such periodicals as the *Princeton Review*, the
Journal of the Exegetical Society, the *Old and New Testament
Student*, *Christian Thought*, and the *Homiletic Review*. The
titles of a few will indicate their character: "Chronology of
Kings of Israel and Judah," *Presbyterian Review*, April, 1880;

" The Logical Methods of Professor Kuenen ;" " The Historical Situation in Joel and Obadiah." In view of the general
acquaintance of students with these, we need do no more than
refer to the critical acumen, mental grasp and power of discriminating statement, which they reveal. In merited recognition of his learning and judgment, he was invited
to prepare a large number of articles for the *American
Supplement to the Encyclopædia Britannica.* The list
includes such weighty topics as " Bible," " Canon
of Scripture," " Daniel," " Israel," " Pentateuch,"
" Prophets," " Septuagint," " Tabernacle." It does not, of
course, lie within the scope of a paper like this to enter into
any detailed estimate of this work. It is our purpose to call
attention rather to the rich fruitage of a thoughtful mind that
has been increasingly productive. And withal, we have
hitherto passed by reference to all the historical matter concerning Auburn Seminary, including a General Catalogue of
the Seminary which he has published. Sufficient has been
written to give the reader some idea of Dr. Beecher's mental
diligence and achievement. To know his power one must
follow him as he goes unhesitatingly and undeviatingly
through the thick of conflicting opinions and theories to the
central question, and to *that* gives a clear and independent
answer, or as he opens the way step by step through tangled
and obscure regions of history or interpretation. We pass to
note briefly some of his qualities as a preacher, a teacher and
friend. Dr. Beecher makes no claim to be an orator. His
pulpit utterances command attention by reason of their
thoughtfulness and evident sincerity. He usually preaches
without manuscript, has his subject thoroughly in hand, and
speaks in a conversational tone. He is didactic in method,
quiet in manner, and leaves the hearer often to make his own
application of the truth unfolded. His original, striking,
truthful interpretations of Scripture fasten attention and leave
lasting impressions. Had nature blessed him with such gifts
as a speaker as he already possesses as a thinker, it is questionable if he could be spared from the pulpit.

Among the early impressions which a student receives from
him as a teacher are those of thoroughness, fairness and ac-

curacy.   There is nothing especially magnetic in his class-room; but he soon inspires confidence and the highest respect. Notably does one soon realize that he has his subject fully at command, and with the utmost fairness to all who disagree, makes clear the grounds of his own judgment.   He is conservative, yet from no fear of anything but the truth itself.   As earnestly and ably as he has contended with the conservative critics of the day for the unity of the Pentateuch and its Mosaic authorship, he would as willingly accept the very opposite of either of these conclusions if they could be substantiated by evidence.   In his wisdom he refuses to make the truth of God dependent simply upon historical criticism; and yet he stands with the conservative side, because facts and truth seem to him to support that side.   His accuracy is enviable; and yet severe as he is with himself in this regard, he is very forbearing with students who find Hebrew slow and difficult work.   Naturally, he has from the students an ever-increasing esteem.   In no class-room of the same department of work can students be more satisfactorily guided or helped to safe conclusions in the great biblical questions of the day. This is saying much, and no invidious comparison is meant. It is simply the estimate of an old pupil who now has the privilege of working side by side with an honored teacher.

To whom Dr. Beecher is a friend, he is a friend indeed. Genial, sincere, disposed to see the good in every man— patient, modest, faithful—such are some of his marked qualities.   He is rather reticent, but helpful in advice, because cautious in judgment.   He is a man of comparatively few words, but these are usually to the point, and therefore sufficient.   His long service to Auburn Seminary has been a blessing in every way to the institution, and the earnest wish of all its friends is that he may yet be spared many years to carry forward the noble work which thus far has been so successfully done.

THE GENESIS OF THE HEAVENS AND THE EARTH AND ALL THE HOST OF THEM.*† I.

By Prof. JAMES D. DANA, LL. D.,
Yale University, New Haven, Conn.

The subject before us is the bearing of the results of Nature's teachings on the character of ancient cosmogonic records. And since but one document has sufficient completeness and authority to merit consideration in this respect, and that is the opening chapter of the Bible, it is essentially a comparison between the teaching of God's Word and the teachings of Nature, or His works.

The cosmogonies of Babylonia and Egypt would be of great interest if we had them in detail. The fragments thus far gathered afford some striking coincidences with the biblical record. In the Babylonian, according to the deciphering of tablets by the Assyrian scholar, the late Mr. George Smith, the coincidences exist in the general arrangement; in the idea of a god speaking; in the idea of universal waters answering to "waters" in the second verse of Genesis; in the mention of the stars as appointed to determine the year; in the introduction, after the announcement of each creative work, of the eulogistic expression "delightful," answering to good in Genesis. "God saw that it was good." But with all this concordance, the religion of the earliest Babylonians was multifariously polytheistic, and it, therefore, seems probable that they had derived these ideas from some earlier monotheistic document or tradition.

In the oldest Egyptian cosmogony there is also the ascription of speech to God. Besides this, the resemblances include

---

* A lecture delivered at Yale College, March 29, 1890.

† The views on the first chapter of Genesis contained in this article are not different from those published by the author in the Bibliotheca Sacra for April, 1885. But the subject is more expanded and somewhat differently presented, and some collateral points are introduced.

the idea of a chaos at the beginning; the stirring of the primeval waters by the divine breath; the creation of light before the sun—the Egyptian god, Thoth, being said to have given the world light when all was darkness, "and there was no sun," and in a recognition of the moulding hand of the Deity. Egypt has been claimed, from the character of some early records, to have been in an early, if not its earliest, state almost monotheistic, though later diverging widely from this.

The Assyrian tablets read by Mr. Smith were from the palace of King Assurbanipal, and, therefore, not older than 673 years before Christ. But there is reason for believing, says Mr. Smith, that the original sources of the doctrines were not less than 2000 years B. C. However this may be, the three cosmogonies, the Babylonian, the Egyptian, and the Mosaic, are like lines converging backward toward a more ancient and original tradition as a common source. And the convergence also toward monotheism affords a strong support of the view that a purely monotheistic system of cosmogony, like that of the Bible, was the original.

The idea of monotheism in that early age could not have been a natural growth or slow development; for the tendency of human reason, under the influence of the various causes of fear, dread, awe, in the world, would have been all against it. There could have been no source short of divine inspiration. The systems of religious belief that have held sway among the nations have not been slow developments, but instead, the enforced ideas of a few individuals whose high qualities gave them the power and position of great leaders. And in the implanting of the idea of the one God, the same must have been true. God enlightened the prophet, fitted him for His divine work, and exalted him thereby into a man of authority. The slowness of the Jews in accepting the idea of monotheism, notwithstanding the line of prophets, proves the impossibility of its being a natural growth. It was divinely nurtured, as well as divinely implanted. It made little progress outside of the Jewish nation before the advent of Christ, the Divine Teacher, who came as a light to the world.

To the same divine origin must we trace the only monotheistic cosmogony; and it has its right place as the opening chapter of a history of the development in man of the idea of One God.

We come now to the biblical narrative and a comparison of its announcements, with the records placed by the same Divine Author in the earth's structure, and the declarations of His will and the display of His wisdom in Nature's laws.

By way of introduction, an abstract of the first chapter of Genesis is here given.

After the opening words of the first verse, "In the beginning God created the Heaven and the Earth," we read as follows:—

On the *first* day there was the appearance of Light. The account says the spirit of God moved or brooded over the deep or abyss (called also "waters"), and God said, "Let Light be, and Light was."

On the *second* day the firmament was made in the midst of the waters, to divide the waters from the waters—the waters below from the waters above the firmament.

On the *third* day the waters of the Earth were gathered together into one place, and dry land appeared, which work God pronounced good.

There was also a second work on this day, the creation of *plants*, "and God saw that it was good."

On the *fourth* day the lights, the sun and moon and stars, were "made," to divide the day from the night, and "for signs, for seasons, for days and for years."

On the *fifth* day "the waters brought forth" abundantly every moving thing, and the fowls of the air.

On the *sixth* day "the Earth brought forth" the cattle, the creeping thing, and the beasts of the earth.

Again, on the same day, God said, "Let us make Man in our image, after our likeness."

Having pronounced each previous work severally "good," the whole creation at the end is pronounced, in like style, "very good;" and then come the closing words, "'THUS THE HEAVENS AND THE EARTH WERE FINISHED, AND ALL THE HOST OF THEM.' And, on the seventh day, God rested from all His work which He had made."

Before proceeding with the interpretation in the light of existing facts, I wish to say again that I believe the record to be a divine record. I believe not only the first verse to be true, but each verse to be worthy of its place in the Bible. I would not separate this first verse from its pronounced theism, and call the next an adapted fable, meaning thereby that it is little worth studying and interpreting: for I find no evidence of this in the chapter itself, which has God's approbation stamped on each day's work, nor in the events announced when viewed with the aid of modern science. If the narrative must be regarded as one of several documents that were compiled to make up the early portion of the Bible, as some biblical scholars hold, I would still claim for it a place among the earliest and most extraordinary of historical records, and none the less divine, none the less worthy of study.

Again, I would ask you not to approach the subject prejudiced with the oft-repeated statement that geology is an immature science; has made many mistakes and may be expected to make many more; or by the equally common remark that the chapter was not intended to teach natural or physical science; or by the companion remark that all attempts to use science in interpretation are, and will always be, failures. The feeling often seems to be that science is profane, the Bible divine, when in fact all truth is equally divine.

You probably never heard of any one going to the Bible for scientific instruction. The fact is that the first chapter of Genesis does not teach science. It gives simply the order of events in creation and God's agency in those events. Only half of it is open to geological argument or illustration; and the arguments appeal to but few geological facts; moreover, they are facts that no geologist doubts. Geological facts and reasonings have no reference to any work of the six days, except that of the third, fifth and sixth.

The Bible says, speaking of the fourth day's work: Let the waters be gathered together into one place, and let the dry (land) appear, and "it was so;" and geology echoes "it was so." The Bible gives the order of the several creations—first, plants; next the lower animals; next the higher; and lastly, Man. And geology says "it was so;" in other words, that the successive events in the geological history of life correspond in a general way with these announcements in Genesis. This is so far a harmless use of geology. What it has to say beyond this is a wonderful revelation with regard to the systems of life; but this is supplementary illustration, not part of the geological argument.

Geology proves that there are discrepancies between science and the record; discrepancies with regard to the kinds of plants which made up the first life of the globe, and on some other similar points. If it states these discrepancies and explains them, it does its duty; and it is very certain that any assertions it may make on the subject will be based on well-established facts.

The interpretation of the word *day* appeals to geology for its testimony; and the testimony received is that there were no twenty-four hour days in the history of creation at any time; and it says this knowing it to be beyond all question true.

To the words, " Let the earth bring forth the grass, the herb yielding seed;" "let the waters bring forth the moving creature;" "let the earth bring forth the living creature after his kind, cattle and creeping thing," geology makes no objection. It accepts them as not teaching the direct creation of species by a divine fiat, but their creation by some other method; for this is in the language. As in Nature, so in the Bible: nowhere is it taught that species were made by special divine acts for each—Man excepted.

About the work of the first, second and fourth days, geology has nothing to say. The recorded events are out of its range. Physical science is naturally appealed to for facts corresponding with that of the first day; but the second and fourth days are left to reasonable exegesis and judicious conjecture.

Now, let us take up the chapter believing that geology is honest and knows what it says, and that science of whatever kind is presenting facts when it claims to present facts; and believing that the chapter is *all*, not merely the first verse, good theism; and that the brief review of the majestic march of events before Man makes a wonderfully fitting prelude to God's message to man of law and love, constituting the Bible.

The interpretation which I present is, with small exceptions, that of Professor Guyot, till recently Professor of Physical Geography at Princeton.   His first published work on the subject appeared just before his decease, in 1884*, but his first communication to me of his views took place in my own house thirty-four years before, soon after his arrival in this country from Switzerland.

It is an interesting fact with regard to Professor Guyot's interpretation of the chapter that, although he had pursued for a while theological studies at Berlin, the views were not a result of an effort to harmonize the Bible and science.   He was preparing, at Neufchatel, over fifty years since, a course of lectures on General History, he being Professor of History in the Swiss University, and thought to commence it with an introductory lecture on Cosmogony, or the world before Man, for which astronomy, biology and geology, afforded facts.   He worked out the order of events without a thought of the first chapter of Genesis.   When his cosmogony, thus deduced, was completed, it flashed upon him, he says, that it set forth essentially the same order of events as the cosmogony of the Bible.   He then took up Genesis for careful study, and the explanations which he has published were the result. This is the right way to approach the subject.

To proceed with the discussion.

It is necessary, at the outset, to recognize two fundamental principles in the interpretation.

First—*A physiological fact bearing on the character of the ancient document.*   The history, if a communication from the Deity to man, should have in its words the limitations that necessarily pertain to a human scribe.   Man's comprehension of an idea communicated by another is limited by the amount and character of his knowledge and beliefs, and the terms or expressions he would use in transcribing it would be thereby determined.   For example, the expression ''plants'' means to an ordinary man ordinary plants, such as he sees about him. Having the impressions of the natural world grown into him, he could not have grasped the general idea of a plant, and recognized the essential attributes in the simplest of species,

---

* Creation, or the Biblical Cosmogony in the Light of Modern Science.   140 pp. 12mo., 1884. (Charles Scribner's Sons.)

however the idea might have been expressed. So again, the idea of space about the earth would necessarily take shape in the mind as that of a solid firmament with men who never had any other idea on the subject, even if the author imparting the idea were divine. Further, man, in his limited experience, would naturally have conceived only of completed results after each fiat, even if the language communicated to him were as adverse to it as the expressions, "Let the waters bring forth;" "let the earth bring forth."

Secondly—*The creative works mark off grand epochs in creation's history.*—To comprehend the narrative, if it be divine, and discern the truth pervading it, we must enter into its spirit. We must understand that it contains but brief announcements of the grand steps of progress in the earth's genesis. Each step in the progress to be of sufficient importance to make one of the eight—those of the eight fiats—ought to correspond to the introduction of some new phase or idea of fundamental significance. Such it must be if written by a man of supreme intelligence and exalted philosophy. Such it must be if God is the author. A method of interpretation that puts among the eight an event not of this epochal character should be received with doubt.

I pass now to the narrative.

First—*The system in its arrangement.*—Of the six days of Genesis, the first three are like the last three in having *light* as the work of the first of the three days, and in having *two* great works on the last of the three. There is, thus, a parallelism in movement between the two halves, or the first and second triads. On the first day, the light was the *light* of the universe, dependent on the constitution of matter; on the fourth day, the first of the second triad, it was the *light* from the sun, moon, and stars to the earth.

Further, the first triad includes the events connected with the *Inorganic* history of the earth, the last of which, on the third day, was the arrangement of the lands and seas. The second triad is occupied with the events of the *Organic* history, from the creation of the first animals to man.

Further, the third day, or the last of the first triad, ends with the creation of plants as its second great work; and this creation of plants was the introduction of the new element, Life, a new creation, inconceivably above the physical forces of dead matter before existing, betokening the grand line of progress during the succeeding era. So on the sixth day, the last of the second triad, the second great work is the creation of Man, a being made in the image of God, and destined through His spiritual nature to immortal progress.

Thus, as Professor Guyot explains, the last day of each era, the Inorganic and the Organic embraced one work typical of the era and another prophetic of the future.

This system of arrangement is not the student's fancy. It is in the record profoundly, and the fact displays purpose in the author of the document and knowledge of philosophy beyond that of man.

This system may be better understood from the following scheme:—

I. Inorganic History.
- 1st Day. Light.
- 2nd Day. The firmament dividing the waters from the waters.
- 3d Day.
  - 1. The appearance of dry land in the seas.
  - 2. The creation of plants.

II. Organic History.
- 4th Day. Light to the earth from the sun, etc., to divide the day from the night.
- 5th Day. Creation of the inferior animals, with fishes, birds, aquatic reptiles.
- 6th Day.
  - 1. The creation of mammals or quadrupeds, with other reptiles.
  - 2. The creation of Man.

III. 7th Day. God's day of rest; Man's redemption.

The beginning: the formless earth; verses 1, 2.*—The first verse of the chapter, besides proclaiming God the creator of the "heaven and the earth," teaches that the beginning of the heaven and the earth was the beginning of the existing

---

* [1] In the beginning God created the heaven and the earth. [2] And the earth was waste and void; and darkness *was* upon the face of the deep. And the Spirit of the God brooded upon the face of the waters.

universe. So says science also, as far as its facts and safe reasonings reach back. There was a beginning, says geology, to man; and farther back, to mammals, to birds and to reptiles, to fishes and all the lower animals, and to plants; a beginning to life; a beginning, it says, also, to mountain ranges and valleys, to lands and seas, to rocks. Hence science takes another step back, and admits or claims a beginning to the earth, a beginning to all planets and suns, and a beginning to the universe. Science and the record in Genesis are thus one. This is not reconciliation; it is accordance.

It is not uncommon to separate the first sentence of the chapter from the rest, making it to refer to a beginning time indefinitely far back of the first day of the described creation. There is no warrant for this in the document itself. The announcement, "In the beginning God created the heaven and the earth," is immediately followed by a description of the events of the creation announced, and particularly that of the earth. And at the end of the document it is added, "Thus the heavens and the earth were finished, and all the host of them," affirming that the creation of the heavens and the earth announced in the opening words was completed.

The words of the first and second verses relating to the earth imply that "in the beginning" it was "without form and void," or, as another translator has it, "formless and naught," or as translated in the Septuagint, "invisible and uncomposed." If the "beginning" was the beginning of creative works, the beginning of the universe, the earth was literally "formless and naught," "invisible and uncomposed."

The waters over which the Spirit brooded: LIGHT *the creation of the first day;* verses 3–5.* — The actual condition of the earth at "the beginning" is partly indicated by the fiat of the first day: "Let light be, and light was." The light was not that of the sun, for the sun is first mentioned on the fourth day. It must, therefore,

---

* [3] And God said, Let there be light: and there was light. [4] And God saw the light, that *it was* good: and God divided the light from the darkness. [5] And God called the light Day, and the darkness He called Night. And there was evening and there was morning, day first.

have been light in its essence or nature, and therefore the first light of the universe, for, once existing, there could be no second creation of light in the universe. The phenomena of light have been proved to be a result of molecular action, and to be dependent upon fundamental qualities of matter as it is now constituted. Man has found that the laws of heat and of electrical and chemical action are so involved with those of light that all these conditions are convertible and one in molecular origin. Since light has, therefore, no existence apart from molecular action, its creation was not the creation of an element, or of a something admitting of independent existence. And as light, heat, electricity are results of molecular activity, the fiat was the initiation of activity in matter, till then inert. Moreover, the fiat must have preceded the existence of water and of earth, of liquid or solid or gaseous compounds of every kind. For light is manifested in the making of such compounds. Our electric lighting is produced through the decomposition of water, and the same light was manifested at the first origin of water.

We thus learn that Light, at the command " Let Light be," was the signal of creation begun; of physical and chemical changes begun that were to evolve systems of worlds, and, within these systems, suns and planets; and, therefore, the signal of the beginning of the " generations of the heavens," or of the development of the universe. Before the fiat, the " earth" must have been literally " formless and naught," or " invisible and uncomposed;" and the " waters" over which " the Spirit of God brooded" before the fiat, " Let Light be," were literally a " deep" or " abyss" in utter darkness, not literal waters.

The latest readings of science thus declare, as emphatically as the Bible, that on the first day " Light was." Here is accordance between science and the Bible; a most marvelous accordance supposing the chapter not inspired; a delighting, soul-stirring accordance to the man of faith in God's word and works.

Before passing on, I will say a word with reference to another view of the earth's condition when creation begun which has been often set forth. It supposes that the earth was in a state of chaos, cold as the intense cold of space, dark, bare, and desolate, and that the creation recorded in Genesis consisted in giving it light and heat, continents and seas, plants and animals, and lastly man.

But such a frigid, frozen globe would have been almost cloudless. Its skies at night would have been studded with stars, and brightened by the changing moon, and now and then streaked by meteors, making heat and light by friction in their movement through the upper air. Darkness would have been impossible. During the day the sun would have shone over the chaos with rays undimmed by cloud or mist, making a well-lighted earth; and why not a well-warmed earth. Under such circumstances the fiat " Let Light be" becomes meaningless.

You may say that the sun, also, was then a dark chaotic globe. The supposition is easily made. But the conditions supposed are an impossibility in the face of existing physical and astronomical knowledge. The earth and sun and stars are one in system. The earth could not have been in existence before the sun. The sun was never a dark globe.

The evening and the morning; day first, v. 5.—The word *day* in the chapter, with the accompanying expression, *evening and morning*, naturally suggests days of twenty-four hours; and many translators still assert that the Hebrew will not admit of any other signification. But the subject or the occasion sometimes reasonably influences interpretation where the literal rendering is not disputed. We must here have in mind, and realize, that the narrative speaks not of some laborer working by the day and resting at night, but of the infinite God, who measures time by no rolling atom in space; who allows over a thousand years for the maturing of some of the plants with which he has adorned this globe; who secures his ends not by violence in the briefest moment —man's criterion of greatness—but by the still and prolonged action of His own irresistible power, evolving vast and varied results through seemingly trivial agencies, in which and by which He executes His will. With correct views on this point, we cannot fail to recognize that days of twenty-four hours are as much opposed to the spirit of the Bible cosmogony or any true cosmogony as they are to the majesty of the Deity Himself and the declarations of His workings in the earth's structure.   Moreover, it is hardly possible that Moses, who wrote—see the 90th Psalm, which is ascribed to Moses— "A thousand years in Thy sight are but as yesterday when it is past," and "Before the mountains were brought forth, or ever Thou had formed the earth and the world, even from everlasting to everlasting, Thou art God," entertained so belittling an idea of the Creator and His work.

Further, the word *day* is used in the account in four different senses, as it is in our own language, and a fifth is introduced in a following verse.   (1) In verse 5 God called the light day; (2) close of verses 3, 5, 8, 13, the evening and morning were one day before there was a sun to mark off days; (3) verse 16, the sun is appointed to rule the *day*, and the lesser light to rule the night—a day of twelve hours; (4) verse 14, the sun is appointed for signs and for seasons and for *days* and years —days of twenty-four hours; again, in the second chapter, 4th verse (5), the whole period of creation is spoken of as the day in which the Lord God made the earth and the heavens. We have, therefore, the light called day; days before there was a sun; days of twenty-four hours; days of twelve hours; and the whole period of creation a day.   Thus there is sufficient authority for whichever use of the word the subject requires.

The expression "evening and morning" indicates, by a familiar metaphor, the beginning and consummation of each work.   It was used for the first day, which was preceded by darkness, but which strictly had no evening.   Night is the natural prelude to the day and day's work.   The time before a work begins is like a night or darkness as respects that work; its commencing progress is the dawn; its consummation is the meridian.   In illustration of this, I cite a fact from the *Journal of the Deputation of Missionaries of a Tour around Hawaii*, published at Boston in 1825 (page 137).   It is there stated that the Hawaiians, when they wish to express the existence of anything from the beginning, say that it has been so "mai ka po mai," *from the night till now*.   Their traditions refer the beginning of things to *night*, and the present state they call *day*, or *state of light*.   Thus the uncivilized people and the civilized are alike in usage.

[To be continued.]

EXPOSITORY PREACHING.*

By Rev. WILLIAM M. TAYLOR, D. D.,
New York City.

1. By expository preaching I understand the presentation in simple and clear phraseology of the meaning of the section of Holy Scripture that is under consideration as viewed in its relation to the purpose of the writer and the context in which it is found; then the distillation therefrom of the principles of permanent importance which underlie the section, and the enforcement of these in their relation to the life of the present day.

2. Every sermon, in my judgment, ought to be an outgrowth from the exposition of the text. But the exposition of a book of Scripture ought to be prosecuted in regular course at one of the services on each Lord's day. This used to be, and very largely is still, the habit in Scotland, and it has greatly contributed to the scriptural intelligence of the churches there.

3. In the prosecution of this work as of others, there will be special aptitudes in the man,—or the reverse,—but I think that no gifts other than those that may easily be acquired by a man of average ability are needed for doing it successfully.

4. The preparation that is most required will involve a familiar acquaintance with the grammar and idioms of the original languages, a patient investigation of the relation of each clause in the section to all the rest, and of the section itself to the object which the author has in view. Add to this a knowledge of the preacher's own heart, an acquaintance

* These suggestions were sent to the Editor in response to the questions concerning Expository Preaching with which the readers of the STUDENT have been made familiar in the " Symposium " on that subject which appeared in the May and June issues. The article of Dr. Taylor arrived too late for insertion with the other communications, and its excellence, together with the well-known ability of its author in the line of Expository Preaching, will be a sufficient warrant for presenting it by itself in the present issue.

with the circumstances and needs of his people and a spirit of prayer and a man so furnished will be in my judgment well furnished for the work.   But he must not suppose that it is easier to preach after the expository than after the so-called topical manner.   Exposition to be successfully done will require greater study than the preparation of a topical sermon.

5. I should recommend those who wish to prosecute the expository method to begin with the narrative portions of the Bible, both for their own sakes and for the sake of the education of their hearers.   The four Gospels, or the historical and biographical portions of the Old Testament, or the book of the Acts of the Apostles might be recommended to a beginner; then the Epistles and then the Prophets.   Excellent courses of exposition might be found in the Parables and Miracles of our Lord, in separate biographies of one or two of the Apostles, and in the lives of Joseph, Moses, David, Daniel and the like.

6. I do not know of any special reasons why at this day this method should have prominence; but it seems to me that one great purpose of preaching in any age is the explanation and enforcement of the Word of God, and there are some special advantages from doing that in the expository way which are and ought to be obvious to every preacher.   For one thing, it would bring both preacher and hearer into direct contact with the Word of God; for another, it would afford opportunity for the treatment of subjects which otherwise might be overlooked, and for exposing evils existing among the people without the preacher's laying himself open to the imputation of having purposely chosen the subject for any personal or local reason.

I have not had time to give to the subject the attention which it deserves; but you will find my views on it set forth at length in the VIIth Lecture of my first Yale course on preaching which has been published by Randolph and Co., under the title of "The Ministry of the Word."

OLD TESTAMENT WORK IN BERLIN.

By Owen H. Gates, Ph. D.,

Berlin, Germany.

What is being done in Berlin cannot fail to be of interest to students in America. This proposition, true in its whole breadth, can be narrowed down step by step, becoming constantly more emphatically true, till the statement is reached, that what the Professors in Berlin University offer in the way of lectures upon the Old Testament must be of interest to students of the Old Testament at home. Some will come to the University for study; more will read the views propounded here; all will feel the influence that directly or indirectly emanates from this centre of thought. Without presuming to be an artist, the writer proposes to show a photograph of what is offered here, and give some details that cannot be learned except from one who has been on the ground.

There are in the Theological Faculty three Professors who lecture upon Old Testament topics: August Dillmann, Paul Kleinert, and Hermann Strack, who is yet Professor Extraordinary. Dillmann is sixty-seven years old, has held Professorships at Tübingen, Kiel and Giessen, and was called to Berlin in 1869. Kleinert is fifty-three years old, and has been in Berlin since 1863—since 1864 in the University. His lectures are chiefly upon Practical Theology. Strack is forty-two years of age, and has been Professor in the University since 1877. There have been no changes in this department since the then *Privat Docenten* Nowack and Vatke left about ten years ago.

The following sketch is gathered form the Verzeichniss of Lectures for the last ten years, and from what one can personally observe during a couple of Semesters.

Strack has lectured every summer during this period, upon Introduction. Every winter he offers a course in Hebrew Grammar; Hebrew is a study very properly taught in the gymnasium, where the student who is preparing for the ministry works hard at it for three or four years; the offer of this course by Strack is therefore only a concession for the benefit of those who from exceptional causes have failed to take it up before entering. The number of such is small, but it is still necessary to provide for them. As for Exegetical work, Strack lectures frequently upon Isaiah, giving the course every third or fourth term. He also reads, somewhat less frequently, upon Job, Psalms, Proverbs and Genesis. In connection with these longer courses he usually offers a public course—once a week—in which he takes up shorter, but equally interesting sections of the Old Testament. A year ago he lectured on the poetical passages in the Pentateuch; last winter upon sections in Leviticus; this term on portions selected from Exodus. He has also gathered a little company for the study of Jewish literature; it is named, a trifle ambitiously perhaps, "Institutum Judaicum." They meet weekly, and read sections of the Talmud from texts edited by the Professor himself. From various sources are brought together items of interest as to Jewish belief and practice.

Strack's chief work, after that upon the *Codex Babylonicus Petropolitanus*, has been upon Hebrew Grammar, and it is natural that in his Exegetical courses he emphasizes grammatical points; it is also natural that his references are to his own Grammar along with Gesenius'. Driver's Hebrew Tenses he cites frequently. His lectures are rendered especially valuable to us by the fact that he assumes that his hearers are near the beginning of their course, or are somewhat sluggish. It hurts one's pride sometimes to be sure, but after all, a strange land and language do make one act stupid, however bright he may be, and make him appear ignorant, however wise he may be. He uses simple words, writes out the Hebrew words he explains, repeats references, spells proper names, and delights to show his familiarity with English authorities.

Another consideration that renders his help valuable for Americans, is his conservative attitude with regard to Old Testament problems; by this is meant a relative—not absolute conservatism; if indeed the very term conservatism does not so necessarily imply some progress, as to forbid the use of the word "absolute". While Strack has little sympathy with "Wellhausen and Co", he is equally emphatic in opposition to the view, "no longer held except by some scholars in England and America", that Moses is the author of the Pentateuch. In regard to Inspiration he expressed himself in somewhat this way. "I believe in Inspiration most thoroughly, but this belief is the result of my study. It is not right to come to the study of the Old Testament with a preconceived notion of Inspiration; careful examination of the Bible will lead up to such belief, but only at the close of the examination can it be fairly formulated, as a preliminary to Dogmatic Theology."

Strack presents some points of resemblance to Prof. Franz Delitzsch. Such is his conservative position; such his work for the Jews; and such, what concerns us most here, his interest in the American students in the University. This has led him to announce for next term a Seminar or Institute for English speaking students, similar in purpose at least to that conducted for years by Prof. Delitzsch. This promises to be of utmost value to us, and is to be recommended to new comers.

In turning to Dillmann, one finds numberless contrasts to Strack; contrasts that concern physical and mental traits alike. He is as deliberate in movement, in utterance and in thought, as Strack is quick and nervous. He wears no beard; has perfectly white hair, and a wonderfully childlike face. One is a little surprised at first to find his manner somewhat irritable, and he is gratified to discover that after all Dillmann is kind and obliging.

He lectures each Winter upon Introduction; his standard Summer course is Old Testament Theology; from this he has since 1880 varied in reading History of Israel in 1882 and 1889, and in offering, so it seems, nothing but one Exegetical course in 1884 and 1886. The lectures upon the History of the Old Testament Text, which forms a part of the course on Introduction, he delivers as a "public" course on Saturdays. Likewise "Jewish Antiquities" he reserves for a weekly course in connection with Old Testament Theology. His Exegetical work has been divided between Genesis, Isaiah, Psalms and (down to 1883) Job. Isaiah is explained every Winter, and in the Summer term Psalms and Genesis alternate. Dillmann conducts the Old Testament Seminar for practical work in Exegesis. Last Winter Ecclesiastes was read, this Summer Nahum, Zephaniah and Habakkuk are being read. These Seminars are, in every department, a valuable part of the course, revealing as they do the Professor's mode of thought, the process of elaborating views that appear in lectures as complete, and above all requiring the students to formulate their opinions, and express them clearly, then maintain them or gracefully yield them. This last advantage of course does not apply to English speaking students, who usually attend only as listeners.

Dillmann's style of lecturing is remarkably simple, clear and straight-forward. He attempts no pleasantry as does Harnack; uses few rhetorical figures; is somewhat sluggish in manner; and appears constantly to regard his task as an unpleasant and burdensome one. He is earnest in support of his opinions, yet betrays no impatience with his opponents. Now and then he quietly asserts their unreasonableness and stupidity, but only "in passing"; as the big dog, annoyed by a little dog, caught him in his teeth, shook him, dropped him again and went on his way as if nothing had occurred. Not that all Dillmann's opponents are little dogs—by no means, though he does characterize one of them as "der kleine A."

Truthfulness requires the admission that it is difficult for a new-comer to understand Dillmann, and to retain interest in his lectures. With Harnack it is a sufficient reward for attendance to look at the man, though one understands little. With Dillmann a front seat is absolutely necessary and considerable independent interest in the theme. His voice is low, his eyes usually closed; he seldom repeats a thought, so that a sentence lost often means the whole train of thought lost. But one rapidly becomes accustomed to him, and then there is a feast of good things spread before him every hour.

Dillmann's position as a theologian is too well known to need definition. His Introduction, History and Old Testament Theology, are all of course based on his views of Critical questions. To one who is prepossessed with what is here

known as American conservatism, these courses offer many
novelties; and sometimes one is unwilling to accede to his
statements. At other times, and they come far oftener, the
lecturer's keen appreciation of the place and meaning of the
Old Testament in the plan of salvation; his reverent acknowl-
edgement of God's hand in history; his comprehension of the
character of His influence upon the human mind—all this
gladdens the heart of the hearer, and he wonders if, after
all, it is necessary to contend for the old position, when the
new one is so satisfying. In Biblical Theology, the crown
of an Exegete's work, Dillmann *assumes* his position; he for
the most part lays aside contention, and the excellencies of
the critical position are apparent. It is indeed a pleasure to
draw away for an hour from all thought of polemic and
strife, and listen as an earnest, honest, learned man explains
the Bible; as so expounded, the Old Testament contains no
fewer treasures, though some that we had called precious
stones, are not so regarded.

Kleinert delivers one Exegetical course each term. His
favorite subject is the Psalms; others are Isaiah, Genesis and
Job. If the writer says nothing further of him, it is simply
because he has heard none of his lectures and so has nothing
to offer.

In connection with Old Testament work, though not a part
of it, should be mentioned numerous courses of lectures upon
the Semitic languages, and especially Schrader's course in
History of the Ancient Orient. The lecturer is peculiar, and
somewhat rambling,—he winters in Egypt, summers in Nineveh, stopping a night or two in Jerusalem or Damascus on
the way; but for a rapid sketch of the subject, and more the
course does not purport to be, it is very profitable.

Add to the rich lecture courses the extraordinary advantages offered by the Library, and one is not astonished at the
large numbers of students that are attracted here from America. The influx of German Old Testament views into the
United States would be alarming if they were dangerous;
would be laughable if they were not so valuable; is hopeful,
for—but this sketch should be simply a statement, not a plea.

SUGGESTIONS FOR THE STUDY OF PAUL'S TEACHING REGARDING THE PERSON AND WORK OF CHRIST IN THE EPISTLES OF THE IMPRISONMENT (COLOSSIANS, EPHESIANS AND PHILIPPIANS).

By Prof. GEORGE B. STEVENS, Ph. D., D. D.,

Yale University, New Haven, Conn.

The three Epistles of Paul named above form a group by themselves, and have a certain kinship and inner unity which make it desirable that they should be studied together. They were written (probably in the order named) while the apostle was a prisoner at Rome (*cf.* Acts xxvii.), during or about the year 63 A. D.* Their composition within the same period of the apostle's life, during which his mind was largely occupied with the same reflections, is sufficient to account for their many points of similarity.

Colossians and Ephesians resemble each other most closely. They are both more doctrinal than Philippians, which was addressed to a church to which the apostle was peculiarly attached, and with which he had very confidential relations. This is, above all others, Paul's epistle of friendship and thanksgiving. Colossians is polemic, being directed against certain errors which combined elements of Essene Judaism and Gnostic speculation, and which the apostle regarded as especially derogatory to the true doctrine of the person and work of Christ. Ephesians is more like a doctrinal treatise, whose purpose is not so much to attack as to instruct and edify. It results from this difference that Colossians treats more of the *person*, Ephesians more of the *work* of Christ.

---

* I here state the common opinion in which I concur, not forgetting that many distinguished scholars (as Meyer, Reuss and Weiss) maintain that Colossians and Ephesians were written from Cæsarea (*cf.* Acts xxiii., xxiv.), and Philippians only from Rome. Bleek and Lightfoot place Philippians before the other two. Among those who hold the genuineness of these epistles, dates ranging from 60 to 63 are assigned to them.

The former is more specific, the latter more general in character. Philippians introduces doctrinal definition only incidentally, but it so happens that in this way the most important passage of all, in its bearing upon Christology, is found in that letter (Phil. ii., 5–11).

As has been already implied, the doctrine which is most fully developed in this group of letters is that of the person and work of Christ. The growth of heresies at Colossæ, which tended to degrade Christ from His kingship over the Church and the world to the rank of a creature, was the immediate occasion for the apostle's turning his attention especially to that subject.

As a guide to the systematic study of Paul's teaching concerning Christ and His work in these epistles, I have made the following analysis and grouping of the material, arranging the points in a logical and progressive order. Verses which bear indirectly, and yet in an important manner, upon the topic under consideration are placed in parenthesis. It is thought that this method of arranging the teaching of the epistles will enable the student to fix clearly in mind their most essential ideas.

1. *The Divine purpose of salvation in Christ.*
   Eph. 1 : 5 ; 2 : 10 ; 3 : 11.
2. *Creation wrought through Christ.*
   Col. 1 : 16 (17).
3. *The Divine Fulness (Pleroma) which dwells in Christ.*
   Col. 1 : 19 ; 2 : 3 ; 2 : 8–10 ; 2 : 17–19.   Eph. 3 : 8.
4. *Christ's essential Divinity.*
   Col. 1 : 15 (17).   Phil. 2 : 6.
5. *His incarnation and humiliation.*
   Phil. 2 : 6–8.
6. *The exaltation of Christ.*
   Col. 3 : 1.   Phil. 2 : 9–11.   Eph. 1 : 20–22.
7. *His sacrifice and sufferings.*
   Eph. 5 : 2.   Phil. 3 : 10 (*cf.* Col. 1 : 24).
8. *His work of reconciliation.*
   (a) Between Jews and Gentiles (Eph.)
   Eph. 2 : 13–16 (*cf.* Col. 2 : 14–15 ; 3 : 11).
   (b) Between God and man (Col.)
   Col. 1 : 20–22.
9. *The Headship of Christ over the Church.*
   Col. 1 : 18.   Eph. 1 : 22 (23) ; 4 : 7–13 ; 4 : 15 (16) ; 5 : 23 (24, 25).

10. *The " Cosmic significance" of Christ.*
   Eph. 1 : 10 ; 1 : 22.
11. *Christ as the object of faith.*
   Phil. 3 : 9. Eph. 3 : 17.
12. *The identification of believers with Christ in His death and resurrection.*
   Col. 2 : 12, 13 ; 2 : 20 ; 3 : 1 ; 3 : 3.
13. *The life of fellowship with Christ.*

Col. 1 : 27, 28 (*cf.* 4 : 3 ; Eph. 3: 4).	Phil. 1 : 21.	Eph. 2 : 6.
" 2 : 6, 7.	" 3 : 12.	" 3 : 17.
" 2 : 11.	" 3 : 14.	" 3 : 19.
" 3 : 3, 4.		" 4 : 13.
" 3 : 15, 16, 17 (24).		

14. *The future life with Christ.*
   Col. 3 : 4.   Phil. 1 : 21-23 ; 3 : 10, 11 ; 3 : 20, 21 ; 4 : 5.

THE LIFE AND TIMES OF THE CHRIST,

BASED ON LUKE.

By William R. Harper and George S. Goodspeed,

YALE UNIVERSITY.

(Copyrighted, 1890.)

STUDIES XXIX. AND XXX.—THE PEOPLE AND THE KINGDOM OF
GOD.—LUKE 12 : 54-13 : 21.

Remark.—It is desirable that in beginning each "study" the entire passage
assigned be read over rapidly and the main divisions of the narrative noted.

I. EXAMINATION OF THE MATERIAL.

[It will be noted that the following order is observed invariably in this work; (1) the
verse or section is read and its contents stated in a general way; (2) important or difficult words and phrases are studied; (3) a complete statement of
the contents of the verse or section is formed in view of the work already
done; (4) the religious teaching is sought.]

§ 1. Chapter 12 : 54-59.

1. Read the passage, note the subject suggested: *The Multitude warned.*
2. The following words and phrases call for study: (1) *in the west* (12 : 54), why in
   that quarter? (2) *heat* (12 : 55), (a) cf. margin, (b) why from the south? (3)
   hypocrites (12 : 56), (a) like Pharisees, (b) led by them; (4) *interpret*, lit.
   "test"; (5) *this time*, (a) when the Christ is present, (b) as the signs would
   show; (6) *of yourselves* (12 : 57), out of your own observation and thought
   apart from either (a) the signs, (b) the Pharisees, your leaders, (c) Jesus'
   teaching; (7) *judge*, "determine" and consequently perform; (8) *for* (12 : 58),
   i. e. this is the time to decide and do, "for"; (9) *adversary*, (a) does this refer
   to God, Christ, the law, or (b) is it merely part of the drapery of the parable
   which teaches one great truth?
3. A condensed statement of the thought should be based on the three divisions of
   the passage: (1) vs. 54, 55, 56, (2) v. 57, (3) vs. 58, 59. The student may
   make the statement after studying these divisions.
4. The teaching of the section lies in (1) the necessity for decision on religious matters, (2) the urgent need of immediate decision when the Christ is present.

§ 2. Chapter 13 : 1–5.

1. The subject may be stated as : *A lesson of Repentance.*
2. Important words and phrases are : (1) *told him* (13 : 1), i. e. since he had been speaking about punishment (12 : 58, 59) ; (2) *were sinners,* etc., (13 : 2), could Jesus have been addressing Galileans ? (3) *in like manner* (13 : 3), either (a) by the sword, or (b) by the Roman hostility, or (c) violently, in punishment, or (d) as certainly ; (4) *think ye,* etc., (13 : 4), did they not think so ?
3. The thought of the passage is briefly stated as follows : *When told of the cruel slaughter of worshiping Galileans, he replied, Neither they nor those crushed by the tower in Siloam were therefore great sinners, but you too shall so perish unless you repent.*
4. The religious teaching here gathers about the need that *all* who hear the call of the Christ should turn to him in repentance.

§ 3. Chapter 13 : 6–9.

1. Read and note the subject : *The worthless Fig tree.*
2. Study the following : (1) *in his vineyard ;* (2) *vinedresser ;* (3) *three years ;* (4) *cut it down ;* (5) *cumber ;* (6) *this year.*
3. The passage condensed may be as follows : *He told them the parable of the worthless fig tree which the owner commanded to be cut down. But the keeper secured a year's delay in which by working with it he hoped to get fruit.*
4. The student may consider carefully the religious thought in the passage.

§ 4. Chapter 13 : 10–17.

1. Is not the subject, *A Work of Healing on the Sabbath?*
2. The following words and phrases are of special interest : (1) *spirit of infirmity* (13 : 11), (a) cf. 13 : 16, (b) how explain this case of possession? (2) *saw her* (13 : 12), what may be inferred as to her state of mind from her presence there? (3) *said to the multitude* (13 : 14), (a) why not to Jesus? (b) censure upon the woman as well as Jesus? (4) *hypocrites* (13 : 15), why plural? (5) *his ox,* (a) as the law was interpreted to allow, (b) argument from lower to higher; (6) *multitude rejoiced* (13 : 17), recalls the Galilean ministry.
3. Criticise the following statement of thought : *While teaching in a synagogue on the Sabbath he heals a deformed woman. The ruler angrily bids the people be healed on some other day, but Jesus replies, You loose and water your cattle on this day, why not let this daughter of Abraham go free from Satan's bond? Thus he shamed the opposers and delighted the people.*
4. Is it not taught here that an undue exaltation of the letter of religion may lead to positive opposition to its true spirit and best expression ?

§ 5. Chapter 13 : 18–21.

1. The student, after reading, may state this subject.
2. Important words and phrases are : (1) *therefore* (13 : 18), how connect this with preceding section? (2) *whereunto shall I liken,* a common formula of Jewish teachers; (3) *his own garden* (13 : 19), peculiar to Luke's account; (4) *three measures* (13 : 21), is this (a) merely the usual quantity, or (b) symbolic of man's threefold nature, or (c) symbolic of the three great races of man ?

3. The following condensation is suggested : *In view of the healing of the woman and its results, he said, The Kingdom of God, like the mustard tree, will grow from small beginnings into great size. Like the leaven hid in meal it will pervade and transform the world.*

4. The student may thoughtfully consider the religious teaching of the passage.

II. CLASSIFICATION OF THE MATERIAL,
1. Contents and Summary.

1) **The Contents.**   The following table of contents is to be mastered.

THE PEOPLE AND THE KINGDOM OF GOD.

§ 1. THE MULTITUDE WARNED.
§ 2. A LESSON OF REPENTANCE.
§ 3. THE WORTHLESS FIG TREE.
§ 4. A WORK OF HEALING ON THE SABBATH.
§ 5. THE GROWTH OF THE KINGDOM ILLUSTRATED.

2) **The Summary.**   The student may prepare the summary on methods already suggested and illustrated.

2. Observations upon the Material.

212) 12: 54–56. Jesus argues that the signs of the coming of the Kingdom of God are as clear as well-known weather signs.*

213) 12: 57. The people do not exercise their own strong sense of what God would have them do.†

214) 12: 54, 55, 58, 59. The intimation is that there are difficulties gathering about the nation which ought to be foreseen and avoided.

215) 13: 1, 2. This conversation would seem to have occurred out of Galilee.

216) 13: 1, 2. The inference is that these men were rather pleased with the slaughter of these Galileans.‡

217) 13: 3, 5. Jesus lays emphasis not on the wrong idea that the Jews had of the relation of calamity to sin but on the universal liability of all to calamity unless they repented.

218) 13: 7. This parable seems to teach that God had long been seeking the fruit of obedience from the nation in vain, and that their continued existence depended on this fruitfulness.

219) 13: 6–9. The parable is one of judgment.§

220) 13: 7. A hint is given of God's larger possessions among men outside of the nation.‖

* Since they were capable of distinguishing the face of the sky . . . . it could only be from a lack of good-will that they left wholly unnoticed the rain and the vital warmth which in these days had been imparted in the Kingdom of God. *Van O.,* p. 208.

† He still hopes that their own sound sense of right may teach them the truth. But this could only be the case, if they got rid of the influence of their pharisaic leaders, whose alienation from His religio-ethical ideal made it impossible for them to be reached by any demand for a profound internal regeneration. . . . It was Jesus' constant endeavor to separate the people from their leaders. *Weiss,* III., 147.

‡ Very probably these Galileans were thus ruthlessly murdered because of their real or suspected connection with the nationalist movement, of which Galilee was the focus. It was as if these Jews had said to Jesus : Yes, signs of the times and of the coming storm ! These Galileans of yours, your own countrymen, involved in a kind of Pseudo-Messianic movement, a kind of "signs of the times rising," something like that towards which you want us to look—was not their death a condign punishment ? This latter inference they did not express in words, but implied in their narration of the fact. *Edersheim,* II., p. 222. ab. ed., p. 363.

§ The obvious purpose of the parable is to enforce the warning: "Except you repent," etc.; to intimate, that is to say, that the judgment of the Jewish nation was impending. Bruce, *Parabol. Teaching,* p. 428.

‖ The parable before us is one of those parts of our Lord's teaching in which is latent universalism. . . . . We see in it an anticipation of Paul's apologetic for his Gentile Gospel, as apparently liable to the objection of setting aside the election of Israel. Bruce, *ibid,* p. 429.

221) 13: 10, 17. Jesus has entered upon a popular ministry in Perea.*
222) 13: 14-16. The opposition of the authorities and the replies of Jesus seem to be
more pronounced and intense than in the
earlier controversies.
223) 13: 14. The reply of the synagogue ruler
is a testimony to the reality of the mira-

cle.
224) 13: 11, 16. The woman seems to be regarded as a victim of demoniacal possession.†
225) 13: 18. Jesus saw in the preceding work
and its accompanying circumstances
an illustration of the growth of the
Kingdom both mightily and quietly.

3. Topics for Study.

Some of the most important and related " observations " are collected and organized here for further study.

1) **Signs of the Times.** [Obs. 212-214, 217, 218, 225]: (1) Consider the possibly
close relation of the teaching in Lk. 12 : 54-59 to 11 : 29-36. (2) Observe the
general thought—the signs existing are sufficient but are overlooked. (3)
Enumerate them, ‡ e. g. (a) John's work, (b) the teaching of Jesus, (c) the
political situation, (d) social life. (4) Determine now carefully just what these
signs meant. (5) Note the predicted consequences of the neglect of these signs
to the nation. (6) Inquire into the realization of (a) that which the signs por-
tended, (b) the result of the national neglect of the signs.

4. Religious Teaching.

Is not the dominating religious thought of this passage that of a *message to dull
hearts?* (1) they ought to recognize the meaning of events around them which
are calling on them to repent and be reconciled to God (12 : 54-13 : 5); (2) they
will surely be destroyed if they do not do God's will (13 : 6-9); (3) they are
making the spirit of God's law inoperative while they exalt the letter (13 : 14-
16); (4) the Kingdom of God will move on in spite of them (13 : 18-21).

STUDIES XXXI. AND XXXII.—THE OUTLOOK FOR THE KINGDOM.
LUKE 13 : 22-14 : 35.

Remark.—It is desirable that in beginning each " study " (1) the material of the
preceding " study " be reviewed, and (2) the entire passage assigned be read
over rapidly and the main divisions of the narrative noted.

---

* Although Galilee had been abandoned by Him, and Jerusalem had been repeatedly hostile,
we infer from Matt. 19: 2, that he was still heard with gladness in Perea; in fact, some such
wave of popularity must have preceded the entry into Jerusalem. Riddle, *Luke*, p. 210.

† In the case of the infirm woman we seem to be on the debatable borderland between ordinary
diseases and the peculiar class denominated demoniacal. Bruce, *Miraculous Element*, p. 180.
Satan is referred to in general terms as the head of the kingdom of evil, physical as well as
moral, and no inference may be drawn as to the woman's past habits and character. *Ibid*, p. 172.
We mark that hers was not demoniac possession at all—and yet, though she had not yielded, she
had not effectually resisted and so she was "bound" by a "spirit of infirmity," both in body and
soul. *Edersheim*, II., 224 (365).

‡ See *Pulpit Com.*, I., pp. 339, 340.

I. EXAMINATION OF THE MATERIAL.

[It will be noted that the following order is observed invariably in this work; (1) the verse or section is read and its contents stated in a general way; (2) important or difficult words and phrases are studied; (3) a complete statement of the contents of the verse or section is formed in view of the work already done; (4) the religious teaching is sought.]

§ 1. Chapter 13: 22-30.

1. Read over the passage and consider a statement of the subject: *The Question of Salvation.*

2. The important words and phrases for study are : (1) *journeying* (13 : 22), i. e. continuing the journey of 9 : 51 ; (2) *are they few* (13 : 23), (a) because of Jesus' stringent conditions, 12 : 58, 59 ; 13 : 3, (b) because Jesus' followers were so few ? (c) the spirit of the question ? (3) *be saved,* lit. " are being saved " i. e. by being received into the Messianic kingdom on the conditions fixed; (4) *narrow door* (13 : 24), either (a) repentance, (b) obedience and holiness, (c) the Messiah Jesus, John 10 : 7 ; (5) *shall seek,* i. e. when too late ; (6) *shut to the door* (13 : 25), either (a) for the night, or (b) for the feast ; (7) *whence,* i. e. of what family ? (8) *workers of iniquity* (13 : 27), (a) doers of evil in having been so near the Christ and yet not really accepted him, (b) " those in the employ of and receiving the wages of unrighteousness," Riddle ; (9) *the weeping,* etc. (13 : 28), i. e. the most terrible anguish and despair that has ever been ; (10) *they* (13 : 29), i. e. the Gentiles? (11) *sit down,* (a) cf. margin, (b) the Messianic feast ; (12) *last . . . . first* (13 : 30), (a) the Gentiles and the Jews, (b) the Pharisees and the publicans.

3. A suggested condensation of the thought of this passage is as follows : *Continuing his journey he is asked whether the saved are few and replies, See to it that you by striving gain salvation, for some will be too late.   When the door is shut the householder will not admit them, though they urge their acquaintance with him. How great will be the despair when from without you see the Messianic feast enjoyed by the patriarchs and prophets with the Gentiles.   Then positions will be reversed indeed.*

4. The student may state what seems to be the important religious thought here.

§ 2. Chapter 13: 31-35.

1. Decide as to the following subject of the section : *The Warning about Herod and its Answer.*

2. The student may examine the words and phrases here noted : (1) *saying* (13 : 31), (a) was this a genuine message or a fiction of the Pharisees? (b) consider the purpose of it on either supposition ; (2) *go and say* (13 : 32), bearing of this message on the question above; (3) *to-day and to-morrow,* i. e. " for a short time "; (4) *am perfected,* (a) i. e. " reach the goal of this human life of mine," (b) the event referred to? (5) *I must go* (13 : 33), (a) " it is God's will," (b) " that I for a time keep working "; (6) *how often* (13 : 34), at what times in the past ? (7) *left unto you* (13 : 35), (a) omit " desolate," (b) i. e. " left by the Lord to you ; " (8) *until ye shall say,* (a) a few weeks later, or (b) at the second coming ? (c) if the latter consider the meaning.

3. Let the student observe the natural divisions of this passage, e. g. (1) vs. 31-33, (2) vs. 34, 35, make out condensed statements of each, and unite them into one statement of the thought.

4. An impressive religious teaching here is the acknowledgment by Jesus himself of the ability of the human will to reject God's proffers of grace.

§ 3. Chapter 14 : 1-6.

1. The student may read the passage and decide as to the subject.

2. (1) *Rulers of the Pharisees* (14 : 1), see John 3 : 1; (2) *to eat bread*, (a) was he invited, or (b) was it a semi-public feast given to the poor? (3) *watching*, a plot? (4) *before him* (14 : 2), was he there by design ? (5) *dropsy*, the first case of the kind ; (6) *answering* (14 . 3), i. e. their secret device ; (7) *held their peace* (14 : 4), why ? (8) *draw him up* (14 : 5), legally they had decided that it was not to be done.

3. A condensation of the passage is as follows : *He enters the house of a prominent Pharisee to dine, and is met by a man with the dropsy. Replying to the crafty design, he says, Is it lawful to heal to-day ? They do not answer, and he adds; Would you not relieve your own beast ? to which they cannot reply.*

4. The student may state the religious teaching of the passage.

§ 4. Chapter 14 : 7-11.

1. Let the student be prepared by a reading of the section to criticise the following subject : *His Suggestion to the Guests.*

2. Among other important words and phrases note (1) *chose out*, (14 : 7), (a) " scrambled for places," (b) they were left to find their seats ; (2) *friend* (14 : 10), mark of a warmly favorable feeling ; (3) *humbleth himself* (14 : 11), i. e. it must be a real humility.

3. The main thoughts of the passage may be thus expressed : *Beholding the scramble for the best seats, he said, When you are invited out, take the poorest not the best seats, if you would have real honor, when the host shall come to say not " go lower," but " come higher." True humility shall be honored.*

4. A religious thought of the passage lies in the manifestation of the wisdom of cultivating a modest and humble attitude of mind.

§ 5. Chapter 14 : 12-14.

1. Read and note the subject : *His Suggestion to the Host.*

2. Study (1) *shalt be recompensed* (14 : 14), which was probably the purpose of the feast ; (2) *resurrection*, (a) first use of the word in the discourses of Jesus, (b) acceptance of the Pharisaic standpoint.

3. The following is a statement of the thought : *He advises the host to invite to a feast of this kind not those who are able to repay him, but those who are not so able, for then the reward will come from God at the resurrection.*

4. The student may determine the religious thought.

§ 6. Chapter 14 : 15-24.

1. The following phrase is suggested to serve as the subject : *Parable of the refused Feast and the welcome Guests.*

2. The student may study the following words and phrases: (1) *he said* (14 : 15), his motive? (2) *eat bread, etc.;* (3) *certain man* (14 : 16) ; (4) *servant* (14 : 17); (5) *with one* consent (14 : 18); (6) *streets and lanes* (14 : 21) ; (7) *highways and hedges* (14 : 23); (8) *constrain ;* (9) *none . . . . shall taste* (14 : 24).

3. The student may criticise and improve upon the following statement of the thought: *A guest said, Happy are those who feast in the Kingdom of God. He replied, A certain man invited some guests to a great feast, and they all declined to come because of other engagements. He indignantly ordered his servants to gather in the common people, and even homeless tramps, to enjoy the feast, declaring that the others should not be received.*

4. The great religious thought here lies in the fact that while those who have the best right to God's favor refuse it, He will admit all to enjoy it.

§ 7. Chapter 14 : 25-35.

1. Let the student examine carefully the following statement of the subject : *The Conditions of Discipleship.*

2. (1) *His own life* (14 : 26), (a) meaning " his own self-satisfaction," (b) throws light on the meaning of *hateth,* etc.; (2) *have wherewith,* etc., (14 : 28), (a) does any one have enough ? (b) then he must renounce himself and all that he has, cf. v. 26; (3) *whether he is able* (14 : 31), (a) is any one able ? (b) then he must make peace by surrendering; (c) to whom, God or Satan? (4) *so therefore* (14 : 33), (a) conclusion of the whole, (b) throwing light on the preceding parables, (c) one must renounce self to be acceptable to God and able to follow Christ ; (5) *salt . . . . savor* (14 : 34), that which makes a Christian profession valuable is the self-renunciation of v. 33.

3. A condensed expression for the contents of the section is : *He tells the multitudes that they must renounce everything that might stand in the way of following him and endure everything if they would be disciples. Self-renunciation is the only way to succeed in becoming a thorough disciple. It is the only way to come into agreement with God. It is the element in discipleship which makes it valuable.*

4. The prominent thing to be considered here in the religious teaching is the importance of beginning discipleship to Jesus the Christ with renouncing self.

II. CLASSIFICATION OF THE MATERIAL.

1. Contents and Summary.

1) The **Contents.** The following table of the contents of the passage is to be carefully examined.

THE OUTLOOK FOR THE KINGDOM.

§ 1. THE QUESTION OF SALVATION.
§ 2. THE WARNING ABOUT HEROD AND ITS ANSWER.
§ 3. HEALING AT A SABBATH FEAST.
§ 4. THE SUGGESTION TO THE GUESTS.
§ 5. THE SUGGESTION TO THE HOST.
§ 6. PARABLE OF THE REFUSED FEAST AND THE WELCOME GUESTS.
§ 7. THE CONDITIONS OF DISCIPLESHIP.

2) The Summary. The student will compare the following "summary" with the Scripture passage, with a view to criticism and improvement : *As he journeys on, Jesus replies to questioners about the small number of the saved in the Kingdom of God by reminding them of the need for personal endeavor, lest they be left out and others admitted there. To a warning about Herod brought by Pharisees, he replies, My work will go on here longer, and that fox cannot stop it. for it is at Jerusalem, which has rejected me, that I must die. At a Sabbath feast he heals a dropsied man, advises guests to be humble if they would have honor, advises the host to invite the poor if he would gain merit with God, tells them that God will receive the outcasts and the poor if the chosen ones will not accept his favor. He warns multitudes that one must renounce self to be worth anything as his disciple.*

2. Observations upon the Material.

226) 13 : 23. The question seems to have been asked in view of the small number of Jesus' followers.

227) 13 : 25-27. There were those who had an external relation to Jesus the Christ without any real spiritual attachment to him: this would not avail for salvation.

228) 13: 29 ; 14: 21-23. Jesus teaches that others will occupy the place in the Messianic kingdom, from which the chosen people will be excluded.

229) 13 : 31. It is a question whether the message from Herod was an invention of the Pharisees.*

230) 13 : 33. Jesus expects to suffer death at Jerusalem.

231) 13 : 34, 35. The reason for the rejection of the theocracy is that they are unwilling to accept Jesus as the Christ.

232) 14 : 3. Jesus takes the initiative in this case, and the Pharisees are silent.

233) 14 : 7. This seems to have been a semi-

public feast at which there was a scramble for seats.

234) 14 : 8-11. Jesus argues that from their selfish point of view it was worth while to be modest.†

235) 14 : 12. The inference is that this class of guests was bidden to this feast.

236) 14 : 13, 14. Taking the Pharisee's purpose in giving this feast, Jesus urges a better way to gain merit.‡

237) 14 : 18-20. The invited guests by being preoccupied with other pursuits show their indifference to the invitation.

238) 14 : 21-23. The most degraded of the people are not only welcome but urged to come to the feast.

239) 14 : 25, 26. Jesus understood and tested the enthusiasm of the multitudes.

240) 14 : 33. The fundamental condition of discipleship is here plainly stated to be self-renunciation.

3. Topics for Study.

1) Sabbath Controversies. [Obs. 222-224, 232] : The student may compare the scenes of Lk. 13 : 14-17 ; 14 : 1-6 with the experiences of the Galilean Ministry in Sabbath controversy (e. g. Lk. 6 : 1-11) to consider the resemblances and differences.§

* Probably the danger of which these Pharisees spoke may have been real enough, and from their secret intrigues with Herod they might have special reasons for knowing of such. But their suggestion that Jesus should depart could only have proceeded from a wish to get Him out of Perea.—*Edersheim*, II., 301, (418).

† See other explanations of the passage in Plumptre, *Luke*, p. 239. Looking at things from even the low standard of the hypocrite's morals, humility has its uses. Then, having glorified humility in a way that even they could understand, He glides from the sordid picture into a general reflection on the worth of the virtue for the whole of life.—*Lindsay*, p. 180.

‡ The Sabbath feast, given to those who did not need it, had more of ostentation than of piety in it. As a good deed, meant to win merit, it was a mistake, which Jesus with gentle irony corrects. *Lindsay*, p. 180.

§ *Edersheim*, II., p. 223, 303 (364. 419) has some observations on the subject.

2) **The Sentence of Condemnation.** [Obs. 227, 228, 237-240]: (1) Recall the teaching in 12 : 54-59 ; 13 : 1-9. (2) Study carefully 13 : 25-30, noting (a) the two elements, rejection of one and the coming in of the other, (b) who is meant by these parties? (3) Observe the clear statement of 13 : 34, 35. (4) Make a careful study of 14 : 15-24, and consider (a) the persons invited in each case, (b) the essential ground of refusal, (c) the rejection of the guests first invited, (d) the general teaching of the parable. (5) Having made these detailed studies, now gather up the whole into a compact statement. (6) In the light of the foregoing, study 14 : 25-35, and find reasons for the connection of these vs. with it. (7) Consider the severe judicial character of this teaching in the light of the Perean ministry as intermediate between the work in Galilee and the suffering at Jerusalem.

4. Religious Teaching.

May not the great religious thought of the passage be regarded as *Self-Renunciation the one needful condition of discipleship?* Study the thought in the light of the following points. (1) The lack of this was the reason for the condemnation of the Jewish people (13 : 26, 27) ; (2) it was the consciousness of this want of everything, which made the persons of 14 : 21-23 acceptable; (3) the danger of fancied self-renunciation which is after all self-satisfaction, e. g. monasticism; (4) one is totally useless as a disciple unless he practices it (14 : 34, 35) ; (5) it is the only source of peace with God (14 : 32); (6) the student may suggest other considerations.

A "SYMPOSIUM" ON THE FAVORITE BOOK OF THE BIBLE.

It has seemed to not a few persons that while there is great interest in the Bible among Christian people, yet this interest is often narrow, confined to a few portions, or based upon grounds that appeal to something short of the whole nature of man. No little help, it was thought, might be furnished in broadening the outlook of many such persons by obtaining from some of the most capable and large minded ministers and teachers a statement concerning what to them, looking at the matter in a broad way, is the *favorite book of the Bible.* Kind and helpful replies have been received from many to whom requests have been sent by the Editor. Some of them are here given.

From GEORGE W. CABLE, Esq.

My favorite book is John's Gospel. It seems to me the supreme flower of divine truth. It has to me the effect of being written to all the world and all time by one to whom all the other books of the Bible,—histories, psalms, laws, prophecies, gospels, epistles,—were known and had been duly pondered and appropriated. If I could say it so, I should prefer to say that my favorite book is John's Gospel and his First Epistle. It would do my mind no violence to call them one book.

My choice of John's Gospel, please note, is a choice of it *among*—not *out from*—the books of the Bible.

Northampton, Mass.

From Rev. W. H. P. FAUNCE.

The question, What is my favorite book in the Bible? is much like the question, What is my favorite article of food? The answer will depend much on the season of the year, the mood of mind and the state of heart. Judging by the amount of time I have spent in its study and the impression made on my own soul, I must say my favorite book is the First Letter to the Corinthians.

1. It is a marvelously graphic picture of the Christian society in the apostolic age.

2. It is a wonderful revelation of the great heart of Paul, unfolding not only his natural convictions, but even his natural sympathies and antipathies, his method of counsel and advice in difficult matters.

3. It is marvelously practical, being almost a compendium of applied Christianity.

4. It contains in a brief space all the essential historic facts concerning the life and death of Jesus.

5. It contains the finest statement ever made of true Christian liberty, its scope and its limitations.

6. It contains the finest poem of the New Testament, the exquisite description of Christian love.

7. It contains the positive though spiritual statement of the resurrection from the dead, unfolding glorious vistas of the life to come.

8. In its horizon extending from the ministry of Jesus to the judgment day, in its scope dealing with the most complicated problems of individual and social life, in its spirit the very incarnation of Christ—I could lose any other book of the Bible sooner than this.

New York City.

From WM. H. THOMSON, M. D.

In reply to your question which of the books of the Bible is my favorite, I find the answer difficult without qualifications as to particulars.

I find in Genesis every kind of interest, religious and general, which leads me very often to study it, frequently also in connection with the rest of the Pentateuch.   For daily spiritual needs I would choose the Psalms.   The Gospel of John would be my favorite but for critical (not doctrinal) difficulties suggested by its style.

New York City.

From Rev. EDWARD G. SELDEN.

I confess the difficulty of naming *the* favorite book, for special study at any given time makes a book the favorite for the time being.   I have in this way been interested for months in Genesis.   Just now I happen to be interested in the book of Ezra.   It delights me week by week as I take up a fresh chapter, and yet it is not always so prominently in my thought and liking.

I prefer the New Testament to the Old.   Luke I prefer of the synoptics, but John of the gospels.   The epistles in turn have been favorites, but if I were to be shut up to one book—which I suppose is a fair way of testing myself—I should certainly take the Gospel of John.

I would keep that story of Christ's life because it gives at once the loftiest conception of spiritual being as realized in Him, and the profoundest searching of the human heart.   The simplicity and beauty of the narrative are an unceasing wonder and delight.   It is quite possible that one would rise to a higher estimate of the Fourth Gospel if it should become one's sole possession among the sacred writings.

Springfield, Mass.

From Pres. JOHN A. BROADUS, D. D.

As to the question What is my favorite book of the Bible, I should answer, The Gospels.   I think History the most important of all studies, and the Bible consists very largely of History—in fact every portion of it needs to be studied historically.   The center of Bible history is found in the Gospels.   Every thing in the Old Testament in some sense points forward to the Gospel period, and everything else in the New Testament flows out of the Gospels.   Jesus

Christ himself is not only the chief theme of Scripture, but the guarantee of
its authority, the interpreter of its meaning. The Gospels rightly form the
principal subject of youthful study in Sunday Schools, but the most intellectual, cultivated and truly wise will also find the Gospels in the highest degree
interesting, convincing and instructive.

Louisville, Ky.

Contributed Notes.

Genesis XIV. 20; XV. 1.—" And blessed be the Most High God, who hath
delivered thine enemies into thy hand."[A. V.]

" And blessed be God, Most High, which hath *delivered* thine enemies into
thine hand."[R. V.]

" Fear not Abram, I am thy *shield* and thy exceeding great reward."[A. V.
and R. V.]

The critical word in these two passages is *Miggen*. It is pointed as a verb
in the first passage and in the *Piel* form. In the second passage it is pointed
as a noun. The Authorized Version and the Revised Version translate the
verb by " hath delivered" and the noun by " shield." Luther's translation
renders the verb " beschlossen hat" and the noun " schild," while Martin's
French Version renders the verb " a livre," and the noun " bouclier." It is
thus evident, that the most common modern versions are alike in the rendering
of the word or words.

Quite hazardous, then, does it seem to proffer any different understanding
of this word as used in the two passages, or rather a single signification for
them both. Yet the Vulgate translation might naturally awaken inquiry.
The verb is there represented by the absolute construction " quo protegente :"
and the noun is expressed by " protector." The figure of a shield is omitted,
or if at all present, it is in the idea of " hiding," " covering," found in the
verb " protego."   The bold metaphor " scutum" is carefully avoided by the
translator of the Vulgate. Yet there can be no doubt but that he knew the
employment of this figure, as an epithet of God in the Psalms. Turning to
the LXX., we find a similar avoidance of the use of this bold metaphor, found
in modern versions.   The verb is translated by " *paradoke* " and the noun by
" *huperaspizo*." The translation of the noun, although by a verb, reflects
the idea of " shield," since it means " to place a shield over one." Yet it still
stands true, that the translator of these passages, in the LXX. also would not
allow here the boldness in metaphor, which we find in modern versions.

There are certain reasons, deducible from the narrative, why the metaphor
would probably not have been employed.   In that wonderful victory of Abram
over the conquering kings, chief among whom was Chedorlaomer, the patri-
arch was the aggressor. He would attack, not they. His enemies would need
the shield. He needed some power to deliver them into his hands. Hence
the word *Magen* as a verb is correctly translated.   It would also be difficult

to trace any suggestion in the narrative which would unite the word " shield " and " reward," with which it is joined in coördinate relation. The student is also surprised, that in a time so early, before perhaps the shield figured prominently in conflicts, at least with the Hebrews, the word should be turned into metaphor and dignified by so noble a use.

Such reasons, however, are not conclusive. Still they are sufficiently strong to lead one to attempt either to refute them or else to establish on stronger grounds the conclusion they make probable. Assuming that the signification given to the verb is the only one for both passages, that *Magen* as a verb means " to deliver some one or something " into another's power, let us see what is the result.

We must change the Massoretic pointing in the second passage from the noun form to the Poel participle, a Qal form. The translation would then be: " I am the One, delivering (enemies) unto thee and the One, rewarding thee very greatly."

The first objection to this translation would be, that the word *Magen*, when used as a verb, is in the Piel form. If we take as authority the lexicon statements, the matter is settled. But it would not be difficult to trace the reasons, that led Iexicographers to adopt this Piel form. But omitting this, the fact is that there are but three places, including this place, where the consonants of this word must be pointed as a verb. And there is no reason why it must be Piel any more than a Qal form. If so the reasons are not apparent.

Again, it may be urged, that the change is of so little importance that it is waste of words to discuss the matter. Yet it may be found that the accepted view is in opposition to the mode of belief and expression of Abraham's time. This, then, would give another to the many plausible arguments that are urged to place this writing in an age much later than the chronology of the traditional view. But the chiefest reason for considering whether the translation suggested is not the most fitting is to be found in the import the verse assumes by this change. However, before considering this result, let us see the philological and grammatical reasons to support the proposed correction of the text.

It may first be assumed as undoubted, that " shield " cannot be the meaning in the first ˉpassage, and that " deliver " must be there the signification. Secondly, it must be admitted that " deliver " is permissible in the second passage. Choice must be made between it and the rendering " shield." Thirdly, the Qal Participle form is as good a Hebrew word as the Hebrew noun " Shield." No valid reason can be given why one word-form may not be used here as well as the other. Philology cannot settle the question.

From the standpoint of Grammar, it must be conceded also that the syntax of both sentences, whether we point *mogen* or *magen* is equally good and furnish equally familiar Hebrew constructions. Yet the symmetry gained by pointing both words, *mogen* and *sokar* as Qal participles, would lead the grammarian to prefer this pointing. If this be not sufficient to determine choice, we can find no ground in Grammar.

On exegetical grounds, not on those of Philology or Grammar, are we to find the surest motive to induce the change proposed. First, we are surprised that Abram, immediately after he is blessed by Melchizedek in the name of God Most High, Possessor of heaven and earth, makes Jehovah, and God Most High synonymous. Such is the case in his word to the king of Sodom. These are the words: " I have lifted up my hand to Jehovah, the Most High God, Possessor of heaven and earth." There was danger here for Abram.

His statement to the king of Sodom was tribute to the God of Sodom, God Most High. The making this overture to this king was to place the Jehovah faith in peril. It opened a way for Abram to become affiliated to the faiths of the land. Whereas he was separated to Jehovah. The danger is averted by a vision from Jehovah. This is the account; "After these things the word of Jehovah came unto Abram in a vision, saying; Fear not Abram; I am thy *mogen* and thy exceeding great *sokar*," Jehovah uses no synonym. He is not the Most High God. Melchizedek had said, that the one delivering his enemies into his (Abram's) hand was God Most High. Abram had accepted the statement. But Jehovah comes in a vision and settles the matter. The one delivering into his (Abram's) hand enemies, the one rewarding him very greatly is Jehovah. Jehovah thus claims for himself what Melchizedek claimed for God Most High. Revelation becomes thus harmonious. And we are charmed by the loving care of Jehovah over his chosen one, evidenced by a revelation by vision which insured Abram against fatal error.

Vanderbilt University.   PROF. W. W. MARTIN.

Exposition of 2 Cor. VIII. and IX. These two chapters form one grand division of the Epistle, and treat of one subject. They afford, therefore, a convenient passage for continuous exposition. Dr. Marvin R. Vincent, in his excellent little book, "The Expositor in the Pulpit," gives the points of a sermon upon this passage, by the late Dr. Candlish, of Edinburgh. It may seem rash to offer any other arrangement than that of the great Scotch preacher, but the following is my own division of the two chapters, for homiletic use.

Introduction. Justification of the subject as appropriate for the Christian pulpit. The Apostle gives up an entire section of the Epistle to it. In the First Epistle he turns abruptly from the discussion of the high theme of the Resurrection, to this matter of giving. Here his object to urge a liberal offering for the saints in anticipation of the arrival of Titus and two other brethren, sent to receive it. He sets before them

I. *The Example of the Macedonian churches. 8: 1-5.* They gave —:
    1. "Of their own accord." 8: 4.
    2. "According to their power." 8: 3.
    3. Out of "their deep poverty." 8: 2.
    4. As a privilege. 8: 4.
    5. "Their own selves first to the Lord." 8: 5.

II. *He then makes his request for gifts. 8: 7-12.*
    1. Not of commandment. 8: 8-10.
    2. According to ability. 8: 12.

III. *He urges these motives.*
    1. The credit of the church and himself. 8: 10; 8: 24; 9: 2-5.
    2. As a proof of love, and faith, leading to thanksgiving by others, and to glory of God. 8: 8; 9: 2; 9: 11-13.
    3. As a privilege of fellowship. 8: 13-15; 9: 13.
    4. As the completion of Christian character. 8: 7.
    5. As bringing blessed return. 9: 6; 9: 8-11.
    6. Because of example of Christ, and from gratitude to Him. 8: 9; 9: 15.

REV. WM. S. JEROME.

Pontiac, Mich.

Synopses of Important Articles.

Joseph in Egypt.*—Under the title above, Dr. Heinrich Brugsch, the German Egyptologist, contributes an article to the *Deutsche Rundschau* for May. In it he discusses the many questions which are of special interest to students of the Pentateuch. According to Dr. Brugsch, the biblical representations of this period are in such perfect accord with the Egyptian mounments in all the details of life and custom, even in the minutest particulars of the court, that there can be no doubt about their trustworthiness ; yet he thinks that the account, as we now have it, must have been written several centuries after the events occurred, since in some respects the representations of Egyptian affairs agree only with those of a later epoch. For instance, two proper names belong to a time several centuries after Moses. The highpriest of On, Potiphera, whom the LXX call Potephres, bore a name most positively Egyptian. Pu-tiphra means " the gift of Ra," i. e., the Sun ; but its formation belongs to a late epoch in Egyptian history. Egyptian proper names of persons beginning with Puti, " a gift," with the name of a god following, belong to the ninth century B. C., and are not found previously. Dr. Brugsch is, therefore, quite certain that Moses did not write the Pentateuch in its present form, but that the editor chose for Joseph's father-in-law the name of a priest of On of his own time.

"Saphnath Paneah," the name given by Pharaoh to Joseph, likewise had its birth in the ninth century B. C., and was previously unknown. This is true of all Egyptian words beginning with " Sa" or " Se," " he said," followed by the name of a god. " Ef-ouch" means " he lives." So the purely Egyptian name borne by Joseph, " Sa-phrete-ef-ouch," means " God said, he lives," and as in a thousand other examples, the god was the king himself. Much discussion has been evoked by the word "Abrek," which Luther translated " Who is the father of the land." Others have interpreted it variously, as, " Bend the knee," " Prostrate thyself," " Bow thy head," " Rejoice," " The chief of the wise men." Recently the word has been found in a papyrus. It reads, " Ab-re-k-suza-haak," " Thy command is our pleasure," i. e., " we are ready for thy service." Henceforth all conjecture about this word is at an end. Our author is very certain that the Pharaoh who knew Joseph belonged to the Hyksos dynasty. His reasons are: 1. The testimony of George Syncellus, whom he regards as high authority ; 2. The four hundred years' sojourn of the Bible corresponds with the Egyptian chronology, which counts four hundred years between one of the Hyksos kings and Rameses II., whom Dr. Brugsch does not doubt was the foster-father of Moses. Joseph, therefore, lived between 1800 and 1700 B. C. These Hyksos were Hittites, and belonged to the Turanian family. Of this fact their portrait statues leave no doubt.

The interest of this paper culminates in the concluding paragraph. Dr. Brugsch announces, for the first time, the discovery of an inscribed stone found only last winter by an American, Mr. Charles E. Wilbour, a native of

---

* By Rev. Lysander Dickerman, in *Zion's Herald*, June 4, 1890.

Little Compton, R. I. The tablet contains 32 lines, more or less defaced. At its head is the name and title of a hitherto unknown king. " Chit-het," who, in the fourteenth year of his reign, speaks of " the very great misfortune of having no overflow of the Nile for seven years." Certain peculiarities in the style of writing and in the grouping of hieroglyphics assign this stone to the fourth century B. C. Evidently somebody had taken an old story of a seven years' famine and clothed it in modern dress for the purpose of exciting respect for some fourth century divinity. In the reign of this ancient king the seven years of famine had closed with the fourteenth year of his reign. The seven " fat years" had preceded them. The throne name of this king, different from his family name, has been found once, on an inscription over a door in the great pyramid of Sakkara, from which it appears that the king belonged to the first Egyptian dynasty, at least 1,500 years before the time of Joseph. The old story, with the name of the old king, was revamped in the XXII dynasty as a pious fraud by the priests. Dr. Brugsch believes in the real historical character of this newly-found stone, and calls Chit-het " the longest forgotten king of any epoch ;" and he says that the stone will be prized through all time as an important piece of evidence for the actual occurrence of a seven years' famine in the time of Joseph.

Compilation in the Old Testament.*—Few scholars would dispute the statement that recent investigation into structure, composition and style, has revealed the compilatory character of a large proportion of the books of the Old Testament. But few have realized its significance. It must ultimately influence the attitude of modern Christian teaching towards many problems that centre around Holy Scripture. The critical study of such facts as these provokes opposition, and students should have patient sympathy with such opposition, which rises out of reverence for the Bible and fear lest its authority and devotional power may be weakened in the popular mind. Other manifest objections to such study arise, such as want of historical and literary sympathy with the ancient Semitic mind, the unwillingness to let one's vision be modified, the fact that biblical criticism will never escape misunderstanding on the part of those who do not wish to welcome it. If we approach the literary analysis of the Old Testament with a recognition of the moral and religious significance of it as a whole, we will not be harmed but delighted with the new light gained. The books will be found to be largely compilations from the literary remains of many epochs, not written wholes, as ordinarily supposed, referrible to some distinguished name. This is true of the Psalter, which contains poetry from David to the Maccabees ; Ecclesiastes is not Solomonic ; Job, a post-exilic writing ; Proverbs has many groups of sayings welded together ; Isaiah, Jeremiah, Zechariah and Daniel illustrate characteristic phases in the compilatory process. The same is true of the historical books. The Pentateuch is very generally regarded as made up of four sources. We must be ready to allow these facts. It will be found that this element of compilation, so strange and startling, may unexpectedly aid us in our understanding and enjoyment of the books of Scripture. (1) It enables us to reconcile what seem to be confusions of facts, statements and forms of thought and language belonging to different ages, which stand together in the same book. (2) We are carried back to re-

* The full title of the paper is *The Study of the Old Testament, with Special Reference to the Element of Compilation in the Structure of the Books*, by Rev. Professor Herbert E. Ryle, in the *Expositor*, May, 1890, pp. 321-339.

mote antiquity in the original documents and stories which the compiler has left intact. (3) Various lives of tradition and statements of many sources add to the general accuracy of the narrative. Thus the collection of Old Testament books reminds one of an old English cathedral, in which the strangely composite structure reveals the varying taste and sympathies of successive centuries.

Literary criticism of the Bible is more generally accepted in England than with us. Granting the position which is assumed in this interesting article, no one can fail to see that the authority of the Scriptures is in no way weakened, and that there are positive advantages accruing from its acceptance. The writer's remarks about the need that critics have sympathy with the prejudices and fears of the opponents of criticism are just and generous. Indeed, the spirit of the whole is admirable, whatever may be thought of its arguments.

Fasting in Holy Scripture.*—The appointment of stated periods for abstention from all food or particular kinds of food is so far from being characteristic of Judaism or of primitive Christianity, that both are conspicuous in comparison with nearly every form of heathendom by their rigid subordination, and (in some respects) by their absolute disparagement of it. The patriarchs are God-fearing men, but they do not fast. In the rest of the Pentateuch we have (1) Moses' fasting on Sinai, which, like Elijah's and our Lord's, was a fasting with ecstasy, not one of humiliation ; (2) the fast of the Day of Atonement, which criticism constrains us to believe to be not of Mosaic origin, for no reference to it is made either in the historical books or the prophets down to the Exile, and the prophets, indeed, discountenance fasts (Joel's fast is more a rending of the heart than an ecclesiastical form) ; (3) the private vow of a woman (Num. 30 : 13). In the New Testament (1) Jesus' disciples stand out from the religious people of the day by their not fasting, and it is a great error to assume that the "bridegroom taken away" (Mark 2 : 18–20) argues for present fasting, since Christ is in every sense nearer to and more closely united with the true Church now than in the days of His flesh ; (2) Matt. 6 : 16–18 (Luke 18 : 12) gives no sanction to fasting ; (3) neither John, Peter, James or Jude refer to it ; (4) in Matt. 17 : 21 ; Mark 9 : 29 the "fasting" is not a part of the original text ; (5) in Acts the early church, being Jewish in form, fasts (Acts 27 : 9) ; (6) in Paul's epistles, ecclesiastical fasts are not once mentioned. Thus in the New Testament it is nowhere commanded nor represented as a necessary means of grace.

The very interesting and careful consideration of the biblical testimony about fasting which is here given is in Dr. Farrar's best vein.

The Critical Study of the Old Testament.†—The books of the Old Testament present certain phenomena in regard to their style, phraseology, point of view, material, etc. Critical theories are efforts to account for these phenomena. [A brief outline of the analysis of the Hexateuch is given.] The principle underlying this analysis is, the gradual formation of the Hexateuch out of pre-existing sources, these sources being still (in the main) clearly distinguishable in virtue of the difference of style and representation by which they are marked. The indications of an age later than Moses are numerous. One can hardly compare the laws as given in Exodus, Deuteronomy and Leviticus without feeling the impossibility of their having been given within forty years.

* By Rev. Canon Farrar, D. D., in the *Expositor*, May, 1890, pp. 339–351.

† By Canon S. R. Driver, D. D., in *The Contemporary Review*, February 1890, pp. 215–231.

The two representations of the "tent of meeting" in Numbers and in Exodus cannot be denied. The arguments against the position of the critics are unsatisfactory, e. g., (1) the critics themselves differ; a theory reigns for a time and is then overthrown; (2) Deuteronomy, if not the work of Moses, is a forgery. The strength of the critical position lies in the cumulative argument by which it is supported. The analysis rests upon a *combination* of resemblances and differences. The theory of Wellhausen, with certain restrictions, seems to be the most satisfactory. If it be asked, Could not Moses writing under Divine inspiration, have issued the laws without waiting for them to be developed? the answer is; yes; but as a matter of fact, revelation is progressive, and we cannot determine upon antecedent considerations how much or how little it may have pleased God to reveal to a particular agent of his will; to determine this, we must study the history, and the observed facts are consistent with the Wellhausen and not with the traditional theory. There is needed a more comprehensive theory of inspiration, and a wider view of the forces that have coöperated in the production of the Bible. It must be remembered, in all this, that critical investigations concern really, not the *fact* of revelation, but its mode, or form, or course; upon Christian faith and practice they have no bearing whatever.

If you wish to read a really strong advocacy of the Wellhausen hypothesis, without the technical material which generally forms a part of such a discussion,—an advocacy presented reverently and cautiously, read this article.

The Prophecy of Isaiah.*—Isaiah is characterized by the wide scope, the far-reaching perspective and the vividness of his visions; by the brilliancy of his diction, the sublimity of his theism, and the spirituality of his teachings. Isaiah's prophecies are a panorama, in advance, of the great scenes of future history; the outcome is in the lowly person and theocratic rule of the Messiah; the scheme, however, does not end until millennial glory is attained. The sixty-six chapters are all the work of *one* Isaiah: (1) the external testimony is overwhelming against the hypothesis of a duplex authorship; (2) the two portions of Isaiah's prophecies are not only not discrepant, but actually harmonious, and mutually sustain each other; for (a) few new topics are introduced in the latter half of the book; (b) the suffering Messiah is brought in in the first part as well as in the second, and there is no difficulty in supposing Cyrus to have been named long beforehand; (c) there is no distinctive peculiarity in the style or phraseology of the writer in these two portions of the book such as to negative the identity. The theory of a second Isaiah has been propounded to get rid of the prediction of the name of Cyrus and the suffering of Christ, and thus destroy this clinching proof of inspiration and religious doctrine. The tendency to doubt the validity of prophecy as an evidence of the truth of the Bible or as a ground of revelation is to be deprecated. The testimony of prophecy has been emphasized by Isaiah himself, and by the New Testament writers, and by our Lord. The trail of the Edenic serpent can be discerned in the work of those who are throwing discredit upon one of the two main buttresses of biblical truth. The old and well-established opinions must stand. It is time for the alarm to be sounded against the imposture and the effrontery of the pseudo-critic.

We wish that every reader of the STUDENT might read this presentation. It clearly exhibits some of the most striking differences which exist between the old and newer schools.

* By Professor James Strong, S. T. D., Madison, N. J., in *The Methodist Review*, March-April, 1890, pp. 169-183.

𝔅𝔦𝔟𝔩𝔦𝔠𝔞𝔩 𝔑𝔬𝔱𝔢𝔰.

Demons in the Gospel Narratives. An interesting discussion of evil spirits in the Bible is presented by Professor Toy in the *Journal of Biblical Literature* (vol. ix., 1). In considering the phenomena of demonic possession in the Gospels, he finds the basis of the conception in the Old Testament view that extraordinary mental conditions were produced by the indwelling of a spirit sent from God. When the good and bad agencies became distinguished in thought, the evil spirits (1 Sam. 16 : 14) became demons. They are represented as active in the New Testament times, as was natural from the intense ethical and redemptive feeling of Christianity. They are the Old Testament spirits sent from God, here organized, according to the general Jewish development, into a separate body, and united with the evil host of which the devil is the head.

The Gospel of Matthew. Professor Gardiner, in the same journal, makes a careful study of the text of Matthew's Gospel. All know that this Gospel consists of masses of discourses and masses of narratives, which are gathered, each class by itself, without regard to chronological order. An examination of these two parts shows (1) that the quotations in the discourses are from the Septuagint, but in the narratives from the Hebrew ; (2) differences in the vocabulary of the two parts are marked and numerous ; (3) differences exist in grammatical forms and favorite phrases. The theory which Dr. Gardiner frames to account for this state of things is an interesting one. It is that Matthew originally wrote only the account of our Lord's discourses in Aramaic, and subsequently caused this to be translated into Greek, himself adding the narratives in the same language. This view he regards as accounting for the differences mentioned better than any other, and as a satisfactory solution of the puzzling enigmas in regard to this Gospel.

Paul at Ephesus. Canon Hicks, who has in charge the editing of the Ephesian Inscriptions in the British Museum, writes a fresh and interesting article in the *Expositor* for June on "Demetrius the Silversmith, an Ephesian Study." He thinks that he has found the name of the very Demetrius referred to in Acts 19 on a marble slab, and shows how much illustrative material can be drawn from the monuments of Ephesus. There Demetrius is found to be one of the guardians of the temple of Ephesians, and the opposition to Paul is, therefore, not primarily stirred up by a trade disaffection, but by religious prejudice. Canon Hicks suggests a plausible explanation of Acts 19 : 24, where Demetrius is said to be a maker of "silver shrines." The difficulty is suggested by Chrysostom—"How is it possible for shrines (temples) to be made of silver?" Other writers speak of silver statuettes of Diana, but must we understand that whole shrines were thus constructed? The solution is as follows : (1) This is not one of the sections of Acts which relate Luke's personal experiences, but was the result of investigations and compilation of others' materials ; (2) he probably had before him a slab like the one previously mentioned, which represented Demetrius as a "temple-warden" (*neopoios*), "neopoios" having this technical meaning ; (3) or, the source which he used may have first described Demetrius as a "silversmith" and a *neopoios* (temple-warden) ; (4) Luke, not being acquainted with the technical meaning of this word, connected it with the "silversmith" just preceding, and thinking it also descriptive of the trade of Demetrius, paraphrased it as "one who made shrines (*poion naous*) of silver for Diana.'

The Satan of Job. In the article already alluded to, Professor Toy compares the Satan of Job with the lying spirit of 1 Kings 22 : 19–22, referred to by Micaiah. He maintains that there are two differences in the conceptions : (1) the Satan of Job has his independent thought and purpose, while the evil spirit of Micaiah is under the direct control of Jehovah, sent to do His commands ; (2) that the spirit in Kings acts on the minds of men influencing their thoughts, while Satan controls only external conditions. The conception of Satan, therefore, is to be regarded as much later than that of the "spirit from Jehovah." Indeed Dr. Toy regards it as not in any way derived from the former idea, but the product of new conditions which the Exile produced. It was the problem of national suffering in the Exile on the part of the true Israel which demanded solution. Jeremiah, Ezekiel, Isaiah 53 solve it in one way. Zechariah and Job refer it to an adversary (Satan) in heaven, the latter generalizing the particular instance into a universal fact of experience, for the explanation of human suffering. All this is very interesting and plausible, perhaps visionary.

Judaism and Temperance. A writer in the *Jewish World* call attention to the well-known fact of the temperate characteristics of the Jews and refers to the little noticed fact of the omission from the Pentateuchal codes of any restriction on drinking wine. He maintains that this fact shows that already the Hebrews had learned temperance in the use of strong drink so that there was no necessity of making laws on the subject. The training had begun far back in the history of the nation and had developed a "special instinct for temperance." The story of Noah, which he regards as one of the oldest documents in the Bible shows that even then this instinct was vigorous. The thought is certainly a suggestive one and if true, shows the power of early tendencies in the history of a nation to influence its subsequent life.

Romans 6 : 4 ; Colossians 2 : 12. In the *Expository Times* for April a new view of these passages is presented. It is claimed that the article with the Greek word for "baptism" in this verse has been overlooked, when it should really be translated, and that too, as frequently elsewhere, by the possessive pronoun. The rendering proposed, therefore, would be : "We were buried together with Him by His baptism unto death." "Thus the baptism of which the Apostle speaks is Christ's 'baptism unto death' upon Calvary ('I have a baptism to be baptized with') ; and the believer, yielding himself to Christ in faith, becomes so identified with Him, that he is condemned, crucified, and buried together with Him ; quickened, raised up, and glorified together with Him." A similar view is held of the parallel passage in Colossians.

The Human Element in Scripture. In a recent lecture by the Rev. A. J. F. Behrends, D. D., some very vigorous remarks are made on this point. He maintains that the time is forever gone by when the human element in the composition of the Scriptures can be ignored or regarded as incidental. The New Testament has a modern atmosphere, to be sure, but the farther back we go, the more Oriental and pictorial becomes the language, "until it becomes difficult to disentangle the historical from the ideal in the recorded tradition or narrative."

The Writings of Luke. In defending the position just stated, Dr. Behrends cites Luke who not only in his phraseology but also in his method shows no trace of conscious reception of supernatural information. He acted the part of an earnest, patient historical student, claiming no supernatural illumination, and never dreaming that his private letters would become universally recognized authorities. These facts, however, only more firmly establish this authority, for he would have been the first to express doubt about his researches if such doubt existed, and he has incorporated in his pages documents and traditions which with the free use of his historical faculty he regards as trustworthy.

Jesus and Death: John 11: 33. The editor of the *Expository Times* considers John 11: 33, where the difficult phrase "He was moved with indignation in the spirit and troubled Himself" occurs. The question why Jesus was moved with indignation has been answered in many ways, e. g., (1) that it was deep grief not anger, (2) His divine nature was indignant that His human nature gave way to sorrow, (3) the hypocritical conduct or unbelief of the Jews who came out to weep, (4) the thought of the ravages of sin in the world of which this was an evidence. These views are rejected and the position taken that Christ's great aim was to teach men that the only great calamity was death in sin. So he was indignant that they were so extravagantly sorrowful over the death of the body. By this wild grief they both forgot that the only real loss was the loss of a soul and they, also, virtually accused Him and His Father of neglect and cruelty. This view is plausible but imputes to Jesus a want of sympathy with human earthly sorrow, even if it may be short-sighted, which at other times he did not fail to show. Why should he not have rebuked the widow of Nain?

Date of the Apocalypse. An interesting note is furnished to the same journal by Principal Brown whose defense of the post-neronic date of the Apocalypse was summarized in a former number of the STUDENT. He finds a further argument in the mention of "clear glass" in the book. "John mentions 'clear glass,' like 'crystal,' four times. He is the only New Testament writer who speaks of it. Now, though *colored* glass and *opaque* glass were known as far back as the early Egyptian era, it was only in the reign of Nero that clear transparent glass came into fashion. A great demand sprang up at once for it. Hence John, in speaking of it, uses it as we would the railway or telegraph, etc., and by so doing shows that his book was written *after* Nero's reign. Possibly some other allusions of the same kind may exist."

Ecclesiasticus. Reference has been made in the STUDENT to the inaugural address of Professor Margoliouth in assuming the chair of Arabic in the University of Oxford. That address has given rise to not a little controversy. The subject of the paper was the Apocryphal book of Ecclesiasticus. The reputed author of that book is Ben Sira or the son of Sirach. The course and contents of Prof. Margoliouth's essay have been thus summarized.

There are three versions of the book extant,—one in Greek, one in Syriac, and one in Latin. But it is now generally held that the original language was none of these, but Hebrew. Besides the three versions, there occur quotations from the book in the Talmud, which may be directly from the original Hebrew. Some time ago Mr. Margoliouth, along with the late Dr. Edersheim, set himself to reconstruct the original text; whereupon he made the surprising discovery that the original Hebrew must have been in metre. This at once made the reconstruction easier, and placed the reconstructed text on a much firmer basis. He then perceived that the original must have been neither in ancient Hebrew, like Isaiah, nor in middle Hebrew, like Nehemiah, but in modern Hebrew, like the Talmud itself. It was at this point that Mr. Margoliouth found himself in conflict with the results of the Higher Criticism. Ben Sira wrote, admittedly, about 200 B. C. If *modern* Hebrew was the literary language so early as that, it becomes necessary, in order to allow time for the gradual formation of this modern Hebrew, to push back the more ancient language in which Ecclesiastes, for example, or Daniel, is written to a much earlier period than the Higher Criticism allows. It is at this point that the controversy has arisen. Criticisms have been made by Profs. Cheyne, Driver, and Neubauer to which Mr. Margoliouth has made a striking reply in the *Expositor*, completely using up the latter critic while the two former have been compelled to yield some points.

General Notes and Notices.

An interesting discussion is going on in the pages of the *Christian Standard*, the organ of the "Christians" or "Disciples," on the origin and date of the Synoptic Gospels. The starting point of the controversy lay in the somewhat unqualified endorsement of the views of Dr. Bernhard Weiss on the origin of Matthew's Gospel by the Rev. G. W. Longan. These views were criticized with great vigor and keenness of thought from the conservative side by the Rev. Professor McGarvey. The discussion has extended to a general consideration of the critical views of the Gospel narratives. The fact that such interest is taken in questions that are largely critical, and that a denominational weekly newspaper opens its columns to such themes of discussion, argues well for the liberty and the high character of the intellectual life of this body of Christian people.

The chair of Hebrew in the Presbyterian College of London, made vacant by the death of the Rev. Professor Elmslie, was recently filled by the election of the Rev. J. Skinner, Free Church minister of Kelso. The name of Rev. George Adam Smith, M. A., of Aberdeen, whose work on Isaiah was thought to contain some startling views on Inspiration, was early and strongly urged, but this evoked so much opposition that Mr. Smith decided not to become a candidate. The Professor-elect is a graduate of Aberdeen. His career as a student in that university was "one of distinction, uniformly notable, and in some respects unexampled." In New College, Edinburgh, he also held the first place, obtained the Cunningham scholarship, and achieved great distinction in Hebrew. He has been examiner in Hebrew in the Exit examinations, and is the author of "The Historical Connection between the Old and New Testaments," one of the "Bible Class Primers," published by T. and T. Clark. He has been in the active ministry for about ten years.

The brilliant sketch of Berlin University professors and their work which appears in this number of the STUDENT is worthy of a place beside the interesting article of Professor S. Ives Curtiss in the *Independent* of June 12, on Leipsic and its professors of 1873 and onward. In that article after describing F. Delitzsch, Kabnis and Luthardt the giants of that day, Professor Curtiss gives the following amusing and at the same time characteristic sketch of the great New Testament critic, Tischendorf. "In my innocence I thought it would be a great privilege to hear the lectures of such a wonderful man. Professor Delitzsch, whom I consulted, laughed when I proposed to hear Tischendorf; and when I asked the reason why, he replied: 'He is what we call a parade horse.' Nothing daunted I went to hear the famous scholar. About thirty were present. His lecture was a strange jumble of Latin, Greek and German, delivered with great volubility. At the next lecture only about twenty were present. Soon after he was smitten with that paralytic shock which soon put an end to his useful labors."

Bible study in the colleges is making progress. In the catalogue of Washington and Lee University Professor Henry Alexander White, Ph. D. announces the following courses in *Bible History*. The English Bible is used as a text-book of history. The plan of study is similar to that published in the OLD AND NEW TESTAMENT STUDENT. The course is designed to enable the student to gain a clear and comprehensive knowledge of (1) six of the *historical* books of the Old Testament (Genesis, Exodus, Samuel (I and II), and the Kings (I and II); (2) the period of history (both sacred and secular) covered by each book; (3) the literature of that period; (4) the more important topics connected with these books, this history and this literature. More in detail: (1) implies a *general* study of each book in its entirety, with an effort to get the narrated events *in their order* clearly fixed in the mind; the basis of study is the text of the Revised Version of the English Bible; (2) the periods of history covered by Genesis and by Exodus bring the student into contact with the early empires, Chaldea, Babylonia, Assyria, and Egypt; the books of Samuel and of The Kings bring him to the study of the same empires when at a later period they gathered around the Jewish monarchy in its rise and fall; (3) the literature of each period embraces the inscriptions on the ancient monuments and the inspired writings of the Prophets; each book of Prophecy is viewed in its historical setting; (4) the topics connected with this course are, in the main, embraced in the sciences of Archæology, Ethnology, Political and Physical Geography. (Two hours a week.)

The first Summer School for 1890 under the direction of the American Institute of Sacred Literature was held at New Haven from May 22d to June 11. Courses were offered in Hebrew and Cognate Languages, New Testament Greek, the Old Testament and the New Testament in English. Fifty-seven persons were enrolled in these courses. The class in the critical study of the Hebrew text of Haggai, Zechariah and Malachi numbered twenty. Nine men began the study of Arabic, and in three weeks had made good progress in reading the Kuran. Sight-reading classes were carried on in Hebrew, six men reading the Books of Samuel, seven the prophecies of Jeremiah. Eight students formed the beginners' class in Hebrew, four in New Testament Greek. Four others reviewed the elements of New Testament Greek, and four reviewed in the same way the elements of Hebrew. The class in the study of the English Old Testament numbered twelve. Their work was the study of the History of the Kingdom from the beginning to the Captivity. The class in the English New Testament, numbering ten, made a careful study of the later ministry of Christ in Perea and Jerusalem down to the Crucifixion. Besides these regular working classes, popular lectures were offered by Professor Stevens of Yale Divinity School upon the Origin and History of the New Testament Books, and by Professor Harper on Isaiah 40–66, taken up verse by verse. These courses of lectures were each taken by about one hundred persons. Much enthusiasm was aroused. Beginning at so early a date, the school was attended by a much larger number than could have been expected, and the results attained amply justified the endeavor. Many of the earnest thinking Christian people of the city received a new impulse to the study of the Scriptures, and others from abroad carried away with them much profitable and suggestive material, as well as gained an insight into methods of study which they will put into practice in their future work. The second school of the Institute is now in session at Philadelphia, and is very largely attended, the regular membership reaching more than one hundred.

It is well known that The Palestine Exploration Fund founded in London June 22, 1865, is a society for "the accurate and systematic investigation of the archæology, the topography, the geology and physical geography, the manners and customs of the Holy Land, for Biblical illustration." Her Majesty the Queen is patron, and the Archbishop of York is president. Its rules are that it is not to be a religious society nor be pledged to advocate or attack any form of creed, that it is not to adopt nor defend any side in controversial matters, and that its work is to be done on strictly scientific principles. The best guarantee of the excellence of its work is the list of those officers and others who have served it, of whom may be named Sir Charles Wilson, Sir Charles Warren, Major Conder, Canon Tristram, Dr. Selah Merrill, and Laurence Oliphant. In the course of its twenty-five years' existence, the Society, with limited funds at its disposal, has done an immense amount of work, and published the results in books, papers, maps, plans, and photographs, primarily for the benefit of its subscribers, and also for the advantage of all students of the Sacred Scriptures. The fund is about to enter upon a special work, having obtained a firman permitting excavation at 'Ajlan, the Eglon of Joshua. The work of exploring this mound has been placed in the hands of Mr. Flinders Petrie, who won fame in the employ of the Egyptian Exploration Fund. It cannot be too strongly urged that no time should be lost in pursuing these explorations, for the vandalism of the East, and the newly imported civilization of the West, together, are fast destroying whatever records of the past lie exposed.

The importance of the work and the value of its results have led clergymen and Bible students generally to become subscribers to the Fund, but the present opportunity seems to demand an increase of its income. An appeal is now made, endorsed by Rev. Lyman Abbott, D. D., of New York; Professor A. V. G. Allen, of the Episcopal Theological School at Cambridge; Rev. Messrs. Phillips Brooks, D. D., E. E. Hale, D. D., Joseph Cook, and Philip L. Moxom. of Boston; Dr. Selah Merrill, of Andover; President W. F. Warren, D. D., of Boston University; Professors A. P. Peabody, D. D., J. H. Thayer, D. D., C. H. Toy, D. D., of Harvard University; Rev. A. McKenzie, D. D., of Cambridge; and others. Theodore F. Wright has been authorized to receive subscriptions and donations. He announces his willingness to give public descriptions of the field and work of the Fund so far as his duties permit. He earnestly hopes that there are many who will deem it a privilege to assist the Fund in its supremely valuable work. Remittances may be made by check or postal order to him at 38 Quincy St., Cambridge, Mass. Readers of the OLD AND NEW TESTAMENT STUDENT ought to have a large share in contributing to this excellent work.

Book Notices.

Baldwin Lectures.

The Church's Certain Faith. Baldwin Lectures, 1889. By George Zabriskie
Gray, late Dean of the Episcopal Theological School, Cambridge, Mass.
Boston and New York: Houghton, Mifflin and Company. Price $1.50.

This volume was prepared for oral delivery under the auspices of the Hobart
Guild of the University of Michigan, but owing to the illness of the writer
soon after the first draft of them was prepared, they appear for the first time
in this handsome volume. Dean Gray was a loyal member and valiant defend-
er of the Episcopalian communion. He means by the *Church's* Certain Faith
the doctrines and organization of that particular branch of Christendom.
Hence those who think the book a defence of Christianity as such will be disappointed to find much in it with which they cannot agree. The lectures are
popular, dealing with such subjects as What is Belief, What is Christianity,
Who was Jesus Christ, What did Christ found, The Bible. One cannot help
regretting the polemical tone of some of these lectures, particularly that on
the church as Christ founded it, and the slighting way in which other branches
of historic Christianity are spoken of. Those who desire a plain and vigorous
defense of Episcopacy will find it in this book. Many would think that Dean
Gray has underestimated the real power of the Bible in spite of his eulogy of
its influence. All will acknowledge the candor and ability with which the
argument is conducted, although no especial contribution is made to general
Christian apologetics. The author's strength appears not in biblical theology
or exegesis, but in a broad common-sense which looks at questions of life and
religion, apart from scholastic and technical forms of expression and thought.

The Unknown God.

The Unknown God or Inspiration among Pre-Christian Races. By C.
Loring Brace. New York: A. C. Armstrong and Son. 1890. Price $2.50.

The title of this interesting work by Mr. Brace is both attractive and unfortunate. It is attractive by reason of its suggestiveness. It is unfortunate because it introduces that ambiguous and therefore dangerous word "inspiration"
which seems to prejudge the question and alienate the intellectual sympathy
of some readers at the beginning. The real and vital point is just this—
whether "inspiration" in any true sense can be predicated of heathen
religions. The conclusion as to this question would better have come at the
end rather than at the beginning of the investigation. Doubtless Mr. Brace
thought he was using the term in a very harmless sense, and so it may be;
but he could not expect his readers to accept his point of view in so important
a respect, before accompanying him on his researches. Apart from this, however, the book is a very readable endeavor to "see how the men of other races
and times regarded the problems of the universe." Egyptian monotheism,

Babylonian and Greek mysteries and faith, Stoical beliefs, Zoroastrianism, the Hindu and Buddhistic religions, are successively examined. The style is pleasing, the information given quite carefully and accurately presented. The liberalism of the writer and his loose views of the relations of Christianity to other religions have not been noted as they should have been noted by those who have praised this work. The writer is not a close thinker, his conclusions are not by any means warranted by the facts. Yet orthodox and unorthodox writers alike have commended the work to their respective friends. If the position of the writer is accepted by those who commend the book so highly they cannot hold the ordinarily accepted view of Christianity and the Bible. Having given this note of warning to those who may wish to read this volume one may add that while the ground traversed is not so broad or the details so completely presented as by Dr. Pressense in his "Ancient World and Christianity," which is equally accurate—yet, readers will find much helpful material given them here in regard to the life and thought of religious men of old times. The outward form and style in which the book is gotten up is admirable.

Jesus of Nazareth.

Jesus of Nazareth. I. His Personal Character. II. His Ethical Teachings. III. His Supernatural Works. Three lectures before the Y. M. C. A. of Johns Hopkins University, in Levering Hall. By John A. Broadus, D. D., LL. D. New York: A. C. Armstrong and Son. Price 75 cents.

In three lectures of some thirty-five pages each Dr. Broadus presents some interesting thoughts upon the character and permanent significance of Jesus Christ and His work for humanity. They seem admirably adapted to their purpose. The style is simple and flowing; the hortatory and evangelical tone permeate the discussion yet not obtrusively; the points made are vital; the impression which they must have made upon their hearers could not have been otherwise than salutary, and the influence which the printed volume will have will be helpful to inquiring and perplexed minds as well as stimulating to all lovers of the life of Jesus. The first lecture is by all odds the best of the three, and the third the least satisfactory by reason of a certain far away and vague character which appears in the argument. The real questions at issue are not directly and steadily grappled with. Indeed Dr. Broadus' style is conversational, and hence somewhat lacking in proportion. Paragraphs sometimes end quite abruptly, and the links of an argument are not always closely joined. There are many finely expressed paragraphs very quotable, though our space forbids the presentation of any of them. One cannot but admire the transparent candor and fairness which (p. 44) freely allow that Confucius in his statement of the idea of the Golden Rule meant to be taken positively, so that he is really at one with Jesus in this noble sentiment. We are glad to see that the author maintains the conclusion which he wrought out in his excellent commentary on Matthew that the "Lord's Prayer" finds nothing like an adequate parallel in Jewish sources. A charming passage presents the true interpretation of the statements of Jesus concerning non-resistance, oaths, etc. "We must remember that our Saviour was often a field-preacher, or a preacher in public squares" (p. 49). We are not quite sure of a few positive statements concerning minor points which occur in these lectures. Is there any evidence to prove that the inhabitants of Nazareth "were rude and violent, and had an ill-name among their neighbors" (page 11)? It can hardly be argued from the facts given in the Gospels. It is suggested (page 21) that mothers were accustomed to bring their children to a revered rabbi for his blessing. But does not the attitude of the disciples, when Jesus was asked to bless the children, constrain us to say with Edersheim that this relation to them was contrary to all Jewish notions and incompatible with the supposed dignity of a rabbi? One might also be inclined to side with Weiss rather than with our author in his interpretation of the famous passage, " Render unto Cæsar," etc. Jesus' reply was practically a declaration that He did not propose to interfere with the Roman sovereignty of Judea, and so far, at least, Jesus, with conscious purpose, told the questioners and the people generally that He was not the Messiah of their expectations. On page 24 it is said that Jesus was weary "with months of earnest teaching" as He sat by Jacob's well. Doubtless this may have been true, but does not the narrative state that it was the journey that had wearied Him? Dr. Broadus has many " asides" in the course of these lectures, but none is more masterly and interesting than the paragraph in which he shows that the " having all things in common" in the early church was nothing like communism. His discussion of the date and trustworthiness of the Gospels in the third lecture shows a clear understanding of these vexed questions. All the way through the book appear that easy mastery of the great facts and that grasp of fundamental principles which we understand better when we learn from the preface that "the little volume is the fruit of life-time studies, and has been prepared with the author's best exertions, and a great desire to promote 'the knowledge of Jesus, the most excellent of the sciences.'" May it do much good.

The Gospel History.

The Gospel History of our Lord and Saviour Jesus Christ, in a connected narrative in the words of the Revised Version. Arranged by Rev. C. C. James, M. A. London and New York: Macmillan and Co. Price $1.10.

The plan which was followed in making up this little book is stated by the author as follows: " First, I arranged the parallel passages, side by side, as denoted by the best authorities. Then taking the fullest account of each event as the ground-work, I have endeavored to weave into that the additional facts, traits or illustrations which are found in the other narratives; assuming first of all that St. Luke did what he tells us he intended to do, viz., to write his history 'in order.'" Whatever was not thus woven into the thread of the story is placed in a "table of variations" at the end of the volume. These statements together with the title page give a sufficiently definite idea of the book. The arrangement and interpretation of the events do not differ as a general rule from those ordinarily accepted. It is taken for granted that there are two rejections at Nazareth, two cleansings of the Temple. In the narrative of the Last Supper that order is adopted which brings the instituting of the supper after the departure of Judas. The arrangement of Luke's material commonly supposed to belong to a Perean ministry is peculiar and not at all satisfactory. Chapters seven to eleven of John are placed before Luke's chapters ten to eighteen, thus making the raising of Lazarus precede the sending out of the seventy. The book as a whole does not serve the purpose as well as Cadman's "Christ in the Gospels," though its clear print and delicately tinted paper make it very attractive.

Jesus the Messiah.

Jesus the Messiah. [An abridged edition of The Life and Times of Jesus the Messiah.] By Alfred Edersheim, D. D., Ph. D. New York: A. D. F. Randolph and Co. Price $2.00.

Students of the Gospels are familiar with the larger work by Dr. Edersheim which has been before the public for several years. It was the author's purpose at some time to compile from the two volumes filled with materials for scholars a book which should present the results without the processes and authorities so fully supplied there, and thus appeal to a larger circle of readers. This praiseworthy conception has now been carried out after his death by those who were acquainted with his ideas and plans for such an abridgement. They have produced a book of which no one who obtains it can fail to enjoy and profit from the reading. The peculiar feature of Dr. Edersheim's larger book was its employment of Jewish materials to illustrate the life of Jesus. This he did on a scale of thoroughness and accuracy never before surpassed and by it his work has a permanent value. This smaller volume is beautifully printed and the editorial work has been done so skillfully, that henceforth only scholars will need to examine the volumes from which it has been abridged. It is not so full as the works of Geikie or Farrar, but in accuracy and freshness it is far superior to them. It is to be hoped that its sale will be large and its use among our Bible reading classes very widely extended.

The Epistle of James.

The Gospel of Common Sense as contained in the canonical Epistle of James. By Charles F. Deems, D. D., New York: Wilbur B. Ketcham. Pp. 322; price, $1.50.

The author of this book is well known as a preacher and scholar. He has here furnished a series of expository lectures upon this epistle. After an introductory discussion of the authorship, which is assigned to James the brother of the Lord, the son of Mary and Joseph, the chapters are taken up and expounded in order. The presentation is vivid, the language racy, and the points made, vigorous and clear. Now and then comes a bit of fanciful allegorizing as that on the *Father of Lights* (pp. 83–85). We are inclined to think that he overstates the astronomical knowledge of the common people in the first century in connection with 1: 18, when he regards them as understanding the sun's movements. As to the coming of the Lord (5: 7) he thinks that the destruction of Jerusalem may have been referred to. In 5: 13–15, the remark is made that while the particular form of miraculous gifts there mentioned may have passed away, yet even up to the present these "gifts" themselves have been bestowed on certain individuals. In that special case the cure was miraculous. The use of the oil is not regarded by him as remedial. Here it seems that the expositor is scarcely right. The very mention of oil in the connection is enough to show that James regarded it as used to assist in the cure of the sick. The author has not produced a great book. It is a good example, however, of expository preaching, and will be useful to those who would preach from this Epistle.

Current Old Testament Literature.

American and Foreign Literature.

1. *Handbook of Bible Biography.* By Rev. C. R. Barnes. New York: Hunt and Eaton. $2.25.

2. *Jehovah-Jesus: The Divine appearances under the patriarchal, levitical, and Christian dispensations.* By G. F. Townsend. London: Nisbet. 5s.

3. *Historie du Canon de l'Ancien Testament.* Lecons d'Ecriture Sainte professes a l' Ecole superieure de theologie de Paris pendant l' année 1889-'90. By A. Loisy. Tours: Maine.

4. *The old Documents and the new Bible; an easy lesson for the people in biblical criticism. The Old Testament.* By J. P. Smith. London: Bagster. 2s. 6.

5. *Dieu et la Creation.* By L. Guignard. Chartres: Havard.

6. *La Sainte Bible, avec commentaire d' apres dom Calmet, les saints Peres, et les exegetes anciens et modernes. T. 2. Levitique, Nombres, Deuteronomie.* By J. A. Petit. Arras: Sueur-Chauney. 1890.

7. *Cursus Scripturae Sacrae—Commentarius in Ezchielem prophetam.* By J. Knabenbauer. Paris: Lethellieux. 9 fr.

8. *Lives and Times of the Minor Prophets.* By Rev. F. W. Farrar, D. D. London: Nisbet. 2. 6.

9. *Präparationen zu den kleinen Propheten. 3 Hft: Der Prophet Amos.* By J. Bachmann, Berlin: Mayer u. Müller. .8o.

10. *Präparationen zu den kleinen Propheten. Der Prophet Micha u Obadja.* By J. Bachmann, Berlin: Mayer u. Müller. .8o.

11. *Les Resultats de l' exegese biblique.* Le Historie; la religion; la litterature. By M. Vernes. Paris: Leroux.

12. *The Jews under Roman Rule.* Story of the Nations Series. By W. D. Morrison. London: Unwin. 5s.

Articles and Reviews.

13. *The Office and Work of the Old Testament in Outline.* By the Rt. Hon. W. E. Gladstone, in S. S. Times, May 31, 1890.

14. *The Study of the Old Testament, with special Reference to the Element of Compilation in the Structure of the Books.* By Rev. Prof. H. E. Ryle, in the Expositor, May 1890.

15. *Le Livre de la Genese.* By Ch. Piepenbring, in Rev. de l'hist. des religions, Jan.-Feb. 1890.

16. *Die Uroffenbarung nach biblischer lehre u. nach heidenischer Irrlehre [Gen. 1-5].* By O. Naumann, in Der Bew. d. Glaub. Jan.-Apr. 1890.

17. *The Pharaohs of Moses according to Hebrew and Egyptian chronology.* By E. De Bunsen, in P. S. B. A., 12, 4, 1890.

18. *Some Suggestions Respecting the Exodus.* By A. L. Lewis, in P. S. B. A., 12, 4, 1890.

19. *Joseph in Aegypten.* By H. Brugsch, in Deutsche Rundschau. May, 1890.

20. *Pithom und Ramses, oder zur Geschichte des Auszugs,* By H. Brugsch, in Jud. Lit. Blt., 14-18, 1890.

21. *Le Droit de propriete foncier dans les lois mosaiques.* By P. Minault, in Rev. du Christ. prat. III., 13, 1889.

22. *Uber Deut. 18: 15, 18.* By Hoppe, in Ztschr. f. d. Evang. Religionsunt. 1, 2, Jan. 1890.

23. *Die Entstehungszeit des Deuteronomiums.* By A. Zahn, in Liter. Beilage der Deutsch. Evang. Krztg. 1 and 2, 1890.

24. *Gilbert's Poetry of Job.* Review by Budde, in Theol. Lztg. Apr. 19, 1890.

25. *Elie et Achab.* By X. Koenig, in Rev. du Christ. prat. 3, 15, 1890.

26. *Nehemie et Esdras.* Une Nouvelle Hypothese sur la chronologie de l'epoque de la restauration. I. By A. Hoonacker, in Le Museon 9. 2, 1890.

27. *Seyring's Abhängigkeit der Sprüche Solomonis Cap. 1-9 von Hiob.* Rev. by Siegfried, in Theol. Lztg. April 19, 1890.

28. *Some Thoughts on the Structure of the Book of Proverbs.* By Rev. Prof. J. R. Lumby, in The Expositor, June 1890.

29. *Zwei Vorlesungen über die hebraische Poesie. I. Die Naturbetrachtung der hebraischen Poesie.* By V. Ryssel, in Theol. Ztsch. aus d. Schweiz. 2, 1890.

30. *The Measurements of Hebrew Poetry as an aid to literary analysis.* By Prof. Francis Brown, in Jour. of Bibl. Lit., 9, 1, 1890.

31. *Exegesis of Isaiah 7: 10-17.* By Prof. C. R. Brown, in Jour. of Bibl. Lit., 9, 1, 1890.

Current New Testament Literature.

American and Foreign Publications.

32. *The Gospel of St. Matthew.* Expositor's Bible. By Rev. J. M. Gibson, D. D., London : Hodder and Stoughton.

33. *Die Bergpredigt Jesus, wissenschaftlich popular ausgelegt.* By H.G.Ibbeken,2 ausg, Einbeck : Ibbeken. 3.50.

34. *Das vierte Evangelium, e. ,authent. Bericht üb. Jesus v. Nazareth, wiederhergestellt, übersetzt u. erklärt.* By H. K. H. Delff. Husum : Delff. 2.

35. *Jesus and the Men about Him.* By Charles F. Dole. Boston: G. E. Ellis. .50.

36. *Das Gebetsleben Jesu.* By G. Jäger. Leipzig, 1890. 1.

37. *La Legende du Messie.* Precis historique. By V. Du Breuil. Paris : Vanier. 5 fr.

38. *The Epistles of St. Paul to the Colossians, Thessalonians and Timothy ;* with notes. By M. F. Sadler. London : Bell. 6s.

39. *Der 1. Brief d. Johanner.* By Th. Jellinghaus. Basel : Spittler. 1.20.

40. *A Commentary on the Revelation of St. John.* By S. Garrett. London : Hunt. 10s.

41. *The Apocalypse considered as the final crisis of the age.* By T. Ryan. London : Stock 3s. 6d.

Articles and Reviews.

42. *Gregory's Prolegomena to Tischendorf's New Testament :* Vol. III. Review by Gebhardt, in Theol. Lztg. May 3, 1890.

43. *A Study in the First Gospel.* By Rev. Prof. Frederic Gardiner, in Jour. of Bibl. Lit. 9, 1, 1890.

44. *Matthew 18: 20, and the doctrine of the church.* By A. Spaeth, in Luth Ch. Rev., Apr., 1890.

45. *A Point of Grammar in the " Gloria in Excelsis."* [*Luke 2:14.*] Critical note by Prof. L. S. Potwin, in Andover Review. June 1890.

46. *Abortive Attempt to arrest Jesus* [*John 7 : 30-36, 40, 52*]. By Rev. Prin. J. O. Dykes, D. D., in the Expositor, May, 1890.

47. *Stalker's Imago Christi.* Review by Duff, in Theol. Lztg. May 3, 1890.

48. *L'Enseignment de Jesus sur son Retour.* By C. Bruston, in Rev. d. Theol. e. d. Phil. 2, 1890.

49. *Bethsaida and Julias.* By Selah Merrill, D. D., in the S. S. Times, May 3, 1890.

50. *The Site of the Garden of Gethsemane.* By Prof. J. Rendel Harris, in S. S. Times. May 24, 1890.

51. *Testimony of Napoleon I. with regard to Christ.* By Rev. Alex. Mair, D. D., in the Expositor, May 1890.

52. *La Question Juive dans l' eglise a l'age apostolique—Apres la reunion de Jerusalem.* By J. Thomas, in Rev. d. quest. hist. Apr. 1890.

53. *Demetrius the Silversmith. An Ephesian Study.* By Rev. Canon E. L. Hicks, in The Expositor, June 1890.

54. *The First Epistle to the Corinthians.* Review of Commentary by Ellicott and Exposition by Dods. In the Andover Review, June 1890.

55. *Soden's Der Brief an die Philipper.* Review by O. Holtzmann, in Theol. Lztg. April 5, 1890.

56. *Schaefer's Thessalonians and Galatians* Rev. by O. Holtzmann, in Theol. Lztg. Apr. 19, 1890.

57. *Westcott's Epistle to the Hebrews.* Review by Schurer in Theol. Lztg. May 17, 1890.

58. *The Epistle to the Hebrews.* Review of Commentaries by A. C. Kendrick and B. F. Westcott. In the Andover Review, June 1890.

59. *The Epistle to the Hebrews. 17. The New Covenant.* By Rev. Prof. Bruce, in The Expositor, May 1890.

60. *The Epistle to the Hebrews. 18. Shadow and Substance.* By Rev. Prof. Bruce, D. D., in The Expositor, June 1890.

61. *The Jews Under Roman Government.* By Dr. G. Dalman, in S. S. Times, May 10, 1890.

THE

Old and New Testament Student

VOL. XI.   AUGUST, 1890.   NO. 2.

A " SYMPOSIUM " which will attract wide attention is given in the present number of the STUDENT. The subject of it is one of living interest to our age. When such writers engage in it—presidents and professors of theological seminaries and colleges as well as prominent and able ministers and laymen, the opinions expressed will carry great weight. There seems to be substantial unanimity of thought among the majority of those who have the most intimate relation to theological instruction. Something ought to be done—they agree upon that. The difficulty is to determine just what is to be done and how to do it.

THIS conviction of a need for improvement in respect to the study of the English Bible in the theological seminary was earnestly urged from the student's point of view in an article recently published in these pages on "The English Bible: its Place in the Seminary." The writer of that article Mr. Fred. L. Sigmund, is a student not of Union Biblical Seminary, Dayton, O., (as was stated in connection with that article), but of the Wittenberg Theological Seminary, Springfield, O. Both students and instructors recognize the deficiency in the curriculum at this point, but, while so many new subjects of study are clamoring for admission into the already crowded courses, they fail to see how the adjustment is to be made by which more time can be given to the English Bible. May not the difficulty lie further back and the solution also?

Is not the time coming when the seminary will demand that the applicant for admission to the courses of study be proficient in the knowledge of the elementary, if not the more advanced topics relating to the Bible. Will it not soon call upon the College to furnish the student this knowledge? Shall we not see the burden lifted from the theological institutions in some such way as this? The signs of it are in the air. A practical example of what is already doing in this direction is the work offered by the University of Rochester some account of which is given on another page.

THE International Sunday School system is, after all, a great machine. Its past history is easily ascertained and understood. It was only after a severe struggle between conflicting interests and through the indomitable persistence of one man that the organization was effected. It is largely because of the jealousy of certain interests, the vast amount of capital invested, and the great energy and tact of one man, the same man, that the organization is continued. The system has accomplished most wonderful results; nor is the least of these, the preparation of the Bible-world for something better than the system itself has now to offer. The difficulty in the situation—and the existence of this difficulty is recognized far and wide—lies in the fact that the system has not grown in proportion to the results which it has accomplished. There are still great possibilities. Whether these will be realized is doubtful. The less of the machine-element there is, the greater will be the chances for ultimate success. The need now is for cautious, yet progressive advance along new, as well as old, lines. Will the few who have the management of the machinery in their hands be able to hold it? It was an unpleasant symptom that the representatives of a certain influential denomination should demand the appointment of one of their number on the "Lesson Committee," with the expressed threat, that otherwise, the system would be abandoned. Before the next triennial convention we may fairly expect that many and grave complications will arise. However this may be the world owes a debt of gratitude to one man, B. F. Jacobs of Chicago, and to the other men who have been associated with him in the work from the beginning.

HAS not the day come when scholarship and the results of scholarly work shall no longer be kept apart and away from the masses? There are scholars who disdain to speak or to write in any other than a technical way; who feel that they are casting pearls before swine, if they make a statement which may be understood by others than those working in their own specialty. Is not this idea becoming antiquated? Is the popular presentation of scientific truth at all inconsistent with a real appreciation of that truth? One would expect to find in the hearts of the men who have reached the highest point in their departments, a desire to inspire others with an interest in the work which they themselves have done, and in its results. But there are still too many scholars who are utterly indifferent whether any, outside of the few who make up their circle, have any knowledge of the précious truth of which they would be the sole possessors. In the realm of biblical science, this feeling is not so rigid a one as in times past. There has been a growing disposition to break down the wall which stands between knowledge and ignorance, between the few and the many. The contempt of the few for the ignorance of the many has not been greater than the distrust on the part of the many, of the knowledge of the few. But the breach is diminishing, and let us hope that the best men in the ranks of scholarship will begin to feel, as they have never felt, the responsibility which rests upon them in this matter. Of him to whom much is given, much also is expected. Scholars owe it to themselves, to the world and above all to the cause of the science in which they are so deeply interested to promulgate the truth in such form as that it may receive the widest acceptance. There is a sense in which the highest interests of any science are dependent upon the popular appreciation of the results gained in that science; for, in order that men may be raised up who shall be able, as specialists, to make contributions to it, there must be a wide-spread general interest in the subject. There is a responsibility here which cannot be evaded. The specialist owes it to himself and the cause to which he is devoting his life to make the results of his work accessible, at least in part, to the average intelligence of those about him.

THERE can be no true Bible study without reverence. The Bible is, above all things, a book of religion, and all religion has its basis in reverence. The spirit of reverence for God as holy and for His word and works as sacred pervades the Bible. The man who has no sympathy with this spirit cannot truly put himself under the real power of the biblical thoughts and truths. Hence the Bible student must be something more than a mere critic. If he can see only the outward and formal in the Bible, if he is more impressed by the imperfections which are incidental to the human element in the Bible than he is by the great truths concerning God and man which pervade it like an atmosphere and give it a dignity and power above all other books, he will be unable to appreciate the *real* Bible and his study of it will be but a process of destructive criticism practiced upon its outer form—a process which does not penetrate to the heart of the Bible.

WHAT would be thought of a so-called student of classical literature who had an eye only for the defective arguments or grammatical irregularities of the writers of antiquity and no appreciation or sympathy for the poetic thoughts, the high aspirations and the lofty moral truths which, in their writings, are struggling into expression? At least so much as respect for the subject-matter of any study is necessary for its profitable prosecution. And in proportion as that subject-matter rises in dignity and worth, must the respect with which it is regarded by the student of it rise into real reverence. Without this high appreciation of the contents of our studies we cannot maintain our own self-respect or develop a healthy and well-directed enthusiasm in the pursuit of them. Some, indeed, seem to take delight in a merely negative, destructive criticism, but it is always an abnormal and unhealthy pleasure which leads the mind more and more deeply into a cynical temper and towards the pessimism which universal skepticism always tends to develop.

No one can be in the best sense a student of a subject who cannot appreciate that which is highest and best in his branch of study. That which is highest and best in the Bible is the lofty truths of the spiritual life which are woven into the course of divine history and training, of which the Bible is the record and product. The man who has no affinity for these, that is, no reverence for those things which are most truly sacred, must remain blind to that which is most characteristic in the Bible.

We have now entered upon a period of critical Bible study. The various books of the Bible are undergoing the processes of literary and historical research. Light from contemporary sources will be poured in greater fulness upon all the questions of history and criticism which arise concerning the Sacred Scriptures. It is a question of the utmost importance whether this critical process shall be inspired by the spirit of reverence for God and for the religious truth which the Bible enshrines. It is certain that criticism will not cease. Shall it remain reverent? If so we have nothing to fear from it. In the long course of testing and counter-criticism to which it will be subjected it will be able to do nothing against the truth but only for the truth. But an irreverent criticism will do infinite mischief, not, indeed, because it will stay the progress of truth, but because of its disastrous effects upon the minds and lives of those who imbibe its spirit. Just here lies the danger to which in this period when critical methods are supplanting the old dogmatic treatment of Scripture, we are exposed. We believe that great religious interests are involved in promoting biblical study which shall be at once critical and reverent. But every effort to secure this result is confronted with two hindrances: on the one hand, it encounters, and, in the nature of the case, tends to develop in some minds, an iconoclastic spirit,—a temper which finds such delight in discovering something new that those who share it are half ready to cast away all that they had ever been taught to believe. The existence of examples of such extreme reaction from traditional views gives to many the impression that criticism is synonymous with negation and skepticism and will always be industriously used by those who have adopted this opinion and who regard themselves as set for the defense of tradition against all innovations. The effort under discussion meets another hindrance in the attitude and influence of those who resist all re-examination of popularly accepted opinions. In this country we are just now passing through that stage of progress in Biblical science at which the remonstrances of traditionalism—itself power-less to deal with the questions involved—are most numerous and determined against the application of scientific and his-toric tests to biblical questions. This is the experience of all progressive movements and should not be regarded as if it were some strange thing. Thoughtful men see its natural-ness and, within certain limits, its justification. Scholars are well aware that it is but the somewhat late repetition among us of what has happened in other countries.

BOTH these classes of hindrances to a real biblical science will be overcome, not by attack and controversy, but by the slow working out of definite and sure results in a positive, constructive, reverent spirit. The destructive radical will be seen to be extreme and abnormal when he is disowned by criticism itself as not possessed of its true spirit, and the ac-cusations of an inert orthodoxy which resents the disturbance of its mental quiet, will be disproved and disarmed when it is seen that criticism is not destructive of anything that is essential in religion, but is reverent in spirit and positive in results, destroying nothing which can endure the tests of truth and destroying only that it may more securely build again. We repeat: Let us have Biblical criticism, but let it be reverent!

THE LITERARY CHARACTER OF ST. PAUL'S LETTERS. I.

By Rev. Professor E. P. GOULD,

P. E. Divinity School, Philadelphia, Pa.

The most characteristic writings of St. Paul are his epistles to the Romans, the Corinthians, the Galatians, and the Philippians. Those to the Ephesians, and the Colossians, and the pastoral epistles have an importance of their own, but their literary character is so different from the rest, that they would require separate treatment, while the two epistles to the Thessalonians belong to a time when both the thought and the style of the apostle were not as yet matured. In confining our study therefore to these more characteristic letters, we shall sacrifice completeness to convenience of treatment, but we shall see the apostle at his best, or at least, where he is most like himself.

These writings are all letters, and they are real letters, not theological essays, or treatises on conduct and the Christian life, under that guise. Of course, we know that they contain such discussions, but the personal element, the relations between St. Paul and the churches addressed by him, gives character to them all, and interest. They begin with the writer's salutation to his readers, which might easily become a merely formal matter with a different kind of man, but which becomes the means in these letters of informing us as to the general feeling of St. Paul towards all his churches, and of the special regard in which he held each. Now, these salutations are, with one exception, all conciliatory. That is, this is what we should say, if we were to find the same expressions elsewhere, but in this case, I think we shall find that they express the genuine feelings of the apostle, and do not arise from any politic desire to win his readers' suffrages by formal, or undeserved compliments.

No, one of the striking things about the apostle revealed in these letters, is his faith in man on the one hand, and in the power of Jesus Christ to transform men on the other. Not that he is an optimist in the superficial sense of the word, for he sees more clearly than most men the fact of sin in men, its universality, and its terrible power. But he sees also, and says, that this is not the deepest thing in man, that the essential underlying humanity in every man is alien to this overlying and obscuring fact of sin. And in believers, he proceeds always on the assumption of the ultimate victoriousness of the grace of God in Christ, in spite of ugly outbreaks of the sin remaining in them. And so, though his letters are the best revelations that we have of the real imperfections of these early churches, there is no element of hopelessness or cynicism in them, and the apostle is evidently genuine in his good will and appreciation, when he selects the good elements in them as matters of congratulation and thanksgiving.

But the point is, that this genuineness makes itself felt in the expressions themselves. The element is so strong that it impresses itself unmistakably on what he says. And this appears especially, when we compare the different letters together, and see the discrimination used in these greetings. That to the Romans is general in its character, this being a church which he had never visited, and which he knew only by report. That to the Corinthians selects their knowledge and their power of speech, gifts especially belonging to these naturally bright and intelligent Greeks. That to the Philippians emphasizes their love and their loyalty to himself, this being the church most distinguished by the apostle's love. And then there is the exception of which we have spoken, the epistle to the Galatians, in which he proceeds immediately to the matter in hand, because their defection from him overlies everything else in his mind for the time being. But he has only reserved it for a place where it can be used with more telling effect, in the midst of his appeal to them to return to their old faith. (4: 12–20).

In studying the epistles themselves, we must remember the class of subjects with which the apostle had to deal. He was the founder of Gentile Christianity, that is, he was introducing a religion having its roots in Judaism, and its headquarters and principal men among the Jews, into communities separated by broad and well defined lines from the peculiar and exclusive system of Judaism. And the tendency had been to regard Christianity as the final form of Judaism, and necessarily incorporating into itself the main features of that system from which it had sprung. But Paul in carrying it among the Gentiles, had seen the necessity, on the contrary, of making it a universal religion, instead of a national, and hence of dropping everything distinctively Jewish. This had caused the first doctrinal dispute in the early church, the Judaizing party claiming that circumcision, the distinguishing feature of Judaism, was necessary for the Gentile converts to Christianity. Together with this, there arose questions about eating meat offered to idols and the observance of Jewish sacred days, which were of the same general character, and outside of these, questions about the resurrection, the time of our Lord's second coming, the orderly observance of the Lord's Supper, the comparative importance of the various miraculous gifts of the Spirit, the praying of women with uncovered heads, or even at all, in the public assemblies of the church, and the like. These are to-day largely questions of merely antiquarian, or historical interest, having very little relation to the present time. And moreover, the apostle was himself a Jew, and a man of his own time, and forced to discuss these things largely from the local and Jewish standpoint of his readers.

There is thus very much in his letters not specially interesting to us. And the striking thing about them is the way in which he emancipates himself so frequently from these limitations, and so elevates the local and transient into the universal. This matter of circumcision, for instance, and the general relation of Judaism to Christianity, is, or ought to be, a matter of the past, but the general question of forms and their relation to spiritual matters, and the adjustment of the principles of law and grace in the dealings of God with man, are questions always to the fore. And it is just these larger questions that the apostle finds in the matters in dispute between himself and the Judaizers, and it is owing to this, that his epistles have a continual interest and importance as expositions of Christian principle. See, for example, Rom. 1: 25–29, where he contends that circumcision and even membership in the Jewish system is not an outward, but an inward thing; Gal. 3: 26–29, where he emphasizes the oneness in Christ, and the consequent abolition of privileged distinctions between Jew and Greek, slave and free, and even male and female in Him; 4: 7–11, where he contrasts the freedom of the Gospel with all bondage to forms and observances; 5: 6, where he declares form or the absence of form to be matters of pure indifference, and faith working through love, that is, principles, affections, living and powerful motives of conduct, to be essential; and vv. 13–15, where he makes love to be the fulfilment of law.

For examples of the same power of generalization in other matters, see 1 Cor. 1: 17–2: 16, where he makes the question in the Corinthian church about the comparative merits of the preaching of himself and Apollos the occasion for contrasting earthly and heavenly wisdom, which we can abstract altogether from its special setting, and which has become, owing to this, one of the classics of Christian literature; 3: 1–23, where he takes this same division of interest, and makes it the occasion for a statement of the unity of all in Christ, and the consequent unchristian character of all divisions in the church of Christ, which is surely not out of place in these times, however much it may be unheeded; also 8: 1–13, where he takes up the matter of eating things offered to idols, and shows that, since there is no such thing really as an idol, it becomes entirely an indifferent matter, whether one eats the meat which has been offered to them, since a mere fiction cannot defile; but on the other hand, since some have not this knowledge, and are still possessed with a vague idea of the reality of the idol, that what is in itself indifferent becomes important to them; and hence the principle of love, of consideration for others, comes in to complicate what as a matter of individual conduct is perfectly simple. And hence the apostle deduces from this question, which would otherwise be practically uninteresting to us who have no idols to bother us, the profound principle of conduct, that where our conduct influences others besides ourselves, we are to be guided not only by our personal conscience and sense of right, but also by our love to them.   See also 10: 23–11: 1, where the same question is further discussed and especially vv. 24, 31, 33.

Another kindred quality in these letters is the ubiquity of the intellectual element in them.   Discussions of religious matters, both doctrinal and practical, are very apt to be dominated by the merely religious element, with large assumptions, ignoring of important data in the determination of questions, with commonplace and hortatory treatment, as the result.   But really, these questions deal with matters of profound interest and importance, and involve principles lying at the root of things.   And when a really active and powerful mind begins to work upon these, the opportunity for intellectual movement, and the play of the intellectual faculties, is correspondingly great.

Yes, it is one of the distinguishing traits of the apostle's writings, that he always approaches a subject on the side of its relations and principles, so that it is constantly illumined by his mental brightness, and penetrated with his active and powerful reason.   And, as we have seen already, while some of these relations in which he sees the matters discussed are necessarily local and temporary, for the most part he sees them in their permanent and universal relations.   Take for example, his discussion of the universality of sin in the early part of the epistle to the Romans, a subject that easily becomes commonplace by an unclassified enumeration, or a mere general showing.   The apostle immediately invests it with interest by showing us the genesis and special character of sin in the Jew and the Gentile.   He traces the sin of the Gentile world to their false conception of God, and shows how this resulted especially in the sins of lust, the abuse of the sexual relations and passions.

Here is evidently a strong, true mind dealing with the question of cause, first, intuitively grasping the principle, that a great fact, like that of the sin of the polytheistic nations, must be dealt with in its causes, and not simply in its outward aspects, and secondly, having a sense, or feeling, for the true cause.   For, when we come to examine historically the distinctive mark of the sin of the heathen peoples, we shall find it to be just this sexual vice of which the apostle tells us, and that the cause of it is their worship of the pro- creative principle which they found everywhere in nature, and which, with their tendency to deify these forces they embodied in male and female deities and worshiped with lust- ful rites.   And the sin of the Jew he traces with an equal discernment to the severance of knowledge and conduct in their religious life.   They were afflicted with the vice which infects all religions, that they were not able to live up to the high standards which their religious faculty had revealed to them as the law of life, and so came to exalt their knowledge and outward worship of God into the place of that true wor- ship which consists in a spirit exalted by its contact with the true God issuing in a life conformed to His will.

The same presence and dominance of the intellectual ele- ment is discernible in the apostle's further dealing with this matter of the relation between the Jewish and Gentile world as a matter of the Divine dealing with them, that is, of the Divine calling or election, which had seemed to be restricted to the Jews, but now in a remarkable manner seemed to be turned about, and to become almost equally restricted to the Gentiles.   The apostle's handling of the great question of causes for a mysterious fact seems to me here to be very re- markable.   In the first place, he makes the cause of the rejection of the Jews to be the fact, that in the course of time they had lost the faith which he maintains was the original cause of the choice of them as a people, while the Gentiles had come into possession of this which had so long been wanting to them.   And he does not treat this as the merely superficial fact that the one had rejected Jesus, while the other class had in so surprising numbers believed in him, but he deals with the principle which underlies these facts, that the Jews had lost the principle of faith which had really vitalized their religious life in the best periods of their his- tory.   The apostle looks at the subject of faith in a large way, seeing that the object of it may be one religious fact or another, and that the essential element in it is such a vivid feeling of the fact, whatever it may be, that it is able to master the man and control his conduct. Now the Jews had substituted for this on the one hand knowledge, held merely as such in the mind, and resulting in no uplift of the spiritual nature and on the other, conduct which was merely the outward observance of a formal rule of life, and without any enthusiasm of goodness such as is awakened by a true faith.

And then, the apostle goes on to discuss this matter of election itself, which, he says, does not have its final cause in the people elected, but in others whom their election is intended to benefit. Thus the Jews were elected in order that through them all nations might be blessed, and now their rejection is to make way for the Gentiles whom they were unwilling to admit to a share in the blessings of God's people. And the Gentiles have been admitted, not for their own sake, but in order to make way ultimately for the return of God's people. That is to say, God's ultimate purpose is to have mercy upon all men, and his temporary election or rejection, now of this people, and now of that, is simply an incident in the process of this advancing purpose. These two statements taken together make a fruitful discussion of a difficult and delicate matter.

Under this general head of the apostle's pervading intellectuality of treatment, notice especially his power to state a thing in such a way that the statement becomes an argument. Instances of this are to be found all through his writings, but see especially Rom. 2: 25–29. Here the apostle so selects his terms that the inner meaning of circumcision and uncircumcision appears, and the importance of the outward rite disappears in the statement, without any necessity for further argument. See also chap. 6: 2, where he refutes the serious charge of antinomianism made against his doctrine of freedom from the law in a sentence; and v. 16, where he sums up the situation again in the words "slaves of sin." Also 13: 10; 1 Cor. 1: 13; 8: 8; 10: 26; 2 Cor. 10: 1, where he puts the matter of his forbearance towards the unruly members of the Corinthian church, which they called weakness, in its true light in the words "through the meekness and gentleness of Christ" with which he begins his plea; Gal. 2: 14; 4: 9.

Again, under the same general head of the apostle's intellectual quality, his eye for true and striking analogies is quite
remarkable.   Among these, the fittest, as it is the most
familiar, is the comparison of the church to the human body
and its members.   The common term which unites them is
the unity of the members each in a living organism; and
the diversity in unity, the common interest, the inseparable-
ness, the necessity of each part to all the others and to the
whole, which follow from this, are seen and stated with
admirable clearness. See Rom. 12 : 3–8; 1 Cor. 12 : 12–27. See
also the comparison of the church to a building and a farm,
with reference to the work bestowed upon it by the planters
and builders, 1 Cor. 3 : 5–17; the choice of the Greek games
to picture the eagerness and striving of the Christian life,
1 Cor. 9 : 24–27; the figure of the seed and the plant to
illustrate the difference between the earthly body and the
resurrection body, 1 Cor. 15 : 35–38; the comparison of the
illuminating power given to God's messengers to a treasure
in an earthen vase, 2 Cor. 4 ; 7 ; the contrast between the
heir in his minority and the mature son, used to illustrate the
difference between man under the world religions and under
the Christian dispensation, Gal. 4 : 1–10.

[To be continued.]

THE ESCHATOLOGY OF THE KURAN.

By G. H. PATTERSON, PH. D.,

Yale University, New Haven, Conn.

Among the teachings of Mahomet, none has called forth more opposition than his representations of the future state. No small part of this opposition, however, has concerned itself with what are merely the traditions that have gathered around his teachings. It is that which is said in the Kuran about this subject, which should form the standard of judgment and it is a subject that must ever engage the attention of thoughtful men.

1. As to the Judgment Day, it may be said that belief in it is one of the articles of faith in Islam. It is called also the Day of Awakening, the Day of Decision, the Day of Reckoning and similar titles. The time of this day is said to be unknown. "They will ask you about the hour, for what time it is fixed?—say, The knowledge thereof is only with my Lord; none shall manifest it at its time but He; it is heavy in the heavens and in the earth, it will not come to you save on a sudden."* (Sura 7: 186 seq.) However, many signs preceding it are mentioned. These are, the folding up of the sun, obscuring of the moon, falling of the stars, removal of the mountains, and flowing together of seas, and such like portents.

The prophet attempts in many places to show the probability of the Resurrection from the manifestations of God's power in creation. "O ye folk! if ye are in doubt about the raising (of the dead), verily we created you from earth, then from a clot, then from congealed blood, then from a morsel shaped or shapeless, that we may explain to you."

It is said that the angels will not intercede for any on that day save for those whom God pleases, but each will bear his

*Citations from the Kuran are taken from Palmer's translation.

own burden, according as the book that will be presented at the blowing of the trumpet will show. "And the Book shall be set forth, and thou shalt see the sinners in fear of what is in it; and they will say, 'Alas, for us! what ails this Book, it leaves neither small nor great things alone, without numbering them?' and they shall find present what they have done; and thy Lord will not wrong anyone." (18: 47.)

The teaching is that the day will seem very short, but it is spoken of once as "a day, the measure of which is as a thousand years of what ye number" (32: 4); in another place as "a day whose length is fifty thousand years," (70: 4). When the affairs of this day are accomplished, angels will guide the just into Paradise but will drive the wicked into hell, where they will be received by nineteen tormenting angels.

2. For this place of torment there are several names which the commentators assign to particular divisions. They hold that there are seven stages in hell citing the following; "It has seven doors; at every door is there a separate party of them." From the last clause it is concluded that different sects will be in each division.

The following are the names of the divisions with the particular sect assigned to each: "Jahannam," the Purgatorial Hell for all Muslims; "The Flaming Fire," for Christians; "The Raging Fire," for Jews; "The Blaze," for the Sabians; "The Scorching Fire," for the Magians; "The Fierce Fire," huge hot fire for idolaters; "The Abyss," bottomless pit for hypocrites. These words, however, in the Kuran are used to denote hell without reference to such divisions.

The following short selections set forth the tortures of hell. It is said that the wicked "shall broil upon a burning fire; shall be given to drink from a boiling spring! no food shall they have save the foul thorn, which shall not fatten nor avail against hunger." "Verily, the zakkum tree (shall be) the food of the sinful; as it were melting, shall it boil in their bellies like the boiling of hot water." "When they shall be cast therein they shall hear its braying as it boils—it will well nigh burst for rage!" "Verily, those who disbelieve in our signs, we will broil them with fire; whenever their skins are well done, then we will change them for other skins, that they may taste the torment, verily, God is glorious and wise."

Whatever may be said of such representations it is certain that those in the later suras are briefer and *less materialistic.* They are not directed against sin so much as against those who did not believe in the mission of the Prophet, as is shown in the following, "God has promised unto the hypocrites, men and women, and unto the misbelievers, hell fire, to dwell therein for aye; It is enough for them! God shall curse them and theirs shall be enduring woe." The unbelievers will then acknowledge that they were warned, will confess their sins and proclaim God to be just. Mahometan divines claim that all Muslims will go to Jahannam (Gehenna; not Hades the purgatory of the Greeks), where they will remain only to be sufficiently cleansed from their sins that they may enter heaven. But there seems to be little basis for this in the Kuran.

3. In heaven, the Kuran declares, there are seven divisions as in hell, but it is with as little reason. The terms, Abode of Peace, Garden of the Most High, Garden of Eden, Garden of Paradise, etc., applied to the supposed divisions are used interchangeably to designate Paradise.

According to the early suras Paradise is represented as in the following selection: "The similitude of Paradise which is promised to the pious,—in it are rivers of water without corruption, and rivers of milk, the taste whereof changes not, and rivers of wine delicious to those who drink; and rivers of honey clarified; and there shall they have all kinds of fruit and forgiveness from their Lord! (Is that) like him who dwells in the fire for aye? and who are given to drink boiling water that shall rend their bowels asunder?" "Verily, the pious are amid shades and springs and fruit such as they love. Eat and drink with good digestion for that which ye have done."

Thus the early representations of heaven and hell in Islam, though one-sixth of the Kuran is taken up with the details of these, seem to be little else than the projection into the future of what is deemed pleasant or painful here. Paradise then is an intense realization of those things which an Arab of the parched desert would naturally desire; such as, shade, water, fruit, rest, etc., while hell is just the opposite. In that dry and thirsty land no doubt the most effective representation of future bliss is that of bubbling fountains and shady gardens through which rivers flow, in contrast with surrounding conditions and placed in juxtaposition with the representations of future punishment.

But this is not the whole of the Islamatic Paradise; the most objectionable element from a Christian standpoint is the encouragement given to sensuality. About five years after the beginning of the Prophet's mission such representations as the following occur. "Verily for the pious is a blissful place,—gardens and vineyards, and girls of the same age as themselves, and a brimming cup." "Therein are maids of modest glances whom no man nor ginn has ever dishonored." Muir observes that the notices of this voluptuous Paradise belong to a period when Mahomet was living, with a single wife, a chaste and temperate life.

In the ten years following the Hegira, women are referred to only three times. Once it is said, "They shall dwell therein for aye, with pure wives and grace from God," and twice the phrase, "and pure wives for them therein," occurs. Concerning this Muir asks, "was it that the soul of Mahomet had at that period no longings after what he had then even to satiety the enjoyment of? Or that a closer contact with Jewish principles and morality repressed the budding pruriency of the revelation and covered with merited confusion the pictures of the sensual Paradise which had been drawn at Mecca." It is to be noted that the male companions of the female elect are not specified. Will faithful women not renew their youth in heaven as well as faithful men? Concerning this Gibbon observes that, "Mahomet has not specified the male compaunions of the female elect lest he should either alarm the jealousy of their husbands or disturb their felicity by the suspicion of an everlasting marriage."

It is a question whether such material descriptions of heaven and hell are to be taken literally or figuratively. Without the use of metaphysics one can only speak of the future state in the form of poetic description. So the circumstances of this life must to some extent be used to give both form and color to the views of the life to come.   It is very natural then to picture the future abode as a restored Eden, the abode of man before the fall.   Is this then only "Oriental imagery?" If so, what language, one is inclined to ask, would have been used to set forth ideas of a material existence?   What joys do the sensual delights, as set forth in the Kuran, represent? Or what can the following mean?   "He shall broil in a fire that flames and his wife carrying faggots" (for fuel).

As a student of Islam has observed, is there not too much individualizing in such representations?   Perhaps, however, the imagery is not to be pressed too closely, as is often the case with the Hebrew prophets.   Whether the representations are to be taken figuratively or not, it is to be remembered as Carlyle says that, "the indulgences, criminal to us, which he permitted, were not of his appointment; he found them practised, unquestioned from immemorial time in Arabia; what he did was to curtail them."

While the Prophet may thus be vindicated, one can scarcely go as far as Carlyle when he says that "such representations teach the Infinite Nature of Duty; that man's actions here are of *infinite* moment to him, and never die or end at all." It is true, perhaps, that heaven and hell are realities to the Mahometan in a sense in which they are not to others, but is not the radical fault of Islam that constant and urgent appeal to a desire for reward?   Everything is thrown into the future. A mode of existence is set forth rather than the ideas which have influence in the development of character.   Death becomes the center of thought of necessity, as it is likely enough to do in any system.   God is rich without man.   What a contrast between this and the idea that whatever man may accomplish in accordance with God's will and purpose enters with him into the blessedness and the infinite work of God Himself!

Islam appears well when viewed in the light of its time, but if Mahomet was the last prophet and Islam the final religion, as it is claimed to be, then let the present condition of Mahometans be its defense.

THE GENESIS OF THE HEAVENS AND THE EARTH
AND ALL THE HOST OF THEM.† II.

By Prof. James D. Dana, LL. D.,

Yale University, New Haven, Conn.

[Continued from the July number.]

Dividing of the waters, the work of the second day; verses 6–8.*—*The dividing of the waters from the waters by a firmament* is the recorded work of the *second* day. Here there is real difficulty in the interpretation. Professor Guyot, believing the Nebular theory to be consistent with the divine method of creation indicated in the chapter—that is, that in all cases *the fiats initiated slowly developing results instead of producing completed results*—explained the work of this, the second day, in the following manner:—

Between the events of the first day, in which matter was endowed with force, and those of the third day, which related to the arranging of the dry land and waters, there would naturally come in the creation of the earth, and therefore of the universe of which it was a part. The work of the second day should hence have been the dividing up of the active matter diffused through the immensity of space; the subdividing and arranging of it, until the system of the universe had been developed, and ultimately the earth had become a defined sphere, with the "heaven of heavens," or a great expanse, around it. The words describe sufficiently well such a division of the "waters from the waters;" or, perhaps, more strictly, the final result, the earth separated from the diffused matter of space in which, on the first day, it was still involved. But the fiat, the rotation of matter in space, was begun (if this was not part of the work of the first day), and the system

---

* [6] And God said, Let there be a firmament in the midst of the waters, and let it divide the waters from the waters. [7] And God made the firmament, and divided the waters which *were* under the firmament from the waters which *were* above the firmament: and it was so. [8] And God called the firmament Heaven. And there was evening and there was morning, day second.

†Copyrighted 1890 by Student Publishing Co.

of the universe was carried forward toward completion. The earth became defined, among the results, though still an un-furnished earth, without its dry land and seas.

There is great doubt about the meaning of the word firma-ment on the part of the sacred historian. Although regarded generally among the Jews as signifying a solid firmament, it is far from certain that the narrator so considered it. Professor Guyot quotes from verse twentieth of the narrative the ex-pression, "fowl that may fly above the earth in the open firmament," as evidence that the firmament was not regarded as solid.

This "division of the waters from the waters" is usually interpreted as a separation, by an expanse or firmament, of waters of the earth's surface from the waters, that is, the clouds, above; or, of the earth's molten surface from the clouds. But such an event—the mere dividing off of clouds from either waters beneath or liquid rock—is too trivial for a place among the eight great works, and also is out of place on the second day. It accomplished nothing, for it left the earth under the swaddling-band of clouds.

Whether admitting or not the truth of the above-mentioned details in the earth's evolution, we may expect this much by way of interpretation of the obscure statements, that the be-ginning of activity in matter was the beginning of the uni-verse, and that in the making of the universe the making of the earth was involved, and that on the third day the earth was in existence.

Geological facts appear to have some reference to the events of the third day, as has been already stated, and a table, giving the successive eras and periods in geological history, is therefore here introduced for reference.

I. ARCHÆAN TIME. Rocks crystalline. No undoubted fossils. Presence, in the later part, of seaweeds and of em-bryonic forms of animal life suspected; that of seaweeds, because of the presence in some of the rocks of much graphite, which, like coal, is essentially mineral carbon.

II. PALEOZOIC TIME.
    1. ERA OF INVERTEBATES.
        1. CAMBRIAN PERIOD: Invertebrates only; Trilo-bites the highest species.

    2. LOWER SILURIAN PERIOD: Invertebrates only; Cephalopod Mollusks (related to the modern Nautilus) the highest species.

    3. UPPER SILURIAN PERIOD: Invertebrates, and the first of Vertebrates, namely, Fishes; also the first yet discovered of Spiders (Scorpions) and Insects, or terrestrial Invertebrates.

  2. DEVONIAN ERA, OR ERA OF FISHES: Invertebrates (which are continued under new species through the following eras) and Fishes among Vertebrates.

  3. CARBONIFEROUS ERA, OR ERA OF ACROGENS (the Coal Plants) AND AMPHIBIANS: Fishes, Amphibians, and in the last period, the Permian, Reptiles.

III. MESOZOIC TIME, OR ERA OF REPTILES.

  1. TRIASSIC PERIOD: Amphibians, Reptiles, Birds (?), and Marsupial Mammals (related to the Opossum and Kangaroo, but much smaller kinds).

  2. JURASSIC PERIOD: Reptiles, Birds, Marsupial Mammals.

  3. CRETACEOUS (or Chalk) PERIOD: Reptiles, Birds, Marsupial Mammals.

IV. CENOZOIC TIME.

  1. TERTIARY ERA, OR ERA OF BRUTE MAMMALS: Ordinary (non-marsupial) Mammals, or the tribes, comprising Cattle, Beasts of prey, Rhinoceros, etc.

  2. QUATERNARY ERA, OR ERA OF MAN: commences with the Glacial Period.

The appearing of the dry land on the third day; the beginning of continents: verses 9, 10.*—The gathering together of the waters into one place called seas, and, thereby, the appearing of the dry land, was the *first work* of the third day.

Geological readings reach back only to this period of the first dry land—that of the so-called Archæan era, the geography of which era, or the distribution of that first land, is

---

* ⁹ And God said, Let the waters under the heaven be gathered together unto one place, and let the dry *land* appear: and it was so, ¹⁰ And God called the dry *land* Earth; and the gathering together of the waters called he Seas: and God saw that *it was* good.

now pretty well understood. Of the earth in its molten state the science has no facts from observed rocks, and derives its conclusions and conjectures mostly from facts and general principles in chemical and physical science. The previous existence of the earth in a state of fusion, with the water in the condition of an envelope of vapor, the gradual condensation of this vapor making seas, and the emergence of the first dry land are events not now questioned. So, in accordance, the words, "Let the waters be gathered together into one place," imply a gathering together, not an abrupt creation. Moreover, the waters of the oceans make one continuous area; not so the lands.

The creation of plants: verses 11–13.*—The second fiat of the third day commences with the words, "Let the earth bring forth grass, the herb yielding seed, and the fruit tree yielding fruit. In the expressions, "yielding seed," "having seed in itself," the words describe, with wonderful precision, as Professor Guyot observes, the fundamental characteristics of a living species, distinguishing it from mineral or inorganic substances. Beings having powers of growth and reproduction were now facts, and this was the great creation. These powers are exhibited in the simplest plants; and hence the new creation was in an important sense complete, although represented at the first only by the lower tribes of plants.

Obedience to the fiat, "Let the earth bring forth," continued in after time; new and higher species coming forth in succession, and ordinary fruit trees not until the later part of geological time.

The discrepancy between science and the Bible implied in this gradual creation is a real one. But it loses its importance if it is considered that the plant kingdom is the great fact that marks the day. It was *the beginning of life*—a new creation whether expressed in an oak or a seaweed. Some have sought to make a coincidence by supposing that the plants of the

---

* ¹¹ And God said, Let the earth bring forth grass, the herb yielding seed, *and* the fruit tree yielding fruit after his kind, whose seed *is* in itself, upon the earth : and it was so. ¹² And the earth brought forth grass, *and* herb yielding seed after his kind, and the tree yielding fruit, whose seed *was* in itself, after his kind : and God saw that *it was* good. ¹³ And there was evening and there was morning, day third.

coal period were in the mind of the inspired writer as in a
vision.   But the "fruit trees yielding fruit" were not in existence at that era, if we except the species related to our
spruces and pines.   The sacred writer has in view and describes the existing vegetation—and however inspired, the
word plant, communicated to him, could have given no other
idea.

With reference to the introduction of life, science, as is
universally admitted, has no explanation; for no experiments
have resulted in making from dead matter a living species.
We can only say, "God created."   The growing plant is on a
higher level than that of ordinary molecular law; for it controls and subordinates to itself chemical forces, and thereby is
enabled to make out of mineral matter chemical compounds
and living structures which the forces without this control are
incapable of.   Only when growth ceases, and death couse-
quently ensues, does ordinary chemical law, under the aid of
infusorial plants or microbes, regain control, and then decomposition goes forward.   More than this, the living being,
before it dies, produces germs which develop into other like
forms, with like powers; and thus cycles of growth are continued indefinitely.   In making its tissues, the living plant is
storing force for the sustenance and purposes of beings of a
still higher grade—those of the animal kingdom; beings that
cannot live on mineral materials.   There is, hence, reason for
believing that the power which so controls and exalts chemical forces, raising them to the level required by the functions
of a plant, cannot come from unaided chemical forces; and
much less that which carries them to a still higher level, that
of the living, sentient animal.

In the Bible record, the creation of plants preceded that of
animals; and this order is sustained by facts from nature.
For the reason just stated, the plant, as Guyot says, "is
the indispensable basis of all animal life."   It could not
exist without pre-existing plants.   Further, the lower species
of plants are capable of existing in waters hotter than animals
can endure; and, therefore, the conditions of the waters of
the globe would have suited them long before they were fitted
for animal life; very long, because diminution in temperature
must have gone on with extreme slowness.

Professor Guyot observes, further, that, since vegetation uses the animal-destroying gas, carbonic acid, as a means of growth, it served to purify the ancient waters and air, and, hence, was a befitting part of the inorganic division of the history.   He also well says that the living principle fundamental to the plant was prophetic of a higher organic era beyond,—that of animal life.

Distinct remains of plants have not yet been found in the oldest rocks.   These rocks have been so changed by heat that relics of plants would have been obliterated or obscured, had they existed.   But the rocks contain great quantities of graphite, or black lead, a variety of carbon that in some cases (as in Carboniferous slates in Rhode Island, and at Worcester, Mass.) has resulted from the action of heat on coal beds; and this graphite, as many think, may have come from those earliest of plants.

The sun, moon and stars in the firmament; verses 14–19.*— On the *fourth day*, "God said, Let there be lights in the firmament of heaven."   In a subsequent sentence, the words are: "made the two great lights," "the stars also."   But the purpose of the lights is set forth in detail in each of the five verses relating to the day's work: "to divide the day from the night;" to be "for signs, and for seasons, and for days, and years;" "to give light upon the earth;" "to rule over the day, and over the night;" "to divide the light from the darkness;" "the greater light to rule the day, and the lesser light to rule the night."   The great purpose of the sources of light was, therefore, accomplished by them, whether they were "made" or made to appear.   It was fully accomplished when the sun became to the earth the actual source of day and night and seasons, and that would have been when it first shone through the earth's long-existing envelope of clouds.

* [14] And God said, Let there be lights in the firmament of the heaven to divide the day from the night; and let them be for signs, and for seasons, and for days, and years; [15] and let them be for lights in the firmament of the heaven to give light upon the earth: and it was so. [16] And God made the two great lights; the greater light to rule the day, and the lesser light to rule the night: *he made* the stars also. [17] And God set them in the firmament of the heaven to give light upon the earth, [18] and to rule over the day and over the night, and to divide the light from the darkness: and God saw that *it was* good. [19] And there was morning and there was evening, day fourth.

One of the sublimest passages in literature is the reference to the work of the third day in creation, contained in God's answer to Job "out of the whirlwind" (chapter xxxviii.); and, although often quoted, it may well be introduced here: "Who shut up the sea with doors?" "When I made the cloud the garment thereof, and thick darkness a swaddling-band for it, and established my decree upon it, and set bars and doors, and said, Hitherto shalt thou come, but no further, and here shall thy proud waves be stayed."

The final disappearance of that swaddling-band would necessarily have resulted in the event of the fourth day.

In that event, by which sunlight first brightened the earth's surface to quicken and sustain the progressing vegetable and animal life, the earth passed from its period of cloud-swaddled adolescence to that of full expansion and vigor. The sun, through the mysterious action of its light on the green parts of plants, carried forward the process of growth by decomposing one of the most stable of compounds, carbonic acid, and also by decomposing water—work demanding enormous power; and thus it stores away carbon and hydrogen and chemical force for the sustenance of the animal life of the waters and land, while also contributing needed oxygen to the atmosphere. This process is feebly carried on under a thickly cloud-covered sky, because the amount of light then received is not more than a tenth of that which comes directly from the sun under a clear sky. The difference is well seen in any garden by comparing the growths in the open sunshine and those in the shade of a tree. These common facts illustrate the importance to the world of the unveiled sun under which clouds make only passing shadows, and help us to realize the full meaning of the fourth day's work. It marked off a grand epoch in creation's history, of immense importance especially to organic progress, well worthy of a place among the eight great works.

The first appearance of the sun naturally comes after the creation of plants; for the cloud envelope would have continued long after the earth's temperature had diminished to that degree which admitted of the growth of the lower plants. And, besides, it is a natural prelude to the organic era, the sun's light being essential to all higher grades of animal species, though not to the lower.

The work of the fifth day : Let the waters bring forth abundantly ; verses 20–23.*   *The first work of the sixth day : Let the earth bring forth the cattle and the creeping thing ;* verses 24, 25.†
—The *fiat of the fifth day* reads: "Let the waters bring forth abundantly the moving creature that hath life, and let fowl fly above the earth in the open firmament of heaven." It is added: "God created the great sea monsters, and every living creature that moveth, which the waters brought forth abundantly, after their kind, and every winged fowl after his kind." These words evidently have reference (1) to the Invertebrates, or the animals of the lower orders, which characterize, under aquatic forms, the life of the earlier part of geological history; together with (2) Fishes, which are the earliest Vertebrates; and with these (3) the Amphibians, Reptile-like species that have gills like fishes in their young stage, and which date from the early part of the Carboniferous era, and possibly from the Devonian; and (4) Reptiles, especially the aquatic kinds, of the era of Reptiles, many of which, like some of the fishes, were sea monsters of enormous magnitude; and besides these (5) the Birds, which also are species of the Reptilian era.   (The table on pages 85 and 86 will enable the reader to see the general order of succession.)

The precise time of the first birds is uncertain.   The earliest specimens found are from beds of the middle of the Reptilian era (the Jurassic Period).   But fossil birds are extremely rare, because birds are mostly terrestrial species, good food

* [20] And God said, Let the waters bring forth abundantly the moving creature that hath life, and let fowl fly above the earth in the open firmament of heaven. [21] And God created the great sea monsters, and every living creature that moveth, which the waters brought forth abundantly, after their kind, and every winged fowl after his kind: and God saw that *it was* good. [22] And God blessed them, saying, Be fruitful, and multiply, and fill the waters in the seas, and let fowl multiply in the earth. [23] And there was evening and there was morning, day fifth.

† [24] And God said, Let the earth bring forth the living creature after his kind, cattle, and creeping thing, and beast of the earth after his kind : and it was so. [25] And God made the beast of the earth after his kind, and cattle after their kind, and every thing that creepeth upon the earth after his kind : and God saw that *it was* good.

for other animals, and have slender, easily destroyed bones. There is reason for thinking that they may have first appeared in the early part of the Reptilian era.

The *fiat of the sixth day* reads: "Let the earth bring forth the living creature after his kind, cattle, and creeping thing, and beasts of the earth after his kind." These words especially designate the Ordinary Mammals or Quadrupeds, which include the cattle and the beasts of prey, species first known from the beds of the Mammalian era, long after the period of the first birds. Besides these, they may refer also to terrestrial Reptiles, either those which preceded or accompanied the Mammals. The lower Marsupial Mammals may perhaps have been comprised also, since through them the type of Mammals had its beginning. The time of their first appearance was far back in the Reptilian era; whether before or after the first of birds is, as above implied, still uncertain.

In either case, the sixth day's work embraced, as its chief creation, the particular division of Vertebrates to which Man belongs, whose common characteristic, that of suckling their young, was to become in Man the principal means of cultivating those affections, and that spirit of dependence and of subjection to law, which binds society together and man to his Maker.

System in the succession of species.—The various species mentioned as the work of the fifth day, and again those of the sixth day, came forth not as a motley assemblage simultaneously at the word of command, but, as already remarked, in long succession. Guyot, like his friend Agassiz, saw in the facts connected with this long succession, and in those exhibited by living species, evidence of a development, or gradual unfolding, of the kingdoms of life. He found this evidence in the general rise in grade of species from the simple beginnings of early time to the crowning species, Man, and in the parallelism between the geological progress of species and the embryological development of individual species of the same group; and in other principles elucidated by geological and biological history.

To the minds of Agassiz and Guyot, thus taught by nature, the hand of God did not appear to be lifted from His works by such truths. They held that the development was carried forward by the Creator, and looked upon each successive species as existing by His creating act. God was not only at the head as the source of power, but also in every movement, and *creatively* in each new step of progress. And how much more God-like is such a system of development than the making of the fifth-day motley assemblage of life at the spoken word!

The very words in the first chapter of Genesis, as Guyot observes, sustain this interpretation. Nowhere is there taught, as I have said, that abrupt creation of species so generally believed. The narrative reads, with reference to plants, "Let the earth bring forth;" not let certain kinds, or all kinds, of plants exist; but "Let the earth bring forth;" and the creation begun in the fiat on the third day was continued on afterward through the earth's period of growth and development. So, again, with regard to the lower Invertebrates or animals, and the fishes, reptiles, and flying things, it says, "Let the waters bring forth," instituting thus a course of development, and not fixing its limits; and conforming in the command, "Let the waters," to the geological fact that the earliest animal species were all of the waters, and a great part of those that followed them throughout Paleozoic time. Further, for the sixth day's work, it says, "Let the earth bring forth," although the species included the highest class of the animal kingdom, the Mammals. Gradual development, if not actually taught by the chapter, is in accord with its spirit.

We note further that the idea of gradual development is sustained by what the narrative contains with regard to the Inorganic history. The creation of light was not the creation of an elemental substance or property, but the imparting of forces to the particles of matter, and thus initiating change and progress. The dividing of the waters from the waters was not the creation of a particular substance or condition, but the carrying forward of the development until suns and worlds had been evolved, and among the worlds the earth.

Again, the gathering of the waters into one place and the appearing of the dry land was not the sudden creation of dry land, but a further carrying on of changes until the molten earth had become covered with the condensed waters, and had at last its seas and continents: not its finished continents, for the fiat is simply a beginning of work that was to be completed, as in other cases, in future ages.

The creation of Man, the second work of the sixth day; verses 26–31.*—The sacred record says—not " Let the earth bring forth," as in the first fiat of the sixth day, but—" Let us make man in our image, after our likeness," to have " dominion over the fish of the sea, and over the fowl of the air, and over the cattle, and over all the earth." And it adds: " God created Man in His own image, in the image of God created he him."

Science has made no real progress toward proving that the divine act was not required for the creation of Man. No remains of ancient Man have been found that indicate a progenitor of lower grade than the lowest of existing tribes; none that show any less of the erect posture and other essential characteristics of the exalted species.

Made in the image of God, Man was capable of moral distinctions and of spiritual progress; and hence with him began a new era in history, that of " moral freedom and responsibility."†

---

* 26 And God said, Let us make man in our image, after our likeness : and let them have dominion over the fish of the sea, and over the fowl of the air, and over the cattle, and over all the earth, and over every creeping thing that creepeth upon the earth. 27 So God created man in his *own* image, in the image of God created he him : male and female created he them. 28 And God blessed them, and God said unto them, Be fruitful, and multiply, and replenish the earth, and subdue it : and have dominion over the fish of the sea, and over the fowl of the air, and over every living thing that moveth upon the earth. 29 And God said, Behold, I have given you every herb bearing seed, which *is* upon the face of all the earth, and every tree, in the which *is* the fruit of a tree yielding seed ; to you it shall be for meat. 30 And to every beast of the earth, and to every fowl of the air, and to every thing that creepeth upon the earth, wherein *there is* life, *I have given* every green herb for meat : and it was so. 31 And God saw every thing that he had made, and, behold, *it was* very good. And there was evening and there was morning, day the sixth.

† The record in Genesis says : " Let *us* make Man." While there is uncertainty as to the application of the plural us, it is interesting to note, in view of recent opinions, that the learned Jewish commentator and scholar, Maimonides, of the 12th century—and, following him, the late Prof. Tayler Lewis, D. D., of Union College, N. Y.—makes the word *us* to include Nature with

This last being of the grand series was the first that was capable of reaching toward a knowledge of himself, of Nature, and of God. The truth that Man, while of Nature, was above Nature—not an improved brute—was recognized by God in the commission given him as he went forth to duty—verse 28: SUBDUE; HAVE DOMINION. It was a divine announcement of Man's dignity, power and high destiny. The earth which lay at his feet was not for him like grass for the brute, but the first stage on the way to celestial heights.

Man has gone forward in accordance with the commission, and already the winds, the waters and the lightning are at his service, and Nature in every part is yielding him tribute. The brute, whether the lowest or highest, is but a fixed point in existence, without progress, made to come and go and leave his fellows and the world unimproved. But Man, through the expansive spirit within and the sources of strength without, ever reaches onward and upward. His mind is not simply a motive power to his individual body, but a radiant centre of force, fitted to diffuse energy indefinitely around; whether into dead or living matter; and a piece of moving enginery is a thing of life because penetrated by the intelligent spirit of man. All things have become active through the breath that was breathed into the being of the last creation.

The heavens and the earth and all the host of them finished; chap. ii., verse 1.*—The record in Genesis, after the closing expression—" And God saw every thing that He had made, and, behold, it was very good," in which words of approba-

God; God, as the latter says, acting directly, sovereignly, Nature mediately and obediently through the divine word; " from the latter coming Man's body, physical nature, from God his divine life and image."

Such a personification of Nature by the Deity as is here supposed seems to be wholly unbefitting the occasion and the document. Since Nature is the expression of God's will, the new creation should have conformed to that expressed will, even, it might be, to the degree above implied, and have demanded only that communication of new power which was required for a being so divinely exalted. But even this consideration scarcely lessens the degrading effect of such a combination.

* 1 Thus the heavens and the earth were finished, and all the host of them. 2 And on the seventh day God ended his work which he had made; and he rested on the seventh day from all his work which he had made. 3 And God blessed the seventh day, and sanctified it: because that in it he had rested from all his work which God had created and made.

tion were comprised the light, the heavens, the earth and its appointments of lands and seas and mountains and rivers, the "grass and fruit trees," the animals of the swarming waters, the creeping things and Birds, the Cattle and Beasts of the land, and Man, male and female, amid Nature's wealth of beauty and strength—then adds: "Thus the heavens and the earth were finished, and all the host of them." In other words, thus the creation announced in the head-line of the record was finished.

Here is reason enough for not separating the event referred to in the first sentence of the chapter by a long, indefinitely long, interval from the rest. Those who continue by such means to insert a scheme of creation by six days of twenty-four hours do it against the fullest denials from facts in geology. There is no break in the series of events before Man where it has any chance to come in.

The seventh day of rest; chap. ii., verses 2, 3.—"The seventh day, the day of rest, the Sabbath of the earth," is the day now in progress, in which "God's work is," in Guyot's words, "one of love to man, the redemption," the creation of "the new man, born anew of the Spirit, in the heart of the natural man," that the flow of love between man and his Maker, which was interrupted by man's debasement, again may be in perpetual interchange.

Parallel with the week of creation, man, a being of a few short years, has his week; and, by God's appointment as well as Nature's need, his seventh day of rest—of rest from daily toil, but of activity in the higher world of the spirit. The commandment, "Remember the Sabbath day to keep it holy, for in six days the Lord made heaven and earth, the sea and all that in them is, and rested the seventh day," appears to have a loftier sanction after this view of the parallelism between the seven days of divine work and Man's seven days or week.

Such is the grand cosmogonic week described by Moses; and such the corresponding records derived from Nature. These readings of nature are modern ; the facts read are from records made during the ages to which they refer. A century since those ages were beyond the bounds of knowledge or thought. The earth in common belief had no past beyond man's birth day. Science has lengthened time back through indefinite æons. It had no history except in the flats of Omnipotence. Now, a volume of revelation is opening before us in which God has inscribed his wisdom and beneficence all along the ages; and the system of Nature, instead of being the system of the now and of this little sphere, is the system of immensity in time and space.

The degree of accordance between science and the Bible which has been made out should satisfy us of the divine origin both of Nature and the Bible. If one in origin, they should be in essential harmony, and not apart in "cosmognic ideas;" and so they prove to be.

The events of creation recorded in Genesis were known only to the Creator; and the stately review of the ages making the Introduction to the Bible stands there as the impress of the divine hand on the first leaf of the Sacred Book. The leaf carries the history, in sublime announcements, onward to Man; and then, Man in his relations to his Maker, Man's duty and destiny become the absorbing themes.

Nature has her words of hope. For if myriads of ages were used in perfecting a single sphere in space and fitting it for its final purpose, and countless tribes of animals lived and died before the series reached a living soul, Man has reason to believe that this noblest form of life, whose likeness to the Eternal One is such that he is able to interpret and utilize His laws and find delight in the beauty and wisdom of His works, will not, after a few short hours, be blotted out forever. But the sure word of prophecy is given him in the Sacred Book which came as a sequel to the volume of Nature to be Man's special guide to life and immortality.

THE LIFE AND TIMES OF THE CHRIST,

BASED ON LUKE.

By William R. Harper and George S. Goodspeed,

Yale University.

(Copyrighted, 1890.)

STUDIES XXXIII. AND XXXIV.—PARABLES OF GRACE. LUKE 15 : 1–32.

Remark.—It is desirable that in beginning each "study" the entire passage assigned be read over rapidly and the main divisions of the narrative noted.

I. EXAMINATION OF THE MATERIAL.

[It will be noted that the following order is observed invariably in this work; (1) the verse or section is read and its contents stated in a general way; (2) important or difficult words and phrases are studied; (3) a complete statement of the contents of the verse or section is formed in view of the work already done; (4) the religious teaching is sought.]

§ 1.   Chapter 15 : 1, 2.

1. Read the section and consider a subject : e. g. *The new Hearers.*
2. The following are important points for study : (1) *were drawing near* (15 : 1), what was the occasion, (a) the gracious intimations of 14 : 21–23, or (b) the stern admonitions* of 14 : 25–32 ? (2) *murmured* (15 : 2), (a) "kept up a chorus of complaints," (b) note previous instances, Lk. 5 : 30; (3) *receiveth*, (a) either as his constant practice, or (b) is engaging in a ministry to them at the present time, probability of this in view of the "condemnation" of Chs. 13, 14.
3. The following is a brief statement of the thought : *Many publicans and sinners are attracted to him, and at his associating with them, even to eating with them, Pharisees and scribes keep complaining.*
4. Note a religious thought in the objection that he "receiveth sinners," that "the most desolate and broken soul cannot desire any better account of the Saviour's work."

---

* It was precisely those who felt they had no means to build the tower, no forces to meet the opposing King ; and hence they sought resources from One who manifested power, and through Him desired conditions of peace. *Riddle*, p. 277.

§ 2.   Chapter 15 : 3-7.

1. The student may read the passage and state the subject.
2. Words and phrases of importance are: (1) *man of you* (15 : 4), addressing those who were familiar with such employments; (2) *lost one*, this is the state of publicans and sinners; (3) *layeth it* (15 : 5), a picture of (a) exhaustion of sheep, (b) sympathy of shepherd; (4) *cometh home* (15 : 6), thither he takes the lost sheep rather than to the fold; (5) *rejoice with me*, as Jesus expects the Pharisees to do; (6) *I say unto you* (15 : 7), emphatic; (7) *joy in heaven*, even if not on earth; (8) *repenteth*, as apparently was the disposition of those publicans and sinners who sought him; (9) *righteous persons*, (a) the outwardly religious portion of the people, (b) the Pharisees and scribes, (c) for the sake of the argument he takes them at their own valuation.
3. A condensation of the thought is as follows: *In a parable he said, A shepherd will leave ninety-nine of his sheep to hunt for one lost till he find it, and will bring it home on his shoulder gladly calling his neighbors to rejoice with him at finding it. So will there be joy above over a repenting sinner more than over ninety and nine "righteous" people.*
4. The student may state the religious thought here.

§ 3.   Chapter 15 : 8-10.

1. The subject may be stated as *The Lost Coin.*
2. (1) *Ten pieces* (15 : 8), representing (a) each a day's wages, the whole being perhaps payment of a debt, or (b) the woman's favorite ornament; (2) *light a lamp*, the house having no window; (3) *lost* (15 : 9), (a) lost to the use to which she had designed it, (b) so the publicans and sinners are at present of no use to God.
3. Criticise the following statement of the thought: *A woman has lost one of her ten pieces. She searches carefully for it and, finding it, calls in her neighbors to rejoice with her. Thus they rejoice above over one repentant sinner.*
4. Is not a very important teaching here the fact that God cannot use people who are sinning, and only as they repent and turn to him can he employ them in his kingdom?

§ 4.   Chapter 15 : 11-16.

1. The subject of the whole passage (11–32) is *The Lost Son*, of this portion of it, *The Son a prodigal.*
2. The student may examine the following words and phrases with all helps he has at command: (1) *the portion* (15 : 12), (2) *wasted his substance* (15 : 13), unflattering description of publicans and sinners, (3) *husks* (15 : 16), (4) *no man gave.*
3. The thought stated briefly is as follows: *The younger of two sons once said to his father, Give me my share of the property. He took it, went far off, and squandered it. Having nothing left, and in the midst of famine, he went to herding swine and had to be satisfied with their food.*
4. The picture of the course and consequences of sinful living is too clear to need any comment.

§ 5.   Chapter 15 : 17-24.

1. The main subject being *The lost son*, this may be called *The Son a penitent.*
2. Important words are here suggested for study: (1) *came to himself* (15 : 17), he had been beside himself; (2) *Father* (15 : 18), Jesus came to assure the publicans

that God would receive this name at their lips; (3) *make merry* (15 : 23), as the Pharisees ought to do; (4) *for*, etc. (15 : 24), the reason for the commands of vs. 22, 23, it is a recovery of a son from the dead.

3. The student may settle upon a statement of the thought of this passage.
4. What can be more impressive than the representation of the fatherly love of God for his repentant sinning child !

§ 6.　Chapter 15 : 25-32.

1. The student may determine upon a statement for the subject.
2. (1) *Elder son* (15 : 25), representing the Pharisees and scribes, and all who thought as they did; (2) *serve thee* (15 : 29), characteristic of the pharisaic attitude toward God; (3) *this thy son* (15 : 30), (a) not "brother," (b) the pharisee fails to acknowledge the brotherly relation, (c) the right that the elder son had thus to speak; (4) *is thine* (15 : 31), the acknowledgment that Jesus makes of the honorable position of the Pharisees, cf. Mt. 23 : 2 ; (5) *it was meet* (15 : 32), (a) the father's defence, (b) the significance of the ending of the parable here, i. e. mercy, delay of judgment, persuasion to alter their attitude.
3. A presentation of the contents is here suggested : *The elder son came in from the field and learning from a servant that they were rejoicing over the return of his brother angrily refused to come in, and to his father's entreaty complained that in spite of his own exemplary service no rejoicing had been made over him as over this returned profligate. The father replied, Son, this rejoicing was fitting, since your lost brother has come back as if from the dead.*
4. The religious thought lies along the line of the godlessness of religious selfishness which cannot sympathize with the love of God for outcast but repentant sinners.

II. CLASSIFICATION OF THE MATERIAL.
1.　Contents and Summary.

1) **The Contents.** The following table of the contents of the passage is to be carefully examined.

PARABLES OF GRACE.

§ 1.　The new Hearers.
§ 2.　The Lost Sheep.
§ 3.　The Lost Coin.
§ 4.　The Lost Son.
　　　1) The Son—a prodigal.
　　　2) The Son—a penitent.
　　　3) The elder brother.

2) **The Summary.** The student will compare the following "summary" with the Scripture passage, with a view to criticism and improvement : *When many publicans and sinners come to hear him he replies to the objections of scribes and Pharisees by telling* (1) *of the lost sheep for which the shepherd left the rest of the flock until he found it and brought it home, and all were glad;* (2) *of the lost coin for which the woman carefully hunted, and many rejoiced when she found it—so heaven rejoices over the recovery of lost sinners. Again he told* (3) *of the lost son, who took and spent his portion in revelry, and then, when in deepest want,*

returned penitently to his father, who received him with love and rejoicing, to the anger of the elder brother whom his father sought to show how fitting it was to rejoice over the recovery of a brother and a son from the dead.

2. Observations upon the Material.

241) 15 : 1. This was a renewal of Galilean experiences, and was probably occasioned by the gracious suggestions of the preceding chapter.

242) 15 : 3. Jesus proceeded to defend himself for the position which he took in relation to publicans and sinners.

243) 15 : 5. The shepherd here is represented as having a tender, sympathetic interest in the exhausted sheep.

244) 15 : 6. Jesus sought to win the sympathy of the Pharisees and Scribes in his endeavor to help the publicans and sinners.

245) 15 : 7. It seems to be suggested that the recovery of an abandoned sinner is of more importance in God's sight than the righteous life of those who are reconciled with God.*

246) 15 : 8. Nothing more than a vivid picture of the careful search of the woman seems to be conveyed by the details of this parable.†

247) 15 : 8, 9. As in the former parable the publicans and sinners are acknowledged to be mere sheep, and that too, lost, so

here they are likened to insignificant coins, and that too, lost.

248) 15 : 13-16. Jesus does not hesitate to indicate by this picture the way the publicans and sinners have departed from the way and word of God. He does not excuse their sin, but paints it in bright colors.

249) 15 : 17-24. The picture of the father's regard for the penitent son must have had great power with the publicans and sinners themselves in calling out repentance, hope and faith in Jesus and his teaching.‡

250) 15 : 22-24. It is because the son has been recovered from a position where recovery could hardly be expected that the rejoicing is made over him.

251) 15 : 25-32. The picture of the elder son is intended to reveal to the Pharisees their unkind attitude toward the abandoned classes of the day, and, if possible, to stir them to a more noble and worthy sympathy with Jesus in his work on their behalf.

3. Topics for Study.

Jesus' Apology for his Relations with Publicans and Sinners. [Obs. 241–251]:

(1) Consider again the occasion for the assembling of these persons to Jesus.

(2) Note the position that the Pharisees take, and compare a similar position in

---

* He argues with His censors on the assumption that they are as good as they think themselves. He means to say that there is a sense in which a man may rationally rejoice more over the repentance of a notable sinner than over the righteousness of many men who have all their days lived in an exemplary manner, if not absolutely, yet comparatively, sinless. This greater joy over the penitent sinner needs no more explanation than the joy of the shepherd over the sheep which was lost. It is simply an illustration of the great law, according to which all human beings have peculiar joy over lost things found. Bruce, *Parabolic Teaching*, p. 273.

It is utterly insufficient to say that this joy is occasioned by the getting back something that was lost. . . . Now, the shepherd, when he found the wanderer, did not bring it back to the old fold, or replace it with the rest of the flock, but apparently (ver. 6) brought it to his own home. This would seem to indicate that sinners whom Jesus has come to save, and whom *he has saved*, are placed in a better position than that from which they originally wandered. *Pul. Com.*, II., 41.

† Commentators, who indulge in spiritualizing interpretation, telling us that the house is the Church ; and the woman the indwelling Spirit ; and the drachma, man with the image of God stamped upon him, but lying in the dust of sin and corruption ; and the candle the Word of God held forth by the Church, and the sweeping the disturbance caused by the action of the Spirit in the individual and in society, making dust rise and fly about, and turning the world upside down. To our mind, however, this style of interpretation savors of frigidity. *Bruce*, p. 278.

‡ Although the story was first told to self-righteous Pharisees—it must surely have passed from mouth to mouth among the publicans and sinners—it became the palladium of all troubled consciences, the patent of nobility for the debased and the outcast. *Weiss*, II., p. 130.

the Galilean Ministry. (3) Study now the three parables, getting in mind a picture of each in its details. (4) Observe Jesus' conception of the condition of publicans and sinners, (a) they are "lost,"* (b) exhausted, foolish sinners—"sheep," (c) lost to God's use and value in God's world—"coins," † (d) profligate and wicked like the "son," (e) yet they are "sons" and are recoverable. (5) Consider whether the above conception of Jesus (a) to (d) may not be his acceptance of the Pharisaic idea of them for the sake of argument. (6) Note now Jesus' view of the situation, (a) to find the lost sheep and the lost coin, ‡ (b) to show that the "lost son" will be welcomed to God's favor, that in heaven there is joy over repentant sinners, (c) to show the Pharisees that they ought to be glad, too, but that in reality they, with all their privileges, are selfish and unkind, (d) to draw the Pharisees over to his way of thinking about publicans and sinners, (e) to inspire the publicans and sinners with hope and desire of forgiveness and acceptance with God.

4. Religious Teaching.

The student may note the thoughts gathering about the *Picture of God's Love :* (1) out of His free grace He seeks lost sinners, (2) He regards degraded men as God's "lost sons" and welcomes them, when they repent, (3) the selfish exclusiveness of more favored "sons" is kindly but searchingly rebuked.

STUDIES XXXV. AND XXXVI.—PARABLES OF DUTY AND WARN-ING. LUKE 16 : 1-17 : 10.

Remark.—It is desirable that in beginning this "study" (1) the material of the preceding "study" be reviewed, and (2) the entire passage assigned be read over rapidly and the main divisions of the narrative noted.

I. EXAMINATION OF THE MATERIAL.

[It will be noted that the following order is observed invariably in this work ; (1) the verse or section is read and its contents stated in a general way; (2) important or difficult words and phrases are studied; (3) a complete statement of the contents of the verse or section is formed in view of the work already done; (4) the religious teaching is sought.]

§ 1.   Chapter 16 : 1-13.

1. The student, after reading, may note the following subject : *Parable of the unrighteous Steward.*

---

* The state indicated . . . . is one from which recovery is possible. Bruce, *Par. Teach.*, p. 293.
† The value of the coin in the eyes of the possessor is the main point. . . . A lost man is a blank in His treasury. *Riddle*, p. 230.
‡ Jesus, seeing the miserable plight of the lost sheep of the house of Israel, sought to be a Shepherd to them. *Bruce*, p. 266.
The repentance of the meanest of mankind (lost coin), however insignificant in social position or degraded in character, calls forth a sympathetic thrill in the heart of God. *Ibid.*, p. 278.

2. Words and phrases of importance or difficulty are : (1) *unto the disciples* (16 : 1), perhaps especially to those of 15 : 1 who had been moved by the parables of Ch. 15 to follow him ; (2) *what shall I do* (16 : 3), he acknowledges his own knavery ; (3) vs. 3 and 4 are a soliloquy in which the *they* (v. 4) is explained by the *debtors* of v. 5 ; (4) *write fifty* (16 : 6), the method which the steward took was one of many which he might have chosen, this one benefited him only indirectly ; (5) *commended* (16 : 8), i. e. his shrewdness ; (6) *sons of this world*, i. e. those who find their life in the affairs of the present ; (7) *sons of the light*, i. e. those who find their life in that " light " which symbolizes moral and spiritual truth ; (8) *wiser*, make better use of the forces belonging to the sphere and course of their existence ; (9) *and I say* (16 : 9), i. e. " in view of this greater wisdom, bestir yourselves ; " (10) *friends*, so use money as to win the favor of (a) the poor, (b) the angels, (c) God ; (11) *mammon of unrighteousness*, (a) " money that is gained by and so characterized by unrighteousness," (b) had not the publicans so gained their money ? (12) *very little* (16 : 10), like this money ; (13) *faithful in the unrighteous mammon* (16 : 12), i. e. " so used this money which you as wicked publicans unrighteously gained ? " (14) *true riches*, i. e. " grow in right character ; " (15) v. 12 is parallel to v. 11 ; (16) *two masters* (16 : 13), " if you have taken God as your master you must now make money your servant."

3. A summary of the section is as follows : *To his disciples he said, A steward, about to be dismissed for stealing, cleverly scaled down the debts of his lord's debtors, and so put them under obligation to him, much to his lord's amused admiration. For worldly men are much more shrewd in getting on than men of high, moral, and spiritual life. I tell you that you are to use your money so beneficently here as to gain the favor of heaven. Insignificant as mammon is, by your faithful stewardship of it, if you do serve God with it, you shall turn it into a source of true riches.*

4. A great religious thought here lies in the power of benevolence in the use of worldly wealth to bless the life and elevate the character.

§ 2. Chapter 16 : 14-18.

1. The subject may be given as *A Rebuke of the Pharisees.*

2. The following words may be examined : (1) *lovers of money* (16 : 14), and had caught his suggestion about benevolence as the right use of it ; (2) *exalted among men* (16 : 15), i. e. as measured by a human standard only ; (3) *law and prophets* (16 : 16), " in which you think that you have the exclusive right ; " (4) *the gospel*, etc., " the good news that the Kingdom is here, is proclaimed, and even publicans may enter, all may push their way in ; " (5) *but* (16 : 17), " though the good news is made known unto all, still the great moral laws of the past are not relaxed, rather intensified, as for example, divorce, (v. 18) "—and the implication is, how much more strict are the laws against the Pharisees' favorite sin (v. 14) !

3. Criticise the following condensation of the section : *When the avaricious Pharisees scoffed at his counsels, he replied, Your standard of excellence is false and hateful to God. You are no longer the arbiters of religious truth. From John's time the Kingdom of God has been proclaimed and all press into it. Yet the laws of this Kingdom do not relax, rather strengthen the obligations of the old law, as in this case of divorce, for to marry one that has been divorced is to commit adultery.*

4. The student may supply the religious teaching here.

§ 3. Chapter 16 : 19–31.

1. Read and consider the subject : *Parable of the Rich Man and Lazarus.*
2. (1) *now*, etc. (16 : 19), (a) is this parable connected with the foregoing ? (b) if so, it is concerned either with the avarice of the Pharisees (v. 14-18), or with the general subject of the right use of wealth (vs. 1-13) ; (2) *laid at his gate* (16 : 20), (a) and brought into relations with him, (b) did the rich man treat him unkindly ? (3) *even the dogs* (16 : 21), either (a) intensifying, or (b) alleviating his sufferings, (c) in either case degrading ; (4) *Abraham's bosom* (16 : 22), (a) the Jewish name for the state of blessedness, (b) does Jesus vouch for the truth of the representation ? (5) *this flame* (16 : 24), is this to be regarded as literal or figurative ? (6) *receivedst thy good things* (16 : 25), the law of equity must rule ; (7) *great gulf fixed* (16 : 26), i. e. " it is impossible to do what you ask ; " (8) *they will repent* (16 : 30), (a) was the rich man repenting now ? (b) was it natural affection that prompted him ? (9) *if they hear not* (16 : 31), i. e. " the present opportunities of knowing the truth are ample, and no supernatural messenger could permanently improve their selfish lives, if they do not heed what they have."
3. The student may make his own statement of the thought of this passage.
4. Among the many teachings of this section, the primary one may be said to be the absolute necessity of active helpfulness to others as a condition of eternal life.

§ 4. Chapter 17 : 1–4.

1. The student may read and decide on a subject.
2. The following words deserve study : (1) *disciples* (17 : 1), composed as they were of the older and the newer members ; (2) *occasions of stumbling*, i. e. such as are suggested in v. 2 ; (3) *these little ones* (17 : 2), (a) one of these newer disciples, the " publicans and sinners " who had believed? (b) had the older disciples been finding fault with them or holding aloof from them ? (c) were they as a result becoming disturbed, angered ? (4) *brother sin* (17 : 3), (a) as these elder disciples, or (b) as the newer ones, had been doing? (c) they are all " brothers " ; (5) *seven times* (17 : 4), is this literal or figurative ?
3. Criticise the following statement of the contents : *He tells the disciples that doubtless it must be that some will give occasion to others to sin and fall, but that such would better even be drowned in the depths of the sea than cause one of these new disciples to fall. Let them all see to it that they be forgiving to sinning brethren even to the seventh degree.*
4. Are not the dangers suggested here, lest older brethren cause the younger and less experienced ones to fall, and lest the younger be inclined to be too critical of older ones and unforgiving toward them—worthy of thought on the part of all ?

§ 5. Chapter 17 : 5–10.

1. Read and criticise the subject *Parable of the Extra Service.*
2. (1) *Apostles* (17 : 5), had they been in sympathy with the spirit of those in 17 : 1, 2 ? (2) *faith*, in what ? (a) in God as a general condition without specific reference, (b) in Jesus' methods of dealing with publicans and sinners, making them disciples, (c) so that they might practice this forgiveness and avoid the sins of 17 : 1-4 ? (3) *ye would say* (17 : 6), is the implication that they did not have it ? (4) *but* (17 : 7), " you have been asking for an increase of faith, as though that was wanted to make you more forgiving or more willing to enter into my plans, *but* know that it is not faith that is wanted ; " (5) *come straightway*, i. e. " now that you have finished your day's work ; " (6) *make ready* . . . . *and afterwards*

(17 : 8), "do this extra service first;" (7) *all the things commandea* (17 : 10), "even the extra service which I may demand;" (8) *unprofitable*, (a) i. e. "who have done nothing to boast of;" (b) in going to the greatest lengths in forgiving (v. 4), (c) and thus in all other elements of Christian service, (d) the ground of all this, the fact that they are servants by glad consent of one who has saved them.

3. The student may make out the statement of the contents of the section.
4. Is not an important religious thought here the teaching that because we are servants of God we must be willing to do anything which may be required, even extra service, without complaining and without taking praise to self?

II. CLASSIFICATION OF THE MATERIAL.
1. Contents and Summary.

1) **The Contents.** The following table of contents is to be mastered.

PARABLES OF DUTY AND WARNING.

§ 1. PARABLE OF THE UNRIGHTEOUS STEWARD.
§ 2. A REBUKE OF THE PHARISEES.
§ 3. PARABLE OF THE RICH MAN AND LAZARUS.
§ 4. OCCASIONS OF STUMBLING.
§ 5. PARABLE OF THE EXTRA SERVICE.

2) **The Summary.** The student may make a summary of the contents of the passage according to examples already given.

2. Observations upon the Material.

252) 16 : 1. Many of the publicans, his disciples, may have been in exactly the same position as the steward; many may have been in the past as dishonest as he.

253) 16 : 1-7. The method of managing a large estate in Jesus' time is here clearly illustrated.

254) 16 : 8. It is in the "head for business" that the typical "sons of this world" always surpass the true "children of light."

255) 16 : 9-13. If the suggestions are made to the publican-disciples especially, it seems that they are told how to make the right use of their wealth which formerly they had gained by unrighteousness.*

256) 16 : 1-8. The incongruous and unpleasant comparisons of this parable may be explained by the fact that Jesus is addressing repentant publicans and sinners, and taking them on their own ground in a typical case which they could recognize as applying directly to them.

257) 16 : 16. The Kingdom of God had been announced in such a way that not privileged Pharisees but every one might rush into it.

258) 16 : 19, 20. The rich man was at fault because he did not avail himself of the opportunity to help Lazarus as he lay at his gate.†

* This was a most appropriate lesson for the wealthy publicans, men whose moral character had been sapped by previous practice of oppression and knavery. They, having come to Christ, had now to live a new life, and to use their wealth for the Kingdom of God. *Lindsay*, p. 191.

The very thought that their wealth, which was now their own in the sense that they were responsible for it, really did belong to those who had been, consciously or unconsciously, in the complex workings of social life, deprived of it, was an additional warning against using wealth in foolish, selfish fashion. *Ibid.*, p. 192.

† By representing Lazarus as laid at the rich man's gate, He affirms the existence of opportunities of *the most obtrusive sort* forcing themselves on men's attention, and not to be escaped . . . . When once it is understood that Lazarus is but a symbol for ample, urgent, unescapable opportunity, it is seen to be the obvious implication that Dives is one who neglects his opportunities. Bruce, *Parabolic Teaching*. p. 386.

259) 16 : 23-26. The rich man is suffering because he did not so use his wealth in this life as to make friends in the life to come. What brought him to Hades was inhumanity.

260) 16 : 27-31. The teaching here seems to be that the Old Testament ought to be sufficient to teach lessons of humanity and benevolence to those who know and read it. *

261) 17 : 1-4. A very serious crisis seems to have occurred among the disciples themselves consequent on the reception of publicans and sinners.

262) 17 : 5, 6. Jesus would have the apostles know that not by having faith increased but by exercising the faith they have, can these great things be wrought. †

263) 17: 7-10. The harsh representation of God is due to the sentimental and practically selfish attitude of mind in the apostles. They are to be rudely awakened to their duty.

3. Topics for Study.

The topic here given is merely a rearrangement and reconsideration of the " observations " already made.

Teaching following the Parables of Grace. [Obs. 252, 255-263]: (1) Recall the teaching of Ch. 15, and consider the probability of an addition of disciples from the new hearers to the company of Jesus. (2) Observe the propriety of the form in which his teaching (16 : 1-13) is given to such new disciples, (a) publicans and sinners were rich, (b) their moral sense had been weakened by unrighteous doings. (3) Notice the point to which his teaching was directed, . (a) the right use of wealth acquired by dishonesty, (b) the absolute necessity for such right use of wealth (16 : 19-31). (4) Consider the probability of a division among the disciples—the old and the new followers—as being suggested in 17 : 1-4. (5) Think over (a) the spirit of the older disciples as shown in 17 : 1, 5, (b) of the newer ones in 17 : 3, 4, (c) the reply of Jesus in 17 : 2, 3, 4, 6, (d) the emphatic parable of 17 : 7-10.

4. Religious Teaching.

The chief thoughts of the passage seem to gather about *the wise employment of one's property:* (1) though gained in the sinful past by unrighteousness, it may be redeemed and transformed into character by beneficence, (2) the crowning sin which brings spiritual ruin is the neglect of opportunity to do good with money, (3) what applies to wealth may also be true of poverty, the spirit of the poorer disciples seems to have been the reverse of kindly toward the newer ones— hence the warning of 17 : 2, (4) the spirit of unselfishness is to be emphasized, which rich and poor alike must strive to manifest—it is God's standard of eminence (16 : 15).

* For the life of selfishness there is no excuse on the score of ignorance. In making this the lesson of the concluding part, we assume that the request of Dives in behalf of his brethren is indirectly self-excuse. Bruce, *Parabolic Teaching*, p. 395.

It implies that these books were sufficient as a guide of life to all men of right dispositions without any further extraordinary means of grace, and that when they failed, a better result could not be reached by any conceivable means. *Ibid.*, p. 397.

† There was something, it may be, false in the ring of that prayer, an unreal diffidence asking for that as a gift which really comes only through active obedience, and the experience which is gained through it. *Plumptre*, p. 279.

You think the duties I enjoin too hard for your faith, but this shows that you have as yet no faith of the high order you ought to have, for the smallest measure of such faith would enable you to do what seems altogether impossible in the natural world. *Riddle*, p. 251.

The disciples scarce knew what faith was when they pleaded the lack of it as an excuse for not forgiving their brother. *Lindsay*, p. 195.

A "SYMPOSIUM" UPON THE ADVISABILITY OF A NORMAL DEPARTMENT IN THEOLOGICAL SEMINARIES.

One of the objects contemplated in the work of the STUDENT is to advance the interests of Bible study, and to help in opening the way to the wider usefulness of agencies for this purpose already existing. Not a little has been said recently in many quarters of the need of a better knowledge of the Bible as a whole on the part of Theological students. Without disparaging in any respect the work of our Theological Institutions, many of whose teachers are working beyond their strength to supply what they recognize to be the needs of students, it seemed to promise help and light to make inquiries of working clergymen, teachers in college and seminary, Sunday school workers and other intelligent observers. The following questions were sent out and replies are here given.

1. What do you think in regard to the necessity of the minister being a skillful teacher of the Bible?

2. Is it or is it not wise to add a department or a course to our theological curriculum for the purpose of doing this work, and what might be urged as reasons for such a step?

3. Are there not some suggestions which you would be willing to make in regard to the subject in general of the minister as a teacher of the Bible?

From Rev. JOSEPH COOK, D. D.

In reply to your three strategic questions in your letter of May 8, I beg leave to say with all deference towards our eminent theological teachers, that our average American ministry ought to be educated to greater skill in teaching the Bible both to learned and to unlearned hearers. Few preachers in our time are so equipped as to be able to repel by clear and candid reasoning the more novel and subtle attacks of skeptical critics of the Bible. Few are so familiar with the mountain ranges of Scripture as to be able to lead congregations to spiritual heights from which the outlook dispels skepticism. It is absolutely indispensable that the ministry of our day should be able to perform easily and often these two majestic tasks. As to whether theological seminaries need a new department to fit men for this work, I am in some doubt. The chairs of Biblical Theology and of Homiletics ought to cover the required instruction. But the *whole* armor of God is to be put on by spiritual leaders in the church and it is the business of theological seminaries to forge and fit to each other *all* the parts of this armor, even if a few new anvils are required for the perfection of the process. The *use* of armor is the duty of preachers, but the *forging* of it is the duty of their instructors. The Bible is breastplate, helmet and sword.

Boston, Mass.

From Rev. A. J. GORDON, D. D.

Bible-readings, so called, are now largely employed by the lay evangelists of the Moody school. Let scholars disparage them as they will, these Bible-readings conform to right methods ; that of comparative Scriptural study. It is a simple method, to which the Concordance furnishes the principal aid ; but it is an effective method for interesting and instructing the people. We wish that this manner of preaching might largely supplement the present form of formal sermonizing. The demand of President Wayland, that theological students should be "taught to think on their feet," we would reinforce by another ; that they be instructed to expound on their feet, so that having stated their doctrine or proposition they should go from cover to cover of their Bibles in proving and illustrating the same. Yes, I heartily approve of your suggestion.

Boston, Mass.

From Rev. Professor GEO. B. STEVENS, PH. D.

Replying to your favor in regard to the necessity of a course or department in theological seminaries for the instruction of young men as teachers of the Bible I would say, that the subject commends itself to my mind as one of great importance.

Your first question whether it is important that a minister be a skilled teacher of the Bible must surely be answered in the affirmative. My own conviction is that one of the greatest deficiencies in ministers so far as imparting thorough instruction in the Bible is concerned, is found in the fact that they are not thoroughly acquainted with the subject themselves. The courses in theological seminaries have generally been so restricted in their scope that not more than three or four books of the Old and New Testaments respectively have been studied during the course.

These may have been very exhaustively studied and well understood, but such a course of instruction is certainly wanting in that range and comprehensiveness which are necessary to furnish one for effective teaching of the Bible as a whole. It is my belief that there is occasion for some modification in this respect in our theological courses, as ordinarily planned.

I believe, for example, in respect to the New Testament, that every student on his graduation from the seminary should know the things most important to be known about each book of the New Testament ; that he should have its main contents clearly in mind, have clear understanding of its occasion, purpose and leading books, and be able to interpret each passage of the book in the light of this information.

Replying to your second question, it does not seem clear to me that a separate department or new course of instruction with reference to this work is needful. I think however that it should receive attention. Could it not, at least in a measure, be introduced in connection with our teaching of interpretation, by requiring the students to interpret for themselves and to bring before the class examples of their own work in exegesis and to present before the class as if they were called upon to give instruction in the matter in hand the results of their own study, bringing forward such points as they would judge to be of importance in case they themselves were the teachers? It appears to me that by the assignment to students of work of this character in the different branches and departments of our biblical teaching, that something could be done in the direction which your question indicates.

In regard to the third point I would say that the demand has not hitherto been often made that a minister should be a systematic teacher of the Bible. It has been felt to be enough if he could clearly and helpfully interpret its truth in preaching. This demand however will more and more be made of him, since the interest in systematic biblical study is becoming more wide spread. He cannot therefore be too well furnished for work like this, and, even if he should not be called upon to give any systematic course of instruction, the work which he would be required to do in preparing himself to do so would be of great assistance to his use of the Bible in preaching. It would give him a well poised judgment in respect to the force and meaning of the texts which he might employ, and would save him from those extravagances and erroneous emphases which are so commonly connected with the use of individual passages of Scripture. That ministers should be acquainted with the Bible as literature, and with its books in their entire scope and purpose, appears to me to be a matter of the utmost importance.

New Haven, Conn.

From Rev. SMITH BAKER, D. D.

I am convinced more and more that the coming pastor, must be a teacher as well as preacher and also a teacher of teachers and in thus doing he will add to the richness of his preaching as well as qualify his people for greater usefulness. Ministers make a great mistake in not studying the art of Bible-teaching. Among the richest experiences of my ministerial life, is my Bible-class of two hundred members.

I have for years felt a sad deficiency on the part of our theological seminaries in this direction. With a somewhat extensive experience in connection with Sunday school institutes for twenty-five years, I have found the majority of our ministers unqualified to lead their Sunday school teachers, in Bible study or in the methods of teaching. They can make good speeches and read good essays but as for helping the teacher to teach, they knew not how to do it. Indeed some of our most learned men are most deficient in this respect, and it seems to me, with the increasing attention now given to Bible study, that one of the most imperative needs in our theological seminaries is a department in the art of Bible-teaching. To know the truth is not enough. To know how to teach the truth is quite as important.

Lowell, Mass.

From Rev. Prof. J. STEINFORT KEDNEY, D. D.

In response to the questions asked, I can but say, (1) that there can be no question that every minister should be, if possible, a skillful teacher of the Bible. (2) If a department having this for its purpose, or a function of an existing one, could be added to any course of theological study, it would be a *desideratum.* (3) In the Theological School with which I am connected, we shall be glad to receive any suggestion having for its end an improvement of our curriculum in this regard ; though it is difficult to see how a new department could be added to the same without extending our course of study, since the time of our young men is now fully occupied.

Individually I have to say that I should like to see the working of any method of teaching the Holy Scriptures before giving it my unqualified approbation. I see clearly that there are at least three distinct methods of interpreting Holy Scriptures, each having its particular worth, and possible adaptation to a particular class of learners, and yet that there is a certain kind of *information*, which is or should be common to them all, and the basis from which they proceed. It is this last, I take it, that you have specially in view.

Fairbault, Minn.

From Rev. C. R. BLACKALL, M. D.

1. There cannot be any question as to the necessity that every minister of the Gospel should be " a skillful teacher of the Bible." Without that qualification he had far better be earning a living in some other way. The Gospel requirement is that he should be " *apt to teach.*"

2. Every Theological Seminary should have, as part of its curriculum, a department that would prepare its students to *teach*, as well as to *preach*, and this department should include all that pertains to the practical working of Sunday schools, in which a large part of personal teaching is done, not only to the unconverted, but also to church members. So far as my observation extends, comparatively few professing Christians have been so instructed in doctrine that it makes any particular difference where they belong, in church relation, except from social or personal considerations. I regard this as a result of the fact that "doctrinal" preaching and teaching is so generally avoided ; that in so large degree pastors leave the Sunday school teaching and administration to others who are less qualified than themselves to instruct ; and that it is so common to regard "the teaching department of the church" as a separate "institution," with rules and regulations that separate it from the church. It never can be otherwise until pastors are better instructed along these lines, and come to their churches fully equipped by practical as well as theoretical knowledge.

3. The minister ought to be a regular teacher in the Sunday school of his church. Better, as a rule, one sermon and an effective teaching service, than two sermons and no teaching service. Better for him to be "servant to all," in this sense, than to be preacher to a few. In the vast majority of cases, if the pastor does not have the place in " the teaching service" that he ought to occupy, it is mainly his own fault. By the exercise of due activity, without self-assertion ; genuine interest in the work, with capacity to do it, and a reasonable amount of common sense, he can easily become what of right he should be, the leader in all departments of work in his church, and the best organizer of its forces for good.

Philadelphia, Penn.

From Professor WM. NORTH RICE.

In regard to the first question which you ask, it seems to me there can be no hesitation. Every minister ought to be a skillful teacher of the Bible. A minister who is a skillful teacher can often, I believe, accomplish more in a Bible-class than in his preaching. I think there is too much talking at people without giving them a chance to talk back. In the free interchange of thought which a Bible-class allows, the perplexities and difficulties, both theoretical and practical, which are felt by many thoughtful minds, are much more likely to be reached than in the formal sermon. As a rule, I think every minister ought to teach a Bible-class. Aside from the good which he could do in the class, the work would have great value in improving the character of his preaching. We need more expository preaching—less dogmatic, illustrative, and hortatory preaching. The preacher who has acquired in large degree the habit of thought of the biblical teacher, will teach the Bible in his sermons, and not treat the people to miscellaneous essays or emotional exhortations prefaced by a fragment of a sentence of the Bible torn from its context and utterly perverted in meaning. The only purely intellectual qualification of an elder, according to Paul, is to be " didaktikon "—a qualification now too sadly neglected.

In regard to the second question, I speak with more hesitation. I incline to think that the establishment of a Normal Department, or Department of Biblical Pedagogics, distinct from the departments of biblical study, would tend to emphasize unduly the subject of methods. There is something fearful in the cut-and-dried-ness of the less intellectually active among the graduates of Normal Schools. Methods are good, but the best method is a live teacher. While I should think it would be going too far to establish a Normal Department in the Seminaries, it would seem to me very desirable to have the subject of the teaching of the Bible brought before the students in the Seminaries in a course of lectures. Such a course might well serve to impress the minds of the students with the importance of the work; and the subject of methods might be treated in due proportion.

All that I should feel disposed to say on the third question I have said in answering the first.

Wesleyan University, Middletown, Conn.

𝔅iblical 𝔑otes.

The Gospels and Jesus' Infancy. Both the silence and the utterance of the Gospels on the subject of the birth and early years of Jesus have occasioned much discussion and difficulty among students. Why they said so little, why they said so much, are both equally hard to explain. Dr. Gibson, in his exposition of Matthew's Gospel, considers the matter, and maintains with much truth that these very sources of difficulty are also sources and signs of the genuineness and truthfulness of the records as a whole. His explanation of Matthew's reticence is this. The Jews attached great importance to child-life, having eight different words to mark the successive stages of development up to young manhood. Matthew, writing to Jews, would hardly have omitted all but the slight reference to the Infancy if he had been left to himself. He was, therefore, in what he said and omitted, directed by the Holy Spirit. This is a reasonable conclusion. Others, arguing from the earlier dates of Mark and Matthew as compared with Luke, have regarded the omissions as due either to ignorance of these facts on the part of the first generation of Christians or to their comparative indifference to them, the chief interest centering in Jesus' public life. But Luke, the reflective historian of the next generation, is interested in all that pertains to his subject, and investigates the facts concerning the earlier private life. The later generations, with greater curiosity but less fidelity to truth, produce the Apocryphal Gospels with their extraordinary fantastic narratives of the Infancy.

Communism in the Early Church (Acts 2 : 44). In his valuable little book on "Jesus of Nazareth," Dr. J. A. Broadus steps aside from his main theme to consider whether the early Christians can be rightly called Communists. He affirms that the very record proves that they were in no sense so. Peter said to Ananias, "While it remained, did it not remain thine own? and after it was sold, was it not in thy power?" The phrase, "they had all things in common," really meant that they held all their property as for the common benefit. No one *said* that any part of his property was his own; it *was* his own; but he regarded and treated his property as for the benefit of his brethren. In Acts 4 : 32–35 every verb is in the imperfect tense, showing what happened from time to time. One Christian one month, and another the next, would bring money even selling property. It was a case of extraordinary generosity called for by extraordinary needs, all of which ceased when the disciples were scattered abroad. This "magnificent example of Christian generosity" was far from Communism. Many who have been in doubt about this passage will be glad to read the clear and satisfactory remarks of Dr. Broadus which are here summarized.

The Gloria in Excelsis: Luke 2 : 14. The revised version of this verse based on the correct reading of the Greek introduces a variation which changes the whole idea of the latter clause ; "peace, good-will toward men" is replaced by "peace among men in whom He is well pleased." Prof. Potwin examines this phrase in the June number of the *Andover Review*, with the result that while he accepts the new reading of the Greek, he returns to a translation which practically restores the old version. The literal translation of the phrase is, "peace among men of-good-pleasure." The R. V. makes the genitive depend on "men"—"men of-good-pleasure," i. e., "in whom He is well pleased." But Mr. Potwin presents certain objections to this, e. g., (1) the meaning of the phrase is not obvious or natural, (2) the construction is foreign to Greek and hardly a Latinism, (3) it is not clear that it is a Hebraism. He would make the genitive depend on "peace," translating "peace—the peace of good pleasure in men." In support of it he urges (1) the old reading, which is the reading of the Psalter, "peace, good pleasure in men," or "good-will toward men," in which the "in men" depends naturally on the "good-pleasure," and therefore (2) a similar construction is reasonable for the new and correct read-ing of Luke. The argument is interesting, and the points which are made are close and strong.

Luke 9 : 57-62. In the *Homiletic Magazine* for April, 1890, Canon Cheyne discusses what he calls "this strange group of stories," "not easy to harmon-ize" with the view of the character of our Lord derived from other parts of the Gospels. He interprets them from the life of Paul, who certainly imitated Christ in not having "where to lay his head." The illustration of the "let the dead bury their dead," he finds in Paul's view of his conversion as equivalent to a death and a new birth. By "suffering the loss of all things" for Christ he left those who were dead to the changes which the Gospel demanded, to tor-ment themselves with spiritually useless observances. In the third case, the "bidding farewell," the meaning comes out clearly in Paul's immediately not conferring with flesh and blood, but going away into (the desert of) Arabia— "a country where no associations with his past life could interfere with the impartiality of his conclusions." Mr. Cheyne adds that this means for us not to be so absorbed in our little spheres as to forget our connection with the great world, not to keep aloof from the political and social problems of our time on the plea that they do not affect *us*, and further that everywhere there is still room for acting out the saying of our Lord—" He that looketh back (on cherished, but now dangerous, friends, opinions, customs,) is not fit for the kingdom of God."

Biblical Criticism. In the London S. S. *Chronicle* some very sensible remarks were recently made on this subject. The writer called attention to the reassuring words of the Bishop of Oxford, who said, "they had often been told that when some startling novelty had been broached, especially in relation to religious theory, opinions went through three phases—1st, that the new was said to be destructive of the old ; 2d, that it did not make any difference ; 3d, that it was absolutely confirmative of the truth it seemed at first to contradict." The writer added, "So far as a thing is proved true, we guarantee that it will be found harmonious with the truth already proved and received. The 'imperfectly apprehended' is the thing that makes difficulties and stumbling blocks.   The bishop very wisely reminded his audience that 'they were none of them in a position to lay down a hard and fast rule about inspiration.' This we can do—study fully the facts, and then formulate our theory.   The mistake men have made is this, they have constructed a theory, and then sought for facts to support it."   Evidently here is a man who has thoughtfully considered these difficult problems, and is "conservatively liberal" in his attitude toward them.

Music in the Old Testament.   In a lecture by Herr Weber upon music in the Bible some interesting suggestions are made.   He is of the opinion that Moses began the compilation of a collection of National songs, and that the Book of *Jashar* was this work, and took its name from what was probably the first song in the collection, the name *Jashar*, or the book of the just, being a later name. Although the form of the music of Israel may have been influenced by Egypt, they had a general fondness for, and skill in, music.   They used it on every occasion.   The singing among them was chiefly antiphonal, one party or choir replying to another.   The song of Deborah was sung by the poetess and Barak, and the people, probably accompanied by timbrel and dance.   When Jephtha returned from victory over Ammon, " Behold his daughter came out with her companions to meet him with timbrels and dances," with songs of welcome and praise.   Saul and David were also met by women out of all the cities of Israel, singing and dancing and playing timbrels, and *Shaloshim*, three stringed instruments (1 Sam. xviii. 6, 7).   When David had established peace in the country, he had the Ark of God brought to Jerusalem with various instruments of music.

𝔖𝔶𝔫𝔬𝔭𝔰𝔢𝔰 𝔬𝔣 𝔍𝔪𝔭𝔬𝔯𝔱𝔞𝔫𝔱 𝔄𝔯𝔱𝔦𝔠𝔩𝔢𝔰.

The Titles of the Psalms.*—The devotional value of the Psalter is not materially affected by critical questions, yet these latter help to the better understanding of the writer and his times. If dates and authors can be fixed, light will be thrown on the religious life of particular periods in Israelitish history. The titles of one hundred psalms give the author, and, in some cases, the circumstances of composition. (1) The external evidence for these titles is strong. They are more ancient than the Septuagint, and even anterior to the formation of the separate books of the Psalter itself. The evidence is presumptive that they are coeval with the liturgical use of individual psalms, if not with their composition. (2) The internal evidence, when fairly examined in detail, is confirmatory of this conclusion as to their trustworthiness ; e. g., (a) Psalm 90 is claimed by the title for Moses, and in favor of this is the historical groundwork in the psalm, and the language often coincident with that of the books of Moses, while objections even such as the representation of human life as shorter than in the Pentateuch are trivial. (b) Psalm 18 was spoken by David according to the title. The books of Samuel corroborate this ; the historical groundwork in the psalm itself is suitable to it, and there are no objections worth considering. So it is argued of Psalm 51, verses 18 and 19 of which can be reasonably interpreted on such a basis. Twelve other psalms ascribed to David contain nothing opposed to such an ascription, which finds an adequate justification in the language of these psalms themselves. The objection that the identification is too general is answered by the fact that the Psalmist prefers to dwell on the general features of his situation ; this was more congenial to his own pious meditations, and fitted them subsequently for liturgical use. The conclusion is that the high antiquity and external evidence for the titles is corroborated by the internal evidence. They should be accepted as true, except in individual cases, if such exist, where there is clear proof to the contrary. And if David wrote any of the psalms attributed to him, the entire Kuenen-Wellhausen hypothesis of the history of Israel vanishes into smoke.

An argument, with no uncertain sound, in Professor Green's best manner.

The Use of Retaliation in the Mosaic Law.†—Is there, after all, so much of a contrast as has been asserted between the precepts of Jesus (Matt. 5 : 38, 39) and the provisions of the Mosaic law for punishment? (1) Christ himself used force ; He contributed to a government of force, and directed His disciples to do so ; when He is about to touch the great principle of non-resistance, He warns His hearers that He came not to destroy but to fulfill the Mosaic law of force, which He was about to contrast with precepts of His own. (2) The character

* By Prof. Wm. Henry Green, in *The Methodist Review*, July, 1890, pp. 489-506.

† By Austin Abbott, Esq., in *Christian Thought*, April, 1890, pp. 321-333.

of the patriarchal organization must be kept in mind ; until Moses' time there had been no law but that of retaliation ; Moses himself had thus avenged the injury done to a brother Hebrew.   There was no standing army to enforce law ; no national tax by which to make provision for the administration of justice ; no prison-house.   The law of retaliation, under all these circumstances, was admirably adapted to secure the ends of justice.   There were many crimes for which death or bondage would be too severe.   In reference to these Moses said, " an eye for an eye, a tooth for a tooth."   The custom of retaliation gave a blow for a word, mutilation for a blow.   Moses limits this.   His law was not a sanction on cruelty, but a restraint on cruelty.   There must be justice ; it was not to be the wild justice of revenge, but an equal punishment, measured by the offence, hand for hand, foot for foot, etc.   The principles which characterize the Mosaic legislation are : (1) " To maintain the authority of the government by adopting for mutiny, that is to say for idolatry and blasphemy, the punishment of death, just as within each family the father might, by immemorial usage, administer the same punishment against a mutinous son.   (2) To mitigate oppression by requiring restitutions with mathematical precision, and putting limited terms of service in place of unlimited servitude.   (3) To use the common indignation and retaliation aroused by crimes of violence, as the means of effecting immediate but limited punishment, and thus to awaken in place of revenge a sense of equal justice and public protection."

Something has been done, but remains still to be done in showing the great legal principles which underly the outward form of the Mosaic legislation.   This is a most fruitful field of investigation, and one which will bring to others as to the writer of this article a new and fascinating interest in the religious source and the religious bearing of Mosaic law.

The Date of Genesis X.*—The author attempts to show that the genealogical tables in this chapter could have been composed as early as the time of Moses.   The evidence brought forward is external : (1) Certain nations are certainly known to have been mentioned before 1300 B. C., viz., Tubal, Cush, Mizraim, Babel, Erech, Shinar, Assur, Nineveh, Sidon, etc.   (2) The names of certain nations have probably been identified as names of nations known before 1300 B. C., viz., Elishah, Tarshish, Kittim, Lud, Aram, Canaan, etc.   (3) The names of nations which can reasonably be supposed to have existed at or before 1300 B. C., viz., Javan, Meshech, Madai, Dodanim, Gomer, Uz, Togarmah, Ashkenaz, Magog, and the sons of Mizraim, Cush and Joktan.   (4) The names of late nations prove the early composition, viz., of India, Sinim, Persia, that it was written 550 B. C. ; of Minni, Cutha, Sepharvaim and Carchemish, Ararat, etc., that it was written before 750 B. C. ; of Sobah, Tadmor, Tiphsah, Maachah, Geshur, Nairi, etc., that it was written before 1000 B. C.   The writer discusses the different views as to the names as each name is brought up.

A scholarly presentation of material bearing upon a most important phase of the Pentateuchal question,—a presentation, however, which would have been clearer and more satisfactory had authorities and references been more generally indicated in footnotes than in the body of the text.

* By Professor Robert Dick Wilson, Ph. D., in the *Presbyterian and Reformed Review*, April, 1890, pp. 252-281.

The Zend Avesta and the First Eleven Chapters of Genesis.*—While the Jews, during the Babylonian exile, borrowed some ideas from the Persians, the writer maintains that they gave to the Parsees many fundamental principles of faith and many traditions.   It is impossible to say that the Parsic ideas are the original ones, for " at the time when the Parsees were wrapped in legendary rudiments, the Hebrews already stood on the height of monotheism, and possessed a pure conception of the God idea."   References are found in the Avesta to (1) the phraseology, "Be fruitful, and multiply, and replenish the earth and subdue it," etc. (Gen. 1 : 28) in the words addressed to Yima : Propagate my worlds, fructify my worlds, be the nourisher, guardian and sovereign of my earthly creatures ;" (2) the fountain-place, the sources of the rivers (Gen. 2 : 10) ; (3) the deluge in general (Gen. 6. 7, 8) ; (4) to the very details, e. g., " bring fowl with yellow grain and inexhaustible food' (*cf.* Gen. 6: 21) ; cattle and beasts are to come two by two (Gen. 6 : 20) ; around the circuit is to be a high door and a window to illumine the interior (Gen. 6: 16) ; " and Yima did as Ahuramazda wanted" (Gen. 7 : 5) ; "on the top he made nine bridges, in the middle he made six, and below three" (*cf.* Gen. 6 ; 16) ; (4) an evil spirit battles against a good spirit, and leaps from heaven to earth in the shape of a serpent to spoil the creatures ; (5) the two trees and the four rivers of Paradise ; (6) when Meshia and Meshiane are created, Ahura addresses them : " Ye are men, beings of life are ye" (Gen. 2 : 7).   Other minor parallelisms are found.

One need only make such an examination as this to be convinced, if there is need of proof, how widely different the biblical accounts of the beginnings of things are from all others. The difference is mark of divine origin.

* By the Rev. Dr. A. Kohut, in *The Jewish Quarterly Review*, April, 1890, pp. 223-230.

ᚷeneral ᚷotes and ᚷotices.

Inductive Bible study is receiving increased attention from thoughtful and intelligent students and leaders in Bible study. It is well known that the conductors of the Congregational publications on the International Lessons have announced that with the third quarter their lessons will be presented from the standpoint of an inductive system. And now from the West comes a practical example of the working of the method. In the First Congregational Church Sunday School of Minneapolis a class of fifty young ladies and gentlemen are enthusiastically following the plan of the Inductive Bible Study Leaflets in the study of Luke's Gospel. Several other classes in the school are following the same system. It is expected that all the classes will undertake it as soon as there are teachers trained to lead it successfully. Thus the methods outlined in the STUDENT and in the Leaflets are proving themselves thoroughly practical and the work is spreading.

In a little four-page pamphlet the University of Rochester prints its questions for " Honor-work on the English Bible ; the New Testament." The questions number thirty-six, and carry the student over a wide range of topics from biblical criticism and introduction to biblical history and theology. A few of the questions copied here will give an idea of the work required :—1. Why do we regard the New Testament Scriptures as credible historical documents ; and why do we exclude from the New Testament other writings emanating from the early church? 5. Why do we regard the New Testament Scriptures as divinely inspired? 10. With reference to Luke's Gospel give : (1) Facts concerning the life of its author, and his possible indebtedness to Paul ; (2) The general purpose and distinctive features of the gospel ; (3) Some indication of those portions of the gospel narrative that are peculiar to Luke. 20. Epitomize the events in Paul's third missionary tour. What letters were written by Paul during this tour ; and with what purpose? 35. What are the teachings of the Scriptures with reference to (1) The *personality* of the Holy Spirit? (2) The *deity* of the Holy Spirit? (3) The *influence* of the Holy Spirit? (4) The *work* of the Holy Spirit?

𝕭𝖔𝖔𝖐 𝕹𝖔𝖙𝖎𝖈𝖊𝖘.

Paul's Earlier Epistles.

*Four of the Earlier Epistles of the Apostle Paul, viz., First and Second
Thessalonians, First and Second Corinthians.* Greek Text with Expository Notes. By James R. Boise, D. D., LL. D. New York: D. Appleton
and Co.

This beautifully printed volume from the hand of so learned and careful an
exegetical scholar as Professor Boise will be heartily welcomed by students of
the Pauline Epistles. The text employed is Tischendorf's with constant reference to those of Westcott and Hort and of Tregelles. The notes are brief and
rigidly exegetical. "Three points are kept constantly in view—the exact signification of words, the force of the Greek construction, and the logical connection of the sentences." They are intended for students and pastors who
need concise and clear directions and suggestions. Professor Boise understands from long experience as a teacher just how much to say and when to
stop. With this little book and a larger commentary the student of these
Epistles will make good progress in the mastery of the thought of four of the
most varied and peculiarly difficult of Paul's writings.

The Gospel of Mark.

The Gospel according to St. Mark. [Expositor's Bible.] By the Very Rev.
G. A. Chadwick, D. D. New York: A. C. Armstrong and Son. Price $1.50.

Dean Chadwick has given us a book of expository sketches on the Gospel
not an exposition of the book as a book or an expository treatment of the life
of Christ. His treatment is not built upon a theory of the development of
events or of revelation in the ministry of Jesus, neither does it reveal a clearly
defined view of the plan of Mark's writing. He has discussed the episodes,
he has not organized and unified them. The strong points of the book lie
along two lines (1) the sharp and clear discussions of topics, as e. g., fasting,
miracles, and (2) an incisive and spirited style. The book is full of vigor and
life. It merits perusal for the breezy and animated tone that pervades it, not
for any particularly new light or originality of method, which may be discovered.

Schuerer's Jewish People.

A History of The Jewish People in the Time of Jesus Christ. First Divis-
ion. Political History of Palestine from B. C. 175 to A. D. 135. Vol. I.
By Emil Schürer, D. D. Translated by Rev. John Macpherson, Edinburgh:
T. and T. Clark. N. Y.: Scribner and Welford. Price $3.00.

This new volume of Clark's Foreign Theological Library has been delayed
because of the careful revision which Dr. Schürer was giving to the German
original. It is already three years ago or more since the three volumes of the
second Division appeared, which deals with the *internal* condition of Palestine and of the Jewish people in Jesus' time. The author found that in their

revision they were expanded to almost twice the original size, so numerous had the materials become which must be incorporated, and now this first division, which investigates the *external* or political history, will occupy two large volumes of almost 400 pages each, the first of which is now in hand. It is astonishing to think of the rapidity with which this new science of *Neu-testamentliche Zeitgeschichte*, as the Germans cumbrously call it, has come into prominence. Its claims are exceedingly lofty. Schürer declares on the first page of this volume that "no incident in the gospel story, no word in the preaching of Jesus Christ, is intelligible apart from its setting in Jewish history and without a clear understanding of that world of thought-distinction (?) of the Jewish people." Alas for our fathers! We are the people! But without going to such a length it may be frankly allowed that the past generations of Christian scholars have altogether too much ignored the abundant help which a knowledge such as Schürer alludes to offered for the understanding of difficult and dark statements or incidents in the New Testament. One can conceive of many intellectual undertakings of our thoughtful and scholarly clergymen which would not give them half the benefit or afford them half the stimulus that a careful study of Schürer's "New Testament Times" offers to them. They would begin to work their way into the life of the first century and live on friendly terms with Pharisee and Sadducee, walk with Jesus and think as Paul thought in the Jewish intellectual atmosphere and with the Hebrew cast of idea and expression. They would find too an unanswerable argument for the truth and the divineness of the Gospel as they move among its neighbors and look from near at hand upon those who would fain be its peers. The Bible would become alive historically and spiritually as now it is alive only spiritually. That spiritual flavor would by no means be lost, rather intensified—possible dangers to it warded off, its permanence assured. This is bound to be in some measure the result of a patient and thorough study of this new science of which Schürer's book is the latest and best representative.

Theism.

Christian Theism, its Claims and Sanctions. By D. B. Purington, LL. D. New York: G. P. Putnam's Sons.

Christian Theism; a brief and popular Survey of the Evidence upon which it rests; and the objections urged against it considered and refuted. By the Rev. C. A. Row, M. A. New York: Thomas Whittaker. Price $1.75.

The wide spread interest in the theistic argument is the occasion for these volumes. Their aim is to reach the popular mind and meet the objections which are being presented so strongly and persistently by the opponents of Theism. Mr. Row's book is the more simple; while the originality of Mr. Purington's contribution will make it acceptable to those more familiar with the subject. It is significant to note that the intuitional school is not maintaining its ground in the face of modern negative philosophy but that the old fashioned theistic argument reshaped on the modern principles of the ultimate unities of force and reason is taking its place and more than holding its ground against all assaults. Both these books are very attractive in outward form.

The Acts of the Apostles.

The Pulpit Commentary. The Acts of the Apostles. Exposition and Homiletics by the Rt. Hon. and Rt. Revd. Lord A. C. Hervey, D. D. Homilies by various authors, P. C. Barker, R. A. Redford, E. Johnson, R. Tuck, W. Clarkson. 2 vols. New York: A. D. F. Randolph and Co. Price $4.00.

The book of the Acts has not secured the attention which both the Gospels and the Epistles have obtained from modern scholars. The Tübingen school, indeed, has made large use of it in defense of their critical and historical theories but while they have over-emphasized the difficulties and thus led their more conservative opponents to minimize them, the book itself has not received a careful and dispassionate treatment. There is needed for such a task a man familiar with the life and literature of the early church, a scholar like the late Bishop Lightfoot. Such a scholar Bishop Hervey would not claim to be. He has produced a commentary which is careful and painstaking but not especially able. For the general reader and student it is probably as good a book as is at present attainable, being the most recent. But the archæological researches now being pursued into the remains of Asia Minor are opening to us new and most important fields of illustration and argument for the Acts. Something new is coming to light every year. The study of the Ephesian marbles now in the British museum carried on by Canon Hicks is yielding fruit in this direction. The article of Lightfoot printed in his "Essays on Supernatural Religion" on Recent Discoveries illustrating the Acts of the Apostles is a case in point though much has been accomplished since that essay was written. The time is not far distant when our commentaries will all have to be re-written in the light of this new knowledge. This fact together with the need of a more thoroughgoing attention to the critical problems of the book incline one to be somewhat impatient with the cautious and quite commonplace work of the author but probably in comparison with much that has been done his exposition should take a good rank. The homiletic material is as usual abundant and of miscellaneous character and value.

The Epistles of Paul.

An American Commentary on the New Testament. Galatians by Alvah Hovey, D. D.; Ephesians by J. A. Smith, D. D.; Philippians by J. B. G. Pidge, D. D.; Colossians by E. C. Dargan, D. D.; I. and II. Thessalonians by Prof. W. A. Stevens; The Pastoral Epistles and Philemon by H. Harvey, D. D. 2 vols. Philadelphia: American Baptist Publication Society.

With these volumes the enterprise undertaken by the Baptist Publication Society to furnish a complete commentary on the New Testament by Baptist scholars is fulfilled. The various parts are to be now re-arranged into seven volumes and sold at $16.00. Of the present commentaries all are worthy of a place in the series and each partakes of the characteristics of its author. The Galatians by Pres. Hovey is prevailingly theological in tone, the Philippians and Colossians written by active pastors are homiletical and practical. The Thessalonians of Professor Stevens who occupies the chair of New Testament Exegesis at Rochester Theological Institution is the most satisfactory from an exegetical point of view and is one of the best commentaries which has been written upon these epistles. The editor, President Hovey and the publishers are to be congratulated that this series, which contains so many volumes of more than average excellence, is now completed.

Lloyd's Greek Testament.

*Novum Testamentum cum Parallelis S. Scripturae locis vetere Capitu-
lorum Notatione Canonibus Eusebii.* Accedunt tres Appendices. Oxonii:
E Typographeo Clarendoniano. Price $1.50.

This high-sounding title introduces one of the most handy and neat editions
of the Greek Testament which a scholar would care to see. It is Lloyd's edition
of Mill's text, which, as is well known, was a reprint of Stephens's, containing
the "Canons of Eusebius" on one side of the page, and on the other carefully
selected marginal references. It is divided into sections according to Bengel's
division, while of course it also retains the ordinary divisions into chapters and
verses. The text itself occupies 653 pages, and is followed by 200 pages of
most valuable appendices from the hand of Professor Sanday of Oxford.
These appendices are three in number, the first being a collation of the Stephens
text of 1510 with that of Westcott and Hort; the second contains a selection of
certain most important passages where there is a divergence in readings (as,
e. g., in John 1 : 18), a list of the authorities in the manuscripts and fathers
being given—a most valuable aid for the student who is beginning the work of
textual criticism. The third presents the readings of certain versions of the
N. T., namely the Coptic (memphitic), Armenian and Ethiopian. As the
ordinary scholar, to say nothing of the ordinary student in New Testament
criticism could scarcely hope to read these versions, this collation of their
readings on important and disputed texts is valuable. All this material, including text and appendices numbering some 850 pages, is included in a little
book, six and one-half by four inches, with a thickness of three-quarters of an
inch. This wonderful compression is accomplished by the use of thin paper,
which at the same time does not interfere with clearness and beauty in the
typography. It is one of the marvels of book-making produced at the Claren-
don press. The little volume can be carried in the pocket, and it will be found
useful in the library of the scholar.

The Smaller Cambridge Bible.

The Smaller Cambridge Bible for Schools. St. Matthew, by Rev. A.
Carr, M. A.; *St. Mark*, by Rev. G. F. Maclear, D. D.; *St. Luke*, by F. W.
Farrar, D. D. New York: Macmillan and Co. Price, each, 30 cts.

These little books continue the series which was begun by the "Kirkpatrick's Samuel," recently noticed in the STUDENT. They appear at a very opportune time when the attention of so many people is directed to the Gospels
and the life of Christ. They are handy in form, beautifully printed, containing
from 100 to 125 pages and, for the young people in the Sunday school, very
admirable. A comparison with the larger corresponding volumes in the regular Cambridge Bible Series shows that the purpose is not to rewrite or reor-
ganize the material of that series, but by judicious cutting out of matter to
render the books useful to less mature readers as well as to bring them within
the reach of the slenderest purse. Whatever defects belonged to the former
series, would, therefore, be likely to appear here also. It is well known, however, that this series is on the whole admirably edited. It would not be a bad
idea for teachers to supply themselves with these little books in addition to the
lesson-helps furnished them. Farrar's "Luke" is, a recent critical opinion to
the contrary notwithstanding, one of the most helpful smaller commentaries
on this Gospel and in this handy size ought to be used by very many students
of the Life of Christ.

The Gospel of Matthew.

The Gospel of St. Matthew. By John Monro Gibson, M. A., D. D. [The Expositor's Bible.] New York : A. C. Armstrong and Son. Price $1.50

The latest issue in that series of expository volumes which has been often noticed in these pages is one of much interest and value. Mr. Gibson is well-known as a successful minister in the city of London and has already shown his ability in expository work by his volumes on the Pentateuch. The chief elements characteristic of this book are not its freshness or originality or its power of expression though, the latter is considerable. They are its broad, generous spirit, its faithful expository character, and its warm, spiritual tone. Some examples of the author's treatment will best bring out his excellencies and his defects. First, as to his general conception of the book, it is somewhat vague. He accepts the usual view that it was written for Jews. His outline of it and treatment in detail apparently go on the general assumption that the order is on the whole chronological. He does not lay any stress upon the massing of the Words and the Works into two great sections, if, indeed, he would favor the view of the arrangement. Still he affirms also that Matthew's order is that of logic rather than of time, and his constant endeavor to show the connection between contiguous narratives or sayings is admirable. His conception of the critical period in Galilee is faulty. He makes it come before the feeding of the five thousand, and culminate after the journeys to the borders of Tyre and Sidon. The crisis of the Galilean ministry was at the miracle of the loaves. Before that event Jesus was in high favor with the people. After it He and they separated. As examples of Mr. Gibson's liberal spirit, we note that he explains the form of the Temptation by the suggestion that the narrative must be addressed to the imagination as well as to the reason. His conception of it as closely connected with Jesus' messianic work is good, but he does not work the idea out into the details which are on the old common place lines. He thinks that Judas, perhaps, when he was chosen, had the making of as grand an apostle as the rest of them, some were far less "likely." Discrepancies in the narratives are brushed aside as unimportant—"why should we trouble ourselves to reconcile so small a difference" as that in the Jericho miracle? Many other points might be mentioned. But let no one who looks at this book fail to read the section on the Transfiguration, which is the best thing it contains. For insight and apt expression it is admirable. We note one word so rare as to be unintelligible to most people, on p. 270—"timeousness," meaning apparently "timeliness." There are also some disfiguring misprints, and the plates seem to have been worn badly in some places. The book is a helpful addition to an excellent series.

A New Testament Greek Grammar.

The Language of the New Testament. By the late Rev. William Henry Simcox, M. A. [The Theological Educator, edited by the Rev. W. R. Nicoll, M. A.] New York : Thomas Whitaker. Pp. xii. 226. Price 75 cents.

This book is the scholarly discourse of a careful and cultivated student upon the various topics of New Testament Greek grammar. It is not by any means a complete or thoroughly systematized treatise. The author has preferred to sacrifice scholastic utility to entertaining discursiveness. The student of N. T. grammar is, perhaps, to be congratulated that he has done so. After a preface and a charmingly written introduction on the Greek nation and language after Alexander, come seven chapters—fancy a Greek grammar divided into seven chapters only, without sections and side-heads to mark convenient portions for study and memorizing! A good index of texts cited is given, so that the author's remarks and discussions can be utilized by the one who wishes to use the book merely for consultation. It is a question whether the book can be put into the hands of a beginner in New Testament study with much profit. Too much knowledge is taken for granted in its pages. But for one who has read his Testament in the Greek with more or less care and wishes to review, in the light of modern critical scholarship, it will be found very pleasant and profitable reading. A second part in another volume is promised, which will deal with the peculiarities of style in the case of the different writers of the New Testament, and compare more in detail the Hellenistic Greek and that of the New Testament.

The Four Gospels.

The Composition of the Four Gospels. A Critical Inquiry. By the Rev. Arthur Wright, M. A. Fellow and Tutor of Queen's College, Cambridge. London and New York: Macmillan and Co. 1890. Pp. vii. 176.

Here we are presented with an application of the methods of historical and literary criticism to the literary form and material of the Gospels. It is a fearless, uncomproming, thoroughgoing investigation, somewhat crude and violent at some points, needlessly offensive in others, but earnest and honest and devout everywhere. The writer finds an oral gospel at the basis of the Synoptical Gospels, of which three cycles exist. The first is that of Peter, and found in its fullest form in Mark, though parts of it are in Luke and Matthew. The second cycle has its home in Matthew, and consists almost wholly of speeches, sermons and parables. Luke's great section, 9 : 51–18 : 30, makes up the third cycle. The interweaving of these cycles, with the addition of other material, editorial notes, etc., under the hand of many oral catechists and teachers account for the peculiarities and difficulties of the three Gospels. Mr. Wright holds that the three first Gospels were produced in the years 70 to 80 A. D., and John's was written ten years or more after. He maintains that historical criticism completely demolishes the idea that all parts of the Gospel narratives are of equal trustworthiness, but that the same criterion of judgment, rigidly applied, proves that the Gospel of Mark is of the highest authority by reason of its comparatively early and apostolical authority. While he is inclined to the view that Mark wrote the Gospel that bears his name, and also John his Gospel, he denies a similar authority to the book of Matthew. A closing chapter considers the inspiration of the Gospels. Verbal infallibility is denied, while divine inspiration of these writings is affirmed. Inspiration cannot be defined any more than life. The facts must be ascertained, and then the theory moulded. The Gospels cannot be said to give the independent testimony of four men, but their parts generally depend on one —yet they are the witness of the faith of the churches—Matthew's of the Eastern Churches, Luke's of those of the West. " A robuster faith in the Gospels is needed, which instead of always seeking to deny the existence of difficulties or to explain them away, shall freely confess them and learn the lessons which they teach." This book will repay study though one may decline to accept any of its conclusions. Like many such books, it belongs to no side. We would be glad to accept its conclusions on the conservative side, if only we did not have to accept its processes, which carry with them much that is too liberal and quite destructive of other cherished notions. On this account the book is worth examining.

The Bible and Modern Discoveries.

The Bible and Modern Discoveries. With map and illustrations. By Henry A. Harper. Boston: Houghton, Mifflin and Co. 1890. Pp. 536.

That there is need of a popular book giving the results of the wonderful discoveries of the last twenty-five years in lands whose history is connected with that of Biblical history is very certain; that this book, which aims to do this thing, has failed is equally certain. The author would seem to have had the necessary qualifications, if the testimony of Mr. Besant, who writes an introduction is to be accepted; but it must be the feeling of every one who rises from a perusal of the book that he has not accomplished what was undertaken. The material is divided into ten chapters: (1) From the call of Abraham, to the death of Joseph; (2) Israel in Egypt; (3) Joshua; (4) The Book of Judges; (5) 1 Samuel; (6) 2 Samuel; (7) 1 Kings; (8) 2 Kings; (9) 1 Chronicles; (10) 2 Chronicles. One can see at a glance the faultiness of such a division. There is no consideration of the Prophetical books or of the wealth of material which illustrates them. In the historical presentation, there is no evidence of an acquaintance with the results of biblical science. The style is execrable, not adapted either to the wants of the average Sunday school teacher, for whom the book would seem to have been intended, or to those of the better informed student, though much of the material will be of value only to such a one. There is no index of Bible texts; but a list of authorities consulted many of which were long ago antiquated. This book is a fair specimen of what an unscientific mind will do with scientific material. It is a warning to some men, to let such work alone, and to scientists, to do their own popularizing.

Barnes' Handbook of Bible Biography.

Handbook of Bible Biography. By Rev. C. R. Barnes, A. B. New York: Hunt and Eaton. 1889. Pp. 546.

The author has furnished in this volume an explanation of all the names of persons in the Bible with accounts of the lives and characters of those of greatest prominence. He has not, indeed, brought forward any new material but claims to have made his list absolutely complete and to have so organized and condensed the information furnished as to make it more easily accessible than it has heretofore been. He has thus put into available form and within a comparatively narrow compass a vast array of facts which were scattered throughout large and expensive works which could not well be in the possession of most students.

The book is furnished with such illustrations and maps as are necessary to make plain the principal subjects of antiquarian interest. The author has been at pains to cite the authorities upon which he has depended and to give a frank statement of the difficulties which critics find in dealing with the biblical statements regarding the characters treated of. In this part of the work, however, it seems to us, that there is a conspicuous absence of citations from the more recent and commanding representations of biblical scholarship. For example, in treating of the " difficulties " connected with Paul's life, the two books most frequently cited are Bloomfield's New Testament and Haley's Alleged Discrepancies of the Bible, good and useful books, it is true, but not representative of recent critical and historical investigation.

While such a volume is necessarily a compilation, it is still a work requiring much diligence and research for its creditable accomplishment and Mr. Barnes has certainly performed his task in a way which both reflects credit upon himself and gives assurance of his having done a real service to students of the Bible.

The Sermon Bible.

The Sermon Bible. Isaiah to Malachi.   New York: A. C. Armstrong and Son.   Price, $1.50.

This volume completes the Old Testament portion of the admirable series published by the Armstrongs. As has been mentioned in noticing other volumes of the series, the aim is to present the essence of the best homiletical literature of this generation whether published in book form or not. These sermons are arranged according to the books of the Bible, so that they form, also, a running homiletic commentary. The reader must not expect to find much juice along with this sermon essence; but for a collection of the best outlines and suggestions in relation to texts which may have been deemed unproductive as well as for use in homiletic study and criticism, these books are exceedingly well adapted. This volume deals with an intensely interesting portion of Scripture, that covering the prophets, and not a few of the finest modern productions of our great preachers will be found condensed in these pages.

Current Old Testament Literature.

American and Foreign Publications.

62. *Der Geschichte der heiligen Schriften Alten Testaments.* By E. Reuss; 2te Aufl. Braunschweig: Schwetscke. 15.

63. *Daniel et le rationalisme biblique.* Thése. By E. Pilloud. Chambéry; imp. Drivet.

64. *The Scriptural Doctrine of Sacrifice and Atonement.* By Alfred Cave, B. A., D. D. New Edition. Revised throughout and partly rewritten. New York: Scribner and Welford. 4.50.

65. *Was lehrt Luther v. der Inspiration der Heiligen Schrift? Mit d. Reformators eigenen Aussprüchen dargelegt.* By W. Rohnert. Leipzig: Böhme Nachf. .25.

66. *A History of the Jewish People in the Time of Christ.* By Emil Schürer, D. D., M. A. Being a second and revised edition of a "Manual of the History of New Testament Times." First Division. Political History of Palestine, from B. C., 175, to A. D. 135. Translated by the Rev. John Macpherson, M. A. New York: Scribner and Welford. 3.00.

Articles and Reviews.

67. *Wellhausen on the Pentateuch.* By Rev. J. J. Lias, in The Theological Monthly, June 1890.

68. *"Blessed be Abram of the most High God."* By Prof. A. H. Sayce, in Hebraica, July 1890.

69. *The Psalms.* By the Rt. Hon. W. E. Gladstone, in the S. S. Times, June 28, 1890.

70. *Studies in the Psalter. 19. The Thirty-fourth Psalm.* By T. W. Chambers, D. D., in the Homiletic Review, July, 1890.

71. *The Date of Isaiah 12.* By Prof. Francis Brown, in Jour. of Bibl. Lit., 9, 1, 1890.

72. *Dr. Forbes on the authorship of Isaiah.* By Rev. J. A. Selbie, in Expository Times, June 1890.

73. *Immortality in the Old Testament Scriptures.* By Rev. C. D. W. Bridgman, D. D., in Christian Thought, June, 1890.

74. *The Babylonian and Jewish Festivals.* By W. H. C. Boscawen, in Bab. and Orient. Rec., Jan. 1890.

75. *Evil Spirits in the Bible.* By Prof. C. H. Toy, in Jour. of Bibl. Lit. 9, 1, 1890.

76. *"Fasting" in Holy Scripture.* By F. W. Farrar, D. D., in the Expositor, May 1890.

77. *The Language and Metre of Ecclesiasticus. A Reply to Criticism.* By Prof. S. D. Margoliouth, in The Expositor April, May, 1890.

Current New Testament Literature.

American and Foreign Publications.

78. *Geschichte der Pflanzung u. Leitung der christlichen Kirche durch die Apostels.* By A. Neander. Neuer Abdr. der 5. Aufl. 2 Tl. (Bibliothek theolog. Klassiker, 27. Bd.) Gotha: F. A. Perthes. 2. 40.

79. *Buddismo e cristianesimo: studio di religione comparata.* By Raff. Napoli; tip. della r Università. 1890.

80. *Buddha. Sein Leben, seine Lehre, seine Gemeinde.* By H. Oldenberg. 2te Aufl. Berlin: Hartz. m. 10, 50.

Articles and Reviews.

81. *Devils Confessing Christ.* By N. S. Burton, D. D., in The Homiletic Review, July 1890.

82. *Simon Bar-jona; The Stone and the Rock.* By Mrs. T. C. Porter, in the Ref. Quar. Rev., July 1890.

83. *The Miracles of our Lord. 19. The Feeding of the Five Thousand. 20. The Walking on the Sea.* By Rev. W. J. Deane, in the Homiletic Magazine, May, June, 1890.

84. *An Inquiry into the meaning of the Phrase, "Born of water."* By Rev. C. Van der Veen, in the Ref. Quar. Rev., July 1890.

85. *Christian Baptism: Exegesis of John 3:5.* By T. G. A. in the Ref. Quar. Rev., July 1890.

86. *The Evangelistic Symbols.* By F. F. Irving, in The Theological Monthly, June, 1890.

87. *Outlines on the first eight chapters of the Epistle to the Romans.* By Rev. C. Clemance, in the Homiletic Magazine, May, June, 1890.

88. *Zur Osterepistel. 1 Cor. 5: 6-8.* By L. Krummel, in Evang. Kirch.-Ztg. 1890, 14.

89. *2 Timothy 3: 16, 17.* By Tryon Edwards, D. D., in the Homiletic Review, July 1890.

90. *Spirits in Prison.* By W. Wishart, D. D., in the Evang. Repos., July 1890.

91. *Historical Christianity as a Proof of the Reality of Christ's Resurrection.* By the late Rev. S. H. Grisy, in the Ref. Quar. Rev., July 1890.

92. *The Witness of Prophecy to Christ.* By E. S. McKitrick, D. D., in the Evang. Repos., July 1890.

93. *Hatch's Essays in Biblical Greek.* Review by Harnack, in Theol. Ltztg., June 14, 1890.

94. *Mohammed and Mohammedanism.* By Rev. T. G. Flanders in the Univer. Quar., July 1890.

95. *The Presence of Latin Words in the New Testament.* By Rev. Preb. Whitefoord, in Expository Times. May 1890.

96. *Bishop Lightfoot on the New Testament in the Second century.* The Church Quar. Rev., 1890.

97. *Der Religionsunterricht u. der neutestamentliche Kritik.* By A. Jacobsen, in Ztschr. f. d. Religionsunter. 1, 2, 1890.

98. *Martineau's Seat of Authority in Religion.* Review in the Unitarian Review, June 1890.

THE

Old and New Testament Student

| VOL. XI. | SEPTEMBER, 1890. | No. 3. |

A PYRAMID upon its apex is in a state of most unstable equilibrium. A pyramid upon its base is not easily over-turned. Yet many people, in constructing a conception of the Bible or of Christ, insist upon putting the pyramid of faith upon its apex, to the great danger of its overthrow.

If Christ did this, or was that, it is said, I cannot believe in Him as the Divine Saviour of men. If He made intoxicating wine, or if He did not know who wrote every one of the books of the Old Testament, I cannot accept Him as teacher and Lord. If the Bible has in it one scientific or historical allusion that is not in harmony with absolute truth, I cannot accept it as the Word of God. So is the pyramid of faith planted upon its apex.

The folly of such a course is shown by the history of the past. Men once said, "If the world is round, the Bible cannot be the Word of God." Yet we easily believe now in both the roundness of the world and the Divine authorship of the Bible. Later it was said, "If the world was not made, and the fullness thereof, in six days of twenty-four hours each, the Bible is not divine." In this case, also, a way was found to take the pyramid from its apex, and thus to save our faith. How very absurd to go on repeating this process for ever !

THE fact is, this work of making our faith in the divinity of the written Word, or the Word made flesh, rest upon some notion of what we think either is or ought to be, is not only shown, by the history of the past, to be dangerous to faith, but it is

9

unreasonable in itself. It is nothing else than setting up human reason as the final judge in regard to what God has done and can do. It is saying, if there is an incarnation, it must result in such and such facts. If God gives to man a book, it must be a book, the pattern of which I can draw upon my nail. Now, when a thinker who denies the reality of the supernatural in nature or history reasons thus, we say he is a rationalist, and that he is setting his reason up as a judge of God. We say rightly and well. Because he affirms that his knowledge of God is final and complete, or that he knows the universe so thoroughly and so well that he can be utterly sure there is no God in it. Such a claim is the height of conceit and folly. But, after all, is there much difference between such a thinker and the man who claims that he has so far reasoned out God, and so known the Almighty unto perfection, that he can surely say what will be exactly the results when He becomes flesh, or exactly what will be, or will not be, the books which He will cause to be written for men ? From what source can this knowledge be obtained ? Not from God himself ; for He has nowhere told us the truth about these matters. Not from the facts in the life of Jesus, and in the Bible itself; for the question is what these facts really are. To assume, and not to determine, the true character of the facts, is to beg the whole question. The seeming knowledge is only deductions from the data furnished by the human reason. A God is made in the mind, by the mind itself working upon its own philosophical conceptions, and to this God possibilities are assigned in harmony with these conceptions. Then it is easy to say what this God will, or will not, do. But this is only to make reason the judge of God. It is rationalism. This orthodox rationalism is as conceited and absurd as any other.

IT IS much more reasonable, as well as more safe, to rest our faith upon what we know, from the facts in the case, Jesus and the Bible are, rather than upon what we think they are not. Then we place the pyramid upon its base. The Bible claims to be from God. Jesus claims to be from

God. They and their history in the world can only be explained by admitting their claims. If any one feels there are difficulties in the way of believing Jesus and the Bible to be divine, if he is an honest thinker, he will find the difficulties to be vastly greater in attempting to account for them without recognizing them as divine. God is their only satisfactory and complete, and, therefore, their only reasonable and scientific, explanation. That they are divine, however, does not in itself determine, without further study, just what they are in all particulars. It is with them as with nature. God is the only satisfactory explanation of nature. But this established, we do not at once know all that nature is. We study it in all its parts, and in all its workings, to think God's thoughts after Him. So we come to know His works. In like way we must come to know His Word and His Son. We must honestly ask for, and earnestly seek after, all the facts that lie in each, and relate to both, and then must gather from these facts their whole meaning. Thus we never can show, however far our inquiries are pushed, that either is not from God ; but we shall only come better to know what the Divine Man and the Divine Book really are. It is in the interests of this knowledge that the STUDENT was founded and is conducted. Its aim is to find and teach, as far as possible, all the facts of the Divine Man and the Divine Book.

THE author of *God in His World* has some interesting and just remarks on the influence of the prophets in the life of the Chosen People. He maintains that it was the prophetic movement which preserved the vitality and simplicity of the Hebrew faith. It came naturally into contact with the state religion, representing as it did the spiritual freedom of the people. One would expect that the holy city would hate and kill the prophets. But we are ourselves prone to glorify the very features of Judaism that the prophets deprecated, the Mosaic ritual, the temple, and forget the spiritual religion for which prophecy stood. The synagogue was in its inception a prophetic institution, as its form of worship shows, though it fell under the sway of the theocracy when prophecy as a vital power perished.   But, as the writer adds, the prophets themselves were born out of the popular faith and are representatives of that divine historical movement which reveals itself in Israel's history, and which is the root of the writings which we call the Bible.

THE glory of prophecy is its power to infuse a fresh stream of spiritual vigor into established forms of life.   The tendency of organized society is toward institutions, and the peril here is of satisfaction in these monuments of human pride. The writer just referred to declares that the people is blessed which, "generation after generation, has a school of prophets to break up those strictures and to call men back with Isaiah-like yearning to the love of the living God."   Such was the work of prophecy in Israel.   But, in this large sense, there have been prophets in all nations, and these have succeeded or failed, according as they have wrought toward this great end of spiritual regeneration.   Greece had her prophets, but they were satisfied to minister to the "martial and heroic pride" of the nation.   They helped to "disintegrate the old sacred foundations," but they substituted no real divine material in place of what they destroyed.   The Christian preacher is our prophet to-day, and if he is true to his mission, he is ever calling us back to the real, the eternal, the spiritual, interpreting to us the meaning of passing events in this light, and warning us of the transitoriness of all institutional life. Often this prophetic office is held by a man of the people who partakes of the simplicity and clear vision of unsophisticated humanity, and who is hereby able to pierce the shams and expose the hollowness of much that we proudly boast as part of our civilization.   Happy such prophets seldom are, but blessed the people among whom they dwell.

DOES the Christian preacher realize the dignity and glory of this prophetic mission with which he is entrusted ?   Does he come in any way near comprehending his responsibility in this great prophetic office ?   Does he see that this calls upon him to strive after the highest and broadest culture, the largest range of vision and the finest power of insight ? All this—that he may bring God's thought to bear upon the secularisms and crude establishments of human sagacity, riddle them with the sword of the Spirit, and build upon their ruins the foundations of the City of God ?

Let him listen, when he is tempted to ride upon the current of human progress, or find the sources and stimuli for his prophecy in the teachings of merely human thinkers or the doings of merely human energy however striking—let him listen to these words of one of the truest of his own number who has exemplified in very deed these words which he recently wrote for the readers of the STUDENT.

"I think that the teaching of the Bible, or exegetical preaching, is altogether the principal business of the Christian minister. He is God's prophet to the Church and to the world ; and what more important thing can he do than to unfold his Master's message ? Public exegesis, when it is both truthful and useful, is, it seems to me, the highest kind of sacred oratory."

THE LITERARY CHARACTER OF ST. PAUL'S LETTERS. II.

By Rev. Professor E. P. GOULD

P. E. Divinity School, Philadelphia, Pa.

[Continued from the August number.]

But we shall miss the real quality of St. Paul, if we think of him as a mere thinker, a logical machine warranted to be always in order, and to work with surprising exactness, which, I am afraid, is the current view of him encouraged by the use that has been made of his writings. Equally apparent and prominent in his letters is the genuine religiousness of the writer. Of course, any man writing about religious topics is going to display a certain amount and kind of religiousness in his writings. But we have to distinguish between the real article and the counterfeit, and now and then we come upon a man who is what we call a religious genius, one who is so en rapport with spiritual and divine realities that he makes us feel their truth and greatness, not so much by any process of reasoning as by a subtle sense of these things which its possessor is able to impart to others by the mere contact of spirit with spirit. This is the basis of what we call inspiration, and this faculty St. Paul possessed in a marked degree. One of the marks of this genuineness is the presence of the ethical tone, the right emphasis given to conduct in the religious life. And Paul's whole treatment of this is that of a man possessed with this genius for religion. The single fact that he broke with the Jewish law, seeing what no other of the apostles saw, its entire inadequacy to contain the spirit of the new religion, and its real disagreement with it, is a sufficient sign of that inspiration which makes the new ways for humanity to walk in. Put by the side of this his enunciation of faith as the principle of the new life. In order to get the significance of this, notice that he does not mean by faith the acceptance of this or that religious truth as the means of gaining favor with God, but such a belief of any great fact about God as shall inspire in the man a new life, and so create a new spring of life within him. He insists moreover that no outward observances, but only these gracious affections, these high beliefs, this inspired living can commend us to God.

But it is when he leaves this region of principles, exalted though they are, and comes to the personelle of the new religion, and shows us the Christ as the source of this quickened life, that he rises to the height of his subject. Faith in itself is good, even the crude faith of Abraham, but it is the faith of Jesus the crucified which can bring about the wonders that St. Paul is never tired of contemplating. In him he sees a new beginning of the race, the dawn of a new era, in which righteousness shall replace sin; through him the man dies to sin and rises to a new life; he is freed from sin, and made the bondservant of righteousness; in him man becomes conformed to the Spirit of God, and his purposes become those of the Spirit; and yet at the same time, the man under this influence does not become a mere passive recipient of grace, but is quickened into a strenuous and eager pursuit of the things that are high and excellent, and a vigorous conflict with the forces of evil.

Another sign of this true religious feeling is the frequency with which the apostle mounts from practical themes to lofty considerations, and on the other hand descends from lofty themes to practical applications. That is, the spiritual insight which enables him to see that religion means the bringing together of earth and heaven, so that the man who dwells in the region of lofty contemplation and is at home with heavenly things is not thereby divorced from practical life, but really gets the only genuine good out of these when they leaven his life with good. A general proof of this is to be found in the discourses on conduct with which he closes the most profound of his epistles. See Rom. 12–16. Gal. 5 : 13–6 : 18.

In the passage in Romans what a singular elevation is given to the whole discourse by this mingling of the religious and the practical elements! He gathers together the whole impression of the preceding argument in the single phrase, "the mercies of God," and makes that the basis of an appeal to them to make to God the offering of themselves, a holy, living, acceptable, and spiritual sacrifice.   And then see how, starting from this high ground, he presents duty in a large and lofty way.   "Be not conformed to this age, but be transformed by the renewing of your mind;" "not to think of himself beyond what he ought to think, but to think so as to be rightminded;" "for we the many are one body in Christ, and members one of another;" "let love be undissembled; abhorring evil, cleaving to good; in brotherly love affectionate to each other; in honor preferring each other; in diligence not slothful; in spirit fervent; serving the Lord; in hope rejoicing, in affliction enduring, in prayer persevering; communicating to the needs of the saints, intent upon hospitality; bless them that persecute you, bless and curse not; rejoice with them that rejoice, weep with them that weep; be of the same mind towards each other, not setting your mind upon high things, but submitting to lowly things; be not wise in your own conceits; rendering to no one evil for evil; taking thought for things that are good before all men; if possible, as far as you are concerned, being at peace with all men; not avenging yourselves, brethren, but give place to the wrath of God; for it is written, 'vengeance is mine;' I will recompense, saith the Lord.   But if thy enemy hungers, feed him; if he thirsts, give him drink; for in doing this, thou shalt heap coals of fire upon his head.   Be not conquered by evil, conquer evil in your good."

A striking instance of this power to rise from practical themes to lofty considerations, and so to lift the whole subject to a higher plane is found in the familiar eulogy of love in the 13th chapter of 1 Corinthians.   The beauty of the passage in itself is great, but it needs to be seen in its connections, in order to appreciate the power of the apostle to see a practical subject in its higher relations.   He has been talking of the contentions in the Corinthian church about the relative value of the different gifts of the Spirit, such as prophesying, speaking with tongues, and the like, and the claim to distinction conferred by these gifts.   He has just said, "desire eagerly the best gifts," and then he proceeds with the statement, that he has a better way to show them. And this better way is the way of love, the superiority of which he unfolds in this incomparable chapter. Another example is the 3d chapter of 2 Corinthians, where he answers the charge that he brings no letters of commendation, such as the Judaizing teachers opposed to him in the church had, by the statement, "ye are our letters," and then in a beautiful passage developes the contrast between the glory of the new dispensation and the fading glory of the old, in the new life of the Spirit displayed in them, contrasted with the spiritual death which alone resulted from the Mosaic law. And in Philippians 2 : 2–11, in enforcing his exhortation to humility and unselfishness by the example of Jesus, he rises to the very height of his teaching about the pre-existent glory of the Lord.

Still another mark of this religious genius of the apostle is the height to which he rises in his conception of the relation of the believer to God (Christ or the Spirit). Such expressions as "in Christ," "died with Christ," "live with Christ," "in the Spirit," "the Spirit of God dwells in you," "Christ lives in me," "to me to live is Christ," and the like, are the commonplaces of religious speech now, and like many such, have become possibly emptied of much of their meaning. But in the speech of the apostle, marking, as they did, his individual thought of the relation between himself and God in Christ through the Spirit, they show how he, out of his personal experience, had come to grasp that idea of the immanence of God which is the supreme test of the spirituality and truth of our conception of God. He felt that it was not any outward relation established between himself and God in Christ, but an inward relation, the meaning of which was nothing else than the life of God in him.

This combination of intellectuality and the religious faculty would lead us to expect eloquence as the natural result, and such expectation would not be disappointed. There are flashes of it all through his letters, and sometimes there are passages of sustained eloquence which belong to the classics of such speech. For examples of the shorter passages in which the apostle rises above the ordinary level of his style into that fitness and greatness of speech which we call eloquence, see Rom. 1: 14–17; 5: 1–11; 13: 11–14; 14: 6–12; 1 Cor. 3: 21–23; 2 Cor. 3: 17–18; 4: 16–18; 6: 3–10; 11:-22–30; Gal. 2: 19–21; 6: 14–18, which is a very noble specimen of the apostle's best style; Phil. 1: 21–26; 2: 1–11; and finally, the surpassingly beautiful close of this epistle contained in the 4th chapter. The whole passage is worthy to be committed to memory, and some of its expressions have passed into the current speech of Christianity. "Stand fast in the Lord;" "Be of the same mind in the Lord;" "Whose names are in the book of life;" "Let your gentleness be known to all men;" "Be anxious for nothing, but in everything by prayer and supplication, with thanksgiving, let your requests be made known to God; and the peace of God which surpasseth every understanding, shall guard your hearts and your thoughts in Christ Jesus;" "Whatsoever things are true, whatsoever things are noble, whatsoever things are right, whatsoever things are pure, whatsoever things are lovely, whatsoever things are gracious, if there is any virtue, and if there is any praise, take account of these things." "I learned, in whatsoever state I am, therein to be content. I know how to be abased, and I know how to abound; in everything and in all I have learned the secret both to be full and to be hungry, both to abound and to be in want; I can do all things in him who strengthens me."

But, as we have said, St. Paul was capable also of a sustained eloquence. The examples of this are too familiar to need mention. The 8th chapter of Romans, the 13th and 15th of 1 Corinthians are noble examples of his power to transport his readers into regions of high thought and lofty imagination.

We come back finally to the quality in these letters which we mentioned at the outset, the strong personal element which marks them, in spite of the lofty themes discussed in them. St. Paul is writing to churches most of which he had founded, and in which he took the deepest interest. And the admirable thing about his letters is that his interest in persons and in churches is never obscured or overlaid by his interest in subjects, no matter how profound. He is like his master in this, that his heart is moved as quickly by contact with men to deep and tender feelings, as his mind is quickened by large themes to large and true thought.

The two parts of 2 Corinthians are an illustration of the way in which the apostle's style responded to strong personal feeling. He had been very anxious about the state of things in this church. As appears from the first epistle, there had been great irregularities both of conduct and opinion among them. And now the matter had been complicated by the delay of the church to follow some of his instructions under the influence of his old enemies, the Judaizers. Timothy had failed in his mission to them, not being mature enough to stem the tide that had set in against the apostle. And Titus had been sent to represent the apostle in a final attempt to win the church back to its old allegiance. His mission had succeeded with the majority of the church, but a part had held out, and were inclined to say disparaging things about the apostle and what they considered his weakness and want of courage.

The first part of the epistle therefore, addressed to the loyal majority, is full of the anxiety, the relief, the love which identifies him with his churches, the dignity with which he sustains his authority, the perception of important principles involved in the matters at issue between himself and the church, and an air of genuineness, an absence of exaggeration, which makes the whole a powerful appeal to right feeling. He had been meaning to come to them himself, but was detained by his regard for them, which led him to refrain from coming as long as their state of feeling toward him would have made it necessary for him to come with reproaches on his lips. As he says, with solemn asseveration, his object in not coming was to spare them. But he had written to them a letter strongly expressive of his grief, not that he might grieve them, but that they might know his great love and longing for them. Moreover, the wrong done by the recusant member, whose sin and failure to repent had caused all the trouble was not his grievance, but theirs, and that had been the reason of the apostle's severity. And now, that the church had, by the action of the larger part of its members, visited the offender with the consequences of his evil, the apostle enjoins them to treat him henceforth with mercy, assured that he would forgive what they do, and that what he has already forgiven is for their sakes. In place of coming himself, he had sent Titus, and in his anxiety to hear from them, he had left a work which promised greatly in Troas, and had come into Macedonia to meet him. And he gives thanks to God that the result was another triumph of God's grace in him.

Then the apostle comes to the conflict of authority between himself and the Judaizing teachers, and over against the commendatory letters which they had shown to the church, by a fine stroke of genius, he places the statement, that the Corinthian Christians are his epistle, and advances from this to a comparison of the new dispensation represented by himself, and the old law represented by them, set forth in the noble passage beginning with chapter 3: 3. At the same time, he admits that this treasure is committed to earthen vessels, that he bears about in his body the possibility of violent death such as his Lord had suffered, but also the life of the Lord Jesus. But then, this exposure to death in him meant life to them, for whose sake he suffered all things, and it was offset by the certainty of a glorious life in the heavens. We will not follow this noble address any further. It closes with a direct appeal to the church to receive the apostle, and his felicitation of himself and them that the mission of Titus had produced so gracious results in them.

The second part of the letter is very different, being addressed to the contumacious members of the church, and is the sharpest and severest of all the apostle's writings. Chap. 10–13. They brought against him the charge that he is bold in his letters, but weakens and humbles himself, when he is present with them, and that such craft is an exhibition on his part of just that walking according to the flesh which he professes to warn them against. In reply he alleges the well-known spirituality of the weapons employed by him in his warfare against the reasonings of men hostile to God. Moreover, so far as he has shown any such weakness as they allege, any softening of his severity towards them, they must remember that his authority is given him to build up, and not to destroy. He does not propose to apply to himself the standards of measurement adopted by his opponents, who measure themselves by their own standards, but God has given him a standard by which his ministry may be judged, in the ground covered by him as an apostle. Not skipping anything, and not, as these men have done, occupying another man's field, he has come as far as them in his preaching of the Gospel, and hopes to be still further magnified by the same standard in reaching out into the regions beyond them. Again, since they have seen weakness in his refusal to exercise his authority and to lord it over them, he shows that these very signs of weakness are the things of which he boasts. To suffer, instead of using his power to inflict suffering upon others, is to be like his Lord, and is really the source of his power. And finally, since they will have it, he is about to come to them, and then they will see that he represents, not only the Christ who was crucified out of weakness, but the Christ who lives out of power. And yet, when that time comes, he prays that he may find them such that he will, after all, have no opportunity to display this power. This brief sketch is not intended to reproduce the peculiar power of this epistle, but simply as a guide to the thought in reading, since the peculiar mingling and conflict of feeling which constitutes its charm is such as cannot be reproduced.

These letters do not mark an extended literary activity. But they are enough to show us the mental and spiritual quality of the man, whose deeds so far surpass his words, who founded the Gentile churches and gave its distinctive character to Gentile Christianity, and the person revealed, to us in them is evidently a great man, measured by any standard. Suffice it to say, in closing, that the Church has not yet apprehended his greatness, nor fathomed his thought.

BIBLE LEPROSY.

By Professor T. WYTTON DAVIES,

Baptist College, Haverfordwest, Wales.

Since the death of Father Damien our attention has been called over and over again to the awful disease to which in the prime of life he fell a victim. In magazines, the question of its contagiousness has been argued with much learning and with not a little warmth. Many Bible students imagined in reading these articles that they were adding to their knowledge of the Bible, at least of an important Bible disease. Perhaps they were. But one thing which I hope to make clear before I am done is that the Leprosy about which so much has been said is quite a different thing from the disease known by that name in the English Bible, Old Testament and New Testament. But if the two things are quite distinct, why is it that they have one name? Before answering this question of the name, let us try to find out whether the diseases are or are not the same. The simplest way will be to look at the modern disease, so-called "True Leprosy;" then to look at the Bible account of what is there in our English version called "Leprosy." It will be seen that the two things are very different.

As to the modern disease, I will follow the account which Dr. Erasmus Wilson gives in Dr. Quain's Medical Dictionary. Dr. Wilson has written a much fuller account in his book on "Diseases of the skin;" this I have not seen; and there is for our purposes a sufficiently full description in the article referred to.

In all forms of modern Leprosy the parts most immediately affected are the integument (skin and membranes) and nervous system. There are sores outside on the surface of the body, but there are also tubercules formed inside. The liver, kidneys, and alimentary canal are attacked; general waste sets in, which stops only with death. This disease is not merely on the outside, it is organic: awful smells are given out, and sleep is next to impossible.

The disease develops in three special directions—more or less in all three, but, as a rule, more in some one than the others. Drs. Daneelsson and Boeck have written largely on the disease as they have watched it in Norway: they hold that there are only two quite independent kinds (1) Tubercular (2) Anaesthetic.*

The three varieties named by Dr. Erasmus Wilson are as follows:—

1. THE TUBERCULAR KIND, *elephantiasis tuberosa*. In this, red spots cover the body so closely on the face as to give a general redness. These spots are followed by tubercles or pimples which break, after which others are formed. The nasal bones fall in, the eyes are destroyed. There is a swelling of different parts of the body, hands, feet, etc.: then the members get deformed and the voice becomes hoarse.

2. There is the ANÆSTHETIC KIND, *elephantiasis anæsthetica*. In this there are spots and blotches but no tubercles or ulcers. The prevailing character of this is that the system becomes insensitive. You can apply fire or any sharp instrument to the skin, but there is no feeling at all. Yet the internal pains are almost always indescribably keen.

3. The MUTILATING KIND, *elephantiasis nodosa* or *mutilam*. This is more local than the others; its main feature is the loss of the limbs. The fingers and toes, the hands and feet fall entirely away.

Though these three are noticed as if they were quite distinct yet they are found together, in the same districts, and not seldom in the same individuals.

This leprosy has been described by travelers in language strong and hard to read; yet from what I saw in Egypt and in Palestine I consider no words too strong in which to set forth its awfulness. I have seen with infinite pain the open sores, the deformities of face and hands. I have seen the poor creatures going about with several of their limbs altogether gone. I have heard their deep-throated, harsh cry for

*See Keil's Biblical Archæology; 114-16.

help. I have given myself the joy of dropping coins into their out-stretched hands.

This is the leprosy about which so much ado has been made of late; from this Father Damien died. Edward Clifford, the sympathetic biographer of Damien, visited the Sandwich Islands; he describes the faces of the poor lepers as "swelled and drawn and distorted, with bloodshot goggle eyes." He says Father Damien used to smoke in order to deaden the loathsome smell coming from the lepers. In March 1888 Mr. Clifford visited the leper asylum at Agra, India. The faces of the inmates were too dreadful to look upon: those lepers were lame, maimed, and mutilated. They sang lustily under the leadership of an American Baptist missionary, Mr. Jones.* This leprosy prevails largely in our Indian empire; in Palestine and Egypt; in the West Indies; and nearest of all to us, in Norway. In the middle ages it was common in this country, so common that there were in England alone 250 leper hospitals. In Waterford at the present moment, a friend tells me, there is a building marked "Leper House." In a church at Ripon there is a door, now fastened, with the words "Lepers' door" still printed on it. The room into which this door leads was at one time a chapel used exclusively by lepers.

Some have held that Leprosy was introduced into Europe by the Crusaders from Palestine. This is against the voice of history, for in the eighth century there were many leper hospitals in the Frankish kingdom: there were hospitals in Ireland in the ninth century, and in England long before William the Conqueror won Hastings.

This disease was known among the Greeks as *elephantiasis* because it makes the skin rough like that of an elephant. What we now commonly understand by *elephantiasis* is the "Barbadoes leg" or swelling of the lower portion of the body. The other is now called *Elephantiasis graecorum*, or more generally, "True Leprosy."

The common view is that *True Leprosy* is not contagious;

*This must be my friend and fellow student Rev. Daniel Jones, a Welshman not a Yankee. And in our College days Mr. Jones was quite clever at the musical art.

most of the authorities support this view. In the year 1867 the Royal College of Physicians took this matter under special consideration. Evidence was got from every spot affected, and they came to an almost unanimous decision that leprosy is not contagious. Since then, men of the greatest eminence have taken the opposite view. Only in December last Dr. Morell Mackenzie in the "Nineteenth Century" and Dr. Robson Roose in the "Fortnightly Review" argued very strongly for the contagiousness of "True Leprosy." Those who deny this explain the case of Father Damien by inoculation, some of the leprous matter somehow finding its way into the blood. I have seen this explanation in the *Lancet*.

Now I wish you to consider the *Leprosy about which we read in the Bible.* Nowhere is it anything like so fully described in the Bible as in Leviticus 13. Let us attend to this account. Moses, or the author of this part of the Bible, is aiding the people to know the true leper, in order that he may be kept apart. What are the signs? First, we are informed how to know leprosy from spots appearing on the skin. If there is a rising, or a scab, or a white spot, leprosy is present, providing that the plague reaches below the skin, and the hair growing on the part turns white.*

If proud flesh shows itself without previous spots, etc., and if the hair on the part swollen with raw flesh turns white, that is Leprosy, chronic Leprosy, and the person so affected is unclean, and must live outside the camp.†

When a man is wholly covered with white spots, he is declared clean. His being so covered shows that he does not suffer from the serious kind, though this too is called "Leprosy." It answers to what we call "White Leprosy."‡

The care of a man who has a sore following a boil § or a burn ‖ is next examined. If the sore goes lower down than the skin, and if the hair growing on it becomes white, this makes the man unclean.

Then we have to do with the head and the face as covered

*13 : 1–8.   § vs. 18–23.
†vs. 9–11.   ‖ vs. 24–28.
‡vs. 12–13.

by hair and beard. If an eruption breaks out on the head
or under the beard the man has real leprosy, provided that
the sore is lower than the skin, and that the hair turns
yellow.

In vs. 38 and 39 a sort of Leprosy is described which is
quite harmless: it is known by its having a pale, white com-
plexion and is called *bohaq*. This disease is to this day well
known among the Arabs, and, singular to say, they call it by
the very same name bohaq.

Now, it will appear to anyone who compares so-called
"True Leprosy" with the disease spoken of in Leviticus, that
we have to do with kinds of diseases altogether different,
though in all alike the skin is affected, and all are loathsome.
In Leviticus there is not the faintest suggestion of deformity
of limb, or of loss of limbs: we are told of sores breaking
out—nothing more. It is wonderful that diseases so different
in their causes, operation and result, could have been identified. It makes one think of the words of an eminent Italian
physician, "L'opinione era contagiosa, e non la malatha"
(Brunelli). It has been said that the symptoms named in
Leviticus relate to the early history of Leprosy, so that we
should not expect to find the more serious developments of
Greek *elephantiasis* referred to. But Sir Resdon Bennet,
M. D., LL. D., F. R. S., ex-president of the Royal College
of Surgeons, holds that the appearances of the Levitical disease are quite unlike the early showings of "True Leprosy."
He quotes from medieval writers who have given directions
for discovering the approach of Greek *elephantiasis*, and he
proves to demonstration that the Leprosy which they diag-
nose is altogether different from Bible Leprosy.*

If we carefully consult other allusions to Leprosy in the
Bible, we shall see no reason for changing our opinion. The
first Bible mention of it is in Exodus 4: 6, where Moses was
to prove his Divine mission by putting his hand into his
bosom. After taking it out, his hand became "leprous as
snow." There is no difficulty here. In the leprosy of
Miriam, Numbers 12: 10–16, we seem to come upon a
case looking like modern Leprosy. Miriam became "lep-

*See Diseases of the Bible, pp. 32-33.

rous, white as snow." This account agrees with all I have
said. But Aaron pleads on her behalf to their brother Moses
in these words: "Let her not be as one dead, of whom the
flesh is half consumed when he cometh out of his mother's
womb." This is practically the rendering of the Revised
Version, though the two great versions the LXX and the
Vulgate give a different form to the words and seem based
on a different text. What do the above words mean? That
the leprosy of Miriam made her as one half eaten up with
disease, one with the foundation of life sapped? This I
verily believe. But like such a person in what? in being
diseased? I think confidently not, but in being shut out of
ordinary society. So explained, the words present no difficulty to me. We read of Naaman and Gehazi in 2 Kings 5.
Of Naaman we are told only that he was "a leper"—no
more. Of Gehazi more is said, though no more than we
learn from the cases of Moses and Miriam; he was "a leper,
as white as snow." But neither of these persons could have
had an attack of what we now call "Leprosy," for Naaman
still discharged his duties as General of the army of Syria,
and he moved in the royal circle; while Gehazi acted as
servant to Elisha and conversed with the king of Israel after
his infliction.

The leprosy of Uzziah (2 Chron. 26: 19–21) and of the
four who lingered before the gate of the city of Samaria
(2 Kings 8: 3–11) has nothing special—indeed, no description is given at all. After closely looking into all the allusions to Leprosy in the New Testament, I see no reason at
all to change my position, indeed, the position is made
stronger, as the Greek word *lepra* has a more definite meaning
than the Old Testament word *tsarangath*. New Testament
Leprosy shut its victim out of society, except in one instance,
"Simon the Leper," and perhaps he received the name because at one time he had been a leper, but was now recovered.
If he were still a leper, his disease must have been of the
clean type. Of Christ, the great Healer, we are told that he
touched the leper, and "straightway the leprosy departed
from him, and he was made clean." Mark 2: 41–42.

What, in modern speech, are we to understand by Bible

Leprosy? Nothing is more clear than that there are many kinds of Leprosy referred to in the Bible, but all of them are diseases of the skin more or less serious, none of them being particularly perilous to life. The word now in common use among medical men for the *lepra* of the Greeks is *Psoriasis*, a word which Dr. Wilson would confine to eczema, corresponding to its Greek original *Psora*; but which, as a fact, covers all that in the Bible is known as Leprosy. Sir Resdon Bennett is very pronounced in what he says—and *his* words have much weight:

"It may, however, without fear of contradiction be affirmed that scarcely any physician of the present day, can see in the various features of the Levitical disease any but varieties of cutaneous disease of some kind." * An additional proof of the conclusion at which we have arrived is that in the LXX the Greek word *lepra* translates the Hebrew word for Leprosy, *Tsarangath*.† Now this word *lepra* has a very clear and well defined meaning in the writings of the Greek physicians from the time of Hippocrates, who flourished four and one-half centuries before the time of Christ, until medical science passed away from the Greeks. We are quite sure that those who made and favored the Septuagint version regarded the Hebrew *Tsarangath* as a mere disease of the skin. This goes for a good deal. Then the physician Luke employs the same word lepra, and he could not but know what the word meant at his day, and indeed long before and after. Josephus too uses this word, and though he was not like Luke a physician, he had a fair knowledge of the meaning of common Greek words. If the LXX translators, Luke and his fellow evangelists, and Josephus had wished to speak of what to-day goes by the name of Leprosy, they would have used the word *Elephantiasis*, which had this meaning, and to a Greek scholar no other.

Remember again that skin diseases like *Psoriasis* are common in Egypt and Palestine at the present day, while among

* Diseases of the Bible. p. 38.

† I represent the third Hebrew consonant by ng, not because this is its pronunciation, but to show that a consonant is meant, and I know of no more correct way of setting forth this letter, which has two sounds, as the Arabic shows.

the Jews of Egypt, Syria, India, etc., *Elephantiasis* is very rare. In Tangiers, both kinds of Leprosy, biblical and modern, abound, but Jews though common victims of what we argue to be Bible Leprosy, are almost wholly free from modern Leprosy. Is it not also significant that while Greek *Elephantiasis* or modern Leprosy is hereditary if not contagious, Jews in England are entirely free from the slightest taint of it? If this were the disease of their forefathers, it would be natural for them to show at least some traces of it.

In Arabic as in Greek there are two distinct words for Bible Leprosy and modern Leprosy; the former is called *Baratz*; the latter, modern Leprosy, is called *Judham*, which means "maimed" from Jadham, to maim. It is a pity we have the word "Leprosy" in the Bible in a sense altogether alien from the one it has in common speech or in the dictionaries. The Bible has the best right to the word as the latter is from a Greek word *Lepra*, which has the same meaning. Yet it is extremely awkward having a Bible meaning for Leprosy, and another—the commoner by far—altogether different.

Dr. Erasmus Wilson thinks we ought to follow the Greeks by keeping the word "Leprosy" for the Bible disease and *Elephantiasis** for modern Leprosy, *Psoriasis* then standing for what the Greek physicians meant by it. Can we not somehow bring this about? The Welsh language is as unfortunate as the English, for "Gwahanglwyt" (separating disease) stands for the two kinds of diseases, as the English word "Leprosy." As far as I am aware, German is no better off, "*Aufsatz*" covering the same ground as the English word: and there is the same confusion in most modern tongues— even in Hindustanee, as Rev. James Hewlett, M. A., Benares, informs me.

How and when did this confusion arise? Most recent authorities agree in making the Arab physicians responsible for the mistake. These were at their height in the tenth century when Rhazes and Haly Abbas flourished. They occupied

---

*What is now commonly dubbed "Elephantiasis" received this name through a careless mistake of the Arab physicians, and it has no right to the name at all.

themselves almost wholly in rendering into the Arabic speech the works of Hippocrates and Galen, just as the Arab philosophers of the same period translated the writings of Plato and Aristotle. The Greek word "Elephantiasis" which meant what "Leprosy" now means, they rendered by an Arabic word meaning "Bible Leprosy." This was the beginning of the confusion. When the era of the Crusades came round, Europeans were shocked by the the cases of Leprosy they saw in the East. As they gazed at the victims compelled to live apart; and as they surveyed the awful spectacles of misery, they thought at once they saw the "Leprosy" of the Bible. In the vernacular Arabic, long before established in the Holy Land, they found this awful disease spoken of in terms that strictly meant Bible Leprosy. The number of Crusaders was very great and they went out from every country of Europe; their influence is sufficient to account for the mistake which soon became almost universal, and which even now is so widespread that nine out of ten who read in the papers about Father Damien and Lepers' Homes have no suspicion but that they are reading of the disease called "Leprosy" in the Bible.

Old Matthew Poole, the delight of Bible scholars even at this time of day, in his wonderful "Synopsis" (mine is the London, best edition of 1669) points out the distinction between the two kinds of Leprosy. See also his "Annotations" where he more clearly decides for the view taken in this paper. Without naming intervening commentators who nearly all go wrong on this question, just think of an expounder so recent, so scholarly and so commendable as Adam Clark explaining the disease of Leviticus by quoting the orthodox passage from old "Maundrell's Travels." Good old Dr. Gill sees in *Tsarangath* nothing but a Divine infliction different from ordinary diseases, and only Divinely remediable. He is followed by Scott and others. They rest their conclusion on the root of *Tsarangath—tsarang*, which is held to mean "strike." But even accepting this root meaning* which

---

*The meaning "strike" is got from the Arabic; but another Semitic language—the Ethiopic—has the meaning "to make cease," from the same three letters.

is at least doubtful, the inference is unwarranted, as is proved by our word "stroke."

I cannot close this paper without calling attention to the question of "Contagion" and "Heredity."

Bible Leprosy is not contagious if we have properly explained it. There is no instance in Scripture of the disease being caught by contact with another. The common belief that Bible Leprosy is contagious arises from making "unclean" equivalent to "contagious." But that they have different meanings is proved by the fact that every dead body was "unclean," healthy animals and things without life were "unclean." Dr. Erasmus Wilson guided by the Bible account, Dr. Greenhill (quoted by Sir Resdon Bennett) and Sir Resdon Bennett, affirm that Scriptural leprosy is not contagious, and their view seems, out of question, correct.* Why then were lepers to be kept apart?

There are many skin diseases neither dangerous nor contagious which yet are unpleasant, and separation adds to the comfort of persons not so suffering. Many such diseases are caused by the want of cleanliness; and if thus applied to Bible Leprosy of the "unclean" kind it was well to punish the victims in order to make them and others avoid uncleanly habits.

Moreover priests mingled with lepers, and I have already called attention to the freedom with which Naaman and Gehazi moved about in society. When, after the captivity, synagogues were built wherever Jews resided, lepers were not prevented from attending with others,† nor were they excluded from early Christian assemblies.

Is Bible Leprosy hereditary? There is nothing in the Bible to show that it is, nor is there in the subsequent history of the Jews to show that this Leprosy is. And indeed it seems evident that the disease *Tsarangath* as spoken of in the Bible, is neither contagious nor hereditary. Sin is nowhere in the Bible compared to "leprosy," but some of the earliest Chris-

---

* It is but fair to say that according to Dr. Wilson *Tsarangath may* include some kinds of skin diseases that were contagious, such as the itch in which Eiphyta can be conveyed from one body to another.

† Lightfoot's works, Pitman's edition. Vol. XII. p. 172.

tian writers such as Gregory Nazianus, Tertullian, Origen and Augustine the Bishop make frequent reference to this disease as a type of sin. In many modern sermons, references are made which apply to modern leprosy only, and it is to be feared that many of us have "stock" sermons which require altering in this direction. But we would better be correct, however many popular sermons we spoil.

THE TITLES OF THE PSALMS.

By Professor W. HENRY GREEN, D. D., LL. D.,

Princeton, N. J.

There is no book of the Old Testament which so reveals the inmost hearts of the pious under the former dispensation as the Psalter. We learn something of the exterior of their lives in the historical books, though these are for the most part occupied with events affecting the nation rather than those which concern individuals. We learn the obligations laid upon them and the standard of moral and religious duty set before them in the precepts of the law, which, however, are largely symbolical and ritual, and might leave us in doubt whether their spiritual meaning was duly apprehended or the people rested in the husk of outward ceremonial observance. We learn the ideals of a later age in the discourses of the prophets, with their stern censures of prevailing sins and their fearless exposures of men's departures from God and from duty; but they present most prominently the dark features of their own times. How far the evils and the corruptions which they depict with a strong hand were balanced by the true-hearted sincerity and uprightness of the better classes of the people, they do not inform us.

But the Psalter was Israel's manual of devotion. There we see the pious heart pouring itself out before God in the various experiences of life, offering its prayers and praises, uttering its hopes and fears, joys and sorrows, disclosing its inmost feelings toward God and toward men. Here the real spirit of the religion of the Old Testament reveals itself as nowhere else in its profoundest characteristics. And the substantial identity of true religion in every age is most clearly shown by the extent to which these Psalms have been adopted as the hymn-book of the Christian Church as well as of the temple and the synagogue, and supply the language of devotion, of which they offer a most suitable vehicle and powerful quickener.

This universal adaptability of the Psalms gives them a meaning and value quite independent of the persons by whom or the period and occasion in which they were severally produced. They speak directly to every pious heart, and find an answering echo there. Nevertheless, it is not a question of idle curiosity, but one both interesting and important, Who wrote those sacred songs? and What are the circumstances which called them forth? It adds greatly to the interest of any composition to know when and by whom it was written. This is the case even with those Psalms, which are purely didactic or devotional, and contain little or nothing that reflects or is affected by the particular circumstances under which it was prepared, and which would seem equally appropriate as the utterance of a devout mind at any time and in any situation. When, however, as is frequently the case, the psalm contains personal, local and historical allusions, or when it is interwoven with, or, it may be, grows directly out of the individual or national experiences to which it relates, it is important to its correct and thorough understanding that the precise situation should, if possible, be ascertained, which is there depicted. A knowledge of the history and of the actors in it will throw light upon the psalm, and the psalm will in turn illustrate the history, giving a fuller insight into the feelings and actions of those immediately concerned, as these appeared at the time and are set forth by one who was in the midst of that which he describes.

The determination of the authorship of the Psalms and of the age to which they belong is, further, of eminent consequence in tracing the history of the religion of Israel. These utterances of pious souls reveal their conceptions of God and of duty, the character of their worship, both in its outward forms and in its inward exercises, and the body of their religious faith. If the age of the Psalms can be definitely fixed, the contemporaneous religion of Israel is clearly and indubitably mirrored forth in them, and with this its relation to antecedent and subsequent stages of that religion is necessarily linked. So that the testimony of the Psalms becomes an important factor in dealing with the theorizing of revolutionary critics respecting the origin and history of the Old Testament religion.

One hundred of the Psalms are in their titles referred to their reputed authors.

1	(the 90th) is ascribed to	Moses.
73		"	David.
2 (viz., 72, 127)		"	Solomon.
12			Asaph.
11			Sons of Korah.
1	(the 89th)	"	Ethan the Ezrahite.

Are these titles reliable? If they are, the authorship of two-thirds of the Psalms is settled, and the particular occasion on which some of them were composed is further made known. It has been the fashion of late to distrust the testimony of the titles. And yet even critics, as little disposed as Ewald and Hitzig to submit to the trammels of traditional authority, did not venture to set them altogether aside, but confessed that several of the Psalms must be admitted to be the genuine production of David. Thus Ewald speaks of a series of Psalms " which all indications combine to show can proceed from no other and no less a poet than David himself." Critics of the school of Kuenen and Wellhausen, however, have adopted a notion of the gradual development of religious ideas in Israel, which is absolutely inconsistent with the admission that David could have composed Psalms breathing such a pure and lofty spirit as those which are attributed to him. They find it essential to the maintenance of their fundamental hypothesis to set these testimonies peremptorily aside. Kuenen says (Religion of Israel. I. p. 322): " It was no longer possible to disguise the fact that not a single psalm or proverb was guaranteed by these headings to be a production of the age of David and Solomon. At last critics had the courage to say that all those titles without distinction are contradicted by the oldest portions of the historical books. . . It is true that a great portion of tradition is thus set aside. . . As a result of such an application of historical criticism, the age of David and Solomon assumes quite a new character."

In like manner, Dr. Robertson Smith (Encyclopedia Britannica xx. p. 32): "The tradition that David is the author of these two collections (viz., Ps. 3–41, 51–72) comes to us, not exactly from the time of the Chronicler, but certainly from the time when the view of Hebrew history which he expresses was in the course of formation. And it is not too much to say that that view implies absolute incapacity to understand the difference between old Israel and later Judaism, and makes almost anything possible in the way of the ascription of comparatively modern pieces to ancient authors." The plain English of which is that the traditional date of the Psalms is utterly irreconcileable with his critical views of "the difference between old Israel and later Judaism." These views oblige him to maintain that the Psalms ascribed to David and other ancient authors are comparatively modern. Delitzsch very properly says (Comment. .on Psalms, p. 16): "The denial of what has been delivered by historical tradition [in these titles], which has been prevalent since the last decenniums of the preceding century, has now come to be a contemptuous snap-judgment, which would be regarded as madness in any other department of literature, in which the decision was not so biassed by foregone conclusions."

In attempting to arrive at a correct estimate of the value of these titles, a few general considerations bearing on the subject will here be presented. They should in the next place be brought to the test of the internal evidence of the Psalms themselves; but upon this we cannot now enter.

1.   These titles embody the oldest accessible tradition of the origin of the Psalms. They have been from time immemorial a part of the text and have the same external vouchers as the body of the Psalms themselves. Sixty-nine of the seventy-three Psalms entitled David's are attributed to him likewise in the Septuagint, the oldest of all the versions and the most ancient voucher that we possess for the text of the Old Testament next to the Hebrew itself. But, on the other hand, stress has been laid* on the circumstance that four of the Psalms ascribed to David in the Hebrew (Pss. 122, 124, 131, 133) do not bear his name in the LXX.;

* *The Old Testament in the Jewish Church*, p. 111.

and fourteen (Pss. 33, 43, 67, 71, 91, 93-99, 104, 137) are ascribed to him in the LXX. but not in the Hebrew. This, it is said, betrays a tendency in copyists to attach the name of David to Psalms not really his. If four such titles have been added in the Hebrew and fourteen in the Greek since the Septuagint version was made, who can say how many were inserted without authority before that date? And thus suspicion is cast upon them all. Fortunately the Hexapla of Origen here comes to our aid, showing that the Greek versions of Aquila, Symmachus and Theodotion, as well as the Hebrew of his day, were in exact correspondence with the Massoretic text, as we possess it, in this particular. Explicit statements to this effect have been preserved in respect to each of the aforesaid Psalms with the exception of two (Pss. 95, 124), whose titles do not chance to be mentioned owing to the fragmentary condition of the Hexapla. And the Chaldee Targum further corroborates the exactness of the title of Psalm 124* in the Hebrew. It appears, therefore, that there are four instances, and only four, in which the ascription of Psalms to David in the Hebrew is not confirmed by the LXX. These are the only cases consequently in which there is any legitimate doubt respecting the text; and in these the Hebrew has the support of the other Greek versions.

2. It further appears from indubitable evidence that the titles belonged to an age much more remote than this. They were already ancient when the Septuagint version was made. Many of the titles contain musical directions which were intended to guide in the use of the Psalms in the worship of the temple. They indicate the chief musician to whose oversight they were entrusted, and sometimes specify whether they were to be performed by male or female voices, the tune or air to which they were to be sung, and the instruments which were to form the accompaniment. Several of these terms were no longer intelligible to the translators, and are either incorrectly rendered or simply reproduced in Greek letters. In fact, their true sense became obscured long prior to that time. As Dr. Delitzsch correctly remarks (Com. über die Psalmen, p. 16): "The key to understanding them must

---

* The Targum refers Ps. 124 to David, but not Pss. 122, 131, 133.

have been early lost, for they cannot be explained·from the books of Chronicles and Ezra, in which much is said of music, but in which they appear as older constituents of the language revived." And Dr. Robertson Smith admits (Enc. Brit. xx. p. 34): "It is not quite clear whether the Chronicler understood them fully." The only satisfactory explanation of this is that these terms belonged to the musical arrangements of the temple, which were in current use before the exile. These were abruptly terminated by the destruction of the city and the removal of its inhabitants. A long suspension of sacred services followed. And when the Jews were permitted to return to their own land, the reduced numbers and the impoverished condition of the early colonists made a complete reproduction of the ancient order of things quite impossible. Through this enforced disuse the meaning of these technical terms gradually faded from their minds, until it was nearly or wholly lost.

And this accounts for the very remarkable circumstance that musical terms, whether in the titles or occurring elsewhere as Higgaion and Selah, are not attached to all the Psalms, nor to Psalms taken at random, but are limited exclusively to pre-exilic Psalms. However obscure or unintelligible, they are extremely interesting as the sole surviving relics of the musical notation which prevailed in Solomon's temple. They mark the Psalms, in which they are found, as set to music and sung in the manner here indicated ·in that ancient sanctuary. These musical notes are found in two anonymous Psalms (66, 67) of uncertain date, and besides, only in those which are attributed to David and to Asaph and the other Levitical singers. And Psalms of late date belonging to the guild of Asaph, as Pss. 74, 79, are without these notes. They do not occur in any psalm which is demonstrably post-exilic.

Dr. Robertson Smith attributes the decadence of these musical terms to a much later period, and seeks to account for it by the introduction of Greek art consequent upon the conquests of Alexander, when, as he supposes, the old national music was superseded by that of the west. But this obliges him to assume a preposterously late date for the books

of Chronicles, since these terms were but partially understood when they were written.   His hypothesis is moreover
clearly set aside by the facts already recited, showing that
the musical crisis was induced by the exile.

That the musical notation which we have been considering
was pre-exilic, is further established by the psalm of Habakkuk in ch. 3 of his prophecy, with its Selahs and its title and
subscription modelled after the titles of the Psalms: "To the
chief musician on my stringed instruments.   A prayer of
Habakkuk the prophet, set to Shigionoth."   It is to be
observed that both the possessive pronoun, and the fact that
the psalm is an integral portion of the prophecy, indicate
that the inscription is from the prophet's own hand.   Again
in Hezekiah's psalm, in Isa. 38, we find the technical terms
of the Psalter in its closing verse: "We will sing my
songs to the stringed instruments all the days of our life
in the house of Jehovah."   And we are reminded of the
technical phrase in the title of Psalm 60: "Michtam of
David, to teach," by the words prefixed to David's lament
over Saul and Jonathan, 2 Sam. 1: 18, "he bade them
teach *the song of* the bow."

This demonstrable antiquity of the technical titles necessarily attaches likewise to the authors' names, not only
because the latter are consistent parts of the same titles,
but it is a very significant circumstance that the authors'
names invariably follow and never precede the musical
directions.   Any addition made to an already existing superscription would naturally be prefixed to it.   There is an
illustration of this in Ps. 88, which affords the only instance
in the Psalter of a double inscription.   Its original title was,
" For the chief musician: set to Mahalath Leannoth, Maschil
of Heman the Ezrahite."   This psalm belonged to an old
collection antedating the present Psalter, which was denominated " Psalms of the Sons of Korah."   Accordingly, when
it was inserted in our present book of Psalms, the words,
" A Song, a Psalm of the Sons of Korah," were prefixed to
its former title, to indicate the source from which it was
taken.   Now, it is noteworthy that the invariable order is,
" For the chief musician. A Psalm of David," never the
reverse.

3. Allusion has already been made to the existence of partial collections of Psalms prior to the formation of the present Psalter. A fresh corroboration may be thence deduced of the conclusion already reached respecting the antiquity of the titles recording the names of the authors. The Revised Version of the Old Testament has made the English reader familiar with the ancient division of the Psalms into five books. These books indicate in a general way successive stages in the growth of the collection, so far at least as this, that the fourth and fifth books are a later appendix to the first three, a fresh body of temple melodies added to those previously in use. This new accession was probably in great part post-exilic, though containing a few ancient compositions. In the first and older portion of the Psalter titles are the rule, in the subsequent portion they are the exception. Of the first ninety psalms only eight are anonymous; of the last sixty, with the exception of eighteen referred to David and Solomon, all are anonymous.

We can push our inquiries yet one step further in tracing the early history of the Psalms. The first three books, which we have seen to be the older portion of the Psalter, have been formed by the combination of two pre-existing collections, called respectively the Prayers of David and the Psalms of Asaph and of the Sons of Korah. Each of these, as they lie in the present book of Psalms, is divided into two parts by the interposition of a portion of the other between its severed segments. The subscription to Psalm 72 marks the termination of one of these: "The Prayers of David the son of Jesse are ended." By the help of the titles we are able to discover the other collection, Psalms 42–50, continued Psalms 73–89. If, in order to restore it to its original completeness, we bring these parts together by removing Psalms 42–50 from its present place, there will be left Psalms 1–41, 51–72; and we can hardly be mistaken in assuming that this was the original compass of the primitive body of temple melodies known as the Prayers of David, so called because with very few exceptions all were from his pen. Psalm 72 is the only one that is attributed to another; it bears the name of Solomon. Psalm 10 is commonly supposed to be a continuation of the alphabetic acrostic begun in Psalm 9. Psalm 2 is in Acts 4: 25 said to have been spoken by the mouth of David; and the internal evidence strongly favors his authorship. There are but three beside which are not in their titles ascribed to David, viz., Pss. 1, 33, 71.

There is no reason, so far as appears, why this collection may not have been coeval with the reign of Solomon, since it contains nothing which can with any certainty be referred to a later period. We learn from 1 Kings 10: 12 that there were singers connected with the temple service from the beginning; and the elaborate arrangements made by David and Solomon in this respect are detailed at length in the books of Chronicles. It is further explicitly mentioned that in the restoration and purification of the temple worship by Hezekiah at the beginning of his reign the commandments of David in this matter were punctiliously obeyed, and "the Levites sang praise unto Jehovah with the words of David and of Asaph the seer," 2 Chron. 29: 25–30. Snatches are even quoted by Jeremiah 33: 11 from Psalms (106, 107, 136) occurring in what is recognized as the later part of the present book, and yet were sung in the temple in his day.

The genuineness of the Davidic psalms is thus vouched for by this ancient collection of the Prayers of David. That this collection now lies before us in precisely its original compass, and that no unauthorized additions were suffered to gain admission to it, appears from the fact that other Psalms entitled David's are to be found in the subsequent portions of our present book. Though recognized as David's, they were inserted in the more recent portion of the Psalter, and thus the integrity of the primitive collection was maintained. We are hence able to distinguish between those Psalms of David which belonged to the temple liturgy from the first and those which were added to it at a later time. That process was repeated in the final constitution of the book of Psalms, which, as we are expressly told, was performed by the men of Hezekiah in relation to the proverbs of Solomon, Prov. 25: 1. Songs of David not previously in use in the temple worship, and yet adapted for the purpose, were culled from various sources and added as an appendix along with others of more recent origin.

The careful discrimination between Psalms of David and those of the Levitical singers, and between both of these classes and all others, is also calculated to inspire confidence in the accuracy of the titles. This further accounts for the fact that no other names of authors were deemed worthy of preservation besides those of these great masters of song, and justifies the belief that no spurious production would be suffered to rank with what was held in such estimation, or to be entitled David's if it was not really his and known to be such.

But Dr. Robertson Smith seeks to neutralize the testimony of this ancient collection of the Prayers of David. He says:* "The collection may not have been framed from the first exclusively with an eye to Davidic poems. But in process of time it may have come to be called Psalms of David because it contained some of his poems. . . And thus, when the first Psalm book was taken up into a longer collection, each psalm may have received a title derived from the current name of the book in which it was found." The title, "Psalm of David," would thus merely indicate the collection from which it was taken, but would give no assurance that it was really David's or that the compiler of the collection supposed it to be his. There is not only no evidence on which to base this conjecture, but it is disproved by Psalm 72 itself. The subscription to this psalm shows that it was unquestionably in the old hymn-book denominated the Prayers of David; and yet it is entitled a Psalm of Solomon. The title was plainly not derived from the collection in which it had stood, but was descriptive of the individual psalm.

There is a further incidental proof of an interesting kind, that the titles were already attached to the individual psalms before the primitive collection was formed. It is well known that the order of the Psalms among themselves was frequently determined by the recurrence of some prominent word or phrase. Thus Psalm 35 follows 34 because "the angel of Jehovah" occurs in both, 34: 7; 35: 5, 6, and nowhere else in the Psalter. Psalm 51 follows 50, because in each material sacrifices are constrasted unfavorably with spiritual. And so

* *The Old Testament in the Jewish Church*, p. 198.

abundantly elsewhere. Now, it is a most significant circumstance that the link which binds Psalm 56 to 55 is the correspondence between the title of the former and the text of the latter. The former is set to the tune of "the silent dove of them that are afar off;" in the latter the Psalmist exclaims, verses 6, 7, "Oh, that I had wings like a dove, . . . lo, then would I wander afar off." The title must be older than this primitive collection to have influenced the arrangement adopted in it.

4. Considerations have now been adduced from the testimony rendered on behalf of the titles by the ancient versions, from their containing musical terms which became obsolete in the exile or shortly after, and from their antedating the ancient hymn-book of the first temple, which is still traceable as the oldest constituent in the gradual formation of the present book of Psalms. These certainly establish their very high antiquity, and prove them to have been in the responsible custody of those officially charged with directing the musical services of the sanctuary. We have thus a strong guarantee of their accuracy and safe transmission. This is further confirmed by the analogy of other titles in the Old Testament. Those that occur in the books of the prophets are with very few exceptions acknowledged to be trustworthy even by the most revolutionary critics. The alleged length of Hosea's ministry has been doubted, but not that he was really the author of the prophecies to which his name is prefixed. Those who dispute the genuineness of Isaiah 40–66 and the closing chapters of Zechariah, lay stress upon the circumstance that these have no special titles indicating their authors. The burdens of Babylon by Isaiah ch. 13, 14, and Jeremiah ch. 50, 51, have been discredited notwithstanding their titles, but these supply a strong argument of their genuineness, which is abundantly corroborated by additional evidence. Hezekiah's psalm, Isaiah 38, and that of Habakkuk, ch. 3, are unchallenged, and their titles afford an exact parallel to those of the Psalter. That of Habakkuk at least must in all probability have been prefixed by the prophet himself. In the opening verse of the last words of David, 2 Sam. 23: 1, his name is announced as the author. There

is much to favor the opinion that the titles of the Psalms are to be attributed to the writers themselves, who were in the habit of prefixing their names to their compositions; or at any rate, that they were placed there by responsible persons cognizant of the fact thus attested. So that, at all events, there is a strong presumption in favor of the correctness of the statements contained in them, which were allowed to be made and permitted to remain, because their truth was known and acknowledged.

5. The titles cannot be, as has sometimes been alleged, the conjectures of a later age, mere inferences deduced from the Psalms themselves respecting their author and occasion; in which case modern critics would be quite competent to review the grounds of judgment and pronounce upon the correctness of the conclusion. But the specific occasion of Psalms of a general nature, e. g., Psalm 34, is sometimes recorded, though they contain no obvious clue to their origin, the circumstance that gave rise to the train of thought pursued in the psalm not being itself the subject of it nor dwelt upon with any prominence. And, on the other hand, there are Psalms, such as Psalms 20, 48, 83, which seem to suggest their own occasion or afford ready materials for an easy and plausible inference, to which no such titles are attached. The natural conclusion is that the titles were based on extraneous information and not inferred from hints or implications in the Psalms; otherwise the obvious would not have been passed by and the more recondite and obscure have been exalted to prominence. Still less can they have been arbitrary and baseless inventions. Then, why were any Psalms left without them? Unfounded fancies could be readily multiplied without limit; and it would be as easy to invent occasions for all as for a part. And by what lucky accident has it happened that random suggestions, if they were such, find such frequent and striking corroboration when they are examined minutely and in detail?

6. Upon the critical assumption of Kuenen and Dr. Robertson Smith and others of like tenor, it is impossible to account for the reference of so large a number of the Psalms of David in their titles, or for his name being given to the

primitive hymn-book of the first temple, as it subsequently was to the present book of Psalms in ancient times, 2 Macc. 2 : 13 ; Heb. 4 : 7. If David was by way of eminence "the sweet psalmist of Israel," as he is characterized 2 Sam. 23 : 1, if he introduced and regulated the psalmody of the sanctuary, and if he composed a large proportion of the songs that were used in public worship, and set the style for the rest, then it is easy to understand how the whole book came to be popularly called the Psalms of David. *A potiori denominatio fit.* But if in point of fact he wrote none of the Psalms, and the ordering of the service of song attributed to him in Chronicles is an erroneous ascription to him of arrangements made long subsequent to his time, then it remains a puzzle how David ever came to be connected with the preparation of the Psalms in the popular imagination.

The critics here involve themselves in precisely the same difficulty that meets them in their hypothesis respecting the legislation of Moses. The only explanation that Dr. Robertson Smith has to give is that David was famous for his musical skill, 1 Sam. 16 : 18, and is credited by Amos 6 : 5 with inventing instruments of music, though in a connection suggestive only of revelry and of profane uses. Thence it became customary to speak of the temple choirs as using "the musical instruments of David," Neh. 12 : 36. And since the temple music was ascribed to him, the oldest liturgy came to be known in its totality as the Prayers or Psalms of David. This is certainly building a large structure on a very slender foundation. That David was a skilful player on the harp and in that capacity quieted the disturbed mind of Saul, cannot have originated the belief that he was the principal composer of the temple Psalms, if in point of fact he had nothing whatever to do with them. The popular belief must have had some foundation. And if David wrote any of the Psalms attributed to him, however few, the entire hypothesis of the history of Israel's religion framed by the Kuenen and Wellhausen school of critics vanishes into smoke. For they all breathe an elevated and spiritual religion, which, according to the scheme propounded by these critics, could not possibly have existed in David's days.

The forbearance of such as may read this article has been seriously overtasked by this protracted and technical discussion of a theme dry and uninteresting in itself, and yet of no small importance as preliminary to the direct study of the book of Psalms. We have seen the documentary evidence from the ancient versions showing that the titles to the Psalms were a constituent of the text prior to the LXX., the oldest known translation; further, the proof that they were then already so ancient that the meaning of the musical terms associated with them was completely lost; that this musical notation was pre-exilic, a knowledge of its meaning had already begun to fade in the long cessation of its use during the exile, and there is no evidence of its employment subsequently; that these titles are not only limited to the first three books of the present Psalter and such Davidic Psalms as are found in the fourth and fifth books, but they certainly antedate the primitive collection of the "Prayers of David," which carries us so nearly back to the age of the royal Psalmist; that the inscriptions referring particular Psalms to him may well have been prefixed by the author himself, or by some one thoroughly cognizant of the facts regarding their composition. Still more, their trustworthiness thus attested by their high antiquity is confirmed by the analogy of the titles found in the books of the prophets, whose statements respecting the authors of the pieces to which they are prefixed are of acknowledged validity; and from the clear internal evidence that the titles of the Psalms cannot be the conjectures of a later age based on the contents of the Psalms themselves; nor can the traditional ascription of the Psalms to David be accounted for unless some at least are genuinely his. To which it is to be added that the wholesale denial of the existence of Davidic Psalms in the Psalter by the most recent critics is under the constraint of a revolutionary hypothesis respecting the gradual development of Israel's religion, which is still under discussion, and is to be tested by the evidence afforded by these ancient records, and cannot be suffered in advance to shape that evidence into accordance with its own prepossessions.

The full treatment of this subject would demand, what is

of course impossible here, the detailed comparison of individual Psalms with the statements contained in the titles prefixed to them. The writer can only state his own conviction that the result of a careful and unbiassed examination would serve to confirm the preliminary conclusion already reached that these titles are in the general entirely trustworthy, that they deserve our confidence as in the main a reliable tradition respecting the authors of the Psalms and the occasions upon which they were prepared. If in any case the title is clearly incompatible with the psalm to which it is prefixed, it should of course be set aside as erroneous. But where no such incompatibility exists, as it is believed, can be shown in the majority of cases, if not in all, the title should be accepted as a veritable and reliable tradition.

THE LIFE AND TIMES OF THE CHRIST,

BASED ON LUKE.

By William R. Harper and George S. Goodspeed,

Yale University.

(Copyrighted, 1890.)

STUDIES XXXVII. AND XXXVIII.—CLOSING JOURNEYS AND TEACHINGS IN PEREA. LUKE 17 : 11–18 : 30.

Remark.—It is desirable that in beginning each "study" the entire passage assigned be read over rapidly and the main divisions of the narrative noted.

I. EXAMINATION OF THE MATERIAL.

[It will be noted that the following order is observed invariably in this work ; (1) the verse or section is read and its contents stated in a general way; (2) important or difficult words and phrases are studied; (3) a complete statement of the contents of the verse or section is formed in view of the work already done; (4) the religious teaching is sought.]

§ 1. Chapter 17 : 11-19.

1. The student may read the passage and decide on a subject.
2. Important words and phrases are : (1) *to Jerusalem* (17 : 11), a new cycle of narrative ? cf. 9 : 51; 13 : 22; (2) *through the midst*, cf. marg.; (3) *go and shew your-selves* (17 : 14), (a) i. e. act as though you were healed, cf. 5 : 13, 14, (b) a test of faith; (4) *as they went*, (a) lit. "were going," (b) was it a gradual process? (c) they had faith to take Jesus at his word; (5) *when he saw* (17 : 15), (a) he was going to a Samaritan priest, (b) did he go and then return? (6) *at his feet* (17 : 16), (a) was not this a violation of law and disobedience to the command of Jesus? (b) how was it excusable? (7) *were there none found*, etc. (17 : 18), were not the nine fulfilling Jesus' command ?
3. Note the following statement of the thought : *On the border between Samaria and Galilee, ten lepers ask for healing, and are told to go to the priests as if healed. As they go their way, they are healed. One, a Samaritan, returns thankfully to Jesus and is blessed by him, while he reflects upon the failure of the others to show gratitude.*
4. An important religious thought here is the example of faith without expression of gratitude or love. Are we not all of us liable to be thus imperfect ?*

---

* Men have the faith which justifies; they are pardoned and they have the sense of freedom from the burden and disease of sin, and yet their lives show no glow of loving gratitude. *Plumptre*, p. 282.

§ 2.   Chapter 17 : 20, 21.

1. A reading of these verses suggests the subject: *The Pharisees' Question and its Answer.*
2. The following are important points to be considered : (1) *asked* (17 : 20), out of (a) mockery, or (b) speculation ; (2) *with observation,* i. e. "careful and anxious watching ; " (3) *within you* (17 : 21), note the margin and compare the two readings in view of (a) the persons addressed, (b) the context.
3. The student may make his own statement of the thought.
4. It is to be noted that Jesus chides the folly of speculating about the blessed future to the neglect of present facts of life and duty.

§ 3.   Chapter 17 : 22-37.

1. Read and criticise the statement of the subject . *Coming of the Son of Man.*
2. (1) *Disciples* (17 : 22), may they have been deceived by the statement of 17 : 21? (2) *one of the days,* (a) which are past, or (b) which are to come ; (3) *shineth,* etc. (17 : 24), " sudden and universally perceived event ; " (4) *but first* (17 : 25), "this is not coming till " etc.; (5) *in the days of the Son of man* (17 : 26), (a) i. e. when he is about to come, (b) there will be a great catastrophe ; (6) *in that day,* etc. (17 : 31), (a) "when he comes," (b) "do not give a thought to worldly affairs ; " (7) *gain his life* (17 : 38), i. e. at that time ; (8) *be taken* (17 : 34), to join the Son of man ? (9) *where the body is* (17 : 37), i. e. wherever the situation is ripe for the catastrophe.
3. The following condensation of the thought is suggested : *To the disciples he said, " Do not expect the kingdom and its glory now. You are going to suffer trial, and then you will long for my presence. People will assure you that I am here or there, but when I do come it will be like lightning, seen everywhere. But I must first be rejected and die. And as the time approaches, people will be unthinkingly going on their wordly rounds, as when Noah's flood suddenly fell. Remember Lot's wife and let your earthly interests all go. Then will be separation of those together in bed and at the mill." When they asked " where ? " he replied " the vultures gather wherever there is carrion."*
4. The student may state the religious teaching in his own words.

§ 4.   Chapter 18 : 1-8.

1. May not the subject be stated as : *Parable of the Widow and the Judge ?*
2. Words and phrases of special interest are : (1) *ought always to pray,* etc. (18 : 1), (a) was there need of this teaching in view of 17 : 22-37 ? (h) was this to be prayer for the coming consummation ? (2) *judge* (18 : 2), a type of God ? (3) *wear me out* (18 : 5), cf. marg.; (4) *and he is long suffering,* etc. (18 : 7), i. e. "and all the while he is delaying to avenge ; " (5) *faith* (18 : 8), (a) cf. margin, (b) i. e. the faith in the consummation, (c) throws light on the " pray " (v. 1).
3. The student may criticise the following statement of the contents : *He spoke a parable to teach them to continue to pray for his coming, saying, An unrighteous judge was so persistently followed up by a widow that he gave her justice to get rid of her. Shall not God, though he delays, at last surely requite his people ? Still when I come will there be any who are expecting my coming ?*
4. The religious teaching of the passage is clearly this, that the character of God is the permanent encouragement to prayer and the sure pledge of its answer.

§ 5. Chapter 18 : 9-14.

1. Read the passage and note the subject: *Parable of the Pharisee and the Publican.*
2. The student may examine carefully the words and phrases of the section, especially any difficulties which they present.
3. A condensation of this passage is as follows: *Those who were self-righteous, he taught by the parable of two worshipers in the Temple. One, a Pharisee, thankfully reminded God of his good deeds and his superiority to others. The other, a Publican, humbly besought God's mercy on himself, a sinner. This one, said Jesus, departed with God's approval rather than the other, for God humbles the proud and exalts the humble.*
4. The student may determine the religious teaching.

§ 6. Chapter 18 : 15-17.

1. The student may state the subject after reading the verses.
2. (1) *They* (18 : 15), who? (2) *rebuked*, what was their feeling, (a) the common sentiment of the time regarding children, or (b) their reverence for their master, or (c) the interruption of their discoursing, cf. Mk. 10 : 1-16? (3) *of such is*, etc. (18 : 16), (a) i. e. the kingdom belongs to such, (b) is this literal or figurative, (c) explained by the following verse?
3. Consider this presentation of the thought. *When babes were brought to Jesus for his touch, the disciples found fault with it ; but Jesus said, Let the children come. They are the ones who possess the Kingdom of God, and you too must become like a child to enter there.*
4. The student may determine the religious lesson.

§ 7. Chapter 18 : 18-30.

1. Read and consider a subject, e. g. *Jesus and the Ruler.*
2. Important and difficult words and phrases are: (1) *why callest thou*, etc. (18 : 19), (a) is this humility on Jesus's part, or (b) claim to be equal with God, or (c) sharp challenge to the superficial greeting? (2) *one thing* (18 : 22), (a) but three things are commanded, why? (b) is this command a means of perfecting one's self in the religious life, or does it lie at the basis of such a life? (c) how far is it to be literally obeyed by all? (3) *how hardly* (18 : 24), i. e. with what great difficulty ; (4) *enter into*, is this (a) enjoy a future state, or (b) acquire a present character? (5) *house or wife*, etc. (18 : 29, 30), (a) is this literal or figurative? (b) if figurative, is it equivalent possessions in the Christian community (1 Cor. 4 : 15; Acts. 4 : 34; Rom. 16 : 13), or spiritual compensations to the individual (1 Cor. 3 : 22 ; 2 Cor. 6 : 10)? (6) *world to come* (18 : 30), is this (a) the epoch of the Christ, or (b) the future life? (c) cf. and explain also "eternal life " (v. 30).
3. The student may make out a statement of the thought noting these divisions (1) vs. 18-23, (2) vs. 24, 25, (3) vs. 26-30.
4. The great religious thought emphasized here is the absolute necessity of putting Christ and the Kingdom first in our affections and purposes.

II. CLASSIFICATION OF THE MATERIAL.

1. Contents and Summary.

1) **The Contents.**   The following table of the contents is to be made thoroughly familiar.

CLOSING JOURNEYS AND TEACHINGS IN PEREA.

§ 1. THE TEN LEPERS CLEANSED.
§ 2. THE PHARISEES' QUESTION AND ITS ANSWER.
§ 3. THE COMING OF THE SON OF MAN.
§ 4. PARABLE OF THE WIDOW AND THE JUDGE.
§ 5. PARABLE OF THE PHARISEE AND THE PUBLICAN.
§ 6. JESUS AND THE CHILDREN.
§ 7. JESUS AND THE RULER.

2) **The Summary.** The student may exercise himself in making a summary of the passage in one hundred words.

2. Observations upon the Material.

The following "observations" upon the passage invite comparison and scrutiny.

264) 17 : 11. Jesus seems to be upon a border ministry, and it may be owing to a fresh outbreak of hostility rising out of the events and teachings of chapters 14-16.*

265) 17 : 16. It is Luke of all the synoptic Gospels which brings in these favorable references to the Samaritans.†

266) 17 : 18. It is significant that those who went to the Judean priests did not return. Was Jesus in bad odor with the ruling classes?‡

267) 17 : 19. It is characteristic of Luke to record the teaching of Jesus that even a Samaritan, if believing, may be saved.

268) 17 : 27-30. This picture is very like the reality of things just before Jerusalem was destroyed.§

269) 17 : 31-33. Some sudden event, apparently a hostile attack, is to come, at the approach of which servants of the Christ are to be ready to let their property go in the endeavor to escape.

270) 18 : 3. Widows in those times were defenceless, and a prey to wicked men, cf. Isa. 1 : 23; Mt. 23 : 14.

271) 18 : 2-8. The judge illustrates the dealing of God either (a) by contrast, or (b) as in our impatient and wicked way we are prone to regard Him.¶

* We may conjecture that, on leaving Ephraim [John 11 : 54], Christ made a very brief detour along the northern frontier to some place at the southern border of Galilee—perhaps to meet at a certain point those who were to accompany Him on His final journey to Jerusalem. *Edersheim*, II., 327, (Ab. Ed. 436).

† As in the parable of the Good Samaritan, Luke's purpose in the selection of the incident falls in with what may be called the Catholicity of his gospel. *Plumptre*, p. 282.

‡ The suddenness of their cure—what we call its miraculous character—had not the slightest effect in startling the nine Israelite lepers out of their moral torpor. They were glad to be freed from a plague, however the advantage might come. But there was no divine message to them in the deliverance. *Maurice*, p. 269.

Perhaps we may overestimate the faith of these men. *Edersheim*, II., 330 (438).

§ These characteristics of former crises or judgments were strictly verified in the one which befel that age. There was the same incapacity of believing that the holy city could fall, in its inhabitants . . . . The Lord of David, they said, could not mean that David's conquest should be won by sacrilegious Romans. All our Lord's warnings have been directed to remove this expectation from His disciples' minds. *Maurice*, p. 275.

‖ The words manifestly point . . . . to the destruction of Jerusalem as an actual revelation . . . . of the Son of Man. *Plumptre*, p. 286.

Then when the Roman forces should be at hand, there would be no security for Christ's disciples but in immediate flight. *Bliss*, p. 265.

¶ That our Saviour should represent his Father by so unworthy a judge is perplexing, till one notices that it is by way of contrast that he so represents Him. *Bliss*, p. 266.

We must not shrink from saying that . . . . the unjust judge represent[s] God as he *appears* to faith tried by delay . . . . Too anxious to vindicate God, [expositors] do wrong to the tempted, instead of helping them with sympathy and counsel, by indulging in reflections to the effect, "Thus God appears to *unbelief*." No, not to unbelief only, but to faith also in times of trial. Bruce, *Parab. Teaching*, p. 448.

272) 18 : 11, 12. The fundamental religious defect of the Pharisee was self-righteousness.

273) 18 : 15. With this incident ends Luke's great characteristic addition, chs. 10-17, to the life of Jesus. Now he comes back to parallel narratives with Matthew and Mark.

274) 18 : 18. It seems as though the ruler's estimate of Jesus was somewhat patronizing.

275) 18 : 23. His character was not yet hardened into selfishness ; he was sorry that he could not give up the riches.*

276) 18 : 26-28. The disciples are not above the spirit of the Old Testament in relation to riches, Deut. 28 : 1, 11, etc.

3. Topics for Study.

The Perean Ministry. † [Obs. 148-266] : (1) Recall the three steps—might they be called stages?—in the narrative of the Perean ministry, (a) 9 : 51-13 : 21, (b) 13 : 22-17 : 10, (c) 17 : 11-18 : 30. (2) Consider as carefully as possible the course of events in each stage. (3) Estimate the probable length of this ministry from (a) the passover imminent at its close, cf. 22 : 1, (b) the passover before its beginning and events between John 6 : 4, (c) the journey of 9 : 51 (cf. 10 : 38) identical (?) with that of John 7 : 2. (4) Note the attitude taken by Jesus toward the Pharisees. (5) Observe his position toward the people in general, judicial warnings and condemnations. (6) Notice also the severe terms of discipleship and the stern spirit of Jesus generally. (7) Compare with it the teachings of grace toward (a) publicans and sinners, (b) Samaritans. (8) Sum up as to the purpose and results of this ministry and the development of Jesus' work and teaching through it.

4. Religious Teaching.

The student may select a theme, e. g. "Self-sacrifice the true safety and reward of the follower of Jesus the Christ "—or any other which gathers up the sections of these last days in Perea, and work out the various lessons which the passage contains.

STUDIES XXXIX. AND XL.—INTO THE SHADOW OF DEATH. LUKE 18 : 31-19 : 48.

Remark.—It is desirable that in beginning this "study" (1) the material of the preceding "study" be reviewed, and (2) the entire passage assigned be read over rapidly and the main divisions of the narrative noted.

I. EXAMINATION OF THE MATERIAL.

[It will be noted that the following order is observed invariably in this work; (1) the verse or section is read and its contents stated in a general way; (2) important or difficult words and phrases are studied; (3) a complete statement of the contents of the verse or section is formed in view of the work already done ; (4) the religious teaching is sought.]

---

* He was a rich man ; he had not yet discovered that to be a man was more than to be rich. *Maurice*, p. 284.

† It is not possible for us to devote more space to a review of this most important division of the work of Jesus the Christ, though two " studies " might profitably be given to it. The student is therefore requested to devote more than the usual study to this special " topic."

§ 1.   Chapter 18 : 31-34.

1. Read and consider a subject : *The unwelcome Teaching again.*
2. The following are important words and phrases : (1) *understood none* (18 : 34), how explain this (cf. 9 : 45)? (2) *was hid*, by whom?
3. A condensation of the passage may be made by the student.
4. A striking religious thought appears in v. 34—the power of prejudice and preconception in religious matters to hide the clearest statements of fact from one's ind.

§ 2.   Chapter 18 : 35-43.

1. The student may, after reading, decide on a subject.
2. Important and difficult words and phrases are : (1) *drew nigh*, etc. (18 : 35), cf. Mk. 10 : 46 and note explanations, (a) two cities, new and old Jericho, (b) cure was long in the working, so that Jesus went and came back, (c) an inexplicable discrepancy; (2) *son of David* (18 : 38), a messianic title; (3) *rebuked him* (18 : 39), (a) for presumption, (b) in view of what? (4) *all the people . . . . gave praise* (18 : 43), a new attitude toward Jesus.
3. The following is a statement of the contents : *Near Jericho a blind beggar hears a crowd passing, of whom he learns that Jesus is the central figure. Him he begs as the Christ to pity him and restore his sight, and, though rebuked by the crowd, is called and healed by Jesus, amid the glad thanksgivings of the multitude.*
4. A religious teaching here is found in the fact that Jesus permits the blind man to name the gift which is to be granted to him.   His faith determined the blessing.

§ 3.   Chapter 19 : 1-10.

1. After reading the passage note a subject, *The Meeting with Zacchæus.*
2. (1) *Chief publican* (19 : 2), i. e. at the head of the publicans of the district; (2) *rich*, is this extraordinary? (3) *Zacchæus* (19 : 5), how did Jesus know his name? (4) *joyfully* (19 : 6), light on his feeling toward Jesus; (5) *I give* (19 : 8), i. e. " I propose to give ; " (6) *I restore*, a confession of wrong? (7) *for* (19 : 10), the apology for his action, cf. ch. 15.
3. A condensation of the passage is here suggested : *A chief publican named Zacchæus, short of stature, is so anxious to see Jesus as he passes through Jericho, that he climbs a sycamore tree. Jesus, passing, says to him, I lodge with thee. He gladly receives him, and solemnly pledges himself to benevolence, and promises restitution of stolen property. Jesus says, This man, a son of Abraham, may be saved, for I came to save such lost ones.*
4. What a proof of the wisdom of Jesus in offering himself to this publican is the utter surrender which Zacchæus makes of his property and the promise of a new life which showed itself in him.   Love "hopeth all things " and is not disappointed.

§ 4.   Chapter 19 : 11-27.

1. Read and criticise the subject suggested : *Parable of the Pounds.*
2. The student may make out his own notes of the important or difficult words of this passage.
3. Criticise and improve upon the following statement of the thought : *To those who, as they approached the city, supposed that he was to establish the Kingdom at*

once, he said, A prince went far away to receive his kingdom. He left ten ser-
vants each a pound with which to trade till his return, when they reported their
gains—one ten, another five pounds. One brought his pound back, carefully kept,
saying that he feared the prince's exacting demands. To him the prince said,
" If you did, you ought to have put it at interest. Give it to the one who gained
the most, for that is fitting." But those citizens who had rejected his rule before,
he bade to be brought and slain.

4. The religious thought here lies in the fact that while many of the Lord's servants receive the same endowment, they are expected not to make the same return, but to do the best they can, and thereby are they rewarded.

§ 5. Chapter 19 : 28-40.

1. The subject of this passage is, *The Triumphal Entry into Jerusalem.*
2. (1) *Bethany* (19 : 29), cf. John 12 : 1, Jesus probably spent the Sabbath there ; (2) *ye shall find a colt*, etc. (19 : 30), was this (a) more than human knowledge, or (b) was it known to him by observation or previous arrangement? (3) *ever yet sat*, cf. Num. 19 : 1, 2; Deut. 21 : 3; Zech. 9 : 9; 1 Sam. 6 : 7; (4) *the Lord* (19 : 31), either (a) Jehovah, or (b) the Christ, or (c) the master, teacher, cf. 18 : 41; 19 : 8; (5) *spread their garments* (19 : 36), cf. 2 Ki. 9 : 13; (6) *King that cometh* (19 : 38), cf. Lk. 7 : 19; (7) *in the highest*, i. e. in heaven ; (8) *stones will cry out* (19 : 40), (a) so glorious is the sight, or (b) so imperative is the need of testimony.
3. The student may make his own statement of the thought.
4. One teaching in the passage is this, that Jesus the Christ is our King and rejoices in the homage of his servants.

§ 6. Chapter 19 : 41-44.

1. Read the section and criticise the subject: *The Lament over Jerusalem.*
2. Note the following words and phrases: (1) *hadst known in this day* (19 : 42), indicating (a) the opportunity still open, (b) but the hopelessness of Jesus that it would be seized ; (2) *because thou knewest not* (19 : 44), cf. 13 : 34, ignorance born of willfulness.
3. The thought may thus be stated: *Beholding the city before him, he bewailed its blindness concerning what was best for it. It did not see that soon it would be besieged and totally destroyed with its inhabitants, because of this ignorance of him.*
4. The student may formulate the religious teaching.

§ 7. Chapter 19 : 45-48.

1. The subject may be stated as, *Jesus in the Temple.*
2. (1) *Them that sold* (19 : 46), (a) consider the occasion for the trading in the temple, (b) note the spirit of Jesus in casting the traders out—a prophet, the Christ? (c) cf. John 2 : 14; (2) *den of robbers* (19 : 46), how was this accusation true?
3. The student may make the statement of the thought.
4. The religious lesson suggested by the temple scene is of religion made a means of gain. Is there anything of this sort to-day?

II. CLASSIFICATION OF THE MATERIAL.

1. Contents and Summary.

1) **The Contents.** Carefully examine and master this table.

INTO THE SHADOW OF DEATH.

§ 1. THE UNWELCOME TEACHING AGAIN.
§ 2. HEALING OF A BLIND BEGGAR.
§ 3. THE MEETING WITH ZACCHÆUS.
§ 4. PARABLE OF THE POUNDS.
§ 5. TRIUMPHAL ENTRY INTO JERUSALEM.
§ 6. THE LAMENT OVER JERUSALEM.
§ 7. JESUS IN THE TEMPLE.

2) **The Summary.** Study the following summary of the whole passage: *On his way he came to Jericho and healed a blind beggar who had hailed him as the Christ, amid a glad company. As he passed through he lodged with Zacchæus, the publican, who was led to renounce himself and his unlawful gains. The multitude expecting the speedy coming of the kingdom, he told them of a "prince who had to go far away to get his kingdom, leaving his servants money to trade with. On his return he rewards the faithful, and punishes the unfaithful servants and enemies." He proceeds up to Jerusalem as the Christ, letting the multitude thus proclaim him, but weeps over the coming destruction of the city for its blindness. Entering the temple, he cleanses it of traders, and teaches crowds there daily, in spite of the plots of the priests and scribes.*

2. Observations upon the Material.

The student may exercise himself in making observations similar to those already made in previous "studies," on the following verses:

1) 18 : 32.	5) 19 : 14, 27.	9) 19 : 40.
2) 18 : 34.	6) 19 : 12.	10) 19 : 43, 44.
3) 18 : 36, 43 ; 19 : 3.	7) 19 : 13.	11) 19 : 45, 46.
4) 18 : 38.	8) 19 : 35-38.	12) 19 : 47, 48.

3. Topics for Study.

The Last Journey to Jerusalem. (1) Note the state of things, (a) the work in Perea over, (b) the people gathering for the passover, (c) Jesus determined to observe the passover in Jerusalem, (d) takes the main high road through Jericho. (2) Observe the attitude, (a) of the twelve, (b) of the people, (c) of the Pharisees. (3) Consider the entry into Jerusalem, (a) the people hail him as the Christ, (b) he accepts this attitude on their part, (c) and publicly enters as the Christ. (4) Note his teaching on this journey, (a) the parable of the obscure, poor king, who is going to return in power to punish and reward, (b) the servants left to labor, (c) the religious system of Israel to be overthrown and Jerusalem to be destroyed. (5) Consider finally the position of things when Jesus has entered, (a) he offers himself to the nation as its Christ, (b) he is conscious that he is to be rejected, (c) what if he had been accepted?

4. Religious Teaching.

Let the religious lessons of this passage be found in a contemplation of *the Heroism of Jesus*, (a) in waiting and doing the work which lay before him until the hour came, cf. 13 : 31, 32, (b) in advancing steadily into the face of death with full knowledge, (c) in making his claim to be the Christ and offering himself as the Christ to a people who were to reject him—all this without self-seeking, (d) in clearing the temple of those who defiled it, (e) in admonishing and warning even those who were most confident of his success, (19:11).

A "SYMPOSIUM" ON THE "GRADUALNESS OF REVELATION."

Few subjects are of more living interest at the present day in connection with Bible study than that which heads this article. There are few subjects on which there exists so great diversity of statement if not of opinion. It was to ascertain the opinions and statements of some of our leading teachers and preachers and to present them to the readers of the STUDENT that the questions which follow were mailed to the eminent men whose remarks are herewith presented.

It will be noted, alas! with regret by not a few, that since their words were written two of the writers have passed away. Ransom Bethune Welch and Israel E. Dwinell, leaders in the respective communions to which they belonged, are looking upon this great subject we may believe in the brighter light of another life.

The following are the questions submitted:

1. What is meant by the phrase "gradualness of revelation," or "development of revelation?"

2. Is this phrase based upon, or does it imply, a sound and reasonable explanation of the phenomena of revelation? (Will you be kind enough to indicate the grounds upon which the answer rests?)

3. What, in your opinion, will be the results of a widespread acceptance of this position?

From President E. BENJ. ANDREWS, LL. D.

By the gradualness of revelation or the development of revelation we mean, I suppose, precisely what we mean when speaking of development in any department of life or history. We mean the progress from the simple and homogeneous to the complex and heterogeneous. We are not to take this in a sense which would imply that truth has made headway apart from an original personal source of truth, but that it has pleased the Eternal Spirit to reveal to mankind the truth necessary for human conduct and salvation in a gradual way rather than all at once. It will be seen that this is, strictly speaking, not an *explanation* of revelation. It is not a causal law of the phenomena of revelation, but only a formal law. It is probably true that we cannot fundamentally or finally tell why it pleased the Power above us so to proceed. We can, however, partly see, when we reflect that the human mind learns gradually and itself develops slowly. Had the whole New Testament been published so early as the time when the first sentence of the Old was written, it must have remained for ages and generations mostly a dead letter. The more widely the doctrine of progress in revelation is accepted, the better. No ill results of consequence can possibly arise from its prevalence. On the contrary, the other view, which puts all Scripture upon a level of worthiness to be taken as final, is fraught with the utmost danger.

Brown University.

12

From Rev. WASHINGTON GLADDEN, D. D.

(1) I suppose that revelation is God's gracious disclosure of Himself to his children ; and that the law of this disclosure is, " Grace for grace,"—or " Grace upon grace,"—each gift making room for a larger gift. The plant just springing from the earth cannot take much sunshine or rain, but the more it receives of this life-giving ministry the more it is able to receive. God's manifestation of Himself to men has certainly followed this law ; it has been conditioned upon and adapted to their mental and moral receptivity ; and yet it has constantly, by its own action, enlarged this receptivity. There is, obviously, a progress in revelation, from lower to higher forms of spiritual truth ; from a defective morality to a perfect morality. The revelation of the Bible is a progressive revelation ; the light is clearer and the standards are higher in the Gospels than in the Hexateuch.

(2) Certainly. This is only saying that truth is self-consistent. No other explanation of the phenomena of revelation is sound or reasonable. The grounds on which the answer rests are many : I can only point to the words of Christ in the " Sermon on the Mount," repeating, in the most express terms, portions of the old legislation, and substituting for it a higher law.

(3) The result will be a great gain to Christian faith and Christian morality. It is always a gain to the Kingdom of God, when his people are ready to face the facts, and make their theories conform to them.

Columbus, O.

From Professor E. H. JOHNSON, D. D.

What others mean by " gradualness of revelation " or " development of revelation " I would rather they would say. I prefer the phrase " progress of doctrine in the Bible," because this includes increase of knowledge not only by objective communication of truth or revelation, but also by progressive insight or illumination. The importance of covering both processes may be seen in the fact that our Lord vainly sought to communicate by revelation the necessity of his impending crucifixion ; whereas, the understanding of what the crucifixion had accomplished came in by and by solely through insight into the fact and into what Jesus had in advance said about the fact, when at length the Holy Spirit brought this to remembrance and interpreted it. Except perhaps in the case of Paul we are without any intimation that the apostles reached their view of the atonement through new revelations as distinguished from new insight into former revelations.

The phrase you ask me to give a meaning to is therefore " based upon " and " implies a sound and reasonable explanation of the phenomena of revelation," if by revelation is meant only the process of objective communication of truth to the writers of the Bible ; but it is based upon only part of " the phenomena of revelation," if " revelation " is used concretely for the product of revelation and of related processes, as that product is recorded in the Sacred Scriptures. The main ground on which I assert the gradualness of revelation, and of other processes by which the Holy Spirit enabled the writers of Scripture to come into knowledge of religious truth, is the obvious fact that the Scripture is a record of increasing knowledge. The illustration above given shows progress of doctrine in the New Testament. Comparison of the elder with the later Scriptures is even more conclusive. The prediction that the " seed of the woman " should " bruise the serpent's head " did not convey so ample or so definite an idea to the writer of Genesis, as the writer to the Hebrews found in the fact that the Lord partook of flesh and blood "that through death he might bring to naught him that had the power of death, that is, the devil." Justification by faith was not nearly so plain a matter when Abraham's faith was "reckoned unto him for righteousness," as when Paul commented upon this transaction. So of all the wide range of truth latent in the Old Testament, patent in the New.

The all-inclusive advantage of a "wide-spread acceptance of this position" will be that a fact about the Bible will be widely accepted. Our sole interest is in dismissing error and admitting the truth as to the word of God. I think that progress of doctrine in the Bible is already widely recognized. Its further recognition will at least extend the advantages already received from its partial recognition. For instance, biblical criticism recognizes in progress of doctrine evidence of lapse of time and change of situation during the intervals at which the Scriptures were written. So great development of doctrine implies intervals long at briefest, and changes profound at the slightest; whereas absence of development in ideas would bring the pretensions of the Bible into disrepute. An essentially unhistorical literature cannot have proceeded from God. The All-Wise fits his undertakings more perfectly to his ends. In other words, the Bible must be genuinely human if it is to be accepted as genuinely divine.

To acknowledge progress in doctrine is to be in the way of reaching a proximate theory of inspiration. Deficiency was acknowledged by the Master to exist in the law of Moses. But to admit deficiencies is to be armed against the charge of errors in the religious and ethical teachings of the Book.

To recognize progress of doctrine is to secure an effective instrument for the interpretation of the Word. To deny this phenomenon is to involve oneself in every sort of violence to the phenomena of the Scripture, that is, to put on them a false construction, and to elicit from them a false meaning.

In a word, if the fact you inquire about be generally admitted the Bible will be more unreservedly believed and more fully understood.

Crozer Theological Seminary.

From the late Professor ISRAEL E. DWINELL, D. D.

1. The two phrases, "Gradualness of Revelation," and "Development of Revelation," refer I think to two entirely different and inconsistent conceptions. "Development of Revelation" goes on the supposition that a germ of revelation was planted in the race, and that germ has gradually unfolded, taking form from the specific conditions. "Gradualness of Revelation" goes upon the supposition that revelation is something made known from a Revealer, and has been gradually made known according to his wisdom and plan.

The difference between *development* and a *gradual giving* is very marked. A development is from an impulse within; a gradual giving is a process originating from without. The fruits of the country are a development from the original crude fruits of nature. The currency of the country is in no sense a development, but is the result of successive acts of government by a gradual process according to the supposed needs of the country and the wisdom and ability of the government to meet them.

So Revelation, in my judgment, has come into the world by a succession of disclosures from God, as He saw men needed it and were ripe for it. I believe, thus, in the gradualness of Revelation, not in the development of it.

2. I think this theory gives a reasonable explanation of the phenomena.

(a) It harmonizes with the obvious facts and claims of the *record* of Revelation. This is the account which the record itself gives of its origin. It purports to be a record of successive historical disclosures from God, not of successive unfoldings of religious truth in the religious consciousness of men. There is not a word in the Bible that gives countenance to the theory that Revelation is a development from a principle inborn in humanity, or subsequently implanted.

(b) It harmonizes with the *historical, psychological* and *religious facts* of the case. When those to whom God was giving his Revelation were ready for it, He gave the new increment ; and so, on and on, till the Revelation was complete. Here all the historical, psychological, and religious conditions are met, as much as if Revelation were a development from those conditions, and, with as much more wisdom, skill, and *off-look*, as an all-wise and loving Planner is superior to a blind and spontaneous impulse seeking self expression in humanity.

(c) It explains the *unity* and the steady *progress* of Revelation from the dim objects disclosed in Genesis to the sublime results recorded in the Gospel, the redemption of the world by Jesus Christ. If Revelation were a development, there might be unity, doubtless ; but we cannot account for the fact that Revelation holds on its way to the sublimest end possible, out of the ten thousand different directions it might take, except on the supposition that God was presiding over it and shaping it, making it infinitely higher than a development. The theory that God gives the new revelations from time to time, as the Book represents, alone fully accounts for the facts.

(d) This theory harmonizes with the fact, the central fact of the world's history, that the *Son of God has come into the world.* If this fact is admitted, it logically covers all the difficulties and objections ; and it furnishes ample reasons why he should interpose by giving previous subordinate revelations to prepare the way for this supreme one and makes it a success. Those who make all the previous miscalled revelations a development are led by logical and moral reasons both to regard the character and mission of Christ as a development, while, on the contrary, those who believe in the Divine Incarnation hold to a system which morally and logically prepares them to accept the evidence that God has proceeded towards this highest revelation by various subordinate approaches leading up to it, according to the record.

3. I can not see that anything but good, all the way round, would result from this theory. One great advantage resulting from it would be the separation of Christian believers from those who deny the supernatural element in the religion of the Bible, and try to drag it all down to the plane of the nature religions   The adoption of a hybrid theory of development, or evolution, by certain Christian people, furnishes a common ground on which rationalists can stand and work for the overthrow of Christianity as a supernatural system.

Pacific Theological Seminary, Oakland, Cal.

From President Alvah Hovey, LL. D.

1. What is meant by the phrase "gradualness of revelation," or "development of revelation?" The former expression, as I understand it, represents the Scriptures as being a record of religious truth that was revealed to man, little by little, part by part, but with increasing fulness, until the intended sum

of it was completed by the teaching of Christ and his apostles. This view appears to be justified by a comprehensive study of the Scriptures and to be taught by the writer of the epistle to the Hebrews (1 : 1). Yet it must not be understood to affirm that in the process of revelation the less important truths were always made known before the more important, the ritual before the spiritual, the rule of duty before the underlying principle, or *vice versa*. It must not be interpreted to mean that glimpses of a great principle were never given long before that principle was made perfectly clear to religious teachers. Nor must it be supposed to imply that religious truths are incoherent, so that the order in which they were revealed was a matter of no consequence and the revelation of one truth not preparatory to the revelation of another.

But the second expression, " development of revelation," is less satisfactory. For the word ' development' suggests a theory of revelation which is questionable—a theory that the increase of religious knowledge among men was due to the natural unfolding of a germ of truth implanted once for all in the human mind, or in some human mind. This theory seems to me incompatible with the obvious phenomena of Scripture, with any natural interpretation of the language in which the prophets, the apostles, and Jesus Christ himself speak of the truth which they taught.

2. " Is this phrase based upon, or does it imply, a sound and reasonable explanation of the phenomena of revelation?" I would answer this question in the affirmative. For, reading the Bible from Genesis to Revelation with a view to the point in question, it is easy to see that the amount of religious knowledge possessed by the apostles was far greater than that possessed by the Old Testament prophets. And, speaking more in detail, it is easy to see that religious truth was revealed to Abraham which was unknown to Noah, and to Moses which was unknown to Abraham, and to Isaiah which was imperfectly known to Moses. With almost equal clearness it appears that more truth was communicated to Peter before his death than to John the Baptist, and more to the minds of Paul and John than to Peter. The Christian doctrine of God was gradually revealed—the trinity being scarcely suggested to the ancient prophets. The same is true of the doctrine of the Messiah, both as to his person and his work. From the promise in Eden to the birth in Bethlehem, and even to the ascension from Olivet, the light of revelation was gradually increasing until all was made known which could be of real service to men. The same in substance may be said concerning the doctrines of the Holy Spirit, the use of the law, the nature of sin, and the way of salvation. Equally gradual was the revelation of a future life, unless we deny that any intimation of it was given to Old Testament saints, and affirm that it was first and fully brought to light by Christ himself. But even if it were certain that a few truths of the Christian religion were revealed once for all and with perfect clearness by Christ, it would still be true that revelation has been for the most part gradual.

3. " What, in your opinion, will be the results of a wide-spread acceptance of this position?" (a) A deeper interest in the study of the Holy Scriptures. (b) A clearer view of essential religious truth. (c) A more intelligent rejection of obsolete rites and methods of service.

Newton Theo. Institution.

From the Rev. Newman Smyth, D. D.

That there is a growing interest to-day in the study of the Bible is very evident. It is also very evident that with this growing interest there is much confusion of thought and diversity of opinion in regard to the Bible, and the right method of interpreting it. Some things however are gradually becoming clear ; and among them, these. First: that the books which constitute the Bible, being a part of the world's literature must be examined as to their date and authorship and genuineness, in the same manner precisely as all other books. Second: that the Bible is not itself the revelation of God, but the *record* of that revelation in human life and character. The record may not be infallible : it does not claim infallibility, and yet in spite of mistakes and inaccuracies, the fact of the revelation is not thereby obscured nor its value impaired. Third: that the revelation of God in human life and character which the Bible records is gradual and progressive, appearing more fully in the later than in the earlier history of Israel and presenting in consequence a higher standard of righteousness to us, and Fourth: that that revelation reaches its consummation in Jesus Christ, whose character, having its witness in itself, is the greatest of all miracles, making the miracles attributed to him not only possible, but in the highest degree probable ; and which cannot be accounted for except upon the hypothesis, that " He is the brightness of the Father's glory and the express image of his person."
New Haven, Conn.

From the late Professor R. B. Welch, D. D.

It should be stated that Revelation and Inspiration are distinct in form and in fact. To confound the two must lead to confusion in treatment and in conclusion. The question proposed here is concerning Revelation—"the gradualness of revelation." It is not a question concerning the fact or form of inspiration.

Now revelation has to do with knowledge. To reveal is to make known. Revelation is the communication of knowledge. It includes three terms,—the knower or revealer; the thing known or truth to be revealed; and the making known or revealing.

Revelation is then primarily and essentially related to a knowing, personal author—an intelligent, free spirit, self-revealing and so communicating knowledge to intelligent, free spiritual creatures, themselves capable of receiving and appreciating such revelation—a revelation not only originated in a personal intelligence but governed by personal intelligence and guided evermore by an intelligent purpose. In principle and process related to a personal efficient cause and to a personal final cause, it is therefore in a profound sense scientific and rational and in the highest sense a revelation communicating knowledge.

At the outset, it should be noted that the phrase "gradualness of revelation," or "development of revelation" is employed by different persons with diverse and even opposite meanings.

In view of these diverse meanings, is the method or process of revelation gradual?

This we may best ascertain not by speculation but by an inductive study of the history of revelation as it is presented in the written Word and in the living Word—the Scriptures and the Christ; and in the record of creation throughout the physical and moral world, especially the earth and man. This is matter of fact, not of fancy. With this fourfold record before us, we should not err in our research and conclusion.

Yet even here we are confronted with diverse answers according to the different view-points occupied and the fairness and thoroughness of the inductive study.

1. The Theistic View.

Consistently with what has been already said of the significance of revelation, the theist believes and affirms "a gradualness of Revelation" in this high sense,—as a divine process of revealing, not by mere continuity or natural development but by a progress of revelation combining the supernatural and the natural and thus advancing toward a higher and supreme end— supremely wise, supremely good.

At the very first, revelation appears not as development but as an origination—not as simply natural and evolutional but as supernatural and creative: "In the beginning God created the heaven and the earth." The revelation was of an Author not of an Evolver—of a personal, free spirit not an impersonal, necessitated energy.

So the ongoing was not merely natural and evolutional, but supernatural, also, and originating,—"And the Spirit of God moved upon the face of the waters" and transformed the chaos into a cosmos—as the word signifies—regulated, wisely adapted, well ordered—revealing the power, wisdom, goodness and care of a personal Author—a revelation not of evolutional gradualness by mere continuity or development but a gradualness as progressive involving supernatural knowledge and purpose, and revealing that knowledge and purpose by higher and still higher acts combining, now, the natural and supernatural: "And God said, Let there be light and there was light"—superinducing higher forces upon the lower,—chemical and electric forces upon gravity and attraction, and upon these superinducing life, vegetable life, and, higher still, animal life or the living soul, and, still higher, creating man, a person endowed with a rational spirit "in the image of God."

Such is the record in the written revelation—the Scriptures.

Such is the record in the unwritten revelation, e. g., in Scientific Geology, a science inlaid of God in the history of the earth. By such progress there is given to us a revelation advancing even to the complete purpose of God in the completed cosmos—Rom. 1: 20, "Since the creation of the world, the invisible things of God are clearly seen being perceived through the things that are made even his everlasting power and divinity," and Rom. 2: 15. Similar to this, as supernatural and natural, is the order of divine revelation in the written and the Living Word—the Scriptures and the Christ—until the revelation is complete in him.

Such in brief is the theistic conception of revelation, of the divine process and purpose, of the grounds upon which it is based, and of the benign consequences of such a revelation issuing as it does in reverence, love, adoration, loyal service.

2. The Atheistic Theory.

This affirms a process of phenomenal development or gradualness in continuity simply natural and evolutional. It is based upon the postulate of evolution—"Evolution as a law of continuity, as a *universal law of becom-*

ing." This theory has no need of God, the Author and Upholder of all things. It ignores, it rejects him from the Universe.

3. The Agnostic Theory.

This affirms an unknowable force or all-pervading Energy as the impersonal cause or underlying ground of all phenomena. The Agnostic like the Atheistic theory asserts a continuity of development, natural, gradual, evolutional.

Indeed there would be no personal will or wisdom in either case to originate or modify or guide the ongoing development. This agnostic theory leads its chief representative to assert "an Infinite and Eternal *Energy* from *which* all things proceed," (Spencer's Ecclesiastical Institutions, pp. 839, 843), and, again, to assert "Our only course is to recognize our symbols—Mind and Matter—as symbols only of some form of Power absolutely and forever unknown to us," (Principles of Psychology, pp. 159,162, Vol. I.). Pressing his theory, on the ground of evolutional development, Mr. Spencer would retrace the notion of "soul" as distinct from "body" to dreams when, it was supposed, the "other-self" wandered away from the body. From this idea of a double self was evolved the notion that in swoon, death, etc., the "other-self" had gone away on a longer journey than in sleep. This simple idea, according to Mr. S., would lead by natural evolution to all those views of inspiration, resurrection, a future life, etc., and to ancestor-worship which he regards as "the root of every religion"*

But without pursuing further Mr. Spencer's speculations which he applies to revelation and to the doctrines of revelation as an evolutional development, let us turn to trace another theory—diverse from and yet akin to the agnostic, viz.—

4. The Gnostico-Agnostic Theory.

This affirms "a Spirit (or Energy)" as immanent in Nature, and asserts an evolutional continuity or gradualness of development. While it talks of a divine Spirit, it quotes approvingly the agnostic speculations and adopts the practical conclusions of Agnosticism, vacillating between Spirit and Energy, playing fast and loose with these terms, adopting both and employing either, at convenience. (See, Evolution of Man and Christianity, pp. 75, 281.) Asserting revelation as a development continuous and evolutional, it tries all possible revelation by this gnostic and agnostic test, ignoring or ruling out the supernatural, at pleasure. This theory leads Mr. MacQueary in his very recent book (Evolution of Man and Christianity, p. 32), to say, "that I may illustrate my idea (of the divine Spirit) more clearly,—God secretes physical Nature as the snail secretes its shell;" and, again p. 271, speaking of "the fascinating unity which all Nature discloses," he quotes admiringly, "This unity is an expression of the Divine Being. God is one. But in this unity what a bewildering manifoldness! How infinite the changes of form which the Divine Being takes," and much more to the same purpose.

Assuming this all-comprehensive ground of evolutional development he declares, pp. 47, 70, "I am an evolutionist. I believe that man has evolved, *body and soul*, from a lower animal." This theory of a gradual development based upon evolution he applies to the Scriptures, and proceeds to say, p. 117, "We have no more reason to believe that our Genesis (in the Hebrew Scriptures) is inspired than we have to believe that George Smith's 'Chaldean Genesis' is."

---

*See MacQueary's, *Evolution of Man and Christianity*, pp. 129, 258, where he refers approvingly to these speculations of Mr. Spencer's, *Principles of Sociology*, Vol. I. Chapts. VIII–XXV.

On the same evolutional ground, he maintains that Jesus was the son of Joseph and Mary, and that his resurrection from the dead was only myth or fiction, "though it is (he says) the best attested miracle in the history of the world."* Yet he declares Jesus "to be in himself an embodied revelation; humanity in its divinest phrase" (p. 288, quoting W. R. Greg) worthy of and receiving the devout admiration and glad worship of even such men as Ingersoll and Renan, as Lecky, Leslie and Greg, pp. 15, 286–289.

But we need not further trace the application of this theory to the other essential doctrines of Revelation exploding, as he declares, the Scriptural doctrine of the Fall, of the Atonement, of Christ's second coming, and of the final Judgment.

In contradistinction from the theistic which we regard as the true view, stand the atheistic, the agnostic and the gnostico-agnostic theories. The common ground on which these three stand we have rapidly but carefully surveyed. The meaning which they attach to the phrase, "gradualness of revelation" or "development of revelation" is evident. Their wide-spread acceptance would, we think, be unfavorable and perilous to Christianity.

Auburn Theo. Seminary.

* Evolution of Man and Christianity, pp. 218, 229.

Contributed Notes.

The Sinlessness of Christ. St. John VIII. 46. In comparing the life of Jesus Christ with the lives of good and holy men we are as much surprised at what we fail to find as at what we do find.

We look for consciousness of sin, but we do not find any trace of it. From Adam to Malachi this consciousness of sin is painfully manifest in every man's life. No sooner had Adam eaten the forbidden fruit than his own heart condemned him and he hid himself from the presence of the Lord God among the trees of the garden. Cain's answer convicted him of murder. Abraham's lying brought a plague upon Pharaoh and upon his house.

Moses was not allowed to enter the promised land on account of his wrong doing and the 90th Psalm is a doleful confession of his transgression against the Lord. David has filled the Psalter with his wailings for his own sinfulness. Solomon too in the dedication of the Temple has the same confession to make. Isaiah cries out in the bitterness of his soul, " I am a man of unclean lips and I dwell in the midst of a people of unclean lips and mine eyes have seen the Lord of Hosts." And so on through every page of the Old Testament. There is not one of these holy men free from the consciousness of sin, no not one.

We might hope to find a change in the New Testament. The Christian lives under a new covenant. Old things have passed away, all things have become new. But if we expect to find men free from sin there we are sure to be disappointed. St. John the Baptist founds his gospel on the very fact that men are conscious that they are sinners. His cry is Repent, and this cry finds an echo in countless human hearts. They find in their own breasts the consciousness of sin, and they leave the palaces of Jerusalem and the market-places of Judea and go down to the Jordan to wash and be clean. They carry their accuser in their own bosom, and it is to stifle that accuser's voice they go out to the Baptist. Christ's own apostles are among the number of the self-accused. St. Peter is obliged to say " Depart from me for I am a sinful man O Lord," St. John says " If any man saith he hath no sin, he deceiveth himself and the truth is not in him." St. Paul calls himself the chief of sinners.

The greatest saints of Christendom have been the most ready to confess their sinfulness. Some of them have written books revealing the secrets of their hearts and even in the case of the holiest men these books are not pleasant reading. Modern Christians have made the same confession. "I do not know," says a great Frenchman, " what the heart of a felon is; but I know what the heart of an honest man is and it is awful."

Thomas Erskine of Linlathen says that he would not like to see his own life repeated in another man, and he was one of the most holy and blameless men the nineteenth century has seen.

In turning from the lives of such men to the life of Christ we naturally look for some words of confession on his lips, but we do not find them. We do not find one single expression which can be construed to mean that he was conscious of sin. We would naturally look for this confession in his prayers to God, His Father. The Lord's prayer which he gave to his disciples is prefaced by the words " But thou, when *thou* prayest." " After this manner pray ye."

It is the disciples' prayer. It is a prayer for the use of Christians. It is not the prayer he uses when he is praying for himself and so the words "Forgive us our trespasses as we forgive them that trespass against us" do not apply to Him.

On the other hand he defies even his enemies to convince him of sin. They have been watching him and trying to entrap him in his talk but they have signally failed. He can look them in the face and challenge them to point out one single error in his public ministry.

He can do more. He can look God in the face and feel confident that the Father finds no fault in him. Has not God manifested his approval in the voice from heaven which said, "This is my beloved son in whom I am well pleased?" He can say to his Father "I know that thou hearest me always."

The consciousness of righteousness, the blessedness of the man to whom the Lord imputeth not iniquity and in whose spirit there is no guile, this freedom, from the smallest tinge of remorse for sin in thought, in word, in deed, is unique in the history of the world. The holiest men are those who would shrink the most from claiming such exemption. Jesus Christ stands alone. He is the First and the Last who has put forth such a claim from Adam to the present hour.

Another remarkable trait in the character of Jesus Christ is the *absence of Aspiration.*

The most beautiful parts of the Old Testament are the Psalms, and the most beautiful of the Psalms are those in which David lifts himself on the wings of prayer into a holier and a better world. He confesses his sins, but he asks God to purify him, to make him holier and happier and more useful than he has ever yet been. This faculty of aspiration is one of the most spiritual capacities of the heart of man. The best men possess it the most fully. It is the hunger and the thirst after righteousness which Christ himself tells us is blessed for it shall be satisfied. It is that divine discontent with ourselves and the world which weans us from the earth and sets our affections on things above. But while this is necessary for us, it is not necessary and it does not exist in the heart of the Saviour. He does not need to pray to God to make him holy or good. He does not yearn like the saints after heights of virtue that he hath not yet reached. He does not ask the Father to give him strength that he may do his work more faithfully in the future than he has done in the past. On the other hand there is a complete satisfaction with himself and his work. While his disciples are beginning to think that his mission is a failure he knows and feels that everything is being done according to the perfect will of God. He knows and feels that it could not be improved. He has nothing left to hope for. He has nothing to wish for. And so in his communion with his Father he can ask changes to be wrought in the world and among his disciples. But as for himself he only asks that God's will may be done. The ideal and the actual in his life are one and the same. He does not transgress God's law on the one side, and on the other he conforms to it in every point. He does nothing that he ought not to have done, he leaves nothing undone that he ought to have done.

The lives of other men are but fragments. They leave many plans unfulfilled at their decease, and they do many things amiss. But the life of Jesus Christ is a perfect whole. He could say "It is finished" on Calvary. "I came to do thy will O God and I have done it, without transgression, without omission, and now I return home unto Thee."

Blantyre, Glasgow, Scotland.   REV. THOMAS PRYDE, M. A.

𝔖𝔶𝔫𝔬𝔭𝔰𝔢𝔰 𝔬𝔣 𝔍𝔪𝔭𝔬𝔯𝔱𝔞𝔫𝔱 𝔄𝔯𝔱𝔦𝔠𝔩𝔢𝔰.

Are There Traces of Greek Philosophy in the Septuagint?[*] The investigations of this question by German scholars during the years 1830–50 have never been brought to any definite issue and should be continued. H. Hody was the first to assert that foreign philosophy influenced the Seventy. Michaelis found Gnostic ideas in a few passages. Their positions were refuted by Ernesti and Horn. Gfrörer (1831) sought to show that the Septuagint was the source of Alexandrian theosophy. Dähne (1833) went further and maintained that many of Plato's thoughts had found place in this translation and that Philo and the Christian Alexandrians, Clement and Origen, were largely indebted to it in their philosophical ideas. Later these conclusions were disputed by Frankel and Zeller who think that the Seventy had but slight contact with Greek philosophy. Siegfried finds but few traces of this philosophy in the work of the Seventy, as in Gen. 1: 2, while Bickell thinks that the avoidance of anthropomorphism can only be explained by the influence of Greek philosophical conceptions. An examination of several terms of philosophical import such as *psyche, nous, arete* and *kosmos* as used in LXX. tends to the conclusion that Greek philosophy had not influenced the translators. In cases where this seems to be the case, we can by no means be sure that we have the original translation of the Seventy, since the quotations from it by Philo show that the text was thus early corrupted and may, in such passages, have been exposed to modification.

A learned discussion of a difficult but interesting theme. For the author's argument in detail reference must be had to the article itself.

Did St. Paul use a Semitic Gospel?[†] There are four questions connected with St. Paul's relation to the Gospels. (1) To what extent was he familiar with the facts of our Saviour's earthly life? The answer to this question is of great evidential value, since the undoubted epistles of Paul show that he accepted the resurrection as an historic fact and taught the divinity of Christ—all this twenty or twenty-five years after Jesus' death. (2) Was he acquainted with the discourses of the Lord? There are six well-established cases of direct or indirect reference to words of Jesus contained in the Gospels. (1) 1 Cor. 7: 10, *cf.* Mat. 5: 31–32; Luke 16: 18, (2) 1 Cor. 11, *cf.* Luke 22: 19, 20, (3) 1 Thess. 4 and 5, *cf.* Luke 21, (4) Rom. 14: 14, *cf.* the Sermon on the Mount, (5) Rom. 13: 7, *cf.* Mat. 22: 21, (6) 1 Tim. 5: 18, *cf.* Luke 18: 7. Note also 1 Cor. 7: 12, 25 where Paul seems to be acquainted with what Jesus did *not* say. (3) Is there evidence that these discourses existed in a written form in Paul's day? It is highly probable that this is to be answered in the affirmative. The first few verses of Luke's Gospel, which was probably written while Paul was a

* By Prof. J. Freudenthal in *The Jewish Quarterly Review*, April 1890.
† By Rev. Professor J. T. Marshall, in *The Expositor*, July 1890, pp. 69–80.

prisoner at Caesarea, A. D. 58-60, would make this tolerably certain. (4) In what language were these evangelistic fragments written? The difficulties are many in the way of supposing them to have been in Greek. Grant that they were written in the then language of Palestine. This hypothesis bids fair to explain many variations in the Synoptical Gospels—that they are variant translations of a common Hebrew or Aramaic original. Without going into the question at large, the six cases cited above in St. Paul's epistles are examined and of them three bear out the hypothesis, 1 Thess. 5: 1-8; 1 Tim. 5: 18; 1 Cor. 2:24. Therefore it is concluded with much probability that St. Paul used an Aramaic Gospel.

An ingenious argument which suggests much but which as it stands is based on too few facts to claim much credence. The cases cited are, however, very interesting.

Book Notices.

First Corinthians XIII.

The Greatest Thing in the World. By Henry Drummond, F. R. S. E., F. G. S. New York: James Pott and Co.

This charming booklet with its enigmatic title contains Mr. Drummond's exposition of the thirteenth chapter of I. Corinthians. As is the case with all his writings it is simple and clear in expression, evangelical and freshly so in thought, intense in the emphasis of conviction. The division of the chapter is into three parts, the Contrast, the Analysis, the Defence. The Analysis is, of course, that which receives the most attention, and in the keenness of its distinctions and the closeness of its application is admirable. One can do little more than urge all to buy and read the book and then to read it again. The latter suggestion scarcely need be made.

God in His World.

God in His World. An Interpretation. New York: Harper and Brothers.

The author of this book prefers to remain unknown, because, it may be, the general position of the book is too decidedly original to be handicapped by the mention of some familiar name in the theological world as its author. The title fairly represents its contents. The history of God's revelations of Himself in the world of nature and of men is traced from the beginning to the present time. This history is considered not in the dry light of scientific investigation but is suffused with the warm glow of intellectual and religious feeling. The leading idea is that the natural and the supernatural are one,— all is natural because all is supernatural—all is supernatural because all is natural; the universe is not divided into hemispheres. Nature is personified and glorified. Natural law is spiritual law. The principles governing the two worlds are not analogous but identical.

The book is open to severe criticism but any criticism fails to reach the secret of its strength. It fascinates the reader who will submit to be led through its mystical and subtly thoughtful passages. The style is delicate and flowing. There is much insight into life and the history of religious thought. The Bible suffers many new interpretations, some illuminating, some disappointing. All is exceedingly suggestive, dangerously so, many would think. The author deprecates system as partaking of human infirmity and yet is rigidly systematic in the development of his ideas; he inveighs against intellectual ability as short-sighted and yet has written one of the acutest speculative treatises of our age. One does not care to classify the book. It does not invite attack. Its tone is irenic and spiritual. No one can fail to enjoy and profit by it, if it be read with single eye and open heart. One's conception of the unity of things, of the immanence of God, of the meaning of the incarnation and the power of the spiritual Christ will be broadened and beautified by a thoughtful study of this remarkable book.

Revelation.

The Nature and Method of Revelation. By Professor George P. Fisher, D. D., LL. D. New York: Charles Scribners' Sons. Price $1.25.

This is a book the larger part of which discusses one of the most important questions of theological study. What is Revelation? has greatly concerned the minds of students for the past twenty-five years, when the new spirit and methods of biblical research have been so fundamentally altering our conceptions of the Bible. Can the old ideas be maintained in the face of these altered conceptions? Does revelation mean the same to us as to those of the last century? The reply, as found in Professor Fisher's book, is clearly in the negative. The thought of the historical progress of revelation in the Bible, of which so much is made in these chapters, is one, the working out of which into its details has been the task of this generation. It is the most popular feature and perhaps the most useful service of these papers, (for they originally appeared as monthly papers in the pages of a popular magazine) that they have presented in simple and pleasing style this most fruitful conception, that, within the Bible itself, there is a progress from age to age in the thought and apprehension which men had of God and religious truth in Bible times. One need not call attention to the almost revolutionary influence which this idea, thoroughly grasped and applied in theological science, is bound to exercise upon the great problems of religion. The many intelligent persons who read this work will have their own religious horizon broadened and the landscape quite changed by contemplating things from this new point of view. Besides these articles on Revelation, Professor Fisher gives us some more technical articles on New Testament subjects, such as the origin of the Gospels, the Parousia, Huxley on the Gospel narratives etc. They are clearly written, and while scholars would not agree that they are in all respects satisfactory, they indicate that the writer is a well-informed and independent thinker. Indeed the versatility of Professor Fisher as shown in this volume is quite surprising, especially when we remember that he is most widely known as a student of Church History. Here he appears as a theologian and biblical critic of no mean ability. His book is one of permanent value.

Current Old Testament Literature.

American and Foreign Publications.

99. *The Ethnographic Scope of the Tenth Chapter of Genesis.* By Rev. A. K. Glover. Pamphlet. Published by the Author.

100. *After the Exile; a hundred years of Jewish History and Literature. Part II., the coming of Ezra to the Samaritan Schism.* By P. H. Hunter. London; Oliphant. 5s.

101. *Etude d'histoire et d'archéologie. Israel et ses voisins asiatiques. La Phénicie, l'Aram et l'Assyrie de l'époque de Salomon à celle de Sanchérib.* By E. Archinard, Avec 2 cartes dressées par l'auteur. Geneve: E. Beroud & Cie. 1890. 8 fr.

102. *Geschichte der Philosophie des Judenthums.* By J. S. Spiegler. Leipzig. $3.00.

103. *Der Optimismus u. Pessimismus in der jüdischen Religions-philosophie. Eine Studie üb. die Behandlg. der Theodicee in derselben bis auf Maimonides.* By H. Goitein. Berlin: Mayer and Müller. m. 2. 80.

104. *Précis d'histoire des religions. Première partie: Religion de l'Inde.* By L. de Milloué. Paris, lib. Leroux, 1890.

Articles and Reviews.

105. *The Length of the Sojourn in Egypt.* Note by H. B. Pratt, Pres. Quar. July 1890.

106. *Pentateuch Criticism.* In the London Quarterly, July 1890.

107. *Apologetische Beiträge zum Pentateuch.* By A. Zahn, in Reform. Kirchztg. 1890, 1, 3, 8, 9, 10, 11.

108. *Zu den neuesten Verhandlungen über die Pentateuchkritik* [seit 1888] In Evang. Kirch-Ztg. 1890, 20.

109. *Substitutes for the Fourth Commandment.* Editorial note by T. W. Chambers, D. D., in Pres. and Ref. Rev. July 1890.

110. *Driver's Notes on the Hebrew Text of the Books of Samuel.* Review by H. P. Smith, in Andover Review, July 1890; by I. Abrahams, in the Jew. Quar. Rev. July 1890.

111. *Rawlinson's Kings of Israel and Judah.* Rev. by A. Gosman, in Pres. and Ref. Rev. July 1890.

112. *Judah and Babylon: a study in Chronology.* By Rev. Prin. Harding, in Expository Times, July 1890.

113. *Recherches bibliques. XIX. Vérifications documentaires de deux données bibliques relatives à Sennachérib* [II Rois XVII, 13—XIX, 37]. By J. Halévy, in Revue des études Juives janv.-mars. 1890.

114. *Exegetical Notes on the Psalms, 3. Psalm 3; 5.* By Prof. John DeWitt, D. D. in Pres. and Ref. Rev. July 1890.

115. *Exposition of Psalms 42 and 43.* By W. J. Beecher, D. D., in Homiletic Rev., Aug. 1890.

116. *The Sixty-third Psalm.* By Rev. Prof. T. K. Cheyne, in the Expositor, July, 1890.

117. *Studies in the Psalter, 20. Psalm 109.* By T. W. Chambers, D. D., in Hom. Review, Aug. 1890.

118. *Notes upon the Date and Religious Value of the Book of Proverbs.* By C. G. Montefiore, in Jewish Quar. Rev., July 1890.

119. *Orelli's Jeremiah.* Review by R. Y. Thomson, in Pres. and Ref. Rev., July 1890.

120. *Israels Restauration nach der Weissagung Ezechiels 40-48.* By J. Knabenbauer, in Ztschr. f. kath. Theol. 1890, 2.

121. *A Prophet—What is he?* By S. Henning in The Theo. Monthly, June 1890.

122. *Elliott's Old Testament Prophecy.* Review by W. M. McPheeters, in Pres. Quar. July 1890.

123. *Smith's Religion of the Semites.* Review in Sunday School Times, July 12, 1890.

124. *The Apocryphal Scriptures.* By Rev. J. A. Quarles, in Pres, Quar, July 1890.

125. *Was the Book of Wisdom written in Hebrew?* By D. S. Margoliouth, in Journal of the R. Asiatic Soc. of Great Britain and Ireland, April 1890.

126. *The Book of Enoch.* By W. J. Deane, in The Theo. Monthly, June 1890.

127. *The Jewish Sibylline Oracles.* By Dr. S. A. Hirsch, in Jewish Quar. Rev. July 1890.

Current New Testament Literature.

American and Foreign Publications.

128. *Jesus the Carpenter of Nazareth.* By a Layman. London: Paul, Trench, Trubner and Co. 7s. 6d.

129. *The Sermon Bible V. Matthew 1-21,* London ; Hodder and Stoughton. 7s. 6d.

130. *The Expositors' Bible: The Gospel according to St. Luke.* By Rev. Henry Burton, London: Hodder and Stoughton. 7s. 6d.

131. *Paulus vor Agrippa. Apg. 26, 9-29.* Vortrag auf e. Pastoralkonferenz. By Haarbeck. [Aus: Mitteilgn. d. Ev. Gesellsch.] Elberfeld, Buchh. d. Ev. Geselsch. 1890. —15.

132. *The Epistle to the Hebrews ; with Notes by C. J. Vaughan, D. D.* London and New York : Macmillan & Co. 7s. 6d.

133. *Erklärung der Offenbarung des Johannes. Ein Beitrag zur Förderung ihres Gebrauches in der Gemeinde.* By A. Lindenbein. Braunschweig. $ .95.

134. *Christianity and biblical criticism:* a paper, read before the St. John Clerical Association, 1890. By J. de Soyres. Saint John N. B.: J. & A. M. McMillan, 1890.

135. *Die biblischen Vorstellungen vom Teufel u. ihr religiöser Werth. Ein Beitrag zu der Frage : Giebt es e. Teufel ? Ist der Teufel e. Gegenstand d. christl. Glaubens ?* By G. Längin. Leipzig : O. Wigand, 1890. m. 1.50.

Articles and Reviews.

136. *Lloyd's Greek Testament.* Rev. by I. H. Hall, in Pres. and Ref. Rev., July, 1890.

137. *Notes on Dr. Riddle's edition of Robinson's Harmony of the Gospels : being a contribution to a complete Harmony of the Gospels.* [*Concl.*] By Ch. Leaman. Bibliotheca Sacra. April 1890.

138. *Die Bildersprache in den drei ersten Evangelien.* Eine religionsgeschichtliche u. geographische Studie. By K. Furrer, in Ztschr. f. Missionskde u. Religionswiss. 2, 1890.

139. *The Miracles of our Lord. 21. Healing of the Syro-Phenician Woman's Daughter.* By W. J. Deane, in Homiletic Mag., July 1890.

140. *Were there four months before the harvest ? An examination of John IV. 35.* By M. A. Power, in The Dublin Review, April 1890.

141. *In welchen Zusammenhang gehört der Abschnitt von der Ehebrecherin ?* [*Joh. 8; 3-11.*] By P. Seeberg, in Mitthlgn. u. Nachrn f. d. ev. Kirche in Russland 1890, Febr. u. Marz.

142. *The Hallel and Jesus Singing.* By Rev. A. B. Grosart, in Expository Times, July 1890.

143. *New Testament Teaching on the Punishment of Sin. 4. The Fourth Gospel.* By Rev. Prof. J. A. Beet, in the Expositor, July 1890.

144. *Did St. Paul use a Semitic Gospel?* By Rev. Prof. J. T. Marshall, in The Expositor, July 1890.

145. *Judas Ischarioth. Probleme seiner Person und seiner That.* By E. Höhne, in Beweis des Glaubens. April, May, 1890.

146. *The Ethiopian and the Old Testament.* By Rev. Geo. Adam Smith, in Expository Times, July 1890.

147. *St. Paul at Ephesus.* By Prof. W. M Ramsay, in The Expositor, July 1890.

148. *Godet's Studies on the Epistles.* Review by J. S. Riggs, in Pres. and Ref. Rev., July 1890.

149. *The Characteristics of Paul's Style and Modes of Thought.* By Prof. G. B. Stevens, Ph. D., in Andover Review, July 1890.

150. *Pauline Usage of the Names of Christ. III. Its bearing on Questions of Authorship.* By B. Hellier, in The Theo. Monthly, June 1890.

151. *Outlines on the First Eight chapters of the Epistle to the Romans.* [*Rom. 3 : 19.*] By Rev. C. Clemance, in Homiletic Magazine, July 1890.

152. *Christ our Passover. 1 Cor. 5 : 7.* By H. Crosby, D. D., in Homiletic Rev., Aug. 1890.

153. *The Resurrection of the Dead. II.* By Rev. Prof. W. Milligan, D. D., in The Expositor, July 1890.

154. *Note on 1 Corinthians 15 ; 20-28.* By Prof. D. C. Marquis, D. D., in The Pres. and Ref. Rev., July 1890.

THE

Old and New Testament Student

| VOL. XI. | OCTOBER, 1890. | NO. 4. |

THE first year's work of the American Institute of Sacred Literature has been finished (October 1st). Has it come to stay? Ask the eight hundred students who have been enrolled during the year in its correspondence schools of Hebrew, Arabic, New Testament Greek and the English Bible. Ask the thousand students who received instruction during the summer just closing in the various schools held under its auspices. Ask the thousand "special examiners" in every state, and almost every county, who are to-day working up groups of men and women to take the examination to be offered December 30th on "The Life of the Christ." The year, beginning strictly October 1st, 1889, has been but a partial one. The first prospectus was not ready until late in November. Work in several of the departments was not opened until after January 1st. But, in spite of delays and difficulties, the work has developed in a manner which is most gratifying to its friends. The new year promises much in the way of more perfect organization and wider usefulness. May friends of the work, already many, continue to multiply, and may the work of the year be guided by Him who is over all and in all.

FOR the International Sunday-school System, and those most closely connected with its management, we have the most profound regard. Under no circumstances would we knowingly say or do anything which would injure or detract from the great and prosperous work carried on under the guidance of the International Committee. We believe that the present system is to continue in the future as in the past, though, possibly, with some modifications. This regard for the system, and this belief in its future growth, must not, however, blind our eyes to defects which begin to show themselves. The system is not a perfect one. It may be more perfect than any other which can be devised, and yet contain defects of no trivial character. These defects its best friends should desire to have pointed out. When they are recognized, they may be remedied. The one who points them out and emphasizes them in order that they may be seen most clearly, is not necessarily an enemy of the system. He may be one of its best friends. We desire to be understood as occupying the position of a friend,—a friend on the outside, and therefore compelled to speak, if we speak at all, from the outside. What are the defects? Mr. Blakeslee, in his article in the *Andover Review*, has pointed out some of them. We need not here comment upon them. It is sufficient to say that they are difficulties which the International Committee can, if they will, easily remove. Will they not do it? It is from this point of view of friendly suggestion that the "Plan of Bible Study for Sunday-schools" in the present number of the STUDENT (pp. 198–206) is offered.

CHAUTAUQUA—what is there in the world like it? It is not a man, and yet one man, John H. Vincent, has breathed his very soul into it. It is not a place, and yet a spot fairer than that which bears the name would be difficult to find. It is not an institution, and yet its outward form is similar in many respects to that of institutions of various kinds. It is none of these. It is rather a feeling, a spirit, an influence, which pervades the inner soul of all who come within its reach, which lifts men up and leads them to strive for something higher than that with which they are surrounded, which points toward heaven, not, to be sure, as the church points, and still in a way most helpful to the church. This spirit grows; it assumes new and varied forms. It will continue to grow, for its growth has but begun.

THE unsoundness of mind which is manifested in possession by "fixed ideas" is an established phenomenon in medical science. Biblical science has its examples of the same intellectual aberration. It appears in different stages and along different lines. Sometimes the realm of prophecy furnishes the material for these strange and, once established, alas! often ineradicable fancies. In the department of biblical chronology, men fall victims to vain imaginings, and spend their lives in the search after phantasmic harmonies, which reacts upon the mind and judgment, until the last state is seven times worse than the first. The latest example, over which the religious press, with a few exceptions, is enjoying a season of felicitation, is that of the assumed discovery in astronomical science that the particular day on which the sun and moon stood still in the valley of Ajalon was the scene of an extraordinary conjunction of heavenly bodies that accounts for and verifies the biblical statements. The mouths of rationalistic and infidel objectors are henceforth closed. But when we learn that the same discoverer of this wonderful "fact" has also proved beyond all doubt that the lost tribes of Israel are in England, it is with some shadow of a fear of "fixed ideas" that we contemplate the argument in explanation of the great miracle of Joshua. And then, further, we are inclined to ask, What is to be done with Joshua's command to these heavenly bodies and what becomes of the miracle itself, if all this is true? Or, again, how complicated and liable to error the calculations necessary to follow back from the present until that particular day and hour when the phenomena took place! To-morrow some other calculator will discover how his predecessor has blundered and we will be left again to the tender mercies of the rationalist and the infidel.

THE author of a recently published history of Egypt remarks in the preface, "It may appear strange to some readers that I have not treated of the Exodus. The event does not, however, properly belong to Egyptian history. It did not at all affect Egypt, however important it may have been to the Israelites." There are not many of us who will accept the statement that Egyptian history was in no way affected by the contact of Israel; but we shall all agree with the writer that Egypt exerted a great and powerful influence upon Israel. Writers universally acknowledge this point, and yet there has never been made an adequate presentation of the facts in the case. This field of investigation, Egyptology, and its bearing upon Israelitish history and institutions deserves more attention at the hands of American students than it has yet received. We have many classical scholars, many Semitic specialists, but how few Egyptologists. There is almost a "craze" in some quarters in respect to Assyriology. When shall Egyptology take the place in our American work which it deserves? Where are the young men who will take up this subject and devote to it the spirit and the labor which America owes it?

———

THERE is something which lies beneath all methods and systems of Bible study, without which all are worse than useless. It is something far higher than cleverness, something deeper than even earnestness. It is an honest spirit. Unless you are prepared to deal honestly with yourself and with the Bible in your study of it, you would almost do better not to study it at all. The reference here is not merely to an honest facing of any problems or difficulties that may arise. Such an attitude toward biblical questions is certainly necessary for real progress in the overcoming of difficulties. They are not solved by ignoring or denying them. But a deeper honesty than that is the yielding up of oneself to the convictions of truth and duty which the Bible may force upon the mind and heart. Of what good is the best system, if you hide yourself from the results in conduct which the application of it to the Bible brings to light? It is the spirit of men who have most scientifically and brilliantly studied the Bible that has done the most harm not to themselves merely but to the method which they advocate and to the Christian world standing by asking, "What results?" and "Whither does this tend?" It is because many of them have not honestly stood by their method and its issues in life that German biblical scholars are in many quarters justly feared and their methods of interpretation opposed. Scientific critical Bible study, if its guidance be sincerely followed to the very end and its outcome in the practical religious life obeyed, will be found to be far more fruitful in a Christian life that is well-rounded and developed, than anything that is the genuine fruit of more imperfect Bible study. It must be so by as much as the new method is better than the old.

ONE phase of this subject is especially important to preachers of the Bible. They have their special temptations along this line. They are constantly drawn by the immense suggestiveness of the Scriptures to the use of biblical material in a way hardly warranted by an honest spirit of devotion to the real meaning and purpose of that material. This is popularly called the "accommodation of texts" to themes which are quite remote and disconnected from their original purport. How far this "accommodation" may go is a question possibly open to debate. There are men rash enough—to say the least—to defend it to any extent. But is it not most in accordance with the honest use of the Bible to avoid utterly this dangerous and in the end unprofitable habit? It is strongly said somewhere by Dr. Dale of Birmingham, "There should be a conscience in the study as well as in the counting-house. To attempt by skillful manipulation to get a better meaning out of a text than it contains is as fraudulent a proceeding as to attempt by skillful manipulation to get a better meaning out of a cheque than it contains." Such habits *are* dangerous in their effect upon the student and preacher. On the whole they are without real and permanent profit to the people. They "do not pay" intellectually or spiritually. Be wise by being honest in handling the Word of God in your study and in your pulpit!

A PLAN OF BIBLE STUDY FOR SUNDAY-SCHOOLS.

By the Editor.

Some Sunday-schools and many Bible-classes are looking about for a systematic scheme of Bible study, which, if diligently pursued, shall produce results more numerous and more definite than those ordinarily obtained. It is too much to expect that any particular plan or system, however excellent, shall prove satisfactory to all. This cannot be claimed even of the International Sunday-school system. Different systems and methods are needed to meet different necessities and demands.* The plan which is here proposed would include two distinct series of courses: the first, a series of Comprehensive or Outline Courses; the second, a series of Special Courses on particular books or subjects.

I. A SERIES OF COMPREHENSIVE OR OUTLINE COURSES.

Of the Comprehensive or Outline Courses there might be five. These should be so arranged as practically to cover the main points of both Old and New Testament material. Of each course there should be at least *three* grades or forms, in order that the entire school might be engaged upon the same subject and by the same plan, and the work at the same time be adapted to individuals of different ages and attainments. (1) The first form, for children *five to nine years of age*, should be made as simple as possible, but the entire ground should be covered. No one who has not tested it by a systematic and comprehensive method can appreciate how comparatively

* In the "Andover Review' for October (1890) the Rev. Erastus Blakeslee has indicated clearly some of the difficulties which beset the system now in general use, and, in a modest and most sensible way, has set forth certain principles and details of a a plan which has suggested itself to him in the course of long years of active Sunday-school work. On several occasions the present writer has compared notes with Mr. Blakeslee upon the subject under consideration. Our views both as to the system and method have been practically the same, though differing somewhat in application. The plan herewith presented will be found, therefore, to include also the substance of Mr. Blakeslee's suggestions, and is published with his approval.

easy it is to put a child, five or six years old, into possession of a connected outline history of the life of Jesus. (2) The second form, for children *ten to fourteen years of age*, while still simple, may be made to include at least three times as much material as was contained in the first form. This is possible, because (a) the child has now reached an age when the mind is ready to grasp not only facts but teachings, and (b) the work done four or five years before, developed by the courses which have followed, furnishes a magnificent basis on which to build. (3) The third form of presentation, for young people *fifteen to nineteen years of age*, though still an outline, may be made tolerably exhaustive. It is possible in this form to include (a) many additional facts omitted in previous forms, (b) the detailed bearing of many teachings which in previous forms had only been hinted at, (c) systematization and generalization of facts and principles which had not before been attempted.

The five Comprehensive Courses are as follows:—

1. Outline of New Testament History: The Life of the Christ.*—Of the three forms, (1) The *first* would cover the chief facts of the Christ's life organized into great periods, the emphasis being laid upon the *deeds* of the Christ; (2) the *second* would cover the same ground in greater detail, introducing a larger element of the Christ's *words* in their connection with His deeds; (3) the *third* would make a still more comprehensive study of the same material, the emphasis being laid upon the *words* of the Christ.

2. Outline of Early Old Testament History and Messianic Prophecy.—This course should cover the history given in the Bible down to the death of Solomon and the Division of the Kingdom, and should lay emphasis upon the general preparatory character of the history with reference to the coming of a Deliverer: (1) The *first* form of presentation should limit itself simply to the lives of the great men of the period, e. g., Noah, Abraham, Isaac, Jacob, Joseph, Moses, Joshua, Samuel, Saul, David, Solomon, and the points in which these resemble that of the Christ; (2) the *second* should take

---

* The outline sketched by Mr. Blakeslee, in the article referred to, will indicate clearly the plan here contemplated.

up (a) the history of the nation Israel, (b) the great events in that history and their significance, and (c) the more important passages containing prophetic truth; (3) the *third* should include (a) still more of the details of the history, (b) a general study of the literature of the period, e. g., the Psalms of David, and of the literature which furnishes the history of the period, and (c) the gradual growth and development of the Messianic idea.

3. *Outline of Later Old Testament History and Messianic Prophecy.*—This course should begin with the Division of the Kingdom and continue to the close of the Old Testament canon, outlining the history, exhibiting the character of the work of the prophets in that history, indicating the reasons for God's attitude toward Israel throughout the history, and developing the relation of the whole to the coming of the Christ: (1) The *first* form, as in the preceding courses, should take up only the great lives, e. g., those of Elijah, Elisha, Jonah, Amos, Hosea, Isaiah, Jeremiah, Ezra, Nehemiah, the teachings of these lives and the points of resemblance, if any exist, with that of the Christ; (2) the *second* form should present an outline of the history, and the place of the prophets in that history; (3) the *third* form should give the history in still greater detail, the teachings of the various prophets, and a general idea of the non-prophetic literature and work of the period, e. g., Job, Proverbs.

4. *Outline of New Testament History: Period of the Apostles.*—Of the three forms of this course, (1) the *first* should cover the Acts and the historical matter in the Epistles, emphasis being laid upon the *deeds* of the apostles; (2) the *second* should cover the same ground in greater detail, embracing more of the *teachings* of the apostles as contained in the Acts and the Epistles, and tracing the growth of the early church; (3) the *third* should make a still more comprehensive study of the same material, the emphasis being here laid upon the Apostolic teachings in the Epistles.

5. *Outline Studies in the Biblical Teaching of Redemption.*—The three forms of this course should be arranged on the following principles: (1) The subject should be presented in its historical growth; (2) each form should cover in a year's study

six biblical periods, (a) the patriarchal, (b) the Mosaic, (c) the early prophetic, (d) the later prophetic, (e) the Gospel, (f) the Apostolic; (3) each form should increase in comprehensiveness, and the emphasis be laid, in the first on the teaching as it appears in biblical *life*, passing in the second and third to its presentation in biblical *preaching*.

Remarks.   1.   Each course should be, as indicated, an outline course. The entire ground must be covered in order that the more careful work which is to follow may be done intelligently. Is it necessary to have a general idea of a chapter as a preparation for the accurate study of a verse? or of a book, as a preparation for the accurate study of a chapter? Just so it is necessary to have a general idea of the whole scope of biblical history and literature in order to be able to deal satisfactorily with any particular portion of that history or literature.

2.   The advantage of covering the same ground in this progressive manner, rather than in taking up in each period an entirely new kind of work, will be apparent to anyone who will but give the matter careful thought. Nothing is truer than that one never really masters a subject the first time he covers the ground. Repetition, not however without variety and progress, is the great principle of education.

3.   The fifth course, as will at once be seen, is a review of the four preceding it. This review will serve the triple purpose of (1) fixing more firmly all that has been studied, (2) showing the relation of the various parts to each other, and (3) welding all the parts into a whole, thus giving to it definiteness, vividness and completeness.

4.   There should be required from the very first (1) independence in work, and (2) definiteness in results. There is no better method of securing these than the use of the note-book and pencil, or, in the case of younger pupils, such an arrangement of the material in the lesson-leaflet or quarterly as will permit the results of investigation to be written in the leaflet itself. For an older pupil to write out in his own language the substance of a given verse or paragraph, or for a younger pupil to write out the answers to questions, so worded as (a) to require a careful study of the verse before the answer can be determined, and (b) to call for the substance of the verse, is an exercise of the greatest disciplinary value, and one which will arouse the enthusiasm of all who undertake it.

5.   The great aim and purpose of all the work should be (1) *to lead the pupil to the Bible*, for it is the Bible which should be studied, and not the opinions of men about the Bible. How often must this truth be reiterated before it shall be accepted in practice by even the majority of those who profess an interest in Bible study? (2) *To familiarize the pupil with the Bible*, its events, its characters, its teachings.

6.   If, now, a child were taken at five years of age, and carried step by step three times through these five courses; if from the beginning the habit of independent investigation were cultivated, and, in every form of every course, definite results were demanded ; consider (if it is possible for one to do so from the standpoint of the chaos and confusion which now reign over all, or nearly all, popular Bible study) what a person thus trained would be prepared to do as an adult.

II.   A SERIES OF SPECIAL, SUBJECT OR BOOK, COURSES.

Having gained a *general* conception of Biblical history, Biblical literature, and Biblical teaching from beginning to end, one is in a position to do special work. Here no particular order is necessary. The field is a broad one and choice must be made according to personal inclination or special need. The number of subjects is beyond possibility of description. Only a few may be mentioned. These are the courses from which the Bible classes in the Sunday school year after year might select.

I.   OLD TESTAMENT SUBJECTS.

1.   Early Hebrew History and Institutions, including (1) a study of the historical material in the Pentateuch, Joshua and Judges; (2) an examination of the origin and significance of the more important ceremonies and institutions, e. g., the Sabbath, marriage, sacrifice, circumcision; (3) a study of the Hebrew State, the various forms of government under which Israel lived; (4) the study of the relation of the Israelitish civilization to the civilization of other Semitic nations.

2.   The History, and Literature of Israel from Samuel to Solomon, including (1) the Books of Samuel and a portion of First Kings; (2) the period of history which these books cover and the literature of the period; (3) the more important topics connected with these books, this history and this literature.

3.   The History and Literature of Israel and Judah from the division of the Kingdom to the Fall of Samaria, including (1) the study of the circumstances leading to the division; (2) a general examination of the characteristics of the historical books of Kings and Chronicles; (3) the mastery of the particular events under the Israelitish history of this period; (4) a general study of the work and writings of the prophets who labored in this period, viz., Elijah, Elisha, Joel, Amos, Hosea and portions of Isaiah and Micah.

4.   The History and Literature of Israel and Judah from the fall of Samaria to the Fall of Jerusalem (B. C. 587). The details need not be specified.

5.   The History and Literature of the Jews during and after the Exile to the close of the Canon. The details need not be specified.

6.   *Old Testament Legal Literature and Legislation,* including a study of (1) the present form of this literature; (2) the contents as classified according to the prevailing element, in each case, whether hygienic, social, civil or religious; (3) the relation of this literature to other divisions of Hebrew literature; (4) the connection of this legislation with the different periods of Israelitish history; (5) the principles underlying this system compared with those of other ancient legal systems; (6) the Divine element apparent in this literature as distinguished from other similar literature.

7.   *Old Testament Prophetic Literature and Prophecy,* including (1) the study one by one of the prophets from Joel to Malachi; (2) the growth and development of prophecy in the various periods of Israelitish history; (3) the study of prophetic life and growth, prophetic politics, prophetic history-writing, prophetic ethics and theology; (4) the study of the principles of prophecy; (5) the study of the fulfillment of prophecy in the New Testament.

8.   *Old Testament Poetical Literature and Philosophy,* including the study of (1) the lyric element as found in the Psalms; (2) the Book of Proverbs; (3) the Book of Job with the various problems which it presents; (4) the Book of Ecclesiastes; (5) the scope and contents of Old Testament Wisdom.

9.   *Principles of Old Testament Interpretation,* including (1) the *general* principles underlying the work of interpretation, e. g., the interpretation of figurative language, the relation of circumstances of person, place, time, etc., to the meaning of the passage; (2) the *special* principles of interpretation, e. g., the principles of typology, of prophecy, the theophanies.

10.   *Biblical Theology of the Old Testament,* including (1) a study of the teachings of each Book on the more important topics of theology; (2) a study of the growth and development of each of these doctrines in connection with the history of the nation.

II. NEW TESTAMENT SUBJECTS.

1. The Synoptic Gospels including among other points the following; (1) a rapid preliminary outline of each Gospel; (2) a comparison of the three Gospels with a view of ascertaining the differences as well as the characteristic elements of each; (3) on the basis of this comparison a study of (a) the origin and literary relations of the Synoptics, (b) the special type of teaching found in each, (c) the doctrine of the Kingdom of God which all reveal; (4) the study of this last great teaching in the light of the present.

2. The Writings of John, including, (1) the consideration of the contents and plan of the Gospel; (2) the view of the Christ which it discloses; (3) this portrait compared with that of the Synoptics; (4) the additional views of truth and life in the early church given in the Epistles and the Revelation; (5) a more or less careful examination of the literary and historical questions connected with these writings; (5) the bearing of the teachings of these writings on current thought.

3.   The Acts of the Apostles, including the study of (1) the progress of the early church through the several periods which appear in the Acts; (2) the life of the early Christian communities as there revealed; (3) the historical and literary questions arising in connection with the book; (4) the comparison of the church and individual life of to-day in the light of these teachings.

4.   The Life and Writings of Paul, including (1) the study of the biblical material which will give a clear and comprehensive outline of Paul's life, an outline which should be mastered; (2) the filling in of this outline from indirect hints in the Epistles etc.; (3) the taking up in historical order of each of the Epistles to determine (a) the general outline, (b) the circumstances of composition and historical situation, (c) the great teachings; (4) the consideration of how all this bears on the missionary methods and the theological ideas of the present.

5.   Paul's Epistles to the Corinthians, including (1) a careful and analytical study of the contents of each and their relations to one another; (2) the consideration of questions of authorship and of literary character ; (3) the effort to obtain a clearer picture of the church-life, therein suggested; (4) the classification of the teachings, the gaining of a familiarity with their contents; (5) the application of this knowledge to the present conditions of life and thought.

6. *Paul's Epistle to the Romans,* including (1) a careful, analytical study of the contents; (2) the consideration of questions of authorship and of literary character; (3) the gaining of a clearer picture of the church life therein suggested; for other points, see above.

7. *Paul's Epistles to the Ephesians, Colossians and Philippians.* The treatment would be similar to that of the two preceding courses.

8. *The Epistle to the Hebrews,* including (1) a careful, analytical study; (2) an examination of the historical situation which lies back of the epistle; (3) an interpretation of it in the light of this situation; (4) the classification of the great teachings; (5) the application of them to the present conditions of life and thought.

9. *The Biblical Theology of the Pauline Epistles.* This subject would demand a familiarity with some of those outlined above, viz., Nos. 4 to 8, and should include (1) the collection of biblical statements of doctrine from these epistles and the interpretation of each in view of the context and historical situation; (2) the classification of these statements under appropriate heads; (3) the formulating of statements covering the Pauline teachings on these points.

10. *Biblical Theology of John, Peter and James.* The treatment would be similar to that under No. 9.

Remarks. 1. Will some one say that the work outlined is too great in amount? Remember (1) that these *special* courses are named as courses from which a choice is to be made according to one's preference and circumstances; and (2) that allowing a year to each course, the man or woman, who has received the preliminary training furnished by the Comprehensive Courses, could finish *all* the work indicated before the age of forty.

2. Will some one say that the work outlined is too high in its character, too far above the level of the average Sunday school student, a work better adapted to the wants of a theological seminary? Remember (1) that these courses are intended for men and women who have been prepared for them by having studied two or three times each, five comprehensive courses, covering practically the entire Bible: (2) that every subject here indicated may be

treated in such a manner as to be not only intelligible, but fascinating to an ordinary Bible class.

3. Will some one say that the introduction of such a plan into a Sunday school, is the introduction of diversity and confusion? Remember (1) that the day is coming, and the sooner it comes the better for the interests of sacred Scripture, when the Sunday school will be graded, classes separated, and *order* introduced; (2) that an artificial unity is injurious; and often gained only by the sacrifice of what is essential; (3) that a real unity exists when the same great subject is studied, whether all be engaged upon the same phase of that subject or not ; (4) that, if it is desired, an arrangement can be made by which the entire school, except the Bible-class, may be at work upon the same subject, and the present uniformity practically be preserved.

4. For such a system as this, leaflets, quarterlies and text-books will be required, to aid in the study of the Book, not as a substitute for it. Let these "helps" be as numerous as there are individuals able and willing to prepare them, or publishers able and willing to issue them. Competition will improve the character of all. Different ideas and methods may thus find a place in the great work of Bible instruction.

5. Imagine a Sunday school which for twenty or twenty-five years has followed some such system as this, with its three "Life of Christ" classes, or its three "Early Old Testament History" classes, or its three "Later Old Testament" classes, or its three "Early Church History" classes, or its three "Redemption" classes, and its one to five Bible-classes doing careful work on special subjects,—imagine, we say, such a Sunday-school. Is it a dream? Is it only a dream?

This is but a rough sketch of what lies in the writer's mind. Are there a few Sunday-schools or Bible-classes which will consent to take a step forward toward something of this kind? At a future time the writer trusts that he may be permitted to present the plan more in detail.

THE MYTHOLOGICAL ELEMENT IN JOB.

By Professor W. W. DAVIES, Ph. D.,

Ohio Wesleyan University, Delaware, Ohio.

Leaving inspiration entirely out of the question—not that we deny the inspiration of this or any other book in the sacred canon—and regarded as a human composition, the book of Job is beyond controversy one of the sublimest works in literature, profane or sacred. The author, whoever he might have been, has displayed in this book, a mind not only inspired by the Holy Ghost, but also capable of presenting in the sublimest language the profoundest truths. The poet—for all will agree that whether or not purely historical, the book of Job is poetical in form—soars on the wings of imagination through the heavens, over the waters into the uttermost parts of the earth and penetrates everywhere into the mysteries of the universe. He draws his illustrations from Sheol, earth and sky; now revelling in brilliant pictures from the natural scenery around him; now passing into the realm of pure imagination; now quoting some familiar doctrine from the remote past; now citing some popular belief, clothed in "all the wealth of Eastern imagery, and mingling in his wild cries, strange snatches of long-forgotten astrology."

There are several passages in Job which have occasioned an unusual amount of trouble to the more conservative school of exegetes, and have a great variety of interpretation. I refer to what are often called the mythological references. At first sight, it might seem a little hazardous, if not altogether irreverent to have the term mythological applied to them; even, though they were uttered not as a part of Job's creed, but simply as incidental allusions to some current superstitions, and intended to impress the reader with the majesty and omnipotence of God, against whom it would be vain for Job or any mortal to contend. At the same time no other interpretation affords even a plausible explanation of these places.

It is not our intention to enter at length into a discussion of these mythological allusions. We find them in the litera- tures of all nations; so that even modern science especially astronomy has accepted things as they were; adopting in great measure the nomenclature of the ancients, which was evidently based upon mere fancy. As a proof of this we have only to refer to the signs of the zodiac and many con- stellations, bearing such names as: Draco, Serpens, Aries, Canis, Pisces, etc.

The principal passages which are supposed to contain some astrological references are the following.

> Let them curse it that curse the day,
> Who are ready to rouse up leviathan.
>
> iii. 8.
>
> Am I a sea or a monster,
> That thou settest a watch over me?
>
> vii. 12.
>
> The helpers of Rahab do stoop under him.
>
> ix. 13.
>
> He stirreth up the sea with his power,
> And by his understanding he smiteth through Rahab.
> By his spirit the heavens are garnished,
> His hand hath pierced the swift serpent.
>
> xxvi. 12, 13.

The passage in 7: 12 may be satisfactorily explained without any recourse to the mythological, though it is very possible that a poetic mind might have conceived the idea that the raging, boundless sea was a high monster, furiously lashing and twisting itself in mad fury around the earth. The same might be said of "the helpers of Rahab" in 9: 13.

The other passages are however much more difficult. Let us now examine the following:

> Let them curse it that curse the day,
> Who are ready to rouse up leviathan.

The second parallel of this couplet is very obscure in the A. V. where we read: "who are ready to raise up their mourning." Such a translation, beside being meaningless, is not warranted. The R. V. transliterates the Hebrew without any attempt at translation. The word leviathan is used five times in the Old Testament. Job 3: 8; 41: 1; Ps. 74: 14; 104: 26; Is. 27: 1. There is no difficulty about the true meaning in the last four places, where the word must be taken in its literal sense, i. e., some well-known monster which wreathes and curves itself such as the serpent, crocodile or some aquatic animal; or symbolically for some hostile nation. The description of the leviathan in chapter forty-one points clearly to the crocodile. Though the same word is used in this verse it is certainly difficult to understand its exact import, if taken literally. The phrase "to rouse up leviathan" is clear enough in itself; but as Davidson observes, it is not easy to find a logical connection between rousing up the crocodile and cursing days. Those who cursed days were magicians, who, by their incantations professed to have the power of rendering any day they desired unpropitious. The author of Job not only assumes the existence of such a class, but also attributes to them the power by means of their enchantments to stir up leviathan.

Were we to enquire what possible connection there can be between curses of days and stirring up leviathan, some would reply that those who cursed the day mentioned in the first clause were those who exercised supernatural power over ferocious animals on land and in water, and by their magic arts could call out any of these formidable beasts from their hiding places in the recesses of the wilderness. But such an interpretation when taken in the light of the context seems flat and unmeaning. It not only destroys the train of thought, but also violates the laws of parallelism; for it is well-known that the second parallel ought to be stronger than the first, whereas, to curse a day in such a way as to overwhelm it with calamities is a greater feat than to charm a snake or to tame a crocodile, or even to allure the most formidable monster from the "impenetrable forest."

Some exegetes, following Origen and some early church fathers, feel called upon to spiritualize every passage in the Bible, especially those difficult to interpret, and they see in the leviathan of our verse, a clear allusion to Satan, the old serpent, "the great spiritual leviathan." But as Dr. Evans says; "When it is remembered that the same writers find the same typical significance in the description of leviathan in the forty-first chapter the extravagance of their fancy will at once appear."

14

A third explanation, held by men of all schools, from the most orthodox to the ultra-rationalistic is that we have here an allusion to one of the many popular superstitions current among even the Semitic people at the time when Job was written. Accordingly the leviathan must be regarded as an imaginary monster which devoured or swallowed up the sun and moon, thus producing darkness and eclipses. Such obscurations were regarded with dread, and if not as the direct cause of the direst calamities, yet certainly as intimately connected with them. It is also well-known that there has been, from most ancient times, a wide-spread superstition regarding the eclipses of the sun and moon. We find traces of it in India, China, Assyria, Africa, as well as in North and South America. No little importance should be attached to the fact that "among the Egyptians, with whose institutions the author of this book was well acquainted, eclipses were attributed to the victory of Typhon over the Sun-God." We also know that the crocodile was a representative of Typhon.

From what has been said, it is not probable that the word leviathan has its natural meaning in chapter third; but though we might prove positively that it has and that the clause in question refers simply to snake-charmers and crocodile-tamers, there is still another passage in Job which cannot be disposed of with such an interpretation. I refer to 26: 12, 13, which reads:—

> He stirreth up the sea with his power,
> And by his understanding he smiteth through Rahab,
> By his spirit the heavens are garnished ;
> His hand hath pierced the swift serpent.

Here we have four parallel ideas to illustrate the power of God. The first couplet refers to the sea; the second, to the heavens. The first clause in each verse is perfectly clear; the second in each, exceedingly obscure if not unintelligible if literally interpreted. If however we are justified to see in these two verses a mythological reference, all difficulty disappears and all becomes perfectly clear. These parallel clauses in their very nature must contain similar thought; this is required by the law of Hebrew poetry.

Let us now examine the thirteenth verse. The first parallel represents God's hand as piercing the fierce monster which occasioned the darkness. According to the popular belief, this swift serpent, which the hand of God pierces, had the power to wrap itself around the sun and moon so as to hide them from the eyes of men. But God is omnipotent, not only more powerful than Job and all mankind, but also the conqueror of Rahab which disturbed the peace of the ocean; as well as of the swift serpent, which caused confusion and tumult in the heavens. God pierces this (imaginary) monster, the cause of the obscuration; it loosens its deadly grasp, and the hidden moon, or the eclipsed sun, released from its sinuous folds becomes visible; darkness gives way to the light, and the heavens once more serenely brighten up. The passage thus interpreted becomes perfectly intelligible, while all other explanations are dark, fanciful and inadequate.

We would not have to go far to find the origin of such a superstition. The poetic Eastern mind could easily transform the ever-changing, restless clouds into animated existences. And when these dark monsters of the skies dragged their ugly forms over sun and moon and stars they were readily looked upon as hostile forces dominating the skies. Now, as magicians had the power to charm the snake and crocodile, how easily might the poet extend their powers and imagine that this same class of people, these cursers of the day had influence over these celestial monsters?

The Bible in referring to these superstitious beliefs does in no way set upon them the stamp of truth, any more than it does upon the false ideas regarding providence in its dealings with mankind or the relation of suffering to sin which the friends of Job entertain throughout the book. Their arguments and illustrations, real or fictitious are faithfully recorded, though the former were often at variance with the truth. That the chosen people of God should have shared in some of the superstitious beliefs of the nations surrounding them, at least, in some degree, becomes evident from the stringent laws which Moses enacted against those practicing or countenancing necromancy, magic and other forms of divination. Laws against such practices are sufficient evidence of their prevalence among the people. Besides, there are many incidental references in the Bible to superstitions which were current among the Israelites; as in the story of the witch of Endor; the supposed evil effects of the moon upon men; (Ps. 121 : 6); and the fact that the disciples of our Lord, at one time, thought he was a spirit.

ON EXPOSITORY PREACHING.*

By President JOHN A. BROADUS, D. D., LL. D.,
Louisville, Ky.

It has been suggested that I should say something on this subject, especially with reference to the exposition of historical Scripture. One or two of the preceding writers have cautioned against a too exclusive use of historical passages, thereby implying that some persons find this easy. This is gratifying, for I am persuaded that the great mass of ministers, when attempting an expository discourse, take some doctrinal, preceptive, or devotional portion. No one can overlook the fact that the greater part of the Bible consists of history, much of it biography; and that all the other portions have a historical setting, which we cannot afford to overlook if we wish to make thorough study. Yet some ministers rarely take a properly historical text; or if they do, it is only the introduction that takes account of the narrative, and then a subject is evolved, and treated in the usual fashion. But all mankind are interested in a story, a narrative, an account of actual persons, in their actual life, and exhibiting their distinctive characteristics. If the Bible is so rich in these elements, ought they not to have a large part in our sermons?

But remember that we are not undertaking to write a biblical story, or to give a lecture on Bible history. We are going to make a sermon which must have very practical aims and bearings that determine the whole management of the discourse. Some ministers, who are fond of history, just give a series of Lyceum lectures upon topics or persons of Bible history, lectures that may be brilliant, highly enter-

* This article was prepared to form one of a series of discussions on Expository Preaching which have been from time to time published in these pages. It will be sufficient to refer readers to the May, June and July, 1890, numbers of THE OLD AND NEW TESTAMENT STUDENT for the previous articles, opinions and letters, bearing on the subject.

taining, even instructive in the way of historical discussion, but that do not powerfully impel the hearer toward a religious life, as sermons ought to do.

On the other hand, many are restrained from attempting historical exposition by the persuasion that they have no talent for narration and description. Perhaps the dignity of this periodical may endure a couple of anecdotes, which at least conform to the etymology of that term, for hitherto they have been unpublished. Years ago a singularly able young man came to be pastor where I lived, who was a vigorous and exact thinker, and whose sermons were full of wholesome truth. We were intimate friends, and one day I asked him if he had paid much attention to preaching on the Bible history. He said, Oh, no, because he had no talent in the world for description. He had once tried a sermon on Balaam—which some might think a rather knotty subject to begin on—and making a wretched failure, had never repeated the attempt. It was folly for him to attempt such a sermon, because he could not describe. I insisted that he could do something better than describing, he could take up some person, and analyze his motives and character, so as to make him yield a rich variety of interesting and useful, practical lessons. He could not deny that he was conscious of power to analyze, and so he consented to make an attempt in that direction. It was not two years before this was his favorite class of sermons, and particularly welcomed by his hearers; and he would get in some good bits of description, too, when the subject called for it.

The other anecdote relates to a man who had reached middle age, was a profound thinker, a lecturer rarely equalled, and when he felt at his ease, a preacher of extraordinary power. Shortly after the war closed, he preached a deeply impressive sermon at an association in the country, upon the text, "Wait on the Lord," etc. He, of course, understood it to mean "wait for the Lord," and one of his illustrations was as follows: "The mother or wife sits at her window in the dusk of evening, looking along the road upon which she hopes soon to see her son or husband returning from the war. She is waiting for him." The application is obvious. As we rode away that afternoon I said, "My friend, what made you spoil that pleasant little picture you gave us of the woman sitting at the window in the dusk? You said the mother *or* wife, looking for the son *or* husband; I couldn't see one for the other." "Oh, pshaw!" he answered, "I was a fool for attempting such a thing. I never can make a description, and I never attempt it except through forgetting myself." Upon being asked how he knew he could not, he said that in his first sermon, which was in the presence of his older brother, a minister, he made some little attempt at description, and his brother afterwards told him not to try that again, for he evidently had no turn that way. "So I have always tried to avoid it," he said, "and am ashamed to have been betrayed into the awkward attempt to-day." I took earnest exception, insisting that any man who could state a thought with such clear-cut edges, and make a series of arguments spring into life as he could, might be able to describe a scene, if he would take half as much trouble to prepare for it as he took in preparing his arguments and statements. After much talk, I playfully dared him to make an honest attempt. Some weeks later we met on the street, and he stopped with a smile and told me that the previous Sunday he had preached in a country church a dozen miles away upon the parable of the sower; and as it was just the season for sowing wheat, he thought in preparing the sermon that he would try to make his farmer hearers see the sower as he scattered the grain, and it fell on different kinds of soil. "And I am bound to acknowledge," he said with a pleasant laugh, "that I think I really did succeed. I give it up." Not long after, I went to preach for him at that same church, and dined with an estimable deacon. At dinner we were talking about my friend their pastor, and they needed but little encouragement to tell of one sermon and another as especially remembered and valued. At length the deacon's wife broke out, "And I tell you, I never heard the like of that sermon last fall about the parable of the sower, when he described that man going across the field sowing wheat. Hi! I can see him now." Here was a man of extraordinary abilities, and supremely anxious to preach well, who had gone on to middle age with a mistaken notion growing out of an unlucky suggestion as to his earliest sermon, and yet the very first time he really attempted to describe a scene the success was remarkable.

These instances may lead some to consider a question as to which I have no doubt. Are there not many men, by no means negligent as to self-development, very anxious to do their best, who go on for years thinking they cannot do this, or cannot do that, simply because of some early failure easily accounted for, or some well-meant but unwarranted discouragement? Are there not probably men who live on and die without ever having developed potencies that were really capable of great effectiveness? Ought not a minister who wishes to make the best of himself, while practicing chiefly those methods of preaching in which he most readily succeeds, yet occasionally to try all manner of experiments, and find out other ways in which he may have reasonable success, thereby enriching his own development, and giving the variety so much needed by his heterogeneous audience?

Not every man will excel in expository preaching. But every man can learn to make fairly interesting and really helpful expository sermons, if he can preach well in any way, and if he will practice this kind of preaching now and then. Only let him make very careful preparation, taking pains to give the sermon unity, decided movement, vivacity, and abundant practical applications. For one, I am quite sure that expository preaching will become increasingly popular in our country throughout the next generation of ministerial life. Without saying more, I may mention a few specimens of historical exposition which are easily accessible, and in their several ways might be particularly helpful:—

Candlish on "Scripture Characters," and also on Genesis; Bruce on "The Training of the Twelve," which has just appeared in a new edition ; the half-dozen volumes of William M. Taylor, particularly those on David and on Paul; Hanna's Life of Christ, which consists of expository sermons; and it is matter of special gratification that the Christian Literature Society (35 Bond Street, New York City) can now furnish volumes of Chrysostom, who is to wise students the most instructive and stimulating of all expository preachers.

THE INTER-TESTAMENT LITERATURE.

By Prof. GEORGE H. SCHODDE, Ph. D.,

Columbus, Ohio.

One of the results of modern methods of Bible study has been that the literary remains from the period that intervened between the close of the Old Testament canon and the beginning of the New are regarded with entirely new eyes. They are no longer looked upon as curiosities of literature without any practical value for Scriptural research. They have been discovered to be important sources of information, not only for the understanding of the intellectual and religious development in Israel in that period when their sacred writings had received a recognition as never before, and had become actually, and not only theoretically, the leading factors and forces in this development, but also for the elucidation of contemporary Jewish thought in the days of Christ and the apostles, without which many of the problems of New Testament theology and New Testament exegesis are unintelligible in their entire bearings and import.

The change in the estimate of these writings, which include not only the so-called Apocrypha, i. e. the books found in the Greek but not in the Hebrew Old Testament canon, but also the apocalypses and other writings of both Palestinian and Hellenistic Judaism, is owing chiefly to the introduction into modern biblical research of that idea which has been the most fruitful of results, both good and bad, in the scientific investigations of the day, namely, the idea of historical development. The Scriptures are no longer regarded merely as a collection of dogmatical *dicta probantia*, but revelation has been a growth, and one that stands in the most intimate relation to the development of the people in whose midst it became a reality. While it cannot be denied that the modern method of Bible study in its one-sided application has led to naturalizing and naturalistic schemes of the re ligion revealed in the Scriptures, yet in its legitimately sober application a much more correct idea of the actual course and character of revelation at its various stages has been secured than was possible from the standpoint of former days. In unfolding Scripture not merely as a revelation, but also as the history of a revelation, the inter-Testament literature has a value and importance of its own, even if these writings in a certain sense are only secondary and auxiliary.

It is a matter of considerable discussion as to the extent to which even temporary thought and literature influenced the sacred writings, more particularly those of the New Testament. It has been the function of biblical study in its modern phases and methods to emphasize more than was done by the scholars of an earlier generation the human side of revelation, the human factors, forces and surroundings, whose presence can be detected in the character and contents of the Scriptures. Indeed, in this point probably more than in any other consist the characteristic differences between the former and the present ways of interpreting the Word. Under the spell of an extremely mechanical idea of inspiration, which made the sacred writers themselves as mediums of revelation little more than blind instruments, it is certainly true that in earlier generations the methods of Bible study were one-sided by the exclusion of this human side. In our day the tendency is often to the opposite, and the extreme emphasis put upon a principle in itself correct has led to the exaltation of the human element to the detriment of the divine, sometimes even reducing the latter to a minimum. Analyzed to bottom facts, it is just here where what the late Professor Delitzsch called "the deep chasm between the old and the new theology" is to be found.

While it is recognized as fixed and settled that for the material contents of the New Testament the writers were not indebted to the thought or literature of their age, but to the spirit of inspiration, it is equally certain that the shape and manner in which this revelation was given and formulated to a great extent was conditioned by this thought. Being supernatural truth revealed to human minds, it of a necessity assumed such a form that those for whom it was in-

tended could understand it.   And just in this particular the
literature between the two Testaments, as the expression of
the religious thought of Israel, renders most valuable service,
as can be illustrated by a few examples.

The prelude of St. John's Gospel contains the deepest of
Christological thoughts.   Its leading idea is that the Logos,
who from eternity existed with the Father, had entered the
world and become flesh.   The general truth here made prominent is thus the eternal pre-existence of the Logos.   The
vast strides here made over and beyond the Messianic promises of the Old Testament are at once apparent, and it is
difficult to see how a reader of this majestic prelude with only
the Old Testament before him could have understood or appreciated the grand revelation.   This becomes possible only
when at the hand of the literature under consideration we see
that the contemporaries of St. John had become familiar
with similar ideas and views.   Although conservative exegesis
has always been a unit in teaching that the predictions of the
Old Testament clearly ascribe to the coming Messiah a supernatural personality and work, and has seen in such passages
as Micah 5 : 1–5 ; Isaiah 4 : 2 ; Daniel 7 : 13, proofs of the pre-
existence of this Messiah, and although, further, neither in
word nor idea has the Logos of John any connection with the
Logos of Philo's philosophy, but is rather a development
from Old Testament premises, yet it is clear that John's
method of expressing this deep idea is not taken from Old
Testament models, nor is it intelligible from Old Testament
thought and words merely.   As John, like the other writers,
used the language and the rhetoric of his day, as he wrote
primarily for his contemporaries, it scarcely admits of any
doubt that in presenting his grand truth he put it into a
mould and form not shaped after Old Testament models, but
in those constructed by the people in the centuries between
Malachi and the appearance of Christt.

A glance at the literature of that era shows how common it
was for the religious writers to describe persons and things
that occupied an important position in the kingdom of God
as pre-existent before Jehovah from eternity and as being
brought down into the world at the proper time and for the

proper purpose—a line of thought which, it is clear in most cases, was suggested by the Messianic interpretation of Daniel 7: 13. In the second part of the book of Enoch, chapters 37–71, entitled The Parables, and written about the beginning of the Christian era, we have probably the highest theological and ethical conception of the Messiah written by uninspired pen without the New Testament as a basis or source of information. Here an eternal pre-existence is also predicated of Him. In chap. 48: 3 we read: "And before the sun and the signs were created, before the stars of heaven were made, His name was called before the Lord of the spirits." Also in chap. 48: 6: "For this purpose He was chosen and hidden before Him [God] before the world was created, and He will be before Him to eternity." Similar views are found chap. 48: 7; 62: 6, 7; 52: 9 (*cf.* Andover edition of Enoch, p. 46 sqq). Essentially the same ideas are found in IV. Ezra, a Jewish product of the first Christian century, or of even an earlier date. There, e. g. chap. 12: 31, we read: " *Hic est Unctus, quem reservavit Altissimus in finem ;*" also chap. 13: " *Ipse est, quem conservat Altissimus multis temporibus, cf.* also 14: 9. Just as is done in Enoch, this pre-existing state is described as being hidden, e. g. 13: 52: *Sicut non potest hoc vel scrutare vel scire quis, quid sit in profundo maris, sic non poterit quisque super terram videre filium meum, vel eos qui cum eo sunt, nisi in tempore diei.* In the same way other sacred persons and even things are described as pre-existent. Thus in the *Assumptio Mosis,* 1 : 4, Moses speaks of himself as *qui ab initio orbis terrarum praeparatus sum.* In the Apocalypse of Baruch we read of Jerusalem that the city "*preparata fuit ex quo cogitavi ut facerem paradisum et ostendi eam Adamo priusquam peccaret.*" In the book of Jubilees, a haggadic production of the first Christian century, we read that the angels celebrated the Sabbath before the creation. In the *Assumptio Mosis* we read of the temple: " *Repones [libros]* . . . . *in loco quem fecit ab initio creaturae orbis terrarum.* The pre-existence of the Law is one of the leading doctrines of Jewish theology in the New Testament age. *Cf.* Weber's *Theologie des Talmuds,* p. 15, 153, 190 sqq. This form of thought was adopted by early Christian writers and was used by them extensively. *Cf.* quotations to the point from patristic literature given in Harnack's notes on *Pastor Hermas*, 2 : 4, and II. Clem. 14 : 1.

But the advantage of a closer study of the inter-Testament literature for New Testament exposition is by no means quite confined, or even principally confined, to such details in the manner of expressing revealed thought. On the contrary, its greatest benefit lies in the light which it sheds on leading and fundamental problems of New Testament interpretation. It is well known that the Judaism of the time of Christ was by no means an honest development from Old Testament premises. While ostensibly still the theology of Moses and the prophets, yet the system of the Pharisees was radically opposed to that theology. Christ came into antagonism to the official theological teachers of the day, simply because He found that they had departed from the landmarks of the old covenant, substituting in their place dogmas and doctrines of foreign origin. His reformatory work consisted in the attempt to lead this thought back again into the channels of revealed truth; hence His conflict with the Pharisees. When looked at more closely it will be seen that the points of divergency and difference were chiefly two, namely, the carnal conception of the Messiah and His kingdom, and the object of the law as being an end in itself and not the means to an end, i. e. righteousness by the law. The process of the origin and genesis of this thought in Israel, although it cannot be traced in all its ramifications in inter-Testament literature, yet its leading characteristics and many of its details can be found. In this respect such works as the so-called Psalms of Solomon, written shortly after the conquest of Jerusalem by Pompey, 46 B. C., are extremely instructive. In the pages of the New Testament the Jews in opposing Christ's claim to be the fulfillment of the Old Testament promises, seem almost to quote the words of this lyrical collection. Plainly and openly a justification according to works (17: 9–12), a "justification of deeds" (14: 1) is taught. In 9: 9 the essence of New Testament Pharisaism is expressed in the words that "he who doth righteousness gathereth to himself eternal life; but he who does evil is the cause of his own destruction." The Messiah is entirely a mighty earthly ruler, who destroys the enemies of Israel and exalts His people. The unclean and foreigners shall be removed from Zion; the Messiah shall be the new king in Jerusalem, to which place all the saints of the Diaspora shall be gathered. Israel is the first nation, and the others shall be merely drawers of water and hewers of the stone for the favored few. In this way shall be realized the hopes of those who, according to the book of Enoch, "had expected to be the head, but had become the tail." In the light of the views expressed in works of this kind, the historical background of the whole New Testament is seen with remarkable clearness; the *status controversiae* in the Gospels and the Acts are intelligible as historical phenomena; the great argument of St. Paul in favor of righteousness by faith alone, to which he devotes the substance of at least two of his greatest epistles, Romans and Galatians, is seen as to its cause and is better understood as to its character. For, understanding the view which he intends to combat, his counter arguments become all the clearer.

These illustrations could easily be increased. But it is evident from what has been said that the literature in question does much to put the New Testament theology into its proper setting. The thought of the age, of which this literature is the best expression accessible, must be a valuable tool in the apparatus of the New Testament student. The principle of historical interpretation finds in it a good auxiliary, the legitimate use of which cannot fail to help clear up more than one exegetical enigma.

"NEITHER POVERTY NOR RICHES;"

OR THE

TEACHINGS OF PROVERBS REGARDING PROPERTY.

By Rev. EDWARD TALLMADGE ROOT,

New Haven, Conn.

The most pressing moral and social question of the day is that of the distribution of wealth. Thoughtful men are asking as never before, What changes must be made in our laws and in our private living to prevent the complementary evils of riches and poverty? Christians, believing that Christianity alone can solve the problem, will seek the answer in the Bible.

In the Old Testament, next to the Mosaic legislation, the Wisdom literature contains the most valuable suggestions. Unlike the Pentateuch, Psalms and Prophets, the books deal with the individual, not the nation. They ask, What course of life is for my highest good? What is wise? The point of view and motives urged therefore differ. Every person is an end in himself; his true good must never be sacrificed; hence the appeal of Proverbs to self-interest is legitimate. But though starting from a different standpoint, the Hokma reaches the same conclusions. Ecclesiastes shows that wealth cannot satisfy; Job, that wealth is not the reward of righteousness. Proverbs teaches how to avoid poverty by industry and frugality, yet excludes ambition for riches by making wisdom the supreme object of life.

I confine attention in this article to Proverbs. It seems the general impression that its ethical standard is the wordly wisdom of the money-getter. The opposite is true. There is no higher standard in the Old Testament. Riches are given a lower place than in the Psalms. There is no proverb inconsistent with the prayer of Agur.   So a study of Proverbs will show.

Let us ask four questions.*

I.   Is the seeking of riches a legitimate life-purpose?

Proverbs accord with Ecclesiastes, but without attaining its profundity.   Greed of gain is condemned, because it leads to dishonesty or judicial corruption (15: 27; 21: 6; 28: 20), or because riches are fleeting (23: 4, 5; 28: 22; 11: 28).   The positive side is more emphasized.   There is something better to seek, viz., wisdom or righteousness, and these two are one, for he who seeks to realize in his life the world-plan ("wisdom") of God lives according to right. The possession of such intelligent moral character is better than riches (3: 13–15; 8: 10, 11, and 18, 19; 15: 6; 16: 16; 28: 6).   It enables its possessor, though poor, to see through the empty pride of the rich (28: 11).   Happiness can dwell where riches are absent, but flies from the home where love and the fear of Jehovah abide not (15: 16, 17; 16: 8; 17: 1). Virtue wins respect and love, which are better than riches, and which it is implied riches cannot buy (22: 1).   And the supreme test is the judgment certain to come.

> " Riches profit not in the day of wrath ;
> " But righteousness delivereth from death."
> (11 : 4, *cf.* 10 : 2.)

So the true life-purpose is to seek not riches, but wisdom. The issues of life do not depend upon possessions, but on character; the *heart*, therefore, is to be kept above every thing else (4: 23).

> " The beginning of wisdom is, ' Get wisdom ;'
> " Yea, at the price of all thou hast gotten, get understanding."
> (4 : 7, *cf.* 4 : 5, etc.)

II.   But are not riches, while not to be supremely sought, a good which the righteous may expect as a reward ?†

* This is not a selection of passages to prove a theory.   *All* the proverbs which treat in any way of riches, etc., were collected, studied and classified, before a sentence was written.

† So accustomed are we to think of the reward of righteousness as given in a future life, that the question seems of little importance.   But to the Hebrews having no clear doctrine of existence after death, it involved all that questions of eschatology do to-day.   It was the one great theological problem in dispute

Some proverbs seem to teach this, as,

> " Length of days is in her (wisdom's) right hand,
> " And in her left riches and honor."
>
>   (3 : 16, *cf.* 22 : 4.)

But we must not take these alone. The mind of the Sage passes so readily to spiritual value as to suggest that he uses " riches" as the fittest symbol which wisdom gives. In the " Mashal Discourse," 8: 18–21, wisdom seems to guard against a literal interpretation.

> " Riches and honor are with me,
> "Yea, *durable riches and righteousness.*
> " My *fruit is better than gold*," etc.

So the treasure provided to the righteous in 15: 6 is evidently not riches, for the wicked have that and yet have trouble. Only a competence and an inheritance for His children are promised (13: 22 ; 10: 3). [See under III. below.]

We should be more inclined to interpret the promise literally, if Proverbs anywhere without qualification called riches a good. To be sure great wealth gives protection (10: 15); but, on the other hand, poverty saves from attacks from which the rich must purchase safety (13: 8). Other proverbs are half-cynical observations regarding human nature.

> " Wealth addeth many friends ;
> " But the poor is separated from his friend," etc.
>
>   (19 : 4, 6, 7).

If his pupil had said, " Then I will seek wealth, that I may have many friends," the Sage would have replied,

> " What profiteth a friend that loveth not at all times ?
> " Or a brother that is not born for adversity?"

A similar observation which does not approve of the fact is,

> " The rich ruleth over the poor ;
> " And the borrower is servant to the lender."
>
>   (22 : 7).

The moral of which is simply, " Keep out of debt." Finally, the low estimate which the Sage puts on riches is shown forcibly in contrast with his absolute trust in Jehovah (18: 10, 11).

(Ps. 37, 73 and 112 ; Book of Job). The fact of God's moral government seemed to hinge on the answer. But even to-day the error of Job's friends has not wholly disappeared. The moral of E. P. Roe's novels, it has been said, is, " Become a Christian and you will get rich."

15

" The name of Jehovah is a strong tower ;
" The righteous runneth into it and is safe.
" The rich man's wealth is his strong city,
" And as a high wall—in his *own imagination*."

So if the Sages looked on wealth as a reward at all, it was as a very subordinate good.   Thus they agree with the author of Job, whose aim is to show that temporal prosperity is not, and could not, be a reward of piety.

III.   Man must have some property; if he is not to seek riches, how much is he to seek?

In apparent contradiction to the exclusion of worldly ambition is the emphasis placed upon the economical virtues. Sloth and idleness are condemned in the most emphatic terms (6: 6–11; 10: 4, 5; 21: 5; 24: 30–34; 27: 23–27). Note the motive urged:

" He becometh *poor* that dealeth with a slack hand ;
" But the hand of the diligent maketh rich."

Similarly various forms of prodigality are rebuked, because they bring poverty (21: 17; 23: 21; 28: 19).   The virtuous woman is one that clothes her family richly and acquires fields and vineyards (31: 10–31).   Honest labor has advantage over more rapid acquisition, in that the earnings are more permanent (13: 11).   Generous support of religion will bring abundance (3: 9, 10).   If riches are not to be sought, why should desire for them be thus appealed to?   It might be said that we could not expect consistency in detached proverbs.   But such a conclusion could be only the last resort. Perhaps this motive is urged because those here exhorted are not capable of appreciating higher considerations; the slothful is urged to diligence that he may gain the wealth he covets; and when he attains it, the Sage will point out that this was not the satisfaction he really craved, and that he must turn from it to wisdom.   But is there not a better explanation?   May not " rich" here be used loosely?   What is the meaning of *rich*, strictly defined?   Many say " no definition is possible."   It is a " purely relative term."   There is no use disputing about words, but it would be an immense advantage to attach a definite meaning to " rich" and " poor." *Rich,* equivalent to having a larger income than the average in the community; *poor,* equivalent to having a less income.

The average income of any community is, mathematically, what its total income, divided equally, would yield to each family. But it means more than this; for probably the incomes of the majority of the families approximate to this average. They would scorn to be called poor, they are independent, comfortable, self-respecting; but they are not rich; they have the average income, a competence.

Now, in the passage just quoted, "rich" *may* mean simply a competence. It need not mean any more than this to accomplish the purpose of the writer. He speaks from the standpoint of the poverty-stricken sluggard to whom the average degree of comfort seems "riches." Not only may this be, but in some of the passages quoted it evidently *is* the meaning. Thus the beautiful strophe in praise of diligence (27 : 23–27) concludes,

> " And thou shalt have goat's milk *enough* for thy food ;
> " For the food of thy household," etc. And
> " He that tilleth his land shall have *plenty* of bread."
> (28 : 19.)

What is promised is not riches, but a competence.

But there is a passage, the most striking and important in the Hokma, in which the words are used in the strict sense defined above. It is the prayer of Agur (30 : 7–9).

> " Give me neither poverty nor riches.
> " Feed me with the bread of my portion ;
> " Lest I be full and deny thee,
> " And say, Who is Jehovah ?
> " Or lest I should be poor and steal,
> " And use profanely the name of my God."

This carries the premises of the Hokma to their legitimate conclusion. Poverty is an acknowledged evil, riches a vanity and snare, yet man, needing food, shelter, clothing, requires property. How much? Agur voices the thought of all the Sages, The middle state is best. The expression, "bread of my portion," seems to be an allusion to the daily supply of manna, of which " he that gathered much had nothing over, and he that gathered little had no lack." If so, it may be paraphrased, " My portion of the supply which Thou wouldest have distributed equally, as the manna." For a comprehensive study of the biblical ethics of property shows that the truths taught by the miracle of the manna everywhere inspire later teaching regarding property, the truths that all good things come from Jehovah, and that He would have them so distributed that none should be surfeited, none lack. To Agur this is no longer merely God's will, he has made it his own choice. The ideal set forth before the nation has become his personal desire. In doing this, Agur has found a new reason for such distribution. In limiting his desires to a competence for the sake of the community, a man does not lose, he gains. What is best for the community is best for him; what harms it, harms him. Riches tempt to excess, self-confidence, neglect, and contempt of God (*cf.* Job 21: 7-15; 22: 17). Poverty tempts to crime and blasphemous complaints against God (*cf.* Prov. 19: 3; Isa. 8: 21). The middle state means provision enough awakening gratitude, yet not so much that one can forget the necessity of constant industry and God's bounty to renew the supply. Enough for use, not enough to become an idol. To these happy effects on morals and piety, named by Agur, we may add the facts, abundantly proven by observation, that the middle state is most favorable to the development of true manhood, to the highest intellectual attainments, the truest culture and most solid enjoyment.

Perhaps the thought arises, How far did Agur mean this prayer? Many have renounced wealth as the fox did the grapes, or as poets praise the pleasures of country life and take the first train for the city. But the Sages were not cynics. They were serious students of the problem of life. An utterance which so accords with and completes their system of economical morals must be sincere. If, moreover, these Proverbs are inspired, we cannot doubt that this prayer was intended to be the rule of our lives.

IV. How should wealth be used; especially by those whose greater ability enables them to produce more than the average?

The Sage unites with the Prophet in recognizing the just claims of the Priest.

> " Honor Jehovah with thy substance,
> " And with the first-fruits of all thy increase," etc.
>
> (3 : 9, 10.)

This implies a recognized system for the support of religion, and is a hearty exhortation to generous compliance.   Having given the claims of religion their true place at the outset, the Sage turns to his own special mission of pointing out man's duties to himself and his fellows.

Generous benevolence is the truest wisdom, for "mercy is twice blessed." It gives true increase, while niggardliness only impoverishes. Whether shown in positive giving or in refusing to use one's advantages to make gain out of others' necessity, it is equally praised (Prov. 11: 24–26). Not that benevolence will make rich. "He that watereth shall himself be watered;" but what he gave was pity and love, the money being simply its expression; what he receives is love and blessing. That this is the meaning is plain from verse 26, and also from the same paradoxical saying in the 13th chapter, which reminds one of Christ's favorite paradox:

> "There is that maketh himself rich and has nothing ;
> "There is that maketh himself poor yet hath great wealth."*
>
> (13 : 7.)

Compare also 21: 26; 22: 9; 28: 27.

Above all, benevolence is blessed by the favor of God:

> "He that hath pity upon the poor lendeth unto Jehovah ;
> "And his good deed will He pay him again."
>
> (19 : 17.)

True benevolence is the expression of love to God, which because it cannot bestow on Him that needed nothing, reveals itself in gifts to His needy children. Compare Matt. 25: 31–46, which has been called a New Testament exposition of this verse. 14: 21 and 31; 17: 5, and 22: 22, 23, state the converse, that neglect or oppression is an insult to God. So man holds property as a trust. From the unfaithful it shall be taken and given to the faithful steward,—

> "He that augmenteth his substance by usury and increase,
> "Gathereth it for him that hath pity on the poor."
>
> (28 : 8.)

Equally shall he be punished who gives to those who have no need, instead of regarding his surplus as dedicated to the

---

* Possibly *mithasser* means "feigneth himself rich," but the translation of the Revised Version accords with the strict meaning of the reflexive verb, and harmonizes best with the spirit of Proverbs.

wants of those who lack (22 : 16).   Giving should not be delayed with frivolous excuses:

" Who gives promptly gives twice" (3 : 27, 28).

Thus the Sages exhort to the same bearing of the burdens of the weak which so characterizes the Mosaic legislation. They do not say how much a man should give, nor even name the goal which is to set the standard of giving, as does the Pentateuch in holding up the ideal, " No poor in the land." Yet if we honestly accept " Agur's Prayer" as the rule of our lives, we shall not be long in finding the standard. It is not well for a man to have riches, i. e., more than the average in the community.   If his greater talents and advantages give him more, the remedy is in his own hands.   Let his " liberal scattering" at the same time save his neighbor from poverty and himself from riches. This inference the Sages do not draw, though 13 : 7 seems to praise even greater liberality.   In another article I hope to show that this is precisely the standard that Paul sets for Christian giving.

THE LIFE AND TIMES OF THE CHRIST,

BASED ON LUKE.

By William R. Harper and George S. Goodspeed,

Yale University.

(Copyrighted, 1890.)

STUDIES XLI. AND XLII.—CONTROVERSIES IN JERUSALEM. LUKE
20 : 1-47.

Remark.—It is desirable that in beginning each "study" the entire passage
assigned be read over rapidly and the main divisions of the narrative noted.

I. EXAMINATION OF THE MATERIAL.

[It will be noted that the following order is observed invariably in this work; (1) the
verse or section is read and its contents stated in a general way; (2) important or difficult words and phrases are studied; (3) a complete statement of
the contents of the verse or section is formed in view of the work already
done; (4) the religious teaching is sought.]

§ 1. Chapter 20 : 1-8.

1. Read the passage and note a subject, e. g. *Jesus' Authority questioned.*
2. Of words and phrases study the following: (1) *chief priests and the Scribes*, etc.
   (20 : 1), i. e. the representatives of the three orders of the Sanhedrim; (2) *what
   authority* (20 : 2), of prophet, teacher or the Christ? (3) *who gave*, etc. (a)
   inquiry into the basis of the authority, (b) motive of the question? (4) *the
   baptism* (20 : 4), i. e. his work as represented by this symbol.
3. The student may make a condensed statement of the passage.
4. When an inquirer is not honest and sincere, he will get no light from Jesus.

§ 2. Chapter 20 : 9-18.

1. The student may read the passage and decide on a subject.
2. The following important or difficult words and phrases are to be studied: (1) *a
   vineyard* (20 : 9), recalls Isa. 5 : 3-7; (2) *give him of the fruit* (20 : 10), either
   (a) as rent for the land, or (b) as his rightful property, (c) which they neglect
   to produce; (3) *beloved* (20 : 13), characteristic of Luke; (4) *son*, does Jesus

claim here to be God's son? (5) *that the inheritance,* etc. (20 : 14), how could they have imagined any such result? (6) *others* (20 : 16), who? (7) *the stone* etc. (20 : 17), note (a) the figure itself, (b) the original application, (c) Jesus' use of it.

3. A statement of the thought is as follows : *He speaks in a parable of " a vineyard which the owner rented to husbandmen and went far away. He sends three servants in due time to them one after the other to receive the fruits, but all are ill-treated, each worse than the other. The son is, thereupon, sent, but instead of paying him regard, they kill him, hoping thus to possess the vineyard themselves. Will not the owner destroy them and give the vineyard to others ?" When the people reply, " Far be it from him," Jesus adds, " The scripture tells of the rejected stone which was afterward put in the highest place. Fall over it and you shall be sore harmed. Should it fall upon you, you shall be utterly destroyed."*

4. The student may consider and decide on a religious lesson here.

§ 3. Chapter 20 : 19–26.

1. After reading the verses, consider the subject : *Discussion about Tribute.*
2. The student may make a special study of (1) *against them* (20 : 19), (2) *righteous* (20 : 20), (3) *acceptest not the person* (20 : 21), (4) *craftiness* (20 : 23), (5) *image* (20 : 24), (6) v. 25, (7) *before the people* (20 : 26).
3. The summary of the thought is as follows : *At once the authorities, had they dared, would have seized him for his attack on them. They send men to engage him in treasonable discussion. He is asked by them, after compliments to his teaching, whether "giving tribute to Cæsar is according to God's law." He takes a penny and calling attention to Cæsar's image and name thereon, says, " Give to Cæsar what is his, and to God what is His," an answer which amazed and silenced them.*
4. A religious thought of the passage is found in Jesus' principle that we have a duty toward the state as well as toward God.

§ 4. Chapter 20 : 27–40.

1. Criticise the statement of the subject : *Questions about the Resurrection.*
2. Important words are : (1) *Sadducees* (20 : 27), their history and opinions? (2) *resurrection,* i. e. of the body ; (3) *asked,* their motive? (4) *Moses wrote* (20 : 28), cf. Deut. 25 : 5, 6, note the custom ; (5) *that world* (20 : 35), i. e. as distinct from " this world," implying that it is in the era of the " resurrection ; " (6) *Moses shewed* (20 : 37), what light on Jesus' idea of the authorship of Exodus? (7) *all live,* etc. (20 : 38), i. e. (a) " all creatures," or (b) all his children such as in v. 37 ; (8) *well said* (20 : 39), spirit of the reply ?
3. Study the following statement of the contents : *Sadducees who deny the resurrection, come and ask how Moses' law about levirate marriage is to result, in the resurrection, to a woman who in obedience to it, has been married successively to seven brothers. He replies by declaring that " the marriage custom of this world does not apply to the other world of the resurrection life. There is a resurrection, however, as Moses' record of God's pledge to the patriarchs shows, for to have Him as your God means to live." The Scribes applaud his answer, and none dare to question him further.*
4. A religious thought of supreme importance is the assurance that they who are God's shall live unto Him.

§ 5. Chapter 20 : 41–44.

1. The student may read and decide on a subject.
2. (1) *He said* (20 : 41), a new attitude ; (2) *say they*, who ? (3) *David himself saith* (20 : 42), light on Jesus' idea of the authorship of this psalm ? (4) *Lord* (20 : 44), a higher than a human or temporal Christ.
3. A condensation of the verses is as follows : *He asks them, How can the statement be made that the Christ is David's son, when David calls him Lord, saying in the Psalms, " the Lord told my Lord to sit at his right hand till he had subdued his enemies ? " Can he be son and Lord of David, too ?*
4. We are brought face to face with the great assertion that Jesus the Christ is more than a human being. As such, what shall be our relation to him ?

§ 6. Chapter 20 : 45–47.

1. Read the verses and note a subject : *The Final Warning.*
2. (1) *In the hearing*, etc. (20 : 43), significance of this ? (2) *in long robes* (20 : 46), i. e. (a) official pride, or (b) to attract attention ; (3) *love*, etc., all significant of what ? (4) *devour widows' houses* (20 : 47), (a) by their superior knowledge of law, or (b) by religious chicanery.
3. The student may make a brief statement of the thought.
4. Note carefully the course and issue of selfish pride, its presence even in religion.

II. CLASSIFICATION OF THE MATERIAL.

1. Contents and Summary.

1) **The Contents.** The following table is to be made familiar.

CONTROVERSIES IN JERUSALEM.

§ 1. Jesus' Authority Questioned.
§ 2. Parable of the Wicked Husbandmen.
§ 3. Discussion about Tribute.
§ 4. Questions about the Resurrection.
§ 5. The Quotation and its Lesson.
§ 6. The Final Warning.

2) **The Summary.** The student may sum up the several passages into a statement of the whole.

2. Observations upon the Material.

The following " observations " upon the passage are to be criticised.

272) 20 : 1. The work of Jesus in Jerusalem is interrupted and hampered by the controversies into which the religious authorities persist in drawing him.

273) 20 : 2. The design of this question seems to be either (1) to overawe him, or (2) to discredit him with the people.

274) 20 : 4, 5.   The question of John's prophetic authority was not merely a catch question but was an argument from John on behalf of his own authority.*

275) 20 : 2.   Rabbis received their authorization to teach from well-known and accredited masters.

276) 20 : 9.   Jesus even now would endeavor to save the people from the consequences of rejecting him.†

277) 20 : 9-15.   The parable represents in a general way the history of the Jewish Theocracy in its relation to God up to and including its dealing with Jesus.

278) 20 : 13, 41-44.   Jesus seems to claim here that he himself as the Christ is more than man.‡

279) 20 : 16.   The people catch a glimpse of the awful future without being moved thereby to change their ways, and hence Jesus calls their attention to the result (vs. 17, 18).

280) 20 : 25.   The reply of Jesus did not evade the issue, but allowed the duty of paying tribute. He had no design of revolution. By that answer he escaped the danger of Roman hostility but lost the help of the people. §

281) This is the first time that the Sadducees have been brought into relations with Jesus. ‖

282) 20 : 37.   The answer of Jesus shows how deep and new was his understanding and exposition of the Old Testament.

---

* He identified his authority with John's, so far as the greater more than covers the less. They stood upon the same platform, authenticated by the same direct inspiration and accredited by the same power. · · · If John was of God, what he said of Jesus was of God. An acceptance of John's baptism and teaching as heavenly, involved the acceptance of the claims of Jesus who was the end of all John's preaching. *Vallings*, p. 165.

† The very character of this parable showed that it did not proclaim an unalterable fate, but was only a threatening prophecy which the timely repentance of the people, either now or in the days to come, might nullify. It is involved in the nature of the parable, that it does not sketch a history, but exhibits a divine law through the regulations of natural life. The husbandmen must necessarily be discharged if they continue obstinate. *Weiss*, III., p. 245.

‡ What the scribes persistently repelled and in the end condemned him for was his *assertion of Divinity*. In this passage (v. 41) he shows from their own Scriptures that whoever was Messiah *must be Divine*. *Pulp. Com.* II., p. 170.

The account given in this parable of the mission of the son has an important bearing on . . . . the personal self-consciousness of Christ. . . . The son is described as the only and well-beloved son of his father and it is natural to suppose that as that son represents the Speaker, He claims for Himself all that he ascribes to the former. Bruce, *Parab. Teach.*, p. 457.

§ A rigid alternative is put before him : theoretically and practically He must solve the great question which is burning in the heart of every devout Israelite. . . . The usual idea is quite mistaken, which supposes that Jesus evaded the question after all, and got Himself cleverly out of the dilemma. . . . By placing the duty of a subject alongside duty to God, He takes the point from the deceptive alternative, about which Jewish Radicalism boasted. He does not say directly that the duty of submissiveness is conjoined with duty to God, or limited thereby ; but he indicates that the two are in no wise contradictory, but are equally incumbent. . . . With these words Jesus frustrated the plan of His enemies. They could not summon Him for treason before the Roman procurator. But He knew that with these same words He had pronounced His own sentence of comdemnation. This was His final refusal to countenance a Jewish revolution. It was the destruction of all hopes of a political kingdom of the Messiah, and the people could never forgive such a bitter disappointment. *Weiss*, III., pp. 239, 240.

It was an answer which elevated the controversy into quite another sphere, where there was no conflict between what was due to God and to Man. Nor did it speak harshly of the Nationalist aspirations, nor yet plead the cause of Rome. It said not whether the rule of Rome was right or should be permanent—but only what all must have felt to be Divine. *Edersheim*, II., p. 386 (472).

‖ This is, it may be noted, the one occasion in the Gospel history in which our Lord comes into direct collision with the Sadducees. On the whole, while distinctly condemning and refuting their characteristic error, the tone in which He speaks is less stern than that in which He addresses the Pharisees. *Plumptre*, p. 332.

283) 20 : 41–44. Jesus brings out here (1) the folly of those who expected merely a human Christ, (2) the reasonableness of his claim to be more tnan man. *

284) 20 : 46, 47. In this warning, given at so much greater length in Mt. 23, Jesus passed from argument to scorching denunciation of the Pharisees and Scribes. †

3. Topics for Study.

1) **The Political Situation.** [Obs. 280] : (1) Note the existence of Cæsar's rule in Jerusalem (Lk. 20 : 20–25). (2) Learn something of the way this rule was regarded (a) by the people in general, (b) by the Pharisees, (c) by the Herodians. (3) Consider how Jesus was situated in relation to this rule, (a) what was expected of him as the Christ in national affairs, (b) the probable attitude of the Romans in view of this expectation. (4) From this point of view consider the critical importance of this question and its answer (vs. 23, 25). (5) Study the answer of Jesus (v. 25), and decide whether (a) it was an evasion, (b) it was a virtual surrender to Cæsar, (c) it offered a new solution of the problem. (6) If the latter, endeavor to state the principle which Jesus here laid down, and observe the position of the Apostolic Church in relation to it (Rom. 13 : 1– ; 1 Pet. 2 : 13–17 ; Acts. 4 : 19).

2) **Jesus as a Reasoner.** ‡ (1) Recall the part taken by Jesus in the discussions of Lk. 20 : 1–47. (2) Seek examples of the following characteristics in his answers, (a) candor, (b) simplicity, (c) boldness, (d) keenness, (e) gentleness, (f) severity, (g) wit. (3) Inquire as to the evidence of (a) his use of verbal quibbling answers intended to puzzle, (b) arguments based on literal and formal grounds, (c) arguments on broad, spiritual principles, (d) a marvelous insight into the O. T. Scriptures and into the human mind. (4) In a general way sum up the purpose and the results of these discussions as relates to (a) the hostile questioners, (b) Jesus and his disciples, (c) the people.

---

* This, he pointed out to them, was the old faith, the doctrine taught in their own inspired Scriptures. But this was not the doctrine of the Jews in the time of our Lord. They . . . . expected for their Messiah a mere " beloved man." *Pul. Com.* II., p. 170.

The simple solution of the question must be sought for in the fact that the Messiah has no specific dignity, because of His being a descendant of David, but He descends from David in accordance with the promise, for He is chosen by God to that unique dignity without which He cannot bring about the consummation of salvation . . . . So long as the Davidic descent of the Messiah was made the starting point, the ascension of David's throne, in the sense of the political expectations, was the indispensable condition for the fulfilment of His vocation. But if it was once acknowledged that as simply belonging to David's line, he had no claim to that unique dignity, then it was plainly a matter of indifference for the attainment of that end whether He ever ascended the throne of His fathers as popular expectation expected Him to do. *Weiss*, III., p. 201.

† At last He carried the war into their own territory, and convicted them of such ignorance or lack of candor as completely put them to shame before the onlookers. Then when He had silenced them, He let loose the storm of His indignation, and delivered against them the Philippic which is recorded in the twenty-third chapter of Matthew. Giving unrestrained expression to the pent-up criticism of a lifetime, He exposed their hypocritical practices in sentences that fell like strokes of lightning, and made them a scorn and laughing stock, not only to the hearers then, but to all the world since. It was the final breach between Him and them. Stalker, *Life of Christ*, p. 118.

‡ A most attractive and profitable discussion of this subject is found in Stalker's *Imago Christi*, Chapt. 15, " Christ as a Controversialist."

4. Religious Teaching.

The student may select a subject, such as " The Use and the Ethics of Controversy," or " Religion and Politics," or any other with which this chapter is concerned, and work out its teachings.

STUDIES XLIII. AND XLIV.—THE FUTURE. LUKE 21 : 1-38.

Remark.—It is desirable that in beginning this "study" (1) the material of the preceding "study" be reviewed, and (2) the entire passage assigned be read over rapidly and the main divisions of the narrative noted.

I. EXAMINATION OF THE MATERIAL.

[It will be noted that the following order is observed invariably in this work; (1) the verse or section is read and its contents stated in a general way; (2) important or difficult words and phrases are studied; (3) a complete statement of the contents of the verse or section is formed in view of the work already done; (4) the religious teaching is sought.]

§ 1. Chapter 21 : 1-4.

1. Read the verses and observe the subject, e. g.: *The Widow's Offerings.*
2. Following are important words and phrases: (1) *looked up* (21 : 1), from where he was seated, cf. Mk. 12 : 41; (2) *gifts*, not for the poor but for the temple service; (3) *all the living* (21 : 4), how did Jesus know this?
3. The student may make the statement of thought.
4. The religious teaching seems to be that our devotion to God is measured, not by the amount of our gifts, but by the self-denial manifested in them for His service.

§ 2. Chapter 21 : 5-11.

1. The subject of vs. 5-36 is one, i. e. *Teaching concerning the Future ;* read the passage vs. 5-11, and note the subject, *The Prospect of World-commotions.*
2. Important and difficult words and phrases are : (1) *some* (21 : 5), cf. Mk. 13 : 1; (2) *they asked* (21 : 7), cf. Mk. 13 : 3 for the persons and place; (3) v. 7, note two questions (a) "when," (b) "what sign;" (4) *these things* (21 : 7), (a) according to v. 6 they are the destruction of the temple, (b) but cf. Mt. 24 : 3 for the addition of the "end of the age," (c) does the reference in Lk. limit the whole discourse? (5) *he said* (21 : 8), to what does his answer apply? (6) *my name*, i. e. as the Christ; (7) *the time*, for what? (8) *come to pass first* (21 : 9), i. e. before the end; (9) *not immediately*, i. e. one does not follow close on the other; (10) *nation* (21 : 10), are particular nations referred to?
3. A condensation of the thought is : *Jesus answers a comment on the beauty of the temple by predicting its total destruction. They ask the time and the sign of this thing. He replies, " False Christs will try to lead you astray ; great social disturbances and terrible commotions in nature will come long before the end."*
4. The thought of the passage connects itself with the insight into things which Jesus had—they saw the goodly outside, he saw the real truth : what this insight should mean for us.

§ 3. Chapter 21 : 12-19.

1. The student, after reading the verses, may state a subject.
2. Important words and phrases to be studied are : (1) *before*, etc. (21 : 12), cf. Mt. 24 : 9 and reconcile the two passages ; (2) *turn unto you for a testimony* (21 : 13), either (a) testimony shall be rendered to your innocence there, or (b) you shall be enabled to testify to Jesus there, cf. Acts 5 : 29, etc., or (c) your fidelity there will prove a glorious testimony ; (3) *not a hair*, etc. (21 : 18), how reconcile with verse 16? (4) *in your patience*, etc. (21 : 19), "in the exercise of such a spirit, you shall establish yourselves in true life, character."
3. The student may make his own statement of thought.
4. The religious thought in this passage is the revelation of the power of adversity to develop and ripen a character which endures through trust in God.

§ 4. Chapter 21 : 20-33.

1. Read the passage and criticise the subject : *The decisive Sign and its Issue.*
2. The student may study the following important words and phrases : (1) *but when*, etc. (21 : 20), i. e. "the former things have been signs of the distant event *but* now comes the imminent sign ; " (2) *compassed with armies*, cf. Mt. 24 : 15; (3) *then know*, etc., this was what they desired to know in v. 7 ; (4) *things which are written* (21 : 22), where? (5) *until*, etc. (21 : 24), the desolation is to continue *until* another event is to occur ; (6) *times of the Gentiles*, i. e. (a) opportunities of the Gentiles, (b) their opportunities to rule Israel or to accomplish God's judgments, or to avail themselves of God's salvation ; (7) *and there shall be*, etc. (21 : 25), is this (a) " and then, after the fulfillment, there shall be " a consummation, or (b) " and at this time of Jerusalem's encompassment by armies there shall be " etc? (8) *then shall they see* (21 : 27), at the end of this awful season of distress, attending either (a) the fulfilling of the times of the Gentiles, or (b) the destruction of Jerusalem; (9) *Son of Man coming* etc., either (a) in his final advent, or (b) the awful calamity of Jerusalem is His coming, cf. Lk. 9 : 27 ; Mk. 8 : 38; 9 : 1 ; (10) *these things begin*, etc. (21 : 28), i. e. the things of vs. 20-26 ; (11) *your redemption*, i. e. either (a) from the power of the Jewish Theocracy, or (b) from the power of the world at large ; (12) *this generation*, etc. (21 : 32) if the "all things," means the events that include the second advent and final consummation, how interpret this verse? (a) "this race of men or of Israel shall not," etc., (b) the germs of all these events *did* appear in that one generation and so they could be said to be fulfilled; (c) Jesus and his disciples expected this consummation to come in a few years but they were mistaken.
3. Note the following statements of the contents of the passage : *But when you see Jerusalem besieged, then know that the end is come. Hasten from the land. Alas for the weak ! There will be great distress. The people shall be slain or taken captive in the midst of awful disturbances in the natural world, remaining subject, till the Gentiles have had their opportunities. This is the time when I shall come in glory and you shall be redeemed. As the budding of the fig-tree tells of summer nigh, so these events, all occurring in this generation, indicate the coming of the Kingdom. My word alone is sure.*
4. It is suggested here that the coming of the Christ means precisely opposite things to different classes of people. The reason of this and the lesson of it will afford profitable reflection.

§ 5.   Chapter 21 : 34-36.

1. The subject suggested is, *The Final Warning.*
2. The student may examine for himself the important words, especially; (1) *that day* (21 : 34), (2) *prevail to escape* (21 : 36), (3) *stand before.*
3. The student may make a statement of the thought.
4. The lesson of watchfulness of one's self as the best way of watching for the Son of Man is here suggested.

§ 6.   Chapter 21 : 37, 38.

1. Read and observe the subject suggested: *The Work in Jerusalem.*
2. (1) *Every night he went out* (21 : 37), why? (2) *all the people* (21 : 38), note the presence of many visitors at this season ; (3) *early*, significance of this?
3. A summary statement of the passage is: *Daily he would teach before the mass of the people, beginning early in the temple, and at night he lodged in the Mount of Olives.*
4. The student may state the religious teaching.

II. CLASSIFICATION OF THE MATERIAL.

1.   Contents and Summary.

1) **The Contents.** The following table of the contents is to be made thoroughly familiar.

THE FUTURE.

§ 1.   THE WIDOW'S OFFERINGS.
     TEACHING CONCERNING THE FUTURE.
§ 2.   1) THE PROSPECT OF WORLD-COMMOTIONS.
§ 3.   2) THE PROSPECT OF PERSONAL TRIALS.
§ 4.   3) THE DECISIVE SIGN AND ITS ISSUE.
§ 5.   4) THE FINAL WARNING.
§ 6.   THE WORK IN JERUSALEM.

2) **The Summary.** The student may exercise himself in making a careful summary statement of the address of Jesus.

2.   Observations upon the Material.

285) 21 : 3, 4. It is in relation to the offering to God, not the exercise of charity toward the poor, that the widow is commended.

286) 21 : 5-36. Luke's account of the discourse differs in many important respects from those of Matthew and Mark.

287) 21 : 5. The beauty of the Temple in its architecture and adornment was widely celebrated.

288) 21 : 8. The first sign of the coming of the event, though far off, is the appearance of false Christs.

289) 21 : 9. The second sign is the presence of great social and political convulsions.

290) 21 : 11 The third sign is the existence of physical disturbances.

291) 21 : 12-16. The fourth sign is the persecution of the believers.

292) 21 : 20. Luke would seem to be interpreting the dark parallel saying in Mt. 24 : 15 and Mk. 13 : 14. Is it possible that he wrote his Gospel after the event and therefore so plainly stated the real meaning of the enigmatic prophecy of Jesus?

293) 21 : 32. This verse is the critical point of the whole discourse; it suggests that Luke arranged his report of the discourse without reference to any prophecy of Jesus' second advent.

294) 21 : 37, 38. Luke seems here to give a summary statement of the general course of Jesus' work in Jerusalem

3. Topics for Study.

1) **The Discourse of Jesus.** [Obs. 286, 288–293] : The student noting (1) the elements of difficulty in understanding this discourse, and (2) the two principal explanations of it—may work out the topic into its details.

2) **The Jerusalem Ministry.** [Obs. 272, 273, 276, 294] : (1) Recall the purpose with which Jesus entered Jerusalem. (2) Note e. g. in 21 · 37, 38, the general features of the ministry. (3) Observe the opposition of the authorities, the form it took and the effect upon the ministry. (4) Collect the facts in 19 : 47, 48 ; 20 : 1, 19, 26, 45–47 ; 21 : 37, 38 and in a general way determine the results of the work of these days upon the people, (5) Compare Mt. 23 : 37–24 : 1 as indicating his conclusion concerning the results of this ministry. (6) Consider carefully the chronological hints in Mk. 14 : 1 ; John 12 : 1, 12 ; Mk. 11 : 12, 20, with a view to determining the length and order of the events in the ministry.

4. Religious Teaching.

The student will do well to recall in connection with this passage former teachings in Luke, and consider the subject of *watchfulness:* (1) a needful element in the Christian life in view of the coming of the Christ, which is (a) uncertain (b) sudden. (2) The true spirit of watchfulness, (a) not anxiety, or (b) constant thought, but (c) readiness as manifested in fidelity to present duty, and striving after perfection of character.

A "SYMPOSIUM" ON THE "TEN BEST BOOKS FOR THE STUDY OF THE BIBLE."

The experience of men in the use of books is always valuable to themselves. It is much more valuable to those who are beginning to form their libraries and are doubtful as to the selections which they ought to make. A poor book used in the study of the Bible is worse than useless. It is positively injurious. It is likely to lead to the adoption of vicious methods or leave the student with shallow or incorrect conceptions lying at the basis of all his future work. The STUDENT has, therefore, sought to obtain from some scholarly ministers help on behalf of their less experienced brethren in this very line of the best books for Bible study. Some answers, which will be found full of interest, are herewith printed. The thanks of the readers of this journal are due to the writers who have made out these lists for the guidance and profit of all who desire to get and use the best helps in the study of God's Word.

From Prof. GEORGE H. GILBERT, Ph. D.

The ten books which I have found most helpful in the study of the Bible are, I should say :—

1. The Bible.
2. The Lexicon (Hebrew and Greek).
3. The Grammar (Hebrew and Greek).
4. The Greek Concordance.
5. The Greek Harmony of the Gospels.
6. R. D. Hitchcock's Lectures on Church History.
7. Edersheim's Life and Times of Jesus the Messiah.
8. Ewald's History of Israel.
9. Weiss' New Testament Introduction.
10. Weiss' New Testament Theology.

Chicago Theological Seminary.

From Rev. EMORY J. HAYNES, D. D.

If you mean *component parts* of the Bible, I should name Genesis, Exodus, Psalms, Isaiah, the Four Gospels, Romans, Corinthians, 1 and 2 Timothy.

If you mean books on the Bible, aside from the original Greek and Hebrew texts, I should say—

1. Lange's Commentaries.
2. Andrews' Life of our Lord (or Geikie, Farrar, or Hanna).
3. Smith's Bible Dictionary.
4. Cruden's Concordance.
5. Thomson's Land and the Book.
6. Wesley's Sermons.
7. Hodge's Systematic Theology.

8. Schaff's Histories (for the New Testament).

9. Stanley's Jewish Church, or Ewald's History of the Jews (for the Old Testament).

10. Any one of the several "Gazetteers" with maps.

Tremont Temple, Boston, Mass.

From Rev. J. L. JENKINS, D. D.

Ten books that have helped me in Bible study :—

1. Trench's Hulsean Lectures, "The Fitness of Holy Scripture for Unfolding the Spiritual Life of Men."

2. Mozley's Ruling Ideas in Early Ages.
   . Stanley's Jewish Church.

3. Ewald's History of Israel.
   Stalker's Life of Jesus Christ.

6. Stalker's Life of St. Paul.
   Stanley on Corinthians.
   . Lightfoot and Ellicott's commentaries ; all of them.

9. Maurice on St. John's Gospel and Epistles.

10. The Bible Commentary on the Old Testament.

I must add—

11. Bruce's The Training of the Twelve, and also his

12. Parabolic Teaching of Christ, and his

13. Galilean Gospel.

Pittsfield, Mass.

From Rev. Professor J. B. THOMAS, D. D.

I have been delayed in responding to your request, not so much by lack of time as by lack of wit concerning the problem suggested. I never had asked myself such a question, and, after some meditation, have not the slightest confidence in my ability to answer it in a way that will materially advance its solution. So much depends upon the attainments, the aims, and the temper of the individual, that in actual life such an appeal, to a pastor for instance, would be apt to receive widely different answers in single cases. In the absolute sense, I doubt if there are any "ten best."

I name, therefore (passing by concordance, dictionary, and Revised Version, which will occur to everybody), a few books which I think likely to be serviceable to the average Bible student, without assuming that they are pre-eminent or enough. I value highly—

1. The Cambridge Bible for Schools.

2. Edersheim's Life of Christ.

3. Thomson's Land and Book.

4. Arnot on Parables.

5. Trench on Miracles.

6. Conybeare and Howson's Paul.

7. Clark's Handbooks for Bible-Classes.

8. Westcott's Introduction to the Gospels.

9. Conder's Handbook of the Bible.

10. Geikie's Life of Christ.

Newton Centre, Mass.

From Rev. Philip A. Nordell, D. D.

Without knowing particularly the grade of students for whom to select ten useful volumes on Bible study, it is somewhat difficult to make a wise choice. For a person of average intelligence in our churches or Sunday-schools, the ten following works will prove very serviceable :—

1. Geikie's Life of Christ.
2. Geikie's Hours with the Bible.
3. Vincent's Word-Studies in the New Testament.
4. Thomson's The Land and the Book.
5. Godet's Studies in the Gospels.
6. Godet's Studies in the Epistles.
7. Briggs' or Orelli's Messianic Prophecy.
8. Isaiah, by Driver, in " Men of the Bible " series.
9. Sears' The Heart of Christ, or The Fourth Gospel.
10. Farrar's Life and Work of St. Paul.

From the above list I have purposely excluded commentaries and books of reference with which each student can provide himself, according to his need and ability. There may be added to this list a recommendation to every one who wishes to obtain a larger and more thorough knowledge of the Bible to read diligently every month The Old and New Testament Student.

New London, Conn.

ℭoreign ℭorrespondence.

One does not go too far when saying that there are more persons in America who are following with interest the trend of the Hexateuchal discussion than there are in Germany. The scholars seem to have *settled* the question, the masses do not know that there has been 'a question. The majority of the evangelical divines in Germany are as rigid in their adherence to their "Luther" as Americans used to be to their "Clarke" or "Henry." The people either take no interest in biblical questions or accept the traditional views. To be a "rationalist" may in Germany be said to be a hopeful sign, for in contrast with the majority the rationalist is an exponent neither of agnosticism nor indifference. To express this in a general statement, there is no such thing as popular Bible study in Germany. It is not the province of this letter to treat of the unfortunate condition of Germany. Our inquiry shall be concerning the influence this small minority of Teutonic students is having or will have upon the study of the Scriptures in our own country.

It is necessary to confine our inquiries to the existing literature and its probable influence. The possibilities of the future products of German pens no one can estimate. Wellhausen, accepting his own results as final, retires from the discussion of biblical questions and confines his lectures to Arabic archaeology. Orelli, on the other hand, belonging to what may at least be called a liberal school, accepts in Isaiah 53 the possibility of the prophet's having "spoken wiser than he knew." His interpretation we find approved by an eminent professor in Göttingen. Is not this diversity of opinions and tendencies alone sufficient to cause us to question the ultimate end of German thought?

No prominent writer in Germany could be called conservative according to the American standard of "orthodoxy." The most influential theologian in Germany to-day is Harnack of Berlin. He is attracting not only more readers, but his lectures are more largely attended than those of any other man. His recent valuable work, "Das neue Testament um 200," is a sufficient exponent of his position. He is a liberal of the liberals. Hence while his work would be of great value to the most conservative student, if he is trying to follow modern scholarship, it can never meet with the favor in America that it is having in Germany. Weiss is perhaps exercising the most influence in the other direction. His readings of his own "Leben Jesu" are enthusiastically attended. His latest edition of that peerless work is so much better than the old English translation that the English reader is at great disadvantage in trying to gain the writer's best thought. His most recent work, "Einleitung in das neue Testament," which is known in America through the valuable translation published by Funk and Wagnalls is considered even by many Germans to be the best "Introduction" yet written. It may be a surprise to old Leipzig students to know that the staunch views of the much lamented Dr. Franz Delitzsch find now no supporter in that former stronghold of conservatism. A vigorous young scholar, not yet known through his writings, Prof.

Guthe, is gaining quite a following among the students though he expresses views which dumbfound the Lutheran veterans of Leipzig. The already famous young Arabic scholar, Dr. Socin, who has recently gone there from Tübingen is quite as liberal as Guthe. Leipzig has lost its prestige in America, but the reputation of Dr. Delitzsch is only heightened by his recently translated Isaiah and the almost posthumous work, "Messianische Weissagungen." It will be of interest to the numerous admirers of Prof. Delitzsch to know that his work on Prophecy appeared in the book stores the day before his death. Every Bible student knows what a powerful influence this eminent scholar has throughout the student world. How his latest views will affect his numerous followers is an interesting question. The age at which he first gave expression to liberal opinions necessarily prevented his going to extremes. Where will be the goal of those who care to fully follow his studies and reach yet more mature conclusions? There is a rich field of speculation suggested in his last three books. Who of the earnest American students will dare explore its utmost bounds?

Strack and Zöckler's Commentary has not met with the success among Germans that it will doubtless have in America. That a work is conservative is a recommendation to American students; that all the writers are of that school suggests to the critical German that too great efforts have been made to secure such contributors and he is justly suspicious. It is unfortunate that all the writers for this work have not the reputation that its editors and the popular Orelli have. As in Lange's great work true scholarly interpretation has been sacrificed to conservatism. Americans should be very proud of the thoroughly critical work done by Prof. Gregory in his now completed "Prolegomena." Dr. Gregory is an American, at present Professor in Leipzig and has had the honor of being chosen to complete the unfinished work of the great Tischendorf. His volumes on the New Testament text are models of accuracy and will be indispensable to students in that department and in fact to all searchers after internal evidences. Of the other German works which have appeared within the last year it must be said the valuable ones all express extreme views. Wellhausen's "Composition des Hexateuchs und der historischer Bücher" is already known. It is a little surprising to see that an excellent book on the pastoral epistles by Knoke gives to them the latest possible date. Perhaps it will not be out of place here to mention for the benefit of students conversant with German a few of the books published during the last year which have met with the highest approval in Germany. Holtzmann's "Hand Kommentar zum neuen Testament," will be criticized by Americans. It is a popular, but too rationalistic work. Steck, "Galatäer Brief" and Knelling, "Der erste Brief Pauli an Timotheus" are good commentaries. Other critical works, some of which are already known from older editions are Baudissin, "Geschichte des alttestamentlichen Priestertums;" Köhler, "Lehrbuch der biblischen Geschichte des alten Testaments;" Schlatter, "Einleitung in die Bibel;" Baethgen, "Beitrage zur semitischen Religionsgeschichte;" Everling, "Die paulinische Angelologie und Dämonologie;" Schultz, "Altestamentliche Theologie;" Schlottman, "Kompendium der biblischen Theologie der alten und neuen Testaments."

These are but a few of the new works or new editions which have recently found favor abroad. What is to be done with this flood of literature, nearly all pointing in a direction we hesitate to follow? To the settlement of the important questions involved the American student brings now a better equipment than ever before, a deep religious faith, which the German generally lacks, he has the sympathy of thousands of fellow students, he has a waiting public, anxious to hear his results, but he may be, alas, without the grubbing habits which help the German to conclusions. These incentives, despite the necessarily absent quality, are sufficient to urge him to study and thought. Whatever be the results of his efforts, it is not improbable, his more slowly reached conclusions, if he can lay aside his prejudices, will bring him more nearly to the truth than the German has attained. If this be so, that fact and the good he may accomplish by making his results known should stir every student of the Scripture, be he specialist or not, to greater exertions. It should make him open his eyes to what the Europeans are pleased to call "results" and to close them temporarily to the burdensome traditions that prevent free, scholarly work. Prepared then for vigorous effort what will be accomplished? The question, "Whither?" has lately been made popular in America. In biblical study a few possibilities may be suggested, even though it be with hesitation. The conservative American student will probably change many of his views. If he comes to know a different Bible, as many fear, he will know it better. If he lays aside some old interpretations he will not rest till he has new and better ones. He will not go so far as the critics, it may be safely said, but he will learn to use their results for the attainment of more moderate ends. He will be a better man for having made his efforts, he will be a more useful man for having gained his new information, but it must be said he may shock the "pillars" by accepting an uninspired Bible or he may have exactly the same theology, truths, faith that he had when he began. To become acquainted with Truth he must examine the results of scholars even though stared in the face by the possibility of a great change of opinions. Does he care enough for the truth to make the investigation? Trusting to that Guidance to which he looks in his study of "the Word" he will surely attain results and the results will help him and others to better lives.

Hear what the grandest of German scholars of to-day, or rather of yester-day, has said. In the preface to his "Messianische Weissagungen," Dr. Del-itzsch writes, "It is in a critical time in biblical and especially in Old Testa-ment study that the evening of my life is falling. This crisis repels me by the satisfaction its advocates find in destruction, in wholesale denials, in unspirit-ual profanity; but this crisis shall also prove, as did many crises in the time of the apostle Paul, a lever for advancing knowledge, thereby releasing and declaring the elements of truth that are therein. For as primeval creation began with chaos, so in the advance of understanding, and particularly of the spiritual life, from epoch to epoch, the new comes from the chaos of the old. It is not now the business of one alone to bring to completeness this work of sifting, purification, reforming. Therefore let us interest ourselves in this, though our contribution be ever so small."   C. N. ZEUBLIN.

Paris, 25, August, 1890.

𝔅𝔦𝔟𝔩𝔦𝔠𝔞𝔩 𝔑𝔬𝔱𝔢𝔰.

The Word "Prophet." In the *Andover Review* for September an article, by Rev. G. B. Spalding, D. D., discusses the "Hebrew Prophet and the Christian Preacher." He calls attention to the prevalent idea that it is the ordinary view of the prophet that he was "only a predictor," "simply a foreteller," as the preposition *pro* in the word would seem to favor. But he maintains the better, the true view that the central idea of the word is that of one "to whom God reveals Himself and through whom He speaks. The revelation may or may not relate to the future. The prophet is a *forthteller*, not necessarily a *foreteller*. The prophet was the interpreter of the Divine Will. The early English scholars kept to this biblical use of the word. Prophecy was to them synonymous with preaching."

Miracles in the Gospels. The critical study which Mr. Wright has given to the gospels, as shown in his *Composition of the Four Gospels*, has determined him in the view that the Synoptical Gospels contain three cycles of teaching differing in content and date. The first and earliest appears in Mark in its fullest form. It is, from the point of view of historical criticism, the most trustworthy. But the extraordinary fact about the contents of this earliest and most historical tradition is that it is most full of the miraculous element. The later cycles contain the simpler teaching of trust in God and love to man, humility, prayer. The first cycle, which modern research has established in its historical character, is that which most demands a belief in the supernatural. This is exactly the opposite of that which would be expected if the gospel narratives were fictions or legends. The earlier would be the simpler, the later would be overlaid with miracles and wonders.

New Testament Greek. In his exceedingly readable little book on New Testament Greek Grammar, Mr. Simcox utters a note of warning against expecting too much from a study of the grammatical peculiarities of the New Testament. Its Greek he regards "an eminently translatable language." It has very little grammar compared with other Greek. "There is something that the diligent scholar can learn from study of the Gospel in the original; but he must beware of overrating its importance, which is but slight compared with what any diligent reader can learn from any decently faithful translation." What can be gained lies along the line of the beauty or significance of a passage which is heightened by a shade of language that vanishes in the translation, or an untranslatable idiom. Many will be inclined to think that Mr. Simcox overstates the case, especially those careful students of the Greek who think they enjoy "a greater freshness, perhaps a greater keenness of insight in the processes of the minds of the inspired writers." It would seem to them also that emphasis ought to be laid on the real advantages to be obtained from this study rather than upon the dangers of disappointment in expecting too much. Few approach the New Testament in the original with any such expectation.

Ecclesiastes 11: 3. Professor Davison has written in the *Methodist Recorder* protesting against the common misinterpretations of this text, some of which are based upon what reads thus, " Where the tree falleth, there it shall lie." "There is no such text in the Bible. The passage referred to runs thus : ' If a tree fall toward the south, or toward the north, in the place where the tree falleth, there it shall be.' In the context the writer is urging the importance of faithful fulfilment of duty, regardless of consequences in the future which no man can forecast. The proverbial expression of verse 1, 'Cast thy bread upon the waters,' points the same lesson as St. Paul's, 'Let us not be weary in well-doing ; for in due season we shall reap, if we faint not.' 'But,' the preacher goes on to say, 'we cannot tell precisely how future events will be ordered, but it would be folly on that account to stint our labors and kindnesses, like a husbandman staying his hand to gaze into the sky and wonder what the weather will be. The laborer in the field does not know what rain the clouds contain, which way the wind will blow, nor how the tottering tree will fall. The course of events we must be content to leave, and diligently use our own opportunities, sowing such good seed of the kingdom as we can, leaving results with God.' There is, of course, no reference here to the future life, or the fact that man's lot in the next life is fixed at death, as certain popular hymns, and perhaps popular ministers, have been accustomed to suggest. But the whole passage inculcates fidelity to duty while the opportunity is ours, lest the time come when it will be too late (Eccles. xii. 1, 7, 13, 14)."

Paul at Ephesus. The article by Canon Hicks noticed in the STUDENT for July, in which he claimed to have discovered upon the Ephesian marbles in the British Museum the name of the very Demetrius mentioned in Acts 19, has called forth a reply from Professor W. M. Ramsay in the July number of the *Expositor*. Prof. Ramsay highly commends the spirit and method of Canon Hicks' paper, but objects to his conclusions as playing into the hands of those critics who maintain that the narrative in Acts 19 is a forgery. He would place the Demetrius inscription much later, and finds that the motive for the attack on Paul is much more satisfactorily put in the Acts on a trade basis than on a religious basis, as Hicks would have it. The priests were, as a rule, indifferent to the rise of new cults of religion, but Christianity came early into opposition to those businesses which got their trade from the temple services. Ramsay entirely reverses the argument of Hicks concerning Luke's mistake about the making of silver shrines, showing that we have many remains of terra-cotta shrines, and arguing that there must have been similar ones made of silver, the offerings of the rich. That they do not remain is explained by their value and the probable practice of melting them down. He believes that the narrative of this chapter, as of many other chapters in the Acts, will be proved by future discoveries to be most accurate. He has found upon some statues the very cry of the Ephesian mob, " Great is Diana." With the greatest courtesy, yet equal keenness, he thoroughly examines, and seems greatly to weaken, the force of Canon Hicks' conjectures and arguments. The article is worth reading as a whole. An explanation and brief rejoinder is made by Hicks in the following number of the same journal which with great courtesy defends the former positions while acknowledging the weakness and conjectural character of much of the evidence.

General Notes and Notices.

Professor Lyon of Harvard University has spent the Summer in Europe on the mission of purchasing materials for the new Semitic Museum at Harvard. It will be remembered that this museum was rendered possible by the generous gift of ten thousand dollars from Mr. Jacob Schiff, an intelligent Hebrew, and a friend of biblical and Semitic studies.

Rev. Professor Wallace W. Lovejoy has resigned the Chair of Ancient Languages, Old and New Testament Exegesis and Biblical Theology in the Seminary of the Reformed Episcopal Church in West Philadelphia, has accepted a similar Chair in Pacific Theological Seminary of the Congregational Church at Oakland, Cal., and has entered upon his duties.

In the "Expository Times" it is stated, with what comes probably with semi-official authority, that a series of volumes called "The International Theological Library" is a new enterprise, in which the publishing houses of T. and T. Clark in Edinburgh and Scribner's in New York have combined their forces. Under the editorship of Dr. Salmond in Britain and Dr. Briggs in America, great scholars have engaged to write upon great subjects, and a series of volumes are promised which in all probability will take the first place in the true student's esteem. Apologetics has been undertaken by Professor Bruce, the History of Doctrine by Professor Fisher, Symbolics by Dr. Schaff, Comparative Religion by Principal Fairbairn, the Theology of the Old Testament by Professor A. B. Davidson, the Philosophy of Religion by Professor Flint, the Literature of the New Testament by Professor Salmond. The first volume of the series is announced as almost ready. It is by Canon Driver, and its subject is, "The Literature of the Old Testament." In the studies that lie before biblical students it will probably be found indispensable.

The Philadelphia Summer School of the American Institute of Sacred Literature was held this year at the University of Pennsylvania instead of the Episcopal Seminary as in former years. The school opened Thursday, June 12, with a lecture by Dr. W. R. Harper, the Principal of the American Institute of Sacred Literature, on "The Historical Element in Prophecy." The following instructors were present: in the Old Testament: Professors Harper, Taylor, Rogers, Lovejoy and Batten; in the New Testament: Professors Stevens, Gould, Weidner and Stifler; in the Cognates: Prof. Hilprecht. Courses were also given in the English Old and New Testaments. There were about a hundred students in all the departments, and for the most part they studied faithfully, though the very hot weather was a serious drawback to the school. The experience of several years in the Philadelphia School has convinced the managers of the desirability of holding future sessions in a more comfortable place than the heart of a hot city. Steps are being taken to hold the next school at Bryn Maur, one of the finest of Philadelphia's suburbs, ten miles from the city.

The announcement is made that the Rev. Thomas F. Day, of American Fork, Utah, whose communication in the STUDENT for December, 1889, on Bible Study in the Far West described a Utah Summer School of Hebrew, has been appointed Professor of Old Testament Exegesis in the San Francisco Theological Seminary. A second session of the Summer School in Utah was held this year, at which assistance in teaching was rendered by Professor E. L. Curtis of Chicago. It is hoped that this appointment will open the way for larger things in Summer Bible work on the Pacific Coast.

The first installment of a new translation of the Old Testament into German has just appeared. This translation is undertaken by Professors Baethgen, Guthe, Kamphausen, Kautzsch, Kittel, Lic. Marti, Prof. Rathstein, Rüetschi, Ryssel, Siegfried, and Socin. The portion now published is issued gratis for criticism and suggestion. It embraces thirty or more chapters of Genesis, and is from the hand of Professor Kautzsch. The division of the material into the documents P, J, E, etc,, is indicated in the margin of the page. While the Massoretic text is taken as the basis, no hesitation is shown in preferring a better reading, when it appears to be made tolerably certain from the versions or other sources. The aim is to reflect in the translation the high-water mark of German biblical scholarship.

It is interesting to note that Correspondence Classes of Bible Study for women are conducted in connection with Queen Margaret College, Glasgow, which is a college for women. A description of the work is given by Mrs. Robert Jardine in a recent number of the Expository Times :—" There are four classes, in which the books prescribed for the Local Examinations in (1) Common, (2) Junior, (3) Senior, and (4) Higher Subjects, respectively, are studied. Last session these books were : (1) St. Mark, (2) St. Luke, (3) 2 Kings, and (4) St. Luke and 1st and 2nd Thessalonians. At the beginning of the session a plan of study, divided into thirteen lessons, is sent to each pupil, who thus knows exactly what ground is to be gone over each fortnight. A fortnightly paper of questions is received, which, after answering, the pupils send to the tutor. He corrects the answers, adding notes and critical remarks, and the corrected work is returned with the next set of questions. The questions set vary in difficulty, according to the standard reached by the pupils. Knowledge of the words and facts of the Bible is the chief thing looked for in the work of junior pupils ; while those more advanced are expected to display more or less scholarship and critical insight."

Synopses of Important Articles.

The Old Testament and Our Lord's Authority. * The question involved here is one that must be met and settled without delay by the believers in Jesus Christ. Varying conclusions have been reached by those who have considered His expressions regarding the Old Testament in their necessary relation to His nature and person. It is proposed to consider them in connection with a class of facts which come still better within our own sphere; namely, His work for man. Christ's saving work consists of what He has done and the example He has set, this latter including His teaching, which shows us His mind and how to follow Him. In order to maintain the place of Christ as our teacher in that sense which peculiarly belongs to His saving work, we must be careful to assert the resemblance which exists between His own ways of knowing and the knowledge He imparts to us. We had as well deny the correctness of His knowledge as deny that it is human. This is recognized in regard to His strife with evil, His temptation and His growth in obedience, "learning" it "by the things He suffered." Now is there any similar relation between Him and ourselves in the intellectual life? Is His conquest of error and His acquisition of truth of so wholly different a nature that, while in the moral life He is not ashamed to call us brethren, in the intellectual He is not our brother, but something infinitely above us? Such a position divides the constitution of His humanity, making part less human than the rest. It also separates faculties which are inseparable. The intellect and the conscience move not in parallel lines but in woven strands. He must have struggled toward knowledge as toward the establishment of character. Is it objected that as the Lord's moral life was confessedly perfect, so must His intellectual illumination be perfect also? His moral life was perfect but only in quality, not in quantity; moral problems occur to-day to His followers which never presented themselves to Him. So is His knowledge not perfect in point of volume and contents, but a perfect intellectual attitude, according to the general conditions of humanity, toward His whole environment spiritual and sensible. The perfect attitude of the intellect is not merely consistent with the limitations in knowledge which the character of man's state involves, but actually requires them. Christ had the perfect intellectual attitude. Granted that He was not omniscient, what reason for imagining Him endowed with knowledge which would have been useless for His blessed work and which He gives no sign whatever of possessing? You cannot separate this knowledge and say it was religious and hence He must have known the truth about critical questions of the Old Testament. He took the perfect intellectual attitude toward this Scripture—an attitude of reverent freedom. Scientific knowledge of authorship and date are like scientific knowledge of astronomy and geology—matters with which He does not deal. Thus we consider this problem from the moral side and find that our Lord is pledged to no belief which Old Testament criticism of the day calls in question.

This article must be read in detail to grasp its subtle and yet most comprehensive argument. It is one of the freshest and strongest presentations of the question that recent years have seen.

* By Canon Richard Travers Smith, in *The Expositor*, Aug. 1890, pp. 81–101.

Book Notices.

Lux Mundi.

Lux Mundi: A Series of Studies in the Religion of the Incarnation.
Edited by Charles Gore, M. A., Principal of Pusey House, Fellow of Trinity
College, Oxford. From the fifth English Edition. New York: John W.
Lovell Company.

This series of essays has excited much discussion in England. Its authors
are High Churchmen and are popularly supposed to speak in this volume for
their division of the English Church. And a somewhat surprising utterance it
is to those who imagined that the Ritualists were as severe in their theology
as they are strict in their observances. A large amount of liberalism on theological and critical questions has been disclosed by the writers. In theology
the Incarnation assumes the place that the old theology gave to the Crucifixion. In criticism opinions are expressed by the Rev. Charles Gore in his essay
on the Holy Spirit and Inspiration which bring him very near to the school of
Driver and Cheyne. It is about this essay that the conflict has raged most
fiercely, Canon Liddon leading the conservative attack, while from the ultra-
liberals the voice of Mr. Huxley is heard, deriding the compromises and the
half-way measures which are here used to bridge over the gaps which scientific investigation is opening in the orthodox biblical interpretations. The very
fact, however, of attack from both extremes ("Pharisees and Herodians
united" some have said) argues that the views presented in the essay are more
likely to be nearer the truth of things. The positions of the essay are as follows: The Holy Spirit in the Church gives life; this life manifests itself
among other ways in inspiration; this inspiration is disclosed in its finest form
in the Scriptures, especially in the point of view of the writers, which is that
of God's dealings with man; this point of view results in a devotion to fact on
the part of the writers which makes the work pre-eminently historical; yet
though historical, this work may admit an idealizing element which reads
back into past history what was the real purpose of God in it, though it was
not actually manifested at that particular epoch; such inspiration does not preclude the possibility of a mythical element in the earliest Jewish records; all
this idealizing does not exist in the New Testament, where the ideal is become
realized and absolute coincidence is necessary; inspiration has never been defined by the Church, and Jesus Christ in His use of the Old Testament does
not pass on critical questions—a thing which was contrary to His whole method
—indeed, "His utterances about the Old Testament do not seem to be nearly
definite or clear enough to allow of our supposing that in this case He is de-
parting from the general method of the Incarnation by bringing to bear the
unveiled omniscence of the Godhead, to anticipate or foreclose a development
of natural knowledge" (p. 301). This essay will strike many as a piece of
straddling. It is certainly candid, if not convincing to anybody. Those who
are interested in modern religious ideas and their development in special
schools of thinkers will do well to read this volume.

THE EXAMINATION ON LUKE
OF THE AMERICAN INSTITUTE OF SACRED
LITERATURE.

Responses from North, South, East and West. As the date appointed for this examination draws nearer, ministers and Bible-teachers in all parts of America and in many others lands are realizing its value. Almost three hundred beyond the Mississippi have fallen into line as special examiners· The South is represented by each of her thirteen states, Virginia leading with eighteen men who are forming groups. Connecticut leads the list of the Eastern States with examiners in sixty towns, while the following extracts from letters of the Rev. Chas. A. Cook of Bloomfield, N. J., and the Rev. W. C. King of Warren, Pa., voice the enthusiastic support of the Middle States :—

"We are getting to work. Several in my church have committed themselves to the study. In one of the Presbyterian churches here steps are being taken to organize a group and we hope to report good work in Bloomfield."

From Warren :—"I am pressing the matter vigorously. Have written a personal letter to all the pastors and Sunday-school superintendents, and they are to report how many would like the direction and announcement sheets. Will you not furnish me at least one hundred ? Mean to have a class of *fifty*."

From foreign lands. Still more encouraging are the reports from across the borders. On this continent Ontario, Quebec, Prince Edward Island, Nova Scotia, North-west Territory, New Brunswick, Manitoba and British Columbia on the North, and Mexico on the South, have each some who, as individuals or in groups, are anticipating the helpful test of examination by closer study of the weekly S. S. Lessons from the Gospel of Luke. Mr. G. E. ·Williams, Secretary of the Y. M. C. A. of Kingston, Ont., speaks for Canada when he says : " I am greatly interested in the extension of Bible study, and hail any movement having that end in view." Beyond the Atlantic, England, Ireland and Wales have taken up the work ; and in the far East, China, Burmah, India and Syria are led by Japan with five special examiners.

From India the following is of interest :—

"At this station (Ramapatam, Nellore Dist., Madras Pres.) there are only two English-speaking residents, viz., my wife and Miss Emma J. Cummings, M. D. If the examination were held in the language in which all the work in our seminary is done (the Telugu) there might be a good many to take the examination." [The examination will be offered to these students *in Telugu*.]

One Thousand Special Examiners. The number of examiners is now nearly eight hundred, and before this number of the STUDENT reaches its readers the desired number, one thousand, will doubtless be obtained. The names of these examiners, with the territories they represent, will be published in November. The list comprises ministers, Y. M. C. A. secretaries, S. S. superintendents and distinguished Bible-teachers. It is not our desire to limit the number of examiners to one thousand, however, and if any of our readers will send us the names of persons whom they may consider suitable and willing to serve as examiners, we will gladly invite their co-operation. Single applications for examination will also be welcomed, and the applicants will be assigned to the examiner in their locality.

Current Old Testament Literature.

155. *Die Heiligen Schriften d. Alten Testaments*, in Verbindg. m. Baethgen, Guthe, etc. ubersetzt u. hrsg. v. E. Kautzsch, 1 Lfg. Freiburg : Mohr.

156. *La Sainte Bible (texte latin et traduction francaise), commenteé d'après la Vulgate et les textes originaux,* à l' usage des seminaires etc. By L. Fillion, Tours : Mame.

157. *Introduction a' l' étude de l'Ecriture sainte d'après la " Sainte Bible" avec ' Commentaires.'* T. 2. Introductions particulieres aux livres de l' Ancien Testament. By Trochon et Lesètre. Paris : Lethiellieux.

158. *Historische-kritische Einleitung in die Bücher d. alten Testaments hinsichtlich ihrer Entstehung u. Sammlung.* By A. Kuenen. Autoris. deutsche Ausg. v. Th. Weber. 1 Tl. 2. Stück. Die historischen Bücher d. Alten Testaments. Leipzig . Reisland. 6.—

159. *Lehrbuch der biblischen Geschichte Alten Testaments.* By A. Köhler. 2 Hälfte, 2 Thl. 2 Lfg. Leipzig : Deichert. m. 2.40.

160. *Der biblische Geschichte d. Alten Testaments in uebersichtlichen Betrachtungen f. Kirche, Schule u. Haus.* 2 Halfte. Samuel bis Makkabaer. By J. M. Einfalt. Leipzig : Deichert. 3.20.

161. *Les Cinq Livres (mosaïstes) de Moïse.* Traduits texuellement sur l' hébreu, avec commentaires et étymologies (premier livre ; la Genèse avec élimination des textes interpolés, preuves à l'appui de la religion miraculée et idolâtrée du second temple, textes qu'Esra et la grande synagogue ont frauduleusement mis dans la bouche de Moise) par Alexandre Weill. Paris : libr. Sauvaitre, 5 fr.

162. *De Hexaëmero secundum caput primum Geneseos ad literam.* By E. de Gryse. Brugis ; Beyaert-Storie.

163. *Isaac and Jacob ; their lives and times.* By G. Rawlinson ; London : Nisbet. 2s. 6d.

164. *Der Triumphgesang am Schilfmeer. (Exod. 15), ausgelegt u. kritisch untersucht.* By Carl Floeckner, Benthea O. S.: Wylezol.

165. *Die Psalmen. In Bebelstunden.* By K. Gerok. 2x Lfgn. 1 Sfg. Stuttgart : Krabbe. .50.

166. *Präparation Kommentar zu den Psalmen, m. genauen Analysen u getreuer Uebersetzg.* By J. Bachmann. 1 Heft.; Ps. 1-20, Berlin : Schneider. 1.—

167. *Biblical Commentary on the Prophecies of Isaiah.* By Franz Delitzsch. Translated from the fourth edition, with an introduction by S. R. Driver. Vol. 1. Edinburgh ; Clark. 10s. 6d.

168. *Beitraege zur Jesaiakritik. Nebst e. Studie üb prophet. Schriftstellerei.* By F. Giesebrecht. Göttingen : Vandenhoeck und Ruprecht. 5.

169. *Outlines of Prophetic Truth ; viewed practically and experimentally in the light of the divine Word.* I. By R. Brown. London : Partridge. 12 s.

170. *Ueber das Verhaeltnis des naturlichen zum Goettlichen im alten Testament.* By Wagner. Sondershausen : Eupel.

171. *Zur Weltstellung d. israelitischen Volkes.* By Rochall. Leipzig : Faber. .40.

172. *Das Pferd, der Esel, und der Hund in der heiligen Schrift.* Ein Beitrag zur biblischen Archaeologie. By A. Zeller. Plauen : Wieprecht.

173. *Das Buch Judith historisch-kritisch beleuchtet.* By A. S. Weissmann. Wien : Lippe. .80.

174. *The Bible true from the Beginning.* Vol. 3. By E. Gough. London : Paul. 16s.

175. *The Origin of Scripture on its divine and human sides ;* a contribution to the present biblical discussion. By J. Wilson. Edinburgh : Macniven. 1 s.

176. *Current discussions in theology.* By the professors of Chicago Theological Seminary. Boston : Congregational S.S. and Pub. Soc. $1.50.

177. *Der Religion der alten Aegypter.* By A. Wiedemann. Münster i. w.: Aschendorff. 2.75.

178. *Vedisme, Brahmanisme et Christianisme.* La Bible dans l'Jude et la vie da Jezeus Christua d' apres M. Jacolliot ; la personalite du Christ et le Dr. Marius. By de Harlez. Bruxelles ; Soc. gen. de libr. cath. f. 3.

Articles and Reviews.

179. *Le Texte Parisien de la Vulgate latine.*
[Suite]. By J. P. P. Martin,in Le Museon,
9, 3, Juin, 1890.

180. *Mayor's Latin Heptateuch.* Review
by Gebhardt, in Theol. Ltztg. Aug. 23.1890.

181. *Étude sur certains archaismes au
Pentateuque.* By Graffin, in Congres
scientifique internat. des Catholiques,
1888. t. 1, Paris, 1889.

182. *Gihon.* By Th. Chaplin, in Palestine
Exploration Fund, 4, 1890.

183. *Inschriftliche Glossen und Exkurse
zur Genesis und zu den Propheten.* By
Fr. Hommel, in neue kirchl. Ztschr., 1,
6, 1890.

184. *Exodus 1; 11.* By P. de Lagarde, in
Nachrn. v. d. Kgl. Gesellsch. der Wiss.
u. d. Georg-Aug.-Univ. zu Goettingen.
5, 1890.

185. *The Time of the Judges.* By Howard
Crosby, D. D., in Homiletic Review, Sept.
1890.

186. *Noch einmal Sauls Königswahl und
Verwerfung.* By C. H. Cornill, in Ztschr.
f. d. alttestam. Wissensch., x. 1, 1890.

187. *Nehemiah's Wall.* By W. F. Birch, in
Pal. Expl. Fund. Apr. 1890.

188. *Die Namen in Buche Esther.* By
Scholz, in Theol. Quartalschr, 2, 1890.

189. *Psalm lxviii.* By Rev. Professor T.
K. Cheyne, in The Expositor, Sept. 1890.

190. *Studies in the Psalter, 21. The Sixty-
eighth Psalm.* By T. W. Chambers, D.D.,
in Homiletic Review. Sept. 1890.

191. *Der 68 Psalm nach Abfassungszeit
und geschichtlichem Inhalt.* By B.
Behrend, in Magazine f. d. Wissensch.
des Judenth. 2, 1890.']

192. *Selah* [in the Psalms]. By W. Muss-
Arnolt, in The Academy, 6, 1890.

193. *Ecclesiastes. Chapter 12.* By T.
Edwards, D. D., in Homiletic Review,
Sept. 1890.

194. *La Sagesse dans l'Ancien Testament.*

By J. Corluy, Congrès scientifique internat. des catholiques, 1888. t. 1. Paris,
1889.

195. *Version d' Isaïe de R. Saadia.* By J.
Derenbourg, in Ztschr. f. d. alttestam.
Wissensch., x. 1890.

196. *Études d'histoire israélite. Le règne d'
Ézéchiaes.* By E. Renan, in Revue des
deux mondes, 99, 100, 4, 1, 1890.

197. *The Hebrew Prophet and the Christian
Preacher.* By George B. Spalding, D.
D., in the Andover Review, Sept. 1890.

198. *Is the Book of Daniel a Prophecy?* By
John Poucher, D. D., in the Methodist
Review. Sept.-Oct., 1890.

199. *Delitzsch's Messianische Weissagungen.* Review by Siegfried, in Theol.
Ltztg., Aug. 23, 1890.

200. *Der Gottesname Tsur und seine Deu-
tung in dem Sinne Bildner oder Schöpfer
in der alten Judischen Litterature.* By
A. Wiegand, in Ztschr. f. d. alttest.
Wissensch. x. 1, 1890.

201. *Étude sur les genéalogies bibliques.*
By Abbé de Broglie, in Congrès scientifi-
que internat. des catholiques, 1888, t, 1.
Paris 1890.

202. *Welche Lehren bieten uns die sozialen
Verhältnisse im israelitischen Volke?* By
J. Waser. in Kathol. Schweizer-Blätter.
1, 2, 1890.

203. *Siegfried's Die theologische u. die
historische Betrachtung des Alten Testaments.* Review by Budde, in Theol.
Ltztg., July 12, 1890.

204. *Trois letters des Juifs de Palestine.*
By C. Bruston in Ztschr. f. d. alttestam.
Wissensch. x. 1, 1890.

205. *The lost works of Philo.* By F. C.
Conybeare, in the Academy, July 12, 1890.

206. *Brace's Unknown God.* Review by
F. P. Noble, in the Bib. Sac., July, 1890.

207. *Egyptian Ethics.* Translated from
the French of Revillout, in the Bibliotheca Sacra, July, 1890.

Current New Testament Literature.

American and Foreign Publications.

208. *Die chronologische · Reihenfolge, in welcher die Briefe d. Neuen Testaments verfasst sind, insofern dieselbe abzuleiten ist sowohl aus ihrer gegenseit. Uebereinstimmg. u. gegenseit. Verschiedenheit, als aus dem in den späteren Briefen gemachten Gebrauch v. Worten u. Citaten, die in den früheren vorkommen.* By W. Brückner. Von der Teylerschen theolog. Gesellschaft gekrönte Preisschrift. Haarlem, 1890. 6.—

209. *Das Neue Testament des Clemens Alexandrinus.* Ein Beitrag zur Geschichte des neutestamentlichen Kanons. By H. Eckhoff. Schleswig: Bergas.

210. *The Life of Christ.* By F. W. Farrar. With an American appendix giving over 500 translations of non-English matter; an introduction by Taylor Lewis. Boston: Bradley and Woodruff. $3.50.

211. *Zu Matthaeus 5 : 17-20.* Ein Beitrag zur Exegese der Bergpredigt. By G. Tiede, Sprottau: Wildner.

212. *Johanneisches Evangelium.* By H. J. Holtzmann. [Hand-Commentar zum Neuen Testament.] Freiburg: Mohr. 3.

213. *Beitraege zum Verstaendniss d. Johanneischen Evangeliums. v.* Die Heilung d. Blindgebornen durch Jesum. By F. L. Steinmeyer. Berlin: Wiegandt and Greben. 1.80.

214. *Our Lord's miracles of healing considered in relation to some modern objections, and to medical science.* By T. W. Belcher, with preface by Archbishop Trench. 2nd edit. revised. London: Griffith. 6s.

215. *Las Urevangelium.* Studien zur Entwicklungsgeschichte der christ. Lehre u. Kirche. By E. Solger. Jena: Manke. 3.60.

216. *St. Paul: His Life and Times.* (Men of the Bible.) By J. Iverach. London: Nisbet. 2s. 6d.

217. *Der Brief Pauli an die Römer, übersetzt u. erklärt by A. Ebrard.* Nach dem Tode d. Verf's. hrsg. v. Ph. Bachmann, Leipzig: Deichert. 6.—

218. *St. Paul's Epistle to the Galatians.* A revised text with Introduction, notes and dissertations. By Bp. Lightfoot. 10th Edition. London: Macmillan. 12 s.

219. *Der erste Brief Petri, in 20 Predigten*

ausgelegt. By R. Kögel. 3 Aufl. Bremen: Müller. 3.60.

220. *Harmageddon II. Das tausendjaehrige Reich.* [Offenb. Ch. 20.] By P. Cassel. Berlin: Haack. 1.

221. *The Story of the Jews under Roman Rule.* By the Rev. W. D. Morrison. New York: G. P. Putnam's Sons. $1.50.

Articles and Reviews.

222. *Quelques publications recentes sur la Bible.* [consacrées an texte du nouveau Testament ou de la Bible en grec]. By S. Berger, in de Revue theol. et de philos. 3, 1880.

223. *Survey of Recent Literature on the New Testament.* By Rev. Professor Marcus Dods, in The Expositor, Aug. 1890.

224. *The Vatican Codex.* Review by Gebhardt, in Theol. Lztg. Aug. 9, 1890.

225. *Lloyd's Greek Testament.* Review by Gebhardt, in Theol. Lztg., July 26, 1890.

226. *Ueber das Evangelienbuch des Juvencus in seinem Verhaeltniss zum Bibeltext.* By K. Marold, in Ztschr. f. Wissensch. Theol.. 33, 3, 1890.

227. *Die vier Evangelien u. ihre vier Symbole.* By Sepp, in Deutscher Merkur, 28, 1890.

228. *Ewald's Das Hauptproblem der Evangelienfrage.* Review by Holtzmann, in Theol. Lztg., July 12, 1890.

229. *Zur Kritik der Evangelien. 1. Die Beziehung zwischen dem ersten u. dem dritten Canonischen Evangelium.* 2. Bemerkungen über das vierte Evangelium. By A. Jacobsen, in Ztsch. f. Wissensch. Theol. 33, 3, 1890.

230. *Noch Einmal ueber "Epiousios."* [Matt. 6 : 11 ; Lk. 11 : 3]. By F. W. Münscher, in Neue Jahrbchr. f. Philol. u. Paedag., 2, 1890.

231. *Zu Lucas 15 : 18.* By Chr. Crow, in Neue Jahrbchr. f. Philol. u. Paedag., 2, 1890.

232. *Hat Lukas die Paulinischen Briefe gekannt?* By R. Steck, in Theol.Ztschr. aus. d. Schweiz, 3, 1890.

233. *New Testament Teaching on The Future Punishment of Sin. 5. The Synoptic Gospels.* By Rev. Professor J.A. Beet, in The Expositor, Sept. 1890.

234. *The Light of the World.* [John viii. 12]. By Rev. Prin. J. O. Dykes, in The Expositor, Sept. 1890.

235. *St. John 12 : 3.—The word " pistikes."* By E. N. Bennett, in The Classical Review, 7, 1890.

236. *Kuehl's Die Heilsbedeutung des Todes Christi.* Review by Kaftan, in Theol. Lztzg. Aug. 9, 1890.

237. *Was the Resurrection of our Lord Jesus Christ literal, absolute and complete?* By Bishop W. F. Mallalieu, in the Meth. Rev. Sept.-Oct., 1890.

238. *Einen unbekannten Gott.* [Acts 17]. By R. Graw, in Der Bew. d. Glaub. Juni, 1890.

239. *St. Paul's Sermon on Mars Hill and Robert Browning's Cleon.* By A. H. Bradford, D. D., in Christian Thought, Aug. 1890.

240. *Ephesus. A Postscript.* By Rev. Canon Hicks, in The Expositor, Aug. 1890.

241. *Der urchristliche Gemeinder-fassung mit spezieller Beziehung auf Loening und Harnack.* By F. Loofs, in Theol. Stud. u. Krit., 4, 1890.

242. *Galaterbrief und Apostelgeschichte.* By A. H. Franke, in Theol. Stud. u. Krit. 4, 1890.

243. *Voelter's Komposition der paulinischen Hauptbriefe.* Review by O. Holtzmann, in Theo. Lztzg., Aug. 23. 1890.

244. *Zur Erklaerung des Roemerbriefs.* [Cap. 1 to 4]. By C. Willing, in Ztschr. f. Wissensch. Theol., 33, 3, 1890.

245. *Bemerkungen zu 1 Kor. 10 : 34 und Eph. 4 : 8-10.* By J. Dalmer, in Theol. Stud. u. Krit., 3, 1890.

246. *1 Corinthians 15 : 29, 30.* By J. M. S. Baljon, in Theol. Stud. 3, 1890.

247. *The Resurrection of the Dead. 3.* (1 *Cor. 15 : 45, 46.*) By Rev. Professor W. Milligan, in The Expositor, Aug. 1890.

248. *2 Corinthians 3 : 18.* By J. Hoskyns-Abrahall, in the Classical Review, 7, 1890.

249. *On 2 Corinthians 6 : 2-7 : 1.* By Chase and Whiteland, in the Classical Review, 7, 1890.

250. *The Epistle to the Hebrews. 19. Draw near!* By Rev. Professor A. B. Bruce, in The Expositor, Aug. 1890.

251. *The Epistle to the Hebrews. 20. Not of them who Draw Back!* By Rev. Professor A. B. Bruce, in The Expositor. Sept. 1890.

252. *Die Poimenik des Apostel Petrus* (1 *Petri 5 : 1-5), nach ihrer geschichtlichen und praktischen Bedeutung.* By B. Riggenbach, in Theol. Ztschr. aus d. Schweiz, 3, 1890.

253. *Nero Redivivus.* [*Rev. 17 : 8-11*]. By Rev. William E. Barton, in The Bib. Sac. July, 1890.

254. *The Old Testament and Our Lord's Authority.* By Rev. Canon R. T. Smith. in The Expositor, Aug. 1890.

255. *Trichotomy; A Biblical Study.* By S. H. Kellogg, D. D., in The Bibliotheca Sacra, July, 1890.

256. *On the relation of Jewish to Christian worship.* By Rev. Preb. E. C. S. Gibson, in The Expositor, July 1890.

257. *Mead's Supernatural Revelation.* Reviewed by W. H. Ryder, in the Andover Review, Aug. 1890.

258. *Fisher's Nature and Method of Revelation.* Review by E. Y. Hincks, in Andover Review July 1890.

259. *Hints as to Interpretation of Scripture.* By Pres. J. A. Broadus, D. D. in Sund. School Times, July 12, 1890.

260. *Die Bedeutung des Volksthums nach der heiligen Schrift.* By H. Seesemann, in Mitthlgn. u. Nachrn. f. d. Evang. Kir. in Russ. Apr. 1890.

261. *Die Lehre vom Reiche Gottes nach Ritschl, beleuchtet aus den heiligen Schriften des neuen Testaments.* By W. Graeber, in Kirchl. Monatsschr. 9, 9, 1890.

262. *Recent Researches into Bible Lands.* By Prof. G. H. Schodde, in Homiletic Review, Aug. 1890.

263. *Bezetha* By C. R. Conder, in Palestine Exploration Fund, 4, 1890.

THE

Old and New Testament Student

| VOL. XI. | NOVEMBER, 1890. | No. 5. |

To ONE who possesses what may be termed an orderly mind, it must at first appear a strange thing that, in so many cases, Scripture material is not arranged chronologically. One is really puzzled, when he first makes the discovery that the sacred writers did not, for some reason or other, take the pains to put their matter, even when it was historical, in the order in which the events described took place. The facts are so many and so clear that some way must be found to account for them. It is unreasonable to assume that the writer made an effort to put his material in chronological order and failed in the effort. This would reflect too severely on his ability as an author. Nor is it supposable that, in any number of cases, the original writer placed it in chronological order, and that copyists have displaced it. There is sufficient evidence to prove that this has sometimes happened in the case of verses; but no sane man would try to explain in this way the multitude of departures from the chronological order which are known to exist. It must be, then, that the writer did not make an effort to secure chronological order. He certainly might have so arranged his narrative, if he had tried, but he did not try. The fact is, we must conclude, that the question of chronological order did not seem to him an important one. The purpose he had in view could be attained without it. He probably did not consider the question. He had a distinct end in mind, and this end he accomplished. We cannot consider here the nature of the purpose which guided him. It is sufficient to say that it was a purpose independent of modern historical methods,

17

INSEPARABLY connected with this lack of chronological order, and certainly in part responsible for it, is another fact, no less puzzling to the inquiring mind, viz., that in so many instances, the writer has failed to give us any indication of when or where a particular event occurred, or a particular prophecy was uttered. The insertion of four or five chronological statements in the Book of Judges would have saved us from the overwhelming flood of conflicting theories (in all, fifty) which have from time to time been presented in reference to the chronology of this book. It is hardly possible for one to get a correct understanding of the facts concerning Sennacherib in Isaiah 37: 37, 38, until it is known that twenty years elapsed between the events described in these two verses. One wonders why Ezekiel should have been so exact in this matter, while in Isaiah but few sermons have a definite statement of the time of their utterance. What an amount of discussion would have been rendered unnecessary, if a more exact statement had been made somewhere of the time of the residence in Egypt, whether 430, or 230 years. It appears that many of the Old Testament writers exercised little or no care to indicate the time of their writing. Sometimes the date is given, more frequently, perhaps, it is omitted. What shall we say about this fact? It will not do to assume that the date was originally given in every case, and has been lost. It must be that indications of chronology were not essential to the plan of the writer. His work, the thing he sought to accomplish, the idea he endeavored to convey, was, in no sense, dependent upon a date. Let us hold these things in mind, and, at another time, consider one or two other matters which stand closely related with them.

ONE of the apparent miracles of organization and growth in modern times is the Christian Endeavor. The progress of this movement is something almost incredible. Two questions are all the time suggesting themselves: (1) Is this progress to continue? (2) Is the ground, already gained, to be maintained? We believe,—and there are many who share with us the opinion,—that the answer to both of these questions, is largely to be determined by the attitude assumed toward a true and vigorous Bible-study. The thing of all things, essential to spiritual growth—the growth of the Christian must be spiritual, if anything—is Bible-study; not mere Bible reading, but downright study. If the Christian Endeavor is to *grow*, in the greatest and best sense of the word, it must undertake Bible-study as an organic part of its work. It cannot afford to trust this work to the Sunday-school, to the family, or to any other agency. Let all these agencies do Bible work, each in its own way; but let the Christian Endeavor, also, if it would preserve its own existence, organize a work for its membership, a work so arranged as, when done, to furnish the foundation for the superstructure which is now being erected to so dizzy a height, and with such amazing rapidity, as to occasion no small degree of alarm. Many leaders in the work have already expressed this feeling. The recent action of the New Hampshire, Iowa, Wisconsin and other State Conventions certainly points in this direction. It is time, *now*, to act.

In a recent discussion of Babylonian Seals, attention was called to the fact that these seals are marked with emblems of the gods of the Babylonian pantheon. It is curious also to note that the earliest of these seals present a front view, full face, of the deities, while in those which are later the representation is in more or less of a profile. What does this fact signify? Is it that, as the gods were enveloped in greater sanctity, they were removed from the direct contemplation of their worshippers? Does it recall the biblical conception whereby no man can look upon the face of Jehovah and live? Or, should we rather see in it the growing consciousness of sin, as though, by a symbolic representation, the gods would turn their eyes from beholding the guilt of man? Thus it would ally itself with the thought of Adam, who, after his sin, would fain hide himself from God in the thick of the wood. The subject is an interesting one, and perhaps significant of a mode of thought among those ancient peoples which brings them near to their Hebrew brethren.

No thoughtful student of the religious movements of our times can fail to see that they are chiefly characterized by some special attitude towards, or view of, the Bible. Perhaps to say that they are *chiefly* characterized thus is too indefinite a statement and therefore misleading. Certainly there can be no doubt that the positions taken by schools of religious thought in reference to the Bible is the *fundamental* thing about them. This conditions their progress. This determines their direction. That this will finally decide their permanence and usefulness in the world, none can fail to recognize.

THE subjects considered in the "Symposium" contained in the present number of the STUDENT are, from this point of view, of the highest importance. The fundamental questions concerning the fundamental Book—what can be of more burning interest to men of our time? It is believed that the answers there given to the inquiry concerning the great problems of Bible study are not only well-considered but exceedingly helpful. Younger scholars offer their testimony which is found in striking harmony with the conclusions of older and experienced students of life and the Word. The impressive and timely suggestions as to the Bible in its relation to personal life and in its contribution to the knowledge and appropriation of God and of the Christ, are of the utmost value in these days, when the progress in the intellectual study of the Bible is so wonderful and fascinating. It is never to be forgotten that such study is only a means, though an indispensable means, to spiritual growth.

THE question which by all is recognized as vital, in many ways the question of questions, is that of Inspiration. The soberness and vigor with which the writers deal with this is admirable. They do not agree at all points and it is not desirable that they should agree. Some are willing to concede more to biblical criticism than are others. There is a common desire to be rid of the ordinary theological nomenclature which obscures the facts that it seeks to unfold. In many respects the contributions of these scholars show that a new way of looking at this problem has come to us—a way which is farthest from the scholastic, which may rather be termed the vital. It recognizes that it is dealing with a living body not with a dead corpse. Language concerning such a phenomenon must be as living as its subject. It must be ample enough to admit new facts when they appear. A statement has recently been made on this subject by an English scholar which may profitably be considered in connection with those in the "Symposium." It is as follows: "We have no right to prescribe to God the method of His address to men. He employs human instruments, and it is not for us to say how far He will permit the human element—the element of imperfection—to characterize the vehicle of His communications. Let us but be sure that He has spoken to us, and our further questions as to the form and mode of His speech can only be solved by our study of the oracles themselves. *A definition of Inspiration should be the end and not the beginning of our research.*" It may be that none of the writers would entirely agree with this. Some would certainly oppose it. It dwells upon one side of the living organism. It may fail to emphasize duly its other aspects. A modification of it may be accepted from the pen of an American theologian who says: "The important thing is not to get a verbal theory; the important thing is to get a supernatural theory. In relation to God, inspiration is but a part of the supernatural plan of redemption. In relation to the man inspired, inspiration is the supernatural raising of his entire person to the highest power. As to the Book, it is the *result* of this supernatural purpose and process. More than that, the Holy Ghost is *now* with the word to keep it safe, to vitalize it and make it the power of God unto men. The whole thing is supernatural; and yet the human element is as plainly in it as it is in the person of our Lord."

The subject is a great and a complex one. Patience, forbearance, common sense, piety, scholarship, must enter into its discussion. It is not to be doubted that a solution for our time, if not for all time, will come under the guidance and blessing of the living God.

ZEPHANIAH.

By Prof. MILTON S. TERRY, D. D.,

Garrett Biblical Institute, Evanston, Ill.

The prophecy of Zephaniah forms one of the smallest books of the Old Testament, but has a symmetry and an apocalyptic tone which entitle it to high rank among the oracles of the Hebrew prophets. The free appropriation of language and sentiments from Joel, Micah and Isaiah takes from it certain claims to originality, but its scope and plan are obviously the product of the writer's own independent thought, as he was moved of the Spirit to announce the word of Jahveh. That the prophet was descended from king Hezekiah (verse 1) has been a prevalent opinion since the time of Aben Ezra, and is quite probable; but there is no conclusive evidence for this opinion, and the matter is of no considerable importance.

The book is assigned to "the days of Josiah," but no more definite date is given, and the attempts of interpreters to determine the exact time of the prophecy have not been successful. Some maintain that it belongs to the earlier period of Josiah's reign, before the king had undertaken the reforms for which his administration was notable; others date it during the progress of the reforms, and others during the latter part of his long reign of thirty-one years. According to 2 Chronicles (34 : 8) the reformation really began in the eighth year of Josiah's reign, and was continued with greater vigor after the discovery of the book of the law, in the eighteenth year. But notwithstanding the violence of the king's measures, and the temporary suppression of idolatrous usages, it was a notorious fact that the false worship was not effectually destroyed. It revived and flourished again immediately after Josiah's death, and 2 Kings 23 : 26–29, together with the whole testimony of Jeremiah's prophecies, is evidence that the Baal worship and other idolatrous practices were not abol-

ished, but at most only driven into secret, by the rigid
measures of the pious King of Judah and those who were
associated with him in the work of reform.   Hence the mention of such idolatry as is referred to in Zeph. 1 : 4–6 is no
certain proof that the prophecy was uttered before Josiah's
reforms, nor is the expression '' remnant of Baal'' (chap. 1 : 4)
any sufficient evidence that the worship of Baal had already
in great part been destroyed.   As well might one argue that
the words '' remnant of the house of Judah '' in chap. 2 : 7,
prove that the Jews were already in exile.   In short the
prophecy of Zephaniah would fit either the beginning or the
close of Josiah's reign.   If it were made before the reforms,
the allusions to existing idolatry and wickedness would have
been very natural and direct.   But if made towards the close,
about the time that Pharaoh-necho marched against the
Assyrians (2 Kings 23 : 29), these same allusions would have
been sufficiently pertinent, for to every man of the kingdom,
gifted with the discerning insight of Zephaniah, it must have
been apparent that the false worship had only concealed its
face for a time, and was not really abolished. Comp. 2 Kings
23 : 26–28.   If obliged to express a judgment where certainty
is not attainable, we prefer on the whole the later date. This
judgment is based, not on particular allusions like those above
referred to, but on the apocalyptic tone of the whole prophecy,
which may well be supposed to have been prompted by the
military movements of the great nations on the south and
north just before the fall of Assyria, and the deep conviction
that nothing short of national overthrow and captivity would
eradicate the deeply-rooted evils of the kingdom of Judah.
In the signs of the times the prophet recognizes the imminent
'' day of Jahveh,'' day of dense darkness and overwhelming
wrath.

The prophecy is naturally divisible into three parts. The
first is the announcement of a rapidly approaching day of
judgment upon the nations, especially upon Judah, and occupies chapter 1.   The second consists of a hortatory appeal,
based upon the foregoing decree of judgment and the further
prophecy that the heathen powers of the four quarters of the
earth shall be overthrown.   This part extends from chapter

2 : 1 to 3 : 7. The third part completes the book (chap. 3 : 8–20), and consists of a glorious promise of restoration and salvation to the remnant of Israel who are true to Jahveh. These sections embody the three great elements of apocalyptic prophecy, namely, the proclamation of judgment, admonition and encouragement for such as will hear God's word, and the glorious purpose of the Most High to redeem unto himself a holy people and thereby vindicate his administration of the world, and magnify his name.

The following translation exhibits the prophecy under the form of short but quite regular and harmonious parallelisms. The first section falls into six strophes of nearly equal length, presenting so many different phases of the approaching day of wrath. The admonition which follows is divided into the same number of strophes, consisting of so many various arguments and appeals. The third section contains the promise, in four strophes, which present so many different aspects of the future restoration and joy.

THE DECREE OF JUDGMENT. CHAP. I.

I.

2 Gathering I will sweep everything away
From off the surface of the ground, saith Jahveh.
3 I will sweep off both man and beast,
Sweep fowls of heaven, and fishes of the sea,
And things that cause the wicked to stumble;
And I will cut off the whole race of man
From off the surface of the ground, saith Jahveh.

II.

4 And over Judah I will stretch my hand,
And on all dwellers in Jerusalem,
And cut off Baal's remnant from this place,
The name of idol-priests along with the priests,

---

2 *Gathering . . . sweep* :—Two words of different origin and meaning, combined here so as to express not only intensity of action, but also the twofold idea of gathering together for judgment and then sweeping them away into destruction.

3 *Things that cause* :—Probable reference to idols.

4 *Idol-priests* :—Comp. 2 Kings 23 : 5.

⁵ And those that on the roofs bow to heaven's host,
And those that bow down, those that swear to Jahveh,
And those that swear by Milcom,

⁶ And those that turn away from Jahveh back,
And who have not sought Jahveh, nor inquired of him.

III.

Hush, in the presence of the Lord Jahveh!
For near at hand is Jahveh's day,
For Jahveh has prepared a sacrifice,
Has sanctified the ones whom he has called.

⁸ And in the day of Jahveh's sacrifice,
I'll visit on the princes and king's sons,
And on all them that clothe in foreign garb,

⁹ And visit all who leap o'er thresholds in that day,
Who fill their lord's house full of force and fraud.

IV.

¹⁰ And it shall be in that day, Jahveh saith,
A voice of crying shall rise from the fish-gate,
And lamentation from the second ward,
And a great crashing ruin from the hills.

¹¹ Lament, O ye that in the Mortar dwell,

---

⁵ *Roofs:*—Comp. Jer. 19: 13. *Milcom*—The worship of this god of the Ammonites had been made familiar in Jerusalem (1 Kings 11: 5, 7; 2 Kings 23: 13). The decree is against those that swear both by Jahveh and Milcom, not recognizing any important distinction.

⁷ *Sacrifice:*—Slaughter of his enemies. Comp. Isaiah 34: 6-8. *Sanctified*—Set apart and made ready to execute his decrees. Comp. Isaiah 10: 5, 6; 13: 3.

⁸ *King's sons:*—No necessary reference here to Josiah's sons in particular. *Foreign garb*—Costumes adopted from foreign nations.

⁹ *Leap thresholds:*—Enter houses violently, as do those who plunder or collect dues by sheer force. The reference is not to the superstition mentioned in 1 Sam. 5: 5, but to the exactions of the rich and noble, who ground the faces of the poor by requiring these toll-gatherers to collect by force if necessary. Comp. Isaiah 3: 14, 15. These minions of the rich filled their lord's houses with the product of their violence and fraud.

¹⁰ *Second ward:*—A well known quarter of the city. Comp. 2 Kings 22: 14. The wailing from various parts of the city, and the crashing ruin wrought by a desolating army on the hills about the city, furnish a fearful picture of destructive judgment.

¹¹ *Mortar:*—Name of some depression, or hollow within the city, probably

For all the Canaan-people are destroyed,
Cut off are all the silver-laden ones.

[12] And in that day I'll search Jerusalem with lamps,
And visit on the men stiff on their lees,
Those who are saying in their hearts,
Jahveh will neither good nor evil do.

[13] And for a plunder shall their substance be,
Also their houses for a desolation;
And houses they shall build and not inhabit,
Plant vineyards and not drink the wine thereof.

V.

[14] Near is the day of Jahveh, the great day,
'Tis near and hastening speedily along,
The sound of Jahveh's day!
Bitterly waileth there the mighty man.

[15] A day of pouring fury is that day,
A day of cramping pressure and distress,
A day of noisy wreck and ruin dire,
A day of darkness and calamity,
A day of cloud and dense obscurity,

[16] A day of trumpets and of war-alarm,
Upon the cities that are fortified,
And on the lofty battlements.

VI.

[17] And I will bring a pressure upon men,
And they shall walk like those who cannot see.
For against Jahveh they have sinned.
And their blood shall be poured out like the dust,
And their full bodies even as rolls of dung.

[18] Nor will their silver nor their gold have power
To save them in the day of Jahveh's wrath,

---

in the Tyropoeon valley. *Canaan-people*—Not here put for people of Canaanite origin, but of Canaanitish character and qualities, idolatrous, and especially given to traffic. Comp. Isaiah 23 : 8 ; Hos. 12: 8 ; Prov. 31 : 24.

[12] *Stiff on their lees :*—Metaphor referring to old wine which has not been drawn off in a long time ; figure expressive of religious ease and indifference.

[14] *There:*—Where the noise and destruction sweep along. Comp. the vivid conception of the day of Jahveh in Joel 1 : 15–2 : 11 ; Isaiah 13 : 6–16 ; Amos 5 : 18–20.

And in the fire of his zeal shall all the earth be eaten,
For a consumption, yea a fearful doom,
Shall he work on all dwellers of the earth.

THE ADMONITION.   CHAP. II. 1–III. 7.

I.

ch. 2 : ¹ Gather yourselves together, gather ye,
    O nation not an object of desire.
 ² Before the time appointed bringeth forth,
    [Before] the day like chaff has passed,
    Ere yet comes on you Jahveh's burning wrath,
    Ere yet comes on you Jahveh's day of wrath.
 ³ Seek Jahveh, all ye humble of the earth,
    Ye who his judgments have performed;
    Seek righteousness, seek ye humility,
    Perhaps ye may be hidden in Jahveh's day of wrath.

II.

 ⁴ For Gaza shall deserted be,
    And Ashkelon become a desolation,
    Ashdod, at noon-day they shall drive her out,
    And Ekron shall be rooted up.
 ⁵ Ho! Dwellers of the portion by the sea,
    Nations of Cretes, on you is Jahveh's word;
    O Canaan, country of the Philistines,
    Thee I destroy without inhabitant.
 ⁶ And it shall be—the portion by the sea—
    Dwellings of shepherd's caves and folds of flocks.

ch. 2 : ¹ *Gather*—Best understood as a call to penitence and prayer much as Joel 1 : 14 and 2 : 15, 16. *Desire*—Israel is called a "nation not desired" because of having forfeited the yearning love of God by sin, and so becoming an object of loathing rather than of desire. It is better thus to adhere to the meaning which the word *kasaph* has in every other passage where it is found than to attach to it the sense of *shame* or *turned white*, or *pale*, which has no sanction in the usage of the language.

⁴ *Gaza . . . Ekron*—The writer constructs a paronomasia on these names by the words translated *deserted* and *rooted up*, after the manner of Micah 1 : 10–15.

⁵ *Cretes*—Ancient name of inhabitants of Philistia, but why so called uncertain. The most plausible conjecture is that there was some historic or traditional connection of the Philistines with Crete. Comp. Amos 9 : 7.

⁶ *Caves*—Dug-outs occupied by shepherds. Others explain the word as meaning *pastures* or *meadows* occupied by the shepherds.

[7] And it shall be a portion for the remnant of the house of
Judah;
 Upon them they shall graze at morning time,
 At eve they will lie down at Ashkelon;
 For Jahveh, their own God, will visit them,
 And bring their captives back again.

III.

[8] I have been hearing the reproach of Moab,
 And the revilings of the sons of Ammon,
 Who have upon my people cast reproach
 And acted proudly on their boundary.
[9] Therefore as I live, saith Jahveh, Israel's God,
 'Tis sure that Moab shall like Sodom be,
 And the sons of Ammon like Gomorrah;
 The property of thorns and pits of salt,
 And desolation to eternity.
 The remnant of my people shall spoil them,
 My nation's residue inherit them.
[10] This shall be to them for their haughtiness,
 For they reproached and acted with great pride
 Against the people of Jahveh of hosts.
[11] Terrible is Jahveh upon them,
 For he has thinned away gods of the earth;
 And they shall worship him, each from his place,
 All islands of the nations.

IV.

[12] Also ye, Ethiopians,
 The slain of my sword are they.
[13] And he will stretch his hand upon the north,
 And cause Assyria to perish,

[7] *At morning time*—Read *beboqer* instead of *bebhati.* This very simple emendation restores the parallelism which the common reading has destroyed.

[8] *Their boundary*—My people's border, always a matter of contention between the Ammonites and Israel. Comp. Amos 1: 13. Jer. 49: 1. and Judges 11: 24.

[11] *Upon them*—Reference to Moab and Ammon. *Thinned away*—Caused to disappear. *From his place*—Not *in* his place, as if remaining there, contrary to the idea of chap. 3: 10; Micah 4: 1. And Zech. 14: 16; but thronging *from* the place; pouring forth thence. Comp. Micah 7: 17. *Islands*—Comp. Isaiah 41: 1: 42: 4; 51: 5; 60: 9; 66: 19.

And will make Nineveh a desolation,
A dryness like the desert.

¹⁴ And in her midst shall flocks lie down,
All kinds of animal-nations,
Also the pelican and porcupine;
Among her capitals shall they repose;
A voice will in the window sing,
A desolation be upon the threshold;
For naked has he laid the cedar-work.

¹⁶ This is the city, the exulting one,
She that is dwelling in security,
She that is saying in her heart,
I am, and there is nothing more;
How has she a deserted waste become,
A place for beasts to lie!
And every one who passes over her,
Will hiss, will wave his hand in scorn.

V.

ch. 3: ¹ Ho, the rebellious and polluted one,
The city that oppresses;

² She has not listened to a voice,
She has not received discipline,
In Jahveh she has not put confidence,
Unto her God she has not closely come.

³ Her princes in her midst are roaring lions,
Her judges evening wolves,
They do not for the morning leave the bones;

¹⁴ *Animal-nation*—Literally, *every animal-nation*; nation here in the sense of tribe or class. Comp. Joel 1 : 6. Prov. 30 : 25–27. *Pelican and porcupine*—These are fittingly named as given to frequent marshy and waste places. Comp. Isaiah 14 : 23. *A voice*—The singing of birds generally, not of any particular kind of bird or singer. *Naked . . . cedar-work*—The palatial buildings are thought of as so torn down and exposed as to lay bare the costly cedar-work of the interior apartments.

3 : 1. *Rebellious one*—Jerusalem. Having pointed to sweeping judgments to fall on the heathen powers of the west, east, south and north (chap. 2: 4–15), the prophet directs his word of admonition to Jerusalem again, and shows that her many sins call for a like judicial doom.

³ *Leave the bones*—They are so ravenous that they devour all their prey in the evening, and so leave nothing until the morning,

⁴ Her prophets boasters, men of treacheries,
　Her priests stained what is holy, broke the law.
⁵ Jahveh is righteous in the midst of her,
　He will not do a wrong;
　Morning by morning he will give his judgment to the light;
　He fails not, but wrong-doers know not shame.

VI.

⁶ I have cut nations off; their towers are waste,
　I have destroyed their streets so no one passes,
　Razed are their cities, no man there, no dweller;
⁷ I said, "Only fear me; take discipline,"
　And so her dwelling would not be cut off,
　All which I have appointed upon her;
　But they in haste corrupted all their deeds.

THE PROMISE. CHAP. III. 8–20.

I.

⁸ Therefore do ye wait for me, Jahveh saith,
　Unto the day when I rise for the prey;
　For 'tis my judgment to assemble nations,
　That I may gather kingdoms together,
　To pour my indignation upon them,
　Even all the burning fury of my wrath;
　For in the fire of my jealousy
　Devoured shall all the earth be.
⁹ For then to peoples' pure lip will I turn,
　That all of them may call on Jahveh's name,
　To serve him with one shoulder.

⁵ *Jahveh . . . righteous*—The divine administration is contrasted with the people's sinfulness. He will not do a wrong act, but manifest his holy judgments in ever increasing light. Comp. Deut. 32 : 4.

⁶⁻⁷ *I have cut off . . . I said*—The perfects of these two verses point to the already completed acts of the divine administration, on which Jahveh bases his admonition and appeal; and also to the persistent sinfulness of the people of Jerusalem, which justified the sweeping judgment about to come.

⁹ *Pure lip*—Pure language as expressive of the purity of the popular life. The peoples will be converted to purity of heart, thought, life and act, and all this will find expression through the lips. *With one shoulder*—With united strength as of many putting their shoulders together under one yoke or burden.

¹⁰ Beyond the streams of Ethiopia,
    My suppliants, daughter of my scattered ones,
    Shall bear mine offering.

II.

¹¹ That day thou wilt not blush for all thy deeds
    Which thou hast been transgressing against me;
    For then will I remove out of thy midst
    Those of thine that exult in arrogance,
    And thou shalt no more be set high in pride
    Within the mountain of my holiness.
¹² And I will leave a remnant in thy midst,
    A people lowly and impoverished,
    And they shall put their trust in Jahveh's name.
¹³ Israel's remnant will not commit wrong,
    And they will not be speaking what is false,
    Nor in their mouth will tongue of guile be found;
    For they will pasture and lie down to rest,
    And no one making them afraid.

III.

¹⁴ Daughter of Zion, utter shouts of joy,
    Send forth a cry of gladness, Israel,
    Be merry and exult with all the heart,
    O daughter of Jerusalem.
¹⁵ Jahveh thy judgment has removed,
    He has turned off thy enemy.
    The King of Israel, Jahveh, is in thee,
    No longer shalt thou see calamity.
¹⁶ That day be it said to Jerusalem, fear not;
    O Zion, do not let thy hands hang down.

¹⁰ *Daughter of my scattered ones*—Those begotten in the uttermost parts
of the earth (as Ethiopia) by God's people who have been dispersed thither.
These are thought of as converts to the true religion, and bringing offerings to
Jahveh.

¹¹ *Wilt not blush*—Because there will be no disgraceful deeds to blush for.

¹² *Remnant*—This remnant is that same kernel of righteousness, which is
ever seen by the prophets to survive the chastening judgments; a lowly, poor,
often down-trodden class (Comp. 1 Cor. 1 : 16), who trust God and are cared
for as the sheep of a good shepherd.

¹⁷ Jahveh, thy God in thee, strong One, will save,
He will be leaping over thee with joy,
He will be deeply silent in his love,
He will with gladness over thee exult.

IV.

¹⁸ Those grieving for the festal time I gathered,
From thee they were, on whom reproach was cast.
¹⁹ Lo, I will deal with all thy despots then,
And I will succor that which lamely halts,
And that which was thrust out will I collect.
And I will set them for a praise and name
In all the earth, where they have suffered shame.
²⁰ In that time I will cause you to come in,
Yea, in the time of my collecting you;
For I will give you for a name and praise
Among all peoples of the earth,
When I restore your captives to your eyes, saith Jahveh.

¹⁷ *Strong one*—Mighty hero; in apposition with Jahveh. *Leaping with joy*—Figure of exquisite delight. *Silent in his love*—Noticeable counterpart of the active exultation. His joy is not merely that of outward glee, but rooted in that purest love which is silent because of its depth.

¹⁸ *Grieving*—Those who were sad by reason of removal from the appointed festivals so that they could not attend. To gather these home is to end their sorrow. *From thee*—From Israel; they were of God's people. *On whom*— The relative refers to this same people, over whom there was so many times a lifting up of reproach.

¹⁹ *Thy despots*—The oppressors who acted the tyrant over the Israel of God.

A PLAN FOR THE STUDY OF THE BOOK OF ACTS.

By Prof. GEORGE B. STEVENS, Ph. D., D. D.,

Yale University, New Haven.

The history contained in the book of Acts is of the first importance for the student of early Christianity. Here we trace the beginnings of the Church's life, and behold its various conflicts and successes from the day of Pentecost to the imprisonment of the Apostle Paul at Rome. The history covers the years 30–62 or 63, a period which is filled with events which are most significant as illustrating the progress of the Church. The various narratives may be studied from different points of view. The three most important seem to be:—

(1) The relation of the history to the chief actors in it, Peter and Paul.

(2) The Book of Acts as a record of the Church's conflicts and persecutions.

(3) The way in which the events narrated illustrate the expansion of the idea that Christianity was designed for all men on equal terms, and exhibit the effort to carry this idea into effect.

Keeping in mind these three points of view, the student would do well to go through the Acts, and note carefully in a book the bearing of each narrative upon each or all of them.

Taking the three topics in their order, I would make the following suggestions in regard to the method of study:—

I.

(1) Divide the book into the two parts, of which one has Peter for its chief character, the other, Paul.

(2) Collate the principal "acts" of Peter, and carefully define their number, circumstances and character, noting the sphere of his labors.

18

(3) Read all the discourses of Peter together, and determine (a) what was Peter's main subject in preaching, (b) by what arguments he illustrates and enforces it, and (c) what appears to be his attitude on the question of the reception of the Gentiles into the kingdom of God.

(4) Note the bearing of narratives in this portion of the book which do not refer directly to Peter (such as those concerning Ananias, Stephen and Cornelius), and define (a) their relation to the main course of the history in which Peter is the principal actor, and (b) the way in which some of these prepare the way for the introduction of Paul.

(5) Collate the facts narrated about Saul in the part of the book in which Peter still remains the leading character, and carefully estimate their importance for the subsequent work of the apostle to the Gentiles.

(6) Compare the narrative of his conversion in chapter ix. with the two others in the Acts, and with notices of that event in his Epistles (especially Galatians).

(7) In connection with this comparison make a summary of all the points of information which the New Testament furnishes in regard to Paul previous to the beginning of his Gentile mission (chap. xiii.), and define their relation to his work. (See especially Gal. 1 and 2.)

II.

In studying the Acts as a history of the persecutions and hindrances which met early Christianity, it will be useful

(1) To learn from what different classes the opposition arose.

(2) What were the motives of it?

(3) Trace the order in which the hostility of these classes developed, and find the reasons for it.

(4) Carefully note all statements and acts of the apostles which became the occasion of this hostility.

(5) What was the cause and nature of that hindrance which arose from such persons as are mentioned in xi. 3 and xv. 1?

(6) In reading the history of Paul's missionary labors, note (a) the forms and occasions of opposition to his work

from the Romans, and (b) any instances in which the Roman power appeared as his protector, and why.

(7) Paul's trial, imprisonment and voyage to Rome.

III.

If the student pursues the course outlined above, he will be well prepared to trace the development of the idea that Christianity is for all on equal terms, which is the most interesting single truth contained in the whole history. The lines on which it should be traced may be indicated thus:—

(1) The position and teaching of Stephen as foreshadowing Paul.

(2) The process of training and broadening to which Peter was subjected (especially chapters x., xi.)

(3) The conversion of the Samaritans and the Ethiopian chamberlain (chap. viii.)

(4) The conversion, training and commission of Paul.

(5) The mission at Syrian Antioch (xi. 19 sq.)

(6) Study the missionary journey of Barnabas and Paul (chapters xiii., xiv.) with reference to the following points: (a) its course and scope, (b) its events and successes, so far as given, (c) the class which it was principally designed to reach, (d) the means and methods of reaching them.

(7) Study with great care the question that arose about circumcision (chap. xv., and compare throughout Galatians 1 and 2), and the deliberations of the apostles upon it, determining (a) just what the question was, (b) the view of the Pharisaic extremists, (c) the view of the Jerusalem apostles, Peter and James, (d) Paul's view, (e) on what ground they agreed, and (f) to what extent, if any, they remained apart.

(8) Study the second and third missionary journeys, tracing their course on a map, and noting (a) the character and importance of the places visited, (b) where churches were founded, (c) the arguments and other means used by Paul to convince his hearers of the truth of the gospel.

(9) Observe the lines on which Christianity was extended by Paul, and consider how both the directions of its extension, and the character of the centers in which it was planted, indicate the line of its advance in the centuries that followed, even to the present time.

THE PROPHECY CONCERNING IMMANUEL:
ISAIAH VII., 13-17.

By Prof. Edward L. Curtis,

McCormick Theological Seminary, Chicago.

To explain rightly any word of prophecy, one must apprehend the circumstances in which it was spoken, and also the general character of prophetic utterance. Fortunately, we have given the historic setting of this famous passage concerning Immanuel. It is found in the previous verses of the chapter, and also in the narrative of 2 Kings 16: 1–9. The kingdom of Judah was suffering an invasion from the united forces of Israel and Syria. Under these distressing circumstances, the question which must have been uppermost in all minds, was From whence should help be sought—how shall we be rid of our enemies? Two plans seem to have presented themselves: one, that of the people using their own resources, putting their trust in Jehovah their God, looking to Him as their deliverer; the other, that of seeking help through a foreign alliance, and inviting Assyria to come against Israel and Syria. The latter plan was acceptable to Ahaz and the court. The former was that urged by Isaiah. He was confident that the power of Israel and Syria had been over-rated; that their force had already spent itself. He gave this as a Divine message, calling them the two tails of smoking firebrands, contemptible adversaries soon to be broken. If Ahaz would only put his trust in Jehovah, and rely upon Him, all would be well. Jehovah even offered him a sign whereby this fact might be confirmed. Ahaz, however, refused to ask this sign, saying that he would not tempt Jehovah. He was evidently determined to adopt the other policy, that which he finally pursued, of inviting the assistance of Tiglath-pileser, king of Assyria (2 Kings 16: 7–9).

In these circumstances, Isaiah uttered the passage under consideration :—

" Hear ye now, O house of David: is it a small thing for you to weary men, that ye will weary my God also? Therefore the Lord himself shall give you a sign, behold a maiden is with child, and beareth a son, and shall call his name Immanuel. Butter and honey shall he eat, when he knoweth to refuse the evil, and choose the good. For before the child shall know to refuse the evil, and choose the good, the land whose two kings thou abhorrest shall be forsaken. The Lord shall bring upon thee, and upon thy father's house, days that have not come, from the day that Ephraim departed from Judah; even the king of Assyria" (7: 13–17).

" Before, then, the child of a woman, now pregnant, shall be old enough to distinguish between that which is good and bad, not only shall the land of Israel and Syria be devastated by Assyria, but also your land shall be over-run and laid desolate by the contending armies of Assyria and Egypt. You bribe Assyria to come against Israel and Syria, and thereby you invite disaster to your own people." This is the plain meaning of these verses addressed to the house of David, in connection with those that follow. (In the translation given above, I have followed the Revised Version, introducing into the text two marginal readings, which are abundantly sustained by critical authorities, and need no defence. Butter and honey also is the food, and so the sign of the land desolate and forsaken; see verse 22).

So much, then, for one side and meaning of this oracle; it was one foreboding storm and disaster to Judah. But this was not its entire meaning. As fearful as the oracle was to Ahaz and the party at the court, so likewise must it have been hopeful to Isaiah and his friends. Isaiah had two fundamental doctrines which find expression in all his prophecies. The first was that of an impending judgment to befall Judah, the second that of the saved remnant, or the indestructibility of God's people, or the ultimate salvation of the people and city of God. How the former doctrine, that of impending judgment, appeared in our oracle, we have already seen. The latter is seen in the name of the child, Immanuel, God with us. But Isaiah carried also this latter doctrine further than the simple or general conception of the

ultimate salvation of the people. As is seen in other prophecies (9: 5, 6; 11: 1), he presented in connection with it
the promise of a future king of the line of David. An intimation of that person is also found here. It lies in the name
Immanuel. That child, whose early days should be associated
with such disaster, was yet in His name a token of the
indestructibility and ultimate salvation of the people of
Jehovah. Who then was He? To this question there could
be but one answer. Either typically or really He was the
destined king of Israel, the One who, in some mysterious
manner, would be the pledge, if not the actual realization,
of God being with His people.

His mother is indicated by a very indefinite term, i. e.,
"the young woman of marriageable age," for that is the
strict meaning of the original. Possibly she was designed to
be any young woman who, within the time allotted, should
bear a child, to whom might be given the name Immanuel,
and thus might serve as a type of the future king; and thus,
also, would she serve as a type of His mother.

Possibly it may have been the prophet's own wife, for his
child may have been called Immanuel, and (see viii. 18) been
thus a sign of the expected One. Possibly the mother was
nothing more than an ideal figure representing the people of
God. This last supposition is favored by Mic. 4: 10; 5: 3.
At any rate, the New Testament writer, who never distin-
guishes between direct and typical prophecies, was fully
justified in finding this word fulfilled in connection with the
birth of Jesus (Matt 1: 23).

It may now be thought that the interpretation of this passage is too hazy, too indefinite. This leads us then to consider the second point mentioned at the beginning of this
article, namely, the character of prophetic utterance. I
emphasize once for all, the fact that the Hebrew prophet was
a Seer, not a philosopher, not a chronologist, but one who
presented certain ideas without definitely placing them in
their temporal relations to each other. This is illustrated
again and again in the prophetic writings. Many thoughts
are crowded together into one picture, with no mark of the
temporal separation found in their realization. This is the

perspective character of prophecy. It is manifested with especial beauty in Isa. 40–66. "The Divine act of delivering the people from the Babylonian captivity, and their restoration to the promised land, form, with the Messianic redemption and the admission of all nations into the kingdom of God, one great connected picture, closing with the creation of the new heavens and the new earth."

So likewise here the prophet places two thoughts upon one canvas—a coming judgment, a coming redemption. In their midst is a child holding a twofold relation, a sign of ruin and disaster on the one hand, impending and immediate (here, indeed, the prophet is in a certain sense a chronologist); a pledge on the other of God's gracious deliverance in the future. Whether Isaiah expected then and there in his own time that the Messiah would come, he does not tell us. He doubtless was well aware that when and how God would accomplish His purpose could only be known in its fulfilment.

While then giving a sign of God's displeasure to the obstinate, unbelieving house of David, Isaiah placed in connection with it a sign of hope to the faithful of Israel. If his words partook something of the nature of a riddle, their meaning was plain enough to influence human conduct, to warn on the one hand, to comfort on the other. The ultimate reference of Immanuel could escape none who heard the prophet's other discourses, and recognized him as standing as a pledge of Divine deliverance and redemption. (See 8: 8 and 10.) As one writer has suggested, by associating Immanuel with impending ruin and disaster, Isaiah meant to depict most vividly the fatal policy of Ahaz, showing that by his unbelief he had not only disestablished himself (7: 9), but had also mortgaged the hope of Israel. "The child, who is Israel's hope, is born. He grows up, not to a throne, or the majesty which the seventy-second Psalm pictures—the offerings of Sheba's and Seba's kings, the corn of his land shaking like the fruit of Lebanon, while they of the city flourish like the grass of the earth—but to the food of privation, to the sight of his country razed by his enemies into one vast common, fit only for pasture, to loneliness and suffering. Amid the general desolation His figure vanishes from our sight, and only His name remains to haunt, with its infinite melancholy of what might have been, the thorn-choked vineyard and grass-grown courts of Judah." If thus terrible is the meaning of this figure on the one side, on the other, appearing so in the midst of desolation, surrounded with such sad ruin, it would be a sure token that God was still with His people, and whatever disaster might overtake them, in the end His remnant should be saved, and the hope of Israel realized.

EXPOSITORY PREACHING.

By Professor FRANKLIN W. FISK, D. D.,

Chicago Theological Seminary, Chicago.

It is a hopeful sign of yet greater power in the Christian ministry that it is giving its attention more and more to expository preaching. The trend of modern preaching toward what constituted a large element in primitive preaching is indicated, in part, by the increasing number of volumes of expository sermons coming each year from the press, and by the many eminent and popular preachers excelling in expository discourse.

The writer in this article would not presume to instruct his brethren of the ministry, but would simply refresh their memories with a few suggestions respecting the nature, advantages, and methods of expository preaching, which may possibly be of some benefit to young ministers.

It would seem that misconceptions as to what constitutes expository discourse, are somewhat prevalent. They are manifest in the frequently loose and inexact use of the phrase, expository preaching. Running comments, however able, on a passage of Scripture having no unity of thought, cannot properly be called expository discourse. Nor is it necessary that the text include several verses, or even a single verse. A Scriptural phrase may furnish sufficient material for an expository discourse. Often a textual division of a passage is found to be the best for an explanatory sermon, and then the discourse becomes at once textual in plan and expository in development. That which makes a sermon expository is the form of the development of its thought or subject. If the development be mainly expository, the discourse is properly termed an expository sermon.

Of the many advantages of this species of discourse, but little need be said. They are so manifest that it is almost needless to name, much less to enlarge upon them. Yet it may be well to notice two or three of the more important of them.

To the preacher himself the frequent preparation of expository sermons is of great benefit. He is thus kept from yielding to a common tendency to confine one's preaching within a narrow range of Scriptural topics, and so almost unconsciously getting into "ruts" in his pulpit ministrations. He will, at times, be under the necessity of discoursing upon the various doctrines, precepts, histories, and biographies, as they occur in the continuous exposition of a book of Scripture. Thus he will come to have a symmetrical knowledge of Scriptural truth, and his preaching will include a wide range of subjects. It will represent a much larger portion of Scripture than if he confined himself to topical sermons. He will thus become a preacher of the Word rather than of isolated Scriptural topics.

In expository preaching he will be able not only to present a great variety of truths, but also to make such practical applications of them as he could hardly make in topical preaching without the appearance of intentional personalities. So full are many of the books of the Bible—especially the Epistles—of precepts that have to do with the various relationships of human life, that a series of expository discourses upon any one of them will compel the preacher to dwell upon all these precepts as they arise in the course of his expositions, and to apply them to his hearers in all their relations in life.

He will also find that the frequent use of this kind of discourse will tend to render his preaching more attractive. For it will tend to reproduce the Bible in its entirety, and not a few fragments of it. Its charming histories and biographies, interesting and instructive alike to the young and to the old, will have a place in such preaching. Thus the table that he spreads on the Lord's day throughout the year, for the spiritual nourishment of his congregation, will have the attractiveness, variety and abundance that can come only from the bountiful storehouse of all Scripture. Perhaps it is not too much to say that every pastor should aim to have his preaching during a decade or score of years in the same pulpit, represent pretty accurately, and in due proportion, the whole of Scriptural teaching with its remarkable variety of form.

If now we look at the methods of expository preaching, we see that unity is its first law. The passage of Scripture selected, whether a part of a verse or several verses, should have one main thought around which the other thoughts cluster. The aim should be to set forth this thought in its surroundings, and to do this it is necessary that unity preside over every part of the development. The preacher should not for a moment lose sight of the main thought of the passage, and should endeavor in his sermon to reproduce it in its settings. This is often a difficult task when the passage contains several important and apparently dissimilar thoughts, and to do it well, the preacher will find it necessary to study intently in the original, if possible, and with all the helps at his command, the passage itself. And so if he intends to preach a series of expository discourses on a chapter or book of Scripture, the best preparation he can make for such a course of sermons will be a careful study of the entire passage. He will thus have fully in mind what he has undertaken to do, and will be more likely to reproduce the truths he is expounding, in their due proportion.

In making a plan of an expository sermon, the preacher will generally find it best to follow the order of the main thought in the passage. The chief heads need not, however, be as formally expressed as in topical discourse. Then the aim should be to gather from the passage itself the principal materials for the development of these main thoughts. Grammar and lexicon, hard study and commentaries, will bring to light ample materials from which he can select what may best suit his purpose. But care should be taken lest, overwhelmed with multiplicity and complexity of materials, he fail in unity of thought and impression.

As to the place of applying the truth in expository preaching, it may be said, in general, that the truth may be applied as it is unfolded in the progress of the discourse, whenever it is of such a nature as to permit an immediate application. But in such cases, it is often well to make at the close of the sermon a brief application, in which may be passed in review the different points that have been urged. If the sermon be the kind of explanatory discourse termed by some writers, the illustrative, the aim being to unfold Divine truth as illustrated by character in Scriptural history and biography, it is often best, first, to give briefly and vividly the narrative, and then to make the various applications; at other times it is well to apply the truths as they are brought out or suggested in the progress of the discourse.

The above are mere suggestions respecting a species of pulpit discourse in which skill on the part of a preacher can hardly be overrated. The youthful pastor who has come to some just appreciation of the great value of expository preaching both to himself and to his people, who is aflame with the desire to become " mighty in the Scriptures" and will " Give diligence" (literally, make haste) "to present himself approved unto God, a workman that needeth not to be ashamed, handling aright the word of truth," and who will address himself persistently and manfully to become master of expository discourse, will find difficulties vanish before him, and he will have the increasing joy, as the years go by, of growing rapidly in biblical knowledge, and in an instructive and fruitful ministry.

He will also have abundant literature to aid him in his efforts. The modern pulpit is becoming prolific in volumes of expository discourse. Chalmers' " Lectures on the Epistle to the Romans," are admirable models of unity of thought and aim amidst great variety of materials. Robertson's " Expository Lectures on the Epistles to the Corinthians," deserve to be studied for the frequent excellence of their plans, and their fruitful suggestions. In the species of explanatory discourse termed illustrative or descriptive, Dr. William M. Taylor, in numerous volumes, as " David, King of Israel,' " Elijah, the Prophet," has given examples that can hardly be excelled in modern preaching. The ways in which he creates a continual interest in the subject under consideration, and draws from it fruitful practical suggestions, are worthy of careful study. Ex-President McCosh in his " Gospel Sermons," has given several explanatory discourses of the illustrative kind that are of a high order of excellence. Dr. Joseph Parker's volumes, entitled, "The People's Bible: Discourses upon Holy Scripture," as also his "Inner Life of Christ," and "Apostolic Life," are worthy of careful reading as examples of a distinctive kind of expository discourse for which their author is justly celebrated. Dr. J. Oswald Dykes in the "Law of the Ten Words," and in "The Gospel According to St. Paul," has given admirable examples of expository preaching. Dr. Samuel Cox's expository discourses contained in his volumes entitled, "Expositions," are remarkably fresh and interesting both in matter and in manner. In the volume entitled, "Paul's Ideal Church and People," Alfred Rowland, of London University, gives us in a series of forty short sermons, on the First Epistle to Timothy, several admirable plans in expository discourse and worthy of close study by young ministers.

These are only a few of the many volumes of expository sermons that have come from the press of late—the most of them within a few years,—and which are at the service of any youthful pastors, who would become proficient in that most instructive and useful kind of pulpit discourse—expository preaching.

CONTENTMENT AND FELLOWSHIP: *

OR

PAUL'S TEACHINGS REGARDING PROPERTY.

By Rev. EDWARD TALLMAGE ROOT,

New Haven, Conn.

Paul is the formulator of Christian ethics as well as doctrine. He applied the principles taught by Christ to the problems of daily Christian life under the complex conditions of a high civilization. In studying the Christian conception of property in a brief essay one cannot do better than confine attention to his writings.

I. THE LIFE PURPOSE.

Christ's moral teachings center in the idea of a life-purpose (Matt. 6: 19–34). Life should be a seeking, a conscious unity in which every act is subordinated to one great end. Being all-controlling, the life-purpose determines the character. The most important of questions, therefore, is, What is the true life-purpose? Viewed in different aspects the question takes different forms, "Where shall man lay up treasures? Whom shall he serve? For what shall he take thought?" All possible life-purposes may be reduced to two classes, seeking wealth, i. e., food, drink and clothing, and seeking the Kingdom of God. These two are mutually exclusive. The former cannot be the true life-purpose because its objects belong to the sphere of the temporary, because it treats a few of the conditions of life as if they were all, because its objects lie beyond man's control and because its sinfulness is proven by the fruit it has borne among the Gentiles. Therefore the Christian is to lay up treasure in Heaven and serve God by seeking first His kingdom and righteousness. This purpose

* Greek, *Autarkeia kai Koinônia.* Very hard to translate. The R. V. wavers between "contentment" and "sufficiency;" between "fellowship," "contribution" and "communicating."

through God's loving care, will secure all things that he needs.

Paul's teaching is a development and application. The chief passage is 1 Tim. 6: 5–19. Note that he is addressing those who have adopted the Christian purpose and who are in danger, not of willfully abandoning it, but of being beguiled from it by the attempt to seek riches also. He says: To suppose that godliness is a way of gain is a characteristic of ignorant, vain and corrupt men. To seek riches is foolish, harmful and wicked.

(1) Because we brought nothing into this world nor can we carry anything out.

(2) Because even in this life riches are uncertain.

(3) Because such seeking leads to ruinous lusts, all kinds of sin, astray from the faith and into many sorrows. So Paul in his own experience saw the results of covetousness in Demetrius, (Acts 19: 23, ff., compare 16: 19) and in Demas (2 Tim. 4: 10.) Or may have had in mind the cases of Achan, Gehazi and Judas.

Paul classes covetousness with fornication as a sensual sin (Eph. 5: 3, 5, and often). Rightly, for it is the valuing of the material to the exclusion of the spiritual. Both lover of luxury and miser are victims of enslaving lust. He also calls it idolatry, for it substitutes possessions for God as the supreme object of trust and service.

Such being the false, what is the true purpose? "But thou, O man of God, flee these things and follow after righteousness, godliness, faith, love, patience, meekness," etc. Just as others plan and scrape and save every day to add to their hoard; so the Christian is one, who makes every act of every day subordinate and tributary to the attainment of a god-like character; doing nothing, saying nothing, thinking nothing but what will further this end.

The difficult part of this is the "fleeing." If at one stroke we could sever ourselves from the world, it would be easy to be unworldly. But we cannot rid ourselves of the necessity of a certain amount of wealth,—food, clothing, shelter. Seeking these, as means to accomplish our supreme purpose, we are in constant danger of being led by imperceptible degrees into making godliness a way of gain. The problem before the Christian, therefore, is to keep the material in its true place as means to the spiritual,—to "use the world as not abusing * it" (I Cor. 7 : 31). Where draw the line?

II.   CONTENTMENT.

Paul's solution is "contentment."

Since the Christian's purpose cannot overlook the necessity of a certain amount of wealth, his great gain must be not righteousness alone, but "righteousness with *contentment.*" The word in Greek is literally "self-sufficiency." It is used in classical Greek. Plato contrasts it with needing many things. Thucydides uses it of a country which needs no imports. Aristotle defines it as "being all and lacking nothing." Thayer's New Testament Lexicon therefore gives as definition, "a perfect condition of life in which no aid or support is needed."

Now there are two conceivable ways in which a being might attain this perfect condition, either by having infinite power, ability to accomplish every desire; or having finite powers, and limiting desires to those which these powers can satisfy. The latter alone is possible to man; and even this is not, unless man's powers are sufficient to provide for his well-being. Now, man's well-being depends so largely upon spiritual conditions—upon his own will, that "a man's life consisteth not in the abundance of the things which he possesseth." So it is possible, to limit desire for material things. Such limitation is the secret of a happy life; for he alone is rich who has no desire unsatisfied.

This, Paul had learned. Writing to thank the Philippians for their contribution to his needs, he says (4: 11–12), "Not that I speak in respect of want; for I have learned in whatsoever state I am therein to be *content (autarkes).* In everything and in all things, I have learned the secret, both to be filled and to be hungry, both to abound and to be in want." The utterance of a man who sought first the kingdom of God and took no thought what he should eat or drink!

But one may ask, Did Paul regard this as his personal practice or a rule for all? Would he draw no limit except

* *Katachrōmenoi—*perhaps, "to use as the be-all and end-all."

ability, and say that a rich man practices "contentment" provided he lives within his income? Both questions are answered by 1 Tim. 6:8. "Having food and covering we shall be therewith content," or, "in these we shall have enough" (*arkesthêsometha*), By these terms Paul doubtless meant to include the material instruments required by intellectual and æsthetic needs, for his own most cherished possessions were books and parchments. The rule is therefore, to limit expenditures to the least that is required for a healthy body and sound mind.

This idea controlled Paul's life (Acts 20: 33–36). His writings are full of it. Hebrews, 13:5, contrasts such contentment with the love of money. 1 Thess. 4: 11–12, commands quiet, constant industry as a Christian duty, that by a supply of necessities we may have need of nothing.

But why should the limit be drawn at necessities? Why is it not my right and duty to provide myself with all the material advantages which I can procure, so long as I regard them as means? The answer lies in the complementary grace.

III. "FELLOWSHIP."

If I were the only man in the world, it would be my duty to furnish myself with the greatest possible material advantages. But I am not an isolated individual, I am a member of an organism. The root of all sin is to think of myself "more highly than I ought," i. e., to assume that I am anything but a member (Rom. 12; 1. Cor. 12). This community idea is the foundation of all moral duties (Eph. 4: 25–28, etc). The great error of modern Christianity, both practically and doctrinally is that it has substituted individualism for the community idea.

Now the characteristic of a community is that the many members have a common life and "the same care one for another" (1 Cor. 12 and Acts 4: 32). All the powers of each are devoted to the interests of all, they regard all things as "common" (*Koiná*). This "fellowship" (*Koinonia*, i. e., the supremacy in thought, feeling and will of that which is common), is the source of all Christian joy (Acts 2:46), as well as virtue. It is the same as John's favorite precept,

"Love one another." Community of goods, is but one outward expression of this unity of spirit.

"Fellowship" determines what "contentment" shall be. Each member having the same care for every other, will limit his desires to that which all can enjoy—the average income, or supply of "necessities." Yet it becomes a motive to unceasing industry (Eph. 4: 28). Personal necessity might be removed by the possession of a fortune, but one filled with this community spirit will not rest however much he may have given, while his labor can bestow yet more. The motive to labor from love of gain is excluded by Christian "contentment," but only that its place may be filled by the more effective one of life for the community. "Contentment" is one side of Christian love, "fellowship" the other. The former grace is necessary in order that the latter may be possible. This seems the meaning of 2 Cor. 9: 8, "God is able to make all grace abound unto you: that ye having always all contentment (*autarkeia*, R. V. "sufficiency") in everything, may abound unto every good work; as it is written, He hath scattered abroad, he hath given to the poor, etc.

The fullest discussion of "fellowship" is in 2 Cor. 8–9. Comparing this passage with other allusions we learn the significance of the word.

(1) Its ground:—the unity of all in Christ, "One body in Christ."

(2) The underlying principle based on this truth:—"Let no one seek his own, but each his neighbor's good (1 Cor. 10: 24). "Bear ye one another's burdens and so fulfill the law of Christ" (Gal. 6: 2). "So laboring, ye ought to help the weak and to remember the words of the Lord Jesus, how he himself said, It is more blessed to give than to receive" (Acts 20: 35).

(3) Its enforcement:—It must be by each man's conscience. If not voluntary, it is morally valueless; it is not Christian. (2 Cor. 9: 7).

(4) Motives:—Above all Christ's example, who became poor to make us rich, even God's unspeakable gift. (1 Cor. 8: 9 and 9: 15). Also the example of others, the Christian's

reputation, his perfection in grace and the glory of God (2 Cor. 8 : 1–8 and 9 : 1–14).

(5) The result aimed at :—This of course fixes the standard of giving. This result is nothing less than the equality of all Christians in respect to wealth. "For I say this, not that others may be eased and ye distressed; but *by equality*; your abundance being a supply at this present time for their want, that their abundance also may become a supply for your want; that there *may be equality*; as it is written, He that gathered much had nothing over; and he that gathered little had no lack" (2 Cor. 8 : 13–15). "Abundance" means more exactly "superfluity," i. e., excess over that required by Christian contentment; "want" is the amount by which any falls short. Again, as in Agur's prayer, we find the miracle of the manna appealed to as showing how God would have the good things of life distributed. Thus Christian "fellowship" differs from communism not in aim, but in means. It seeks equality without destroying property; relies on love not on law. Startling as this interpretation may seem, the language will bear no other; and it is confirmed by many allusions, e. g., in writing to the Thessalonians, Paul says, "If any will not work, neither let him eat," a command which would have been unnecessary and meaningless except in such a community. Paul's "fellowship" is simply a development and application of the communism of the Jerusalem church, to adapt it to the condition of a scattered and world-wide community.

This grace is emphasized in Paul's epistles. "Communicating to the necessities of the saints" (Rom. 12 : 13, *koinonountes*). "To do good and communicate forget not" (Heb. 13 : 16, *cf.* Philemon 5–7). "Charge them that are rich in the present world . . . that they do good, that they be rich in noble deeds, that they be ready to distribute (*eumetadotous*) willing to communicate, (*koinonikous*)" I (Tim. 6 : 17–18).

But how practically was this grace shown in the early church? "Fellowship" manifested itself in loving hospitality to apostles and evangelists, to delegates from sister churches, and to those whom public or private persecution left homeless and destitute (Heb. 12:2; Rom. 12:13). In the "Teaching of the Twelve Apostles" we find given rules which later became necessary to protect this hospitality from being imposed upon. Again the wants of the poor in each local church were systematically provided for. Widows appear to have been the most numerous class among the needy, and Paul gives detailed instructions for their enrolment among the pensioners of the church (1 Tim. 5:3–16). He would exclude all who could be supported by children, grandchildren or a second husband. A man's first duty was to provide for all naturally dependent on him, that the church relieved of all unnecessary burdens might be able to do more in cases of real need. Not to do this was a violation of "fellowship" worse than apostacy. Ministers of the gospel were another class of the needy. To serve the church, as such, they must be free from other cares; and the church freely receiving their services freely provides for their needs. The very same reason is urged in 1 Cor. 9:11, for support of the ministry, which is given in Rom. 15:27, for contribution to the needy Jewish Christians. So in Gal. 6:6, the word of general import is used, "Let him that is taught in the word, *communicate* unto him that teacheth in all good things." To deprive the church of this privilege is to do it wrong (2 Cor. 12:13). Thus what the minister receives is not a salary, but loving supply of his necessities. Bearing this in mind—that with Paul, "living by gospel," does not mean earning money,—his argument to prove the right of the ministry to receive support loses the mercenary tone which at first it seems to have (1 Cor. 9:6–14).

Finally this fellowship extended beyond the limits of the local church and even of country and race. The great instance of Christian love in the New Testament is the contribution "for the poor saints at Jerusalem." How wonderful the new force brought into the world by Christ, which could constrain inhabitants of the great cities of Antioch, Corinth and Rome to contribute to the needs of unknown people in the obscure province of Judea! Constrain men of the haughty, ruling race and Greeks proud of art and learning, to deny themselves for the sake of barbarians, and, of all barbarians, for the Jews universally distrusted, hated and despised! The world had seen nothing like it. It was a miracle.

Evidently "fellowship" can be perfect only when it is mutual. If one party selfishly takes advantage of the other's generosity, that generosity is doing more harm than good. The grace can therefore be exercised only in a community of persons all practicing "contentment" and "fellowship," all loving and being loved, serving and being served. For those outside of the Christian brotherhood, love however great its yearnings, can do little. So Paul says (Gal. 6: 10) "Let us work that which is good toward all men and especially toward them that are of the household of faith." Even the church is not yet perfect in love. So much of the "flesh" still persists that Christians forget "fellowship" and have law-suits one with another, nay themselves do wrong and defraud their brethren (1 Cor. 6: 1–11).

Others are ready to eat without working, (2 Thess. 3: 10). Or to shift their natural responsibilities upon the church (1 Tim. 5: 8). Because some fail in "contentment" and "fellowship," these graces are more difficult for the rest; and the enforcement of these duties, for self-protection and the welfare of all, occasions friction. The Church is not yet a perfect body in which all the members have the same care one for another; is rather a body diseased by the presence of inert, dead matter, in it, but not of it.

But, though "fellowship" seems often like sowing seeds which are slow to germinate, Paul exhorts, "Let us not be weary in well-doing; for in due season we shall reap if we faint not." The significance of the church, like the corn in the blade, is not what it is, but what it shall be,—"fitly framed and knit together, through that which every joint supplieth," growing into perfect unselfishness like its Head, destined to attain "the measure of the stature of the fulness of Christ."

This is Paul's conception of the Church, his remedy for the long strife of rich and poor—a loving brotherhood inspired by the example of Christ who became poor to make us rich; in which every member limits his own expenditure to the average of the community and employs his surplus wealth or ability in love and wisdom for the common interests of instruction, and preaching, and the relief of every brother's need, in which every local community recognizing the universal body of Christ, cares for every sister church throughout the world, in which the individual instead of being robbed of personality by the constraint of a vast socialistic system is constantly being developed in wisdom and love by the responsibility of planning and doing for himself what ought to be done, and in which this all-pervasive intelligence and devotion, this combined wisdom and mutual love of all, adjusts each one's burden to his ability, and thus attains "equality" —"liberty, equality and fraternity."

'Human nature is diametrically opposed to such a life.' Yes; but what does the Christian life mean, but putting off "the old man with his deeds" and "putting on the new man," even Christ Jesus? 'It is a tremendous task to bring the world, or even the church to such a life.' Yes; our "wrestling is not against flesh and blood but against the powers, against the principalities, against the world-rulers of this darkness." Only heroes can accomplish this warfare. 'We cannot bring all men to this mind, but must remedy social evils by legislation and communistic systems.' Such attempted short-cuts can end only in disaster. Law cannot eradicate selfishness. Individualism is the parent of all heresy; selfishness, the root of all sin; self-absorption, the spring of all misery. Nothing will save the world but their extirpation. Christianity means nothing less than this,— unselfish life in and for the community of the unselfish.

THE LIFE AND TIMES OF THE CHRIST,

BASED ON LUKE.

By William R. Harper and George S. Goodspeed,

Yale University.

(Copyrighted, 1890.)

STUDIES XLV. AND XLVI.—PREPARATIONS FOR THE END. LUKE
22 : 1–53.

Remark.—It is desirable that in beginning each "study" the entire passage
assigned be read over rapidly and the main divisions of the narrative noted.

I. EXAMINATION OF THE MATERIAL.

[It will be noted that the following order is observed invariably in this work; (1) the
verse or section is read and its contents stated in a general way; (2) important or difficult words and phrases are studied; (3) a complete statement of
the contents of the verse or section is formed in view of the work already
done; (4) the religious teaching is sought.]

§ 1. Chapter 22 : 1–6.

1. Read the passage and note the subject· *The Plot and the Traitor.*
2. The following are important words : (1) *which is called*, etc. (22 : 1), light on the
   persons to whom the gospel is written; (2) *Satan entered* (22 : 3), cf. John
   6 : 70; 13 : 27; (3) *captains* (22 : 14), i. e. of the temple guard, cf. Acts 4 : 1; (4)
   were glad (22 : 5), for the reason cf. Mk. 14 : 2.
3. A brief statement of the thought is as follows : *The Passover approaching, the
   authorities consult how to make away with him. Satan inspires Judas, one of the
   twelve, to offer to betray Jesus ; the offer is accepted and a price is fixed. He proceeds to find a good occasion.*
4. An evil mind may live in vain in company with the best and purest associates.

§ 2. Chapter 22 : 7–23.

1. Read the verses and criticise the following subject : *The Last Supper.*
2. The student may note these words and phrases : (1) *day of unleavened bread*
   (22 : 7), i. e. the first day, the 14th Nisan, cf. Ex. 12 : 18 ; Lev. 23 : 5, 6; (2) vs.
   13, 14, compare the judgment you made about Lk. 19 : 30 seq.; (3) *follow him*,
   etc. (22 : 10), consider the reason for this strange proceeding; (4) *the guest
   chamber* (22 : 11), cf. Mk. 14 : 14 ; (5) *with desire have I*, etc. (22 : 15), i. e. "I
   have earnestly desired," a "hebraism ; " (6) *I will not eat it until*, etc. (22 : 16),
   did he eat it with them ? (7) *but behold*, etc. (22 · 21), had Judas eaten with

them? (8) *woe unto*, etc. (22 : 22), is there here (a) compassion, (b) desire to make Judas give up his design?

3. The student may study the following condensation : *When the passover has been prepared in the place he had chosen, Jesus sits down with the twelve. Declaring his eagerness to eat this passover with them, he blesses and divides bread among them saying, " Take this my body ; " likewise wine, saying, " My covenant in my blood for you ; " (saying also, to their astonishment), " For I must die, betrayed by one who is here."*

4. The student may select the religious thought that most fully and clearly is represented in the passage.

§ 3. Chapter 22 : 24-38.

1. A subject of the passage is : *The Table Talk.*
2. (1) *Contention*, etc. (22 : 24), what cause for such a discussion at this time ? (2) *he said* (22 : 25), cf. John 13 for what he had probably done before these words; (3) *but*, etc. (22 : 28), i. e. " although you now have such ambitious ideas, yet I know that you have been faithful ; " (4) *sit on thrones*, etc. (22 : 30), literal or figurative ? (5) *you* (22 : 31), note the plural, i. e. " all you disciples who are here ; " (6) *thee* (22 : 32), as the representative and leader among them ; (7) *turned*, i. e. to God ; (8) v. 36, is this literal or figurative ? (9) *for*, etc. (22 : 37), i. e. you will need to make these preparations for I am to suffer as a felon, and you are my followers ; (10) *enough* (22 : 38), the spirit of this remark ?
3. The student may prepare a brief statement of the thought of the passage.
4. The line of religious teaching running through the passage is that of service to others as the Christian ideal.

§ 4. Chapter 22 : 39-46.

1. The student may state the subject after reading the passage.
2. Words calling for study are (1) *as his custom was* (22 : 39), cf. 21 : 37 ; (2) *the place* (22 : 40), where ? (3) *prayed* (22 : 41), lit. "kept praying," cf. Mk. 14 : 35, 39 ; (4) *remove* (22 : 42), meaning of this ? (5) *cup*, i. e. "destiny of suffering," cf. Ps. 23 : 5 ; 75 : 8 ; Isa. 51 : 17, etc.; (6) *sleeping for sorrow* (22 : 45), cf. Mk. 14 : 37, 38.
3. The condensation of the thought is : *He goes with the disciples to the Mount of Olives and there tells them to pray that they may not be tempted. Going on a short distance, he prays that he may escape the coming experience, if so the Father wills. An angel strengthens him in his overwhelming entreaties. After the prayer, he comes to the sleeping disciples and bids them awake and prepare for the coming trial by prayer.*
4. Consider the spirit and the power of prayer as manifested in this passage.

§ 5. Chapter 22 : 47-53.

1. A subject suggested for these verses is : *The Arrest of Jesus.*
2. The student may study the following with the helps at command : (1) *to kiss* (22 : 47) ; (2) *Jesus said*, etc. (22 : 48), the spirit and motive of the question ? (3) *certain one* (22 : 50) ; (4) *suffer ye thus far* (22 : 51) ; (5) *your hour* (22 : 53) ; (6) *power of darkness.*
3. The thought of the passage may be stated thus ; *Judas comes with a crowd and kisses Jesus who replies, Do you betray me with a kiss ? Friends attempt resist-*

ance ; a man is wounded, but Jesus heals him. He says to the leaders of the crowd, Your preparations are those of thief-takers. You did not molest me in the temple. But it is your hour and darkness rules.

4. The student may decide on the religious thought.

II. CLASSIFICATION OF THE MATERIAL.

1. Contents and Summary.

1) **The Contents.** The following table of contents is to be mastered.

PREPARATIONS FOR THE END.

§ 1. THE PLOT AND THE TRAITOR.
§ 2   THE LAST SUPPER.
§ 3. THE TABLE TALK.
§ 4. JESUS IN PRAYER.
§ 5. THE ARREST OF JESUS.

2) **The Summary.** The complete summary statement of the sections may be made by the student.

2. Observations upon the Material.

295) 22 : 1. The explanation given suggests that the narrative was written for the use of those who were not Jews.

296) 22 : 3-6. The spirit of Judas is regarded by the writer as one of malignity. The money question seems to be an afterthought.

297) 22 : 10. Jesus and the disciples seem to have retired from the city at this time.

298) 22 : 10-12. The special directions given and their peculiar character show the danger which encompassed Jesus, and his care not to be taken before the right time.

299) 22 : 14-23. A comparison of Luke's narrative of the last supper with that of Matt. and Mark shows much divergence in the order and material.

300) 22 : 17. Certain parts of the passover had been observed before Jesus introduced the new institution.

301) 22 : 19, 20. This is Jesus' clearest teaching on the meaning of his death and this is in parabolic form.

302) 22 : 21. The cool deliberate plan of Judas is seen in his remaining with Jesus and the disciples through this scene. He is on the watch for a convenient time (22 : 6).

303) 22 : 24. The contention doubtless arose either in view of their Messianic expectations in general, now apparently to be fulfilled, or in deciding upon the places at the table.

304) 22 : 41-46. Jesus, in this scene, is brought into the closest relation to mankind ; he suffers, is tempted, prays and seeks human sympathy.

305) 22 : 43, 44. There is some doubt about the authenticity of these verses.

306) 22 : 21, 22, 48. Jesus seeks by warning and tender rebuke to bring Judas to his senses even at the very last.

307) 22 : 52, 53. The force which was employed shows the fear that Jesus inspired in the authorities.

3. Topics for Study.

1) **The Passover and the New Institution.** [Obs. 299-301] : (1) Recall the original institution, the passover (Ex. 12 : 1-36), and note the significance of it, (a) a memorial, (b) a sacrifice, (c) a family feast, (d) full of joy. (2) Consider now the relation of the passover to the New Institution of Jesus, (a) its intro-

duction at what point in the passover celebration, (b) its significance in the light of the meaning of the passover as outlined above. (3) Make a study of the New Institution itself to observe (a) the reflection of Jesus' character in it, (b) the reflection of Jesus' method of parabolic teaching in it, (c) an enduring memorial of himself, (d) a permanent testimony to his doctrine, (e) a means of grace and fellowship.

2) Judas Iscariot. [Obs. 296, 302, 306] : (1) Gather the facts in relation to Judas as given in the following passages : Mk. 3 : 19; John 13:29; 6 : 70, 71; 12 : 5, 6; Mk. 14: 10, 11 ; John 13 : 26, 27; 18 : 2; Lk. 22 : 47, 48; Mt. 27 : 3–5; Acts 1 : 16, 17. (2) In view of Lk. 6 : 16 consider why Jesus chose him, whether (a) ignorantly, or (b) hopefully, or (c) designedly (John 13 : 18). (3) Why did he follow Jesus, whether (a) with selfish aims solely, (b) with pure devotion, (c) with mixed motives. (4) Inquire into the causes of his falling away as connected with (a) his being the only Judean disciple, (b) his work, encouraging selfishness, (c) his consciousness of Jesus' insight into his mind (John 6: 70, 71). (5) Consider the cause for his act of betrayal as found in (a) covetousness (John 12 : 6), (b) disappointment (Mk. 9 : 34–37), (c) spite and revenge, (Lk. 22 : 47, 48). (6) What is the explanation of his repentance (Mt. 27 : 3–5)? (7) Make a general summary of Judas' character, (a) its good points, (b) its fatal defects. (8) Is Judas' character exceptional, (a) in its essential elements? or (b) in its special circumstances?

4. Religious Teaching.

The student may take as a subject for the religious lesson, *Jesus' Relation to his Followers* as exhibited in these verses : (1) He enjoys their companionship and seeks their sympathy, 22 : 15, 45 (cf. Mt. 26 : 40, 43). (2) He would win back even one who has betrayed him (22 : 21, 22, 48). (3) He gives himself up to death for them (22 : 19, 20). (4) He bountifully promises them reward for their fidelity (22 : 29, 30). (5) He prays for them in times of trial (22 : 32). (6) Other suggestive points.
What should be our response to this attitude of Jesus?

STUDIES XLVII. AND XLVIII.—THE TRIAL AND CRUCIFIXION OF JESUS. LUKE 22 : 54–23 : 49.

Remark.—It is desirable that in beginning each "study" (1) the material of the preceding "study" be reviewed, and (2) the entire passage assigned be read over rapidly and the main divisions of the narrative noted.

I. EXAMINATION OF THE MATERIAL.

[It will be noted that the following order is observed invariably in this work ; (1) the verse or section is read and its contents stated in a general way; (2) important or difficult words and phrases are studied; (3) a complete statement of the contents of the verse or section is formed in view of the work already done; (4) the religious teaching is sought.]

§ 1.   Chapter 22 : 54–62.

1. The student, after reading the verses. may state a subject.
2. Important words and phrases are : (1) *high priest's* (22 . 54), (a) cf. Mt. 26 : 57, (b) note also John 18 : 13, 15, 16, (c) probability that the two occupied the same house ? (2) *court* (22 : 55), light on the construction of an eastern dwelling ? (3) *maid seeing him* (22 : 56), cf. John 18 : 17 and decide as to these being accounts of the same ; (4) *also*, " this man also as well as some one else," who ? (5) *another* (22 : 58), cf. Mt. 26 : 71 ; John 18 : 25 ; (6) *another confidently affirmed* (22: 59), cf. John 18 : 26 ; (7) *the Lord* (22 : 61), significant as to the date of the Gospel ? (8) *turned and looked,* (a) peculiar to Luke, (b) as Jesus passed from the house to the public trial, (9) *wept bitterly* (22 : 62), i. e. " wept loudly," or " wailed," in bitterness of spirit.
3. The student may make his own statement of thought.
4. An impressive thought is, that even noble impulses, if not buttressed by firm character, bring one into a situation which may overthrow him.

§ 2.   Chapter 22 : 63–71.

1. Read the passage ; criticise a subject : *Jesus before the Jews.*
2. Words and phrases that call for study are : (1) *held* (22 . 69), (a) i. e. as a condemned man, (b) after the scene of Mt. 26 : 59–64 ? (2) *mocked,* (a) lit. " kept mocking," (b) regarding him as condemned in view of Mt. 26 : 64 ; (3) *prophesy* (22 : 64), note their idea of prophecy ; (4) *day* (22 . 66), why wait ? (5) *assembly,* etc., i. e. the " Sanhedrim ; " (6) *council,* etc. (a) cf. Mt. 26 : 59–64, (b) Mt. 27 : 1, (c) deciding as to the relation of Lk. 22 : 66–71 to both of these passages ; (7) *will not answer* (22 : 68), cf. 20 : 1–8 ; (8) *Son of God* (22 : 70), this was the point they were seeking to establish—as the Christ, did he claim divinity ? (9) *ye say that I am,* cf. margin.
3. The student may make his own statement of thought.
4. A religious thought of the passage may be chosen by the student.

§ 3.   Chapter 23 : 1–7.

1. A statement of the subject is suggested : *The accusation before Pilate.*
2. (1) *Before Pilate* (23 : 1), significance of this ? (2) *perverting* (23 : 2), i. e. " leading astray after a false and wicked object of regard ; " (3) *forbidding,* etc., grounds of this charge ? (4) *asked him* (23 : 3), cf. John 18 : 33–38 ; (5) *multitudes* (23 : 4), first hint of a popular uprising against Jesus ; (6) *himself also* (23 : 7), (a) as well as Pilate, (b) where were their usual residences ?
3. The student may give a condensed summary of the thought of the passage.
4. As a practical teaching, observe that a man's right convictions are sure to be assailed by evil motives and the issue cannot be evaded.

§ 4.   Chapter 23 : 8–12.

1. The subject may be given as : *Jesus sent to Herod.*
2. The student is invited to study the following : (1) *exceeding glad* (23 : 8) the spirit exhibited? (2) *answered him nothing* (23 : 9), why? (3) *mocked him* (23 : 11), contempt or resentment ? (4) *sent him back,* on what basis? (5) *at enmity* (23 : 12), on what grounds ?

3. The student may prepare the thought.

4. Note here an example of the deterioration of a character originally open to good influences. How did it come about?

§ 5. Chapter 23 : 13–25.

1. A brief statement of the subject for criticism is: *Pilate's Judgment.*

2. (1) *Pilate called together* (23 : 13), i. e. convened a formal assembly ; (2) *chastise* (23 : 16), why? (3) *Barabbas* (23 : 18), cf. Mt. 27 : 16; John 18 : 40; (4) *gave sentence* (23 : 24), cf. John 19 : 13; (5) *asked for* (23 : 25), lit. "kept asking for."

3. The student may condense the thought.

4. It is instructive to consider the lengths to which a man or a body of men will go when they give loose rein to their evil impulses.

§ 6. Chapter 23 : 26–43.

1. The passage read, suggests the following subject: *The Crucifixion.*

2. Words and phrases of importance or difficulty are : (1) *Simon of Cyrene* (23 : 26), cf. Mk. 15 : 21 ; significance of the choice of this man? (2) *blessed*, etc. (23:29), the chiefest curse would be invoked as the greatest blessing ; (3) v. 31, (a) " if an innocent person must so suffer, what will be done to the guilty?" (b) comparing the attitude of the Romans toward himself now and toward the nation in the future ; (4) *forgive them* (23 : 34), whom? (5) *hath done nothing amiss* (23 : 41), how did he know this? (6) *comest in thy kingdom* (23:42), note significance of this; (7) *paradise* (23 : 43), meaning?

3. The student may make his own condensation of the passage.

4. A religious thought is suggested by the prompt response of Jesus to the prayer of the repentant robber.

§ 7. Chapter 23 : 44–49.

1. The student may read the verses and decide on a subject.

2. (1) *Sixth hour* (23 : 44), i. e. 12 o'clock ; (2) *darkness;* is this (a) supernatural, and yet (b) connected with the earthquake that followed (Mt. 27 : 51), (c) intended to teach what? (3) *whole land*, i. e. (a) that region, or (b) half the world? (4) *veil*, etc. (23 : 45), (a) note physical basis (Mt. 27 : 51), (b) supernatural element, (c) significance—God's abandonment of the temple, unhindered access to God, through death of Jesus; (5) *glorified God* (23 : 47), how much did this mean? (6) *stood afar off* (23 : 49), cf. John 19 : 25.

3. The student may make his own statement.

4. The student may select the great religious lesson.

II. CLASSIFICATION OF THE MATERIAL.

1. Contents and Summary.

1) **The Contents.** To be mastered.

THE TRIAL AND CRUCIFIXION OF JESUS.

§ 1. PETER'S DENIAL.

§ 2. JESUS BEFORE THE JEWS.

§ 3. THE ACCUSATION BEFORE PILATE.
§ 4. JESUS SENT TO HEROD.
§ 5. PILATE'S JUDGMENT.
§ 6. THE CRUCIFIXION.
§ 7. JESUS' DEATH.

2) **The Summary.** This may be carefully prepared by the student.

2. Observations upon the Material.

The student may make " observations " upon the following passages :

(1) 22 : 55	(5) 22 : 69	(9) 23 : 27	(13) 23 : 38.
(2) 22 : 61	(6) 23 : 4, 14, 23, 24	(10) 23 : 28–31	(14) 23 : 43.
(3) 22 : 56–60	(7) 23 : 8, 9	(11) 23 : 33	(15) 23 : 44, 45.
(4) 22 : 66	(8) 23 : 13	(12) 23 : 35	(16) 23 : 46.

3. Topics for Study.

1) **Jesus, the Christ.** (1) Observe the unequivocal statements which Jesus makes in Lk. 22 : 69, 70, (cf. Mt. 26 : 63, 64; Mk. 14 : 61, 62). (2) Analyze them to discover what he claims to be, (a) the Christ, (b) the Son of God, (c) a son of man, (d) clothed with divine majesty and power. (3) Note how the words were understood by his judges, Lk. 22 : 71, (cf. Mk. 14 : 63, 64; John 10 : 33). (4) The significance of this claim in view of the circumstances, his seeming failure and expectation of death.

2) **The Council.** (1) Learn something of the composition, organization and powers of this council (Lk. 22 : 66), called the " Sanhedrim." (2) Observe that Jesus is twice brought before them (subsequent to John 18 : 13), cf. Mk. 14 : 55; 15:1; Lk. 22 : 66. (3) In view of the actions of these gatherings, decide whether they were formal and legal, or irregular and informal, meetings of the Sanhedrim.

3) **The Popular Decision.** (1) Consider the persons composing the "multitudes" of Lk. 23 : 4 (cf. 23 : 13, 18), whether representative of the popular feeling or not. (2) Is it probable that they were seized by a sudden impulse or deceived by false representations? cf. Mk. 15 : 11. (3) Observe their declaration. Mt. 27 : 25. (4) Recall the impression made in the Gospel narratives throughout as to the popularity of Jesus. (5) Endeavor to decide whether (a) the people as a whole rejected Jesus here or (b) a faction of political leaders stirred up the rabble against him.

4) **The Meaning of the Death of Jesus.** (1) Recall Jesus' prophecies of his death, Lk. 9 : 22, 44; 13 : 32, 33; 18 : 31–33. (2) Note his hints as to its purpose and meaning, Lk. 9 : 23, 24; Mk. 10 : 45; Lk. 22 : 19, 20; John 6 : 51; 12 : 32, 33, etc. (3) Examine the apostolic teaching, cf. 1 Peter 1 : 19; Tit. 2 : 14; 1 Tim. 2 : 6; 2 Cor. 5 : 15; Gal. 3 : 13; 1 John 1 : 7. (4) Grasp firmly the *fact* of the "vicarious" death (atonement) of Jesus and then observe the theories which seek to explain it, (a) the moral influence exerted by his death, (b) in Jesus' death God illustrated his character as a moral governor by giving his Son to be punished for sinners, (c) in Jesus' death for sinners God vindicated his righteous character and became reconciled to man, when his Son suffered the penalty of law.

4. Religious Teaching.

The student may select his own subject for the religious teaching—one, however, which gathers up the scenes and subjects of the narrative. The following themes are suggested : (1) The types of character exhibited with the lessons of each, e. g. Peter, Pilate, Herod, etc. (2) Jesus, amidst the scenes and experiences of these last hours, e. g. (a) his heroism, (b) forgivingness, (c) pity, etc., with the obligation these spiritual characteristics lay upon us. Let either one of these (not both) or any other be carefully worked out.

A "SYMPOSIUM" ON SOME GREAT BIBLE QUESTIONS, ESPECIALLY INSPIRATION.

One of the most vital and essential things in the study of any subject is to know clearly and keep well in view the important points about it.   This is particularly true of the Bible, a study of which is in danger of coming to nought or of falling short of what it might accomplish by the choice of what is after all a side issue as the aim of study or by the neglect of those issues which after all are fundamental.   The STUDENT has inquired of the scholars and ministers whose names appear below what, in their opinion, are the *four or five great Bible questions* which are in themselves all-important or of particular prominence at the present day.   It has recognized that among these questions, that of inspiration has a foremost place.   Particular attention has therefore been called to this topic and the suggestions made upon it will be carefully considered.

I. THE GREAT BIBLE QUESTIONS.

From Professor JOHN D. DAVIS, Ph. D.

The subjects of controversy in regard to the Bible as a book are in and of themselves reducible to four : namely, concerning genuineness, authenticity, inspiration and authority.   These questions are all old, but ever new and of supreme present importance.   They are discussed by the believer and the unbeliever, are taught by the book itself in some form or other and more or less explicitly in regard to each and all of its parts.   In what form and to what extent they are claimed is not only a legitimate but a most imperative subject of inquiry.

Attack on these four doctrines, as well as debate concerning them, varies according to the varying science, philosophy and historical knowledge of the different ages.

The first two of these doctrines, as underlying and conditioning the others, are fundamental : are the Scriptures in whole or in part genuine? are they authentic?   At present both are attacked simultaneously and most fiercely with weapons forged in German workshops, with the allegations that numerous glosses of a later age and different spirit are found, that not only supplementary but contradictory accounts are interwoven, that discourses have been manipulated in the spirit of compromise, and that entire books are colored by conceptions not current at the time of the occurrence of the events described.

Genuineness and authenticity being established, the questions of inspiration and authority come up ; otherwise not : and these questions, while not so fundamental, are of first importance in reach of influence on doctrine and character.   Did holy men write under such divine inspiration that the Scriptures not only contain the Word of God, but are the Word of God? and are these Scriptures the sole authority in matters of faith and practice, or is Christian consciousness likewise a standard of truth?

Princeton, N. J.

From Rev. ELDRIDGE MIX, D. D.

I. The first question of importance to the Bible Student is that of the inspiration, and consequent Divine authority, of the Bible itself. That is vital and fundamental. Have we in it that which has come from God? Even though it has come through human instrumentality, has He so inspired it, and guarded it in its transmission to us, that we have in it, without mistake or lack, what exactly expresses His mind and will concerning us? There is little spiritual good to be gained from the study of it, unless we know for a certainty, so as to be satisfied beyond question, that we are dealing directly with God through His written Word.

II. A second question of no less importance, is the interpretation of the Scriptures, as to the principles they inculcate through the letter of the Word which often is of local application and coloring. Very much of the Old Testament is an illustration by example of principles that we ought to put in practice, rather than copy the example itself. So it is with the teaching of our Lord and of His Apostles. How does all its teaching touch us of the present day, and take hold on us, is the all important question.

III. A third thing greatly needing to be done by the Bible Student is to get at the whole of Scripture teaching concerning any particular point, so as not to have partial and one-sided views of truth. Take its teaching in regard to God for example. We do not get its entire conception and representation of Him from either Moses, or David, or the Prophets. What we want is a more perfect welding together of the different and partial representations of Him which together will make a perfect portrait of Him for our beholding. So it is with all other truths. We need to study the Bible in this respect constructively, if I may so express it.

IV. The fourth question relates to the life. It is the question of so studying the Bible as to have as the result a more full and perfect living of the truth. The Scriptures are of comparatively little worth to us,—they fail utterly in fact of fulfilling their purpose, if the Word is not made flesh by us. How then shall our growing knowledge of the Scriptures become to us bread for our eating, to be transmuted into good red blood, and make spiritual fibre and muscle? The great problem is how to yoke the intellect and the heart together in their study, so that they shall work together for the spiritual upbuilding of the whole man.

Fall River, Mass.

From Professor JAMES R. BOISE, D. D., LL. D.

You wish me to state what, in my opinion, are "the *four most important questions relating to the Bible at the present time.*"

I submit the following :

1. Is it the inspired Word of God?
2. Does it present to us clearly the only way of salvation?
3. How may we most profitably study the Bible?

On this question allow me to make a few suggestions.

(1) The Bible should be studied prayerfully. Those who do not study it thus will surely fail to apprehend its most important spiritual teachings. *A natural man (an unregenerate man, psuchikos anthrôpos) does not receive the things of the Spirit of God ; for they are foolishness to him ; and he is not able to know (them), because they are spiritually judged (or examined).* I Cor. 2: 14.

(2) It should be studied critically, with the utmost pains to ascertain the exact meaning of every word, the exact construction of every sentence, and the true line of argument.

(3) It should be studied, if possible, as a whole; with no part left out, no part slighted, with the light from no part eclipsed.

(4) It should be studied with as much knowledge as we can gain of history, geography, antiquities; that is, of the entire surroundings in which each part was written; always bearing in mind the leading aim of the writer, and comparing his views with those of the other writers of the sacred Word, whether in the Old or the New Testament.

4. Can we safely formulate any statements of Christian doctrine on a superficial knowledge of the Bible ?

This is a question of special importance at the present time.

You requested me to mention *four* questions most prominent in my own mind. Allow me to add one more.

5. Does any other knowledge, or any science, compare for a moment in importance with a definite knowledge of the way in which we may become forever " heirs of God, and joint heirs with Christ?"

To any intelligent human being this question requires no answer.

Morgan Park, Ill.

II. THE QUESTION OF INSPIRATION.

The following queries were put to the gentlemen whose communications appear below:

1. What is to be understood by the term " inspiration?"

2. What are the elements which must enter into any doctrine of inspiration?

3. What is the right method of procedure in framing a doctrine of inspiration?

4. What change, if any, has Biblical criticism made necessary in the already existing formulated statements of the doctrine of inspiration?

From Rev. Thos. Scott Bacon, D. D.

1. Inspiration as we are to consider it, is this unique fact that the writings of certain men as collected in the Holy Bible are the Word of God to all mankind. This is a fact which is altogether supernatural, and never was nor could be discovered by our intelligence. So inspiration itself as a fact was revealed directly by God, as first to Moses, " Thus shalt thou say," etc. It is then a mystery as well as a fact and as all facts about God are of necessity. It is beyond human capacity to " find out " these things, or to entirely comprehend them when He makes them known to us for our faith. We are to *believe* with humility and obedience.

2. As is commonly said, there are both the human and the Divine elements in Inspiration. Thus we have the writings of certain men, as Moses, David or the Apostles. But in them we do not so much consider what this or that fellowman of ours thought or knew, as what Another Person—One above us all—is saying to all men. This is indeed such an elevated and spiritual thought that none of us feel all the force which it should have. Yet it is they who with this understanding read those writings most and most attentively, who have the highest sense of this and upon whom it steadily gains. Besides this the most devout and reverent minds are conscious of coming in contact with the thoughts of a fellowman, one of flesh and blood like ourselves,— receiving truth direct from God and communicating it perfectly to us,—yet in much the same way as he would tell us the result of his own thought.

3. If such a doctrine of Inspiration (that is a form of words for stating it,) needs to be framed, I suggest that it should be in the fewest and simplest words,—these as much as may be in the tone and diction of the Holy Scriptures themselves, and also, if possible, in such terms as all the ages of the Church from the Apostles down have used. This last suggestion is not merely sentimentally good. It belongs to the great *principles* of brotherly love and of reverence and faith, which link us to the Gospel and give us a Bible to talk about. All *three* factors in this process should therefore be considered : the Inspirer who speaks, the Prophet who writes and the Church which is "the Witness and Keeper of Holy Writ."

4. I do not know enough about the "existing formulated statements" to answer this. The important thing is, the *fact* that the Spirit of God speaks to us directly in the Holy Bible. This Divine fact and mystery cannot be changed by any man's criticism of the words. It may be denied, or it may be abridged or obscured in some new formulated statement. The former I presume all writers in the OLD AND NEW TESTAMENT STUDENT would deprecate. The latter, I think, would have much the same deplorable effect :—that the Book would then cease to speak to men with the voice of God. This is my decided judgment after, again carefully going over all of the suggestions of such change put forth by some, including the popular theory of Evolution and the so-called "Higher Criticism" of the Hebrew Scriptures.

Buckeystown, Md.

From Rev. Professor JAMES STRONG, D. D.

In response to your interrogatories on the nature of Biblical Inspiration, which I would have preferred to mass together, so as to avoid repetition and confusion, I have time to write but briefly—too briefly, I fear, for the importance of the subject. My views are more fully set forth in the article under the head, "Inspiration" in the *Cyclopædia*, which I prepared myself.

1. *Definition.* Such a special influence of the Holy Spirit upon the sacred writers as to lead them to record statements and teachings intended to be the standard of religious belief and practice for mankind.

2. *Elements.* A careful distinction and harmonious balance of the divine and human coöperation; so that the Bible is at once and throughout the Word of God and yet the word of man.

3. *Doctrine.* To observe that the *materials* for writing were gathered

from various sources, namely, revelation (to the writers or to other parties), historical and general information, memory, and commonsense; while the plan, the method and the phraseology were largely left to the natural but sanctified judgment, habits, special purpose, circumstances and idiosyncrasy of each writer, with only such a preternatural superintendence as to preclude all error in point of fact or meaning.

4. *Adaptation.* The abandonment of the position or nomenclature, "plenary' or " verbal" inspiration, as being both mechanical and unscriptural; unnecessary in theology, and untenable in philosophy and science; misleading and inconsistent with itself. The adoption of these phrases, however, is really a modern phase, carefully avoided at least by the older English theologians, and practically ignored by all sound exegetes.

Drew Theo. Seminary.

From Rev. REUEN THOMAS, D. D.

1. The special use by God of a man or men providentially prefitted to receive such spiritual truth as was necessary to be communicated to the age in which such men lived, in order that through them the age might have a progressive knowledge of God and of Divine Providence.

2. The recognition of prepared men to receive the Holy Spirit's inspiration; a prepared language through which to communicate the truth conveyed to the man's mind; and an age needing and capable of some advance upon the spiritual knowledge and force communicated to it in the past.

3. A study of the admitted spiritual capabilities of human nature; a study of the relations of man to the Spirit of God; and a study of the claims which the Bible makes for itself to meet man's spiritual need, so bringing God, man and the truth into coöperative harmony.

4. The statements need to be less scholastically, less empirically and more Scripturally expressed, specially so as to recognize that in all his operations the Spirit of God communicates his influences through living men filled with a most abundant and exalted life and not simply through a book which apart from men is but a dead letter.

Brookline, Mass.

From Rev. Professor LEWIS F. STEARNS, D. D.

In answer to your questions, I would say:—

1. By inspiration I understand that unique and supernatural influence of God by which the Bible has been made what it is, namely, the means of converting and sanctifying the individual and building up the Church, by bringing them into saving contact with the historical facts, the divine truth, and the spiritual power, of redemption.

2. The following elements, it seems to me, should enter into a doctrine of inspiration:—

(1) A clear statement of its nature. Inspiration is supernatural, as distin-

guished from the ordinary operations of God's Spirit in the souls of believers and in the Christian Church.

(2) A recognition of its purpose,—to secure a means of grace by which the world in all ages may be brought into saving contact with redemption.

(3) A statement of the result. As a whole and in its parts the Bible perfectly answers the purpose of inspiration.

(4) A recognition of the fact that this end has been attained by a large and free use of the natural and human in subordination to the supernatural.

3. The right method of procedure in framing a doctrine of inspiration, is to study the facts of the Bible. But let them be studied in the right way.

The divine factor, and the perfection of the adaptation of the Bible to its end, will be best understood by the continuous and persevering use of it as a means of grace. This implies not only its use by the individual, but an understanding of the Christian consciousness of the Church in all ages as to what the Bible has been to it.

Light will also be thrown upon the subject by the assertions of the sacred writers respecting their own and each other's inspiration.

Finally, we need to study the Bible exegetically and critically. This will be especially useful in bringing out the human side.

4. Biblical criticism has brought us to see, more clearly than used to be the case, the method of inspiration. The chief agency is undoubtedly supernatural. But we have come to see that inspiration has attained its great object by a free use of the natural and human in subordination to the supernatural, in this respect conforming to the general method of God in his introduction of redemption into the world. The Bible is not a document handed down ready-made from heaven, but has been the result of a growth. Biblical critics tell us,—and we may accept their statements as in general true, without committing ourselves to the theories by which they endeavor to explain the facts, —that considerable portions of the Bible have been made up from previously existing materials, and that the Old Testament, at least, has been subjected to several recensions. Inspiration did not suppress the individuality of the sacred writers, but gave free play to it. In matters lying outside the scope of its great purpose inspiration seems to have made no effort to secure that infallibility in detail which certain critics, judging according to the standards of modern scholarship, are inclined to demand. It did not render the sacred writers scientific historians. It did not secure to them that accuracy in unimportant details which is expected from modern historians, though by no means always attained. It did not render them philosophers or men of science. It did not teach them the methods of scientific exegesis and render them accomplished Biblical critics, according to modern standards.

These facts, and others of the same nature, Biblical criticism has brought to light. Different minds judge them differently. The opponents of Christianity welcome them as disproving the divinity of the Bible. But in so doing they ignore the real purpose of the Bible. The advocates of that theory of inspiration which lays the exclusive emphasis upon the supernatural factor in the Bible, are compelled either to deny the facts or to explain them away. But there the facts are, and they are in great danger of doing what Lord Bacon has described as "offering to the Author of truth the unclean sacrifice of a lie." The sober-minded Christian, however, who is not seeking to maintain a theory but to discover the truth, and who is convinced at once of the truth of the facts and of the divinity of the Bible, views the matter in a wholly different light.   To him the facts referred to are a proof of the divine Wisdom which presided over the formation of the Bible.   He sees that the purpose of inspiration is more fully attained by the presence of this human factor.   As a plain book for plain men, a book not to be worshipped but to be used, a book not to satisfy the pedantic requirements of scholars but to make needy souls wise unto salvation, a book for all ages and conditions of men, the Bible is rendered the perfect means of grace which it is by the presentation of its supernatural contents in this human form.

Bangor Theo. Seminary.

Contributed Notes.

The Gathering of the Eagles: A Study of Luke 17: 37, and Matt. 24: 28.   Commentators have regarded this word of Jesus respecting the gathering together of the eagles as a dark saying.   There is a great diversity of view as to what is meant by the " eagles " and by the " body."

A careful attention to the admitted facts in the case may throw some light on the Saviour's use of this proverb.

1.   The discourse in Luke 17: 22–37 was uttered on a different occasion from that of Matt. 24: 4–28 and the succeeding context.   Luke 21: 8–36 is parallel with Matt. 24.

2.   There are some slight verbal differences in the proverb as reported by Matthew and by Luke.   It is likely that Jesus used the same word on the two occasions, and the differences are due to the reporters.   The grammatical sense is substantially the same.

3.   The connection in which the passage stands is also different—or apparently so—in the two discourses.   In Matthew it occurs after a declaration which asserts that there need be no question as to the place where the Son of man is to be seen when he comes.   "If, therefore, they shall say to you, Behold, he is in the wilderness ; go not forth : Behold, he is in the inner chambers ; believe it not.   For as the lightning cometh from the east, and is seen even unto the west ; so shall be the coming of the Son of man.   Wheresoever the carcase is, there will the eagles be gathered together."   In Luke the proverb occurs in response to a question by the disciples.   Jesus, referring to the time of his coming, says : "In that night there shall be two men in one bed ; the one shall be taken and the other left.   There shall be two women grinding together ; the one shall be taken and the other left.   And they answering say unto him, Where, Lord?   And he said unto them, Where the body is, thither will the eagles also be gathered together."

We have, then, the same proverb used on two different occasions, and apparently in two different connections.   We must find an explanation of the proverb that will fit both.   The natural meaning meets the requirement exactly.   It is this: Events occur according to a natural order.   There need be no doubt as to their occurrence or as to their significance when they take place according to the "fitness of things." We are certain that where the carcase is, there will the eagle be. We know that where the eagles are gathered together there will the carcase be found. The one necessarily involves the other.

We are, according to this meaning of the proverb, not to look for any hidden or mysterious reference to spiritual things in the "eagles" or the "body." Our concern is rather with *the relation between the two.* That relation is such that, when we know where one is, we will know where the other is. In Matthew's gospel Jesus means to assert in the use of this proverb that there need be no doubt as to the *where* of his *parousia.* Time, place, circumstance, will fully accord with the event. When he comes, we will be as certain of it as we are certain that where a carcase is, there will the eagles be gathered together.

In Luke's gospel, the question is also, Where? The reference of that question of the disciples is somewhat uncertain. It may be general or particular. They may have intended to ask: Where will these separations take place? How may one be certain that the events predicted are occurring? Or they may have intended to ask: Where will those who are taken be taken to, and where will those who are left be left at?

Whatever the special reference of the question of the disciples may be, the meaning and application of the proverb are the same. If their question be general, then the connection is practically the same as that in Matthew, and Jesus' reply fully expressed would be: Do you ask where my *parousia* will be manifested, and where these separations will take place? You need not ask. There will be no doubt where they will take place. The place and the time will be manifest to all, just as the gathering together of the eagles unerringly indicates the place where the dead body lies.

If, on the other hand, the question of the disciples be more particular; if—as I am inclined to think—they mean to ask: Where will some be taken to, and where will others be left at?—the application is the same as before. Jesus says in effect: You need not ask. Are you ever in doubt as to the place where the eagles gather? You are certain they will be where the dead body is. So as to those who are taken, and as to those who are left. You will be certain about it. Every one in that day will be taken to or left at the place where he naturally belongs. Those who have no thought or care for the coming of the Son of man; who are not watching, nor praying, nor waiting for him; who are like the careless and unbelieving in the days of Noah and of Lot will be left in their appropriate place, the place of the dead, a prey for eagles. But those who watch and pray, who faint not and hold on to faith in my *parousia* will be taken to their place, the place for which they are fit, and which has been prepared for them.

This view of the reference of the disciples' question harmonizes with the succeeding context, in which we have :

1. The need of continued prayer up to the time of the *parousia*, in spite of all temptations to an unbelief which gives up in despair.

2. The need of a profound humility, a child-like spirit if we could enter into the Kingdom of God and share the glories of the *parousia.*

3. The need of the Christ-like spirit, which is willing to sacrifice all earthly things for eternal life.

Those who continue to pray and faint not, who cry for mercy as the publican, who give up all to follow Jesus, will be just as certain to have eternal life and share the blessings of the *parousia*, as it is certain that "Where the body is, thither will the eagles also be gathered together."

REV. E. C. GORDON.

Biblical Notes.

Nero Redivivus: Rev. 17: 8-11. The Rev. William E. Barton, tries his hand on this difficult passage in the *Bibliotheca Sacra* for July. He belongs to the Praeterist School and while agreeing that the beast which was of the seven and is also of an eighth (17 : 11) is Nero and Domitian, confesses that no satisfactory scheme has been made out which reconciles this interpretation with the number of the Roman Emperors. His views may be summed up as follows : (1) It is more natural to begin the Emperors with Augustus than with Julius Cæsar ; (2) this brings the book in the reign of Galba ; (3) Otho and Vitellius whose reigns were very brief are passed over ; (4) Vespasian and Titus are counted as one ; (5) the eighth is Domitian. The writer who is the seer, looking forward, beholds in the eighth a second Nero. The reference to the current superstition need not imply that John believed it ; still it was in a real sense true. As John the Baptist was Elijah, so was Domitian, Nero.

Luke 1: 74, 75. An interesting setting of these verses in the light of historical circumstances is given by Rev. John Reed in the *Expository Times* for September. He says "Zacharias had his own idea of the blessings of the salvation, to be brought to Israel by the "Highest." As a Jew, he shared in the patriotic feelings and hopes of the time. He looked for national independence from the rule of the Romans, and the establishment of a kingdom of Israel, whose glory would eclipse that of any other kingdom. But as a priest, he had a yet dearer hope, of which national independence was only the condition which must precede its fulfilment. The worship of the Temple had often been disturbed by incursions of Roman soldiers. From the tower Antonia, which overlooked the Temple courts, a sleepless watch was kept upon the worshipers. On the slightest appearance of tumult, or suspicion of a plot, the soldiers dashed down among them. On one occasion, at least, the blood of the worshipers was mingled with their sacrifices. The lack of freedom to serve God in His holy house (the verb in 1 : 74 means *to render religious service*, cf. Matt. iv. 10 ; Acts viii. 7 ; Acts xxiv. 14 ; Rev. vii. 15) was an indignity hard to endure, and a constant cause of irritation. Never to be free from the fear of interruption ; never to be without consciousness of being watched by suspicious Gentile eyes, were the worst sorrow and most bitter grievance of the wise and godly priest. The national degradation had its most shameful indignity in that which touched him as a priest most closely. To him the coming salvation would have as its best blessing, and the sign of all others,

liberty to carry on the worship of God without fear.   His song is the true lyric
of a priest.   It is the expression of deep personal feelings and of intense personal hopes."

The Apocalypse. In the year 1886 a German student named Vischer offered
as his thesis a discussion of the composition of the Apocalypse, the boldness
and originality of which has won for it wide acceptance.   Professor Harnack,
to whom it was presented, acknowledged his interest in it in the following
generous fashion.   We quote from Dr. Martineau's translation in his "Seat
of Authority in Religion." "In June last year, the author of the foregoing
treatise, then a student in theology at our University, came and told me that
in working out the theme prescribed for his department, 'On the theological
point of view of the Apocalypse of John,' he had found no way through the
problem but by explaining the book as a Jewish Apocalypse with Christian in-
terpolations set in a Christian frame.   At first he met with no very gracious reception from me.   I had at hand a carefully prepared College Heft, the result
of repeated study of the enigmatic book, registering the opinions of a host of
interpreters, from Irenæus downwards ; but no such hypothesis was to be found
among them ; and now it came upon me from a very young student, who as
yet had made himself master of no commentary, but had only carefully read
the book itself.   Hence my scepticism was intelligible ; but the very first arguments advanced with all modesty, were enough to startle me ; and I begged
my young friend to come back in a few days, and go more thoroughly with me
into his hypothesis.   I began to read the Apocalypse with care, from the newly-
gained point of view ; and it was—I can say no less—as if scales fell from my
eyes.   After the too familiar labours of interpreters on the riddle of the book,
the proffered solution came upon me as the egg of Columbus.   One difficulty
after another vanished, the further I read ; the darkest passages caught a
sudden light ; all the hypotheses of perplexed interpreters—of 'proleptic visions,'
'historical perspectives,' 'recapitulating method,' 'resting stations,' 'recreative
points,' 'unconscious relapse into purely Jewish ideas'—melted away at once ;
the complex Christology of the book, hitherto a veritable *crux* for every historical critic, resolved itself into simple elements." But this theory is so original and revolutionary as not to commend itself to more sober thinkers.   Professor Davidson has said of it, "Such a history of a Jewish Apocalypse is
unexampled.   Further, there could be no thought of the Apostle John in
connection with the book.   The authorship of the Presbyter, mentioned by
Papias, is a purely modern conjecture.   We should have to conclude that the
Christian editor gave out the whole with the design that it should be taken for
the work of the Apostle John, and that his deception succeeded.   This is a
strong assumption, considering that the book was probably known to Papias.
Again, the Christian editor appears to adopt the Jewish views of the rest of
the book, *c. g.* the earthly reign of the saints over the nations (ii. 26 with v. 10,
xx. 4).   When we take into account the known opinions of Papias, Justin, and
Irenæus, and fancy to ourselves the various complections of faith, the crosses,
as we might say, between Judaism and Christianity that must have existed in
the earliest times of the Church, we hesitate to admit that a Christian could
not have written the whole book.   And to mention only one other point : the
theory gives no account of the parallelism between the book and our Lord's
eschatological discourse."

Lachish and Eglon. The excavations of Mr. Petrie in Palestine have been already successful in discovering what he believes to be the true sites of Lachish and Eglon. He passed by the ordinarily accepted sites called Um Lakis and Aijlan and "attacked Tell Hesy, a mound of house ruins, 60 feet high and about 200 feet square. All of one side had been washed away by the stream, thus affording a clear section from top to base. The generally early age of it was evident from nothing later than good Greek pottery being found on the top of it, and from Phœnician ware (which is known in Egypt to date from 1100 B. C.) occurring at half to three-quarters of the height up the mound. It could not be doubted, therefore, that we had an Amorite and Jewish town to work on." This and Tell Nejileh, six miles south, "from their positions, their early age, and their water supply, it seems almost certain, are the two Amorite cities of the low country, Lachish and Eglon." How two other places have got these ancient names attached to them—Um Lakis and Ajlan—he can account for in no other way than by supposing that in the return from the Captivity the Jews were unable to wrest the springs from the Bedawin sheep-masters, and did the best they could to preserve the ancient names by giving them to the places which now bear them. Largely by the pottery and other articles discovered, not by any inscriptions which have been found there, basis is given for writing the history of Lachish. It "was built 1500 B. C. on a knoll close to the spring, and had a wall 28 feet thick. It was an immensely strong fort, intended, perhaps, for shelter against the raids of the Egyptian Tahutmes (Thothmes) I. This was its pre-Jewish stage. Subsequently it fell into ruin, and the deserted hill was used by the alkali burner. This corresponds to the barbaric Hebrew period under the Judges. Again the town was walled, Phœnician pottery begins to appear, and some good masonry —evidently the age of the early Jewish kings. Cypriote influence comes in later, then Greek from about 700 B. C., and onwards. The great ruin of the town was by Nebuchadnezzar, about 600 B. C., and some slight remains of Greek pottery, down to about 400 B. C., show the last stage of its history."

General Notes and Notices.

The Chair of Apologetics and Old Testament Literature in Knox College, Toronto, has just been filled by the appointment of the Rev. R. Y. Thomson, and his induction into the office, with the customary ceremonies, occurred last month.

The death is announced of Rev. James Lyle Bigger, M. A., B. D., Professor of Hebrew and Hermeneutics in Magee College, Londonderry, Ireland, at the early age of thirty-six. Mr. Bigger was appointed to his Chair five years ago. He was greatly interested in the work of the " Hebrew Correspondence School," having himself completed three of the courses, and being, at the time of his death, a student in the advanced course.

The Expository Times, to which frequent reference has been made in the STUDENT, has completed with September its first volume. It is a modest venture in the line of biblical study, and deserves wide success. The articles, while not so full as those in the STUDENT, or dealing with so wide a range of subjects, are yet scholarly and most helpful to ministers and students of the Bible. It admits much homiletical matter, giving indexes of Modern Sermonic Literature, and a unique commentary on the " Great Texts " of Scripture in outlines of many sermons upon them. The well-known firm of T. and T. Clark publish it in monthly parts at 3s. 6d. a year, and it can be procured in this country through Scribner and Welford.

The Winter School of the Boston Local Board of the American Institute of Sacred Literature offers a programme which will interest all Bible Students. A course in " Old Testament Prophecy of the Assyrian Period " of ten lecture-studies will be given by Professor W. R. Harper, beginning Oct. 28th. Prof. Wm. H. Ryder, of Andover Theological Seminary, offers a similar course on " The Closing Events of our Lord's Life." Instruction in Hebrew for beginners and advanced students is given by Professor Harper. Instruction for beginners in New Testament Greek will be in charge of Prof. Buell, and advanced students in New Testament Greek will read the Gospel of John and the Epistle to the Romans with Prof. Thayer of Harvard. The meetings are held in the Young Men's Christian Association Building. It is hoped that many students in and near Boston among the older and the younger people will avail themselves of these opportunities.

Synopses of Important Articles.

Paul's Style and Modes of Thought. * The examination of the way in which Paul thought and expressed his thought is difficult but necessary to establish a sound basis for theological and exegetical conclusions. We find (1) as one prominent characteristic, mysticism. It is seen in the way the believer's relation to Christ is defined which consists in identifying the believer's moral renewal with Christ's death and resurrection, the procuring causes of it, Col. 3 : 1 ; 2 Cor. 5 : 14 ; Rom. 6 : 4. The counterpart of this is the identification of unregenerate humanity with Adam in his transgression. One illustrates Paul's mysticism as much as the other and both should receive similar interpretation. As the ground of identification in one is causal connection, so it is in the other. (2) Another characteristic is personifying, or at least objectifying the truths on which he insists, e. g., Righteousness. It is not a subjective quality, it is a status or relation which God constitutes, Rom. 7 : 4, 11. The same is true of the idea of sin which he presents as a world-ruling power, Rom. 5 : 3, 2 ; 7 : 23, 25. (3) His thought moves in the sphere of legal relations, owing to his Old Testament training, e. g., illustration of marriage contract, adoption, heirship, Rom. 7 : 1, 6 ; 8 : 15, 17. Gal. 4 : 1, 7. This is particularly seen in the undeniable forensic elements of the doctrine of justification. No correct exegesis can ignore this fact. We may not like it but Paul did and put it there. (4) Note the use of parallel, e. g., man cannot be justified by works whether Gentile or Jew but is justified by faith, the parallel between Adam and Christ. The right interpretation of such passages must begin by seeking the fundamental idea to illustrate which the parallel was employed. In Rom. 5 : 12, 21 the undoubted thought is grace abounding not total depravity.

A fresh and stimulating chapter in biblical exegesis, a vein which has been little worked. One notes that the illustrations are taken almost entirely from three great epistles. Professor Stevens should extend his examination to other writings of the great apostle. The article may profitably be compared with those of Prof. Gould in the STUDENT which cover more ground but move in somewhat similar lines. The entire subject is a fascinating one.

On the Relation of Jewish to Christian Worship. † A single question will be considered in connection with this subject—To what extent has the service of the synagogue affected Christian worship? It has been usually thought that the prayer books of the Christian churches have followed the lines of the synagogue worship. The truth is that the synagogue was not a place for worship at all in the real sense of that word. The main features of the service were (1) the reading of the Scripture, (2) the exposition or sermon (*cf.* Mat. 4 : 23 ; 9 : 35 ; Mark 2 : 21 ; Luke 4 : 15.) If there were in the New Testament days a few prayers in the service, they occupied a subordinate position. But in another sphere this service influenced Christian worship. The earliest

* By Professor George B. Stevens in the *Andover Review* July, 1890, pp. 13-25.

† By the Rev. Prebendary Gibson, in *The Expositor*, July 1890, pp. 22-35.

Christian churches were founded in synagogues among those who were familiar with this form of service. When the synagogue rose up against them and they set out for themselves it was natural that the service of instruction was still necessary to them and this they would take from the synagogue. Hence probably the " Liturgy of the Catechumens " originated—a liturgy in which Catechumens might join and at the close of which they departed. This consisted of Scripture reading and exhortation. The testimony of the early Christian writers is to the effect that after this service was over came the prayers and communion in which these novitiates could not yet participate. Theirs was essentially a didactic service, a copy of the synagogue service. · The evidence for this is not inconsiderable.

The subject here considered is one of considerable interest not merely to those churches which use a liturgy but also to other unliturgical bodies of Protestants. The ordinary religious service of these bodies is closely parallel in its essential features to that of the synagogue as here outlined.

Psalms 42 and 43.* These two psalms are manifestly a unit. A study of them to discover the situation and feelings of the writer discloses (1) that he is beside a cataract in the region of the sources of the Jordan (42 : 7, 8) ; (2) that he is in deep trouble, trouble of which the roaring foaming cataract is a symbol ; (3) that in the midst of this trouble he stirs himself to use resources of help, (a) recalling the past (42 : 5), (b) maintaining his faith in God (42 : 7, 9, 10), (c) praying to Him (42 : 6, 12 ; 43 : 5) ; (4) looking more carefully into these troubles, we find that they chiefly concern his forced absence from the temple services (42 : 2, 3 ; 42 : 5, 6 ; 43 : 3, 4) ; (5) these passages (43 : 3, 4) reveal that he is a priest and singer of prominence ; (6) the restraint he is under is that of captivity (43 : 1) by wicked men who taunt him with his misfortunes (42 : 4, 11) —men who are probably aliens, not Israelites, perhaps Assyrians (2 Kings 18 : 13, 22, 30–35) ; (7) thus the spiritual significance of the song is doubled for us when we can trace the author's experience and situation so clearly.

A very clear and satisfactory piece of work, showing the writer to possess an historical sense and imaginative power conjoined with ample scholarship. The article is a model of exegetical ability, and the only criticism that could be passed on it is that the permanent teachings of these psalms are not fully enough developed for what is entitled an "exposition." But this is a pardonable omission in view of the amount of superficial "lessons" which other so-called expositors give us.

* By Professor Willis J. Beecher, in the *Homiletic Review*, August, 1890, pp. 166-170.

Book Notices.

Modern Criticism and the Gospel of John.

Modern Criticism considered in its Relation to the Fourth Gospel: being the Bampton Lectures for 1890. By Henry William Watkins, M. A., D. S. New York: E. P. Dutton and Co. 1890. Pp. xxxix., 502. Price $5.00

The author of this work, in a "prefatory note," remarks that the subject and method of it received the hearty approval of the late Bishop Lightfoot and it was through the suggestion of the latter that he was appointed to deliver the Bampton Lectures for the present year. The plan adopted is simple and quite effective. It is suggested by the remark made by Keim in his History of Jesus that in relation to the Gospel of John our age has cancelled the judgment of the centuries. The judgment of the centuries is carefully and elaborately presented in the first three Lectures. Beginning with the third generation of the second century, with Irenæus and Clement, the author moves back to the second generation and then to the first of the same century, carefully scrutinizing the evidence for the reception of the Fourth Gospel as the work of John the Apostle, and finding the evidence overwhelming in the affirmative, not only as judged by himself but by the most able scholars of our time. He then casts a swift but comprehensive glance at the evidence of the sixteen centuries following, closing with an eloquent passage in which the testimonies of Bede and Bishop Lightfoot are placed side by side. With the exception of the indefinite Alogi, no testimony against the authenticity and genuineness of John's Gospel is found. Lectures four to seven make an exhaustive study of the results of criticism in the present century exercised upon the same subject. The various schools, that of Strauss, that of Tübingen, that of the Partitionists, the negative critics such as Keim, Davidson and Martineau, are first presented. The positive criticism, from Schleiermacher to Weiss, Zahn and Franke are treated with equal fullness. The work of the English scholars, Lightfoot, Westcott, Salmon, and Sanday, receives full statement. The discoveries of the age, such as the works of Hippolytus, Tatian, Caius, the Ignatian Epistles, are carefully outlined and their significance estimated. The concluding lecture enters into more general consideration of the scope and character of the Gospel and its message for our time. The book is a mine of materials for forming a judgment on this great question of the Fourth Gospel. The spirit of it is fair and manly. The style is clear and at times stirring. The plan of it, while allowing little scope for original work on the part of the author, is yet in itself quite original. He must speak through other men's lips, but the conclusions which are evident from the extent, and the variety of the testimony presented, as well as from the ability and prominence of the writers from whom he quotes, stand forth all the more clear and weighty. The book is a kind of water-mark of criticism; that it can be written with any definiteness of conclusion resulting, is the proof that criticism upon this question is no longer doubtful that the Fourth Gospel is the writing of John the Apostle. It affords another argument—one regrets that another should be needed—that criticism of the Scriptures is bringing to light larger and more valuable stores of evidence to sustain the truth and authority of the Word of God.

THE EXAMINATION ON LUKE
OF THE AMERICAN INSTITUTE OF SACRED LITERATURE.

The List of Examiners upon the Gospel of Luke has practically reached one thousand, and still new names are coming every day. All names received before October 20 appear in the list published in this issue of the STUDENT. From many of these we have already most encouraging reports of classes doing earnest preparatory work. There will doubtless be many more examiners enrolled before December 30. A supplementary list will therefore be published in the December number of the STUDENT. The work in the great cities has just begun. Through the ministers' associations twenty cities are being canvassed and much enthusiasm is manifested wherever the subject is introduced. The plan is also under discussion at the Fall conventions of Young Peoples' Societies. The Christian Endeavor Society of the State of New Hampshire have decided to urge the matter in four hundred churches in that State.

Two important changes in the scheme have been made during the past month.

First, the fee has been reduced. It is not the wish of the Institute to allow the fee to debar any from the pleasure and benefit of the examination. To prevent any possibility of this, the fee has been made *a uniform one of fifty cents* for each person taking the examination, whether as a member of a group or as an individual. It is not possible at present to make so small a fee cover the cost of printing, postage and labor, necessary to carry on the examination successfully, but the Institute does not measure the success of the enterprise by its cash receipts, but by quickened brains and responsive hearts the wide world over.

The second change is a broadening of the plan to meet the needs of that large class of persons who would like to try the examination, but through timidity or other sufficient reasons do not wish to have their papers examined, or to try for the certificate of the Institute. Each examiner will be permitted to receive into his class, if he so desires, *any persons, whether of his group or not*, and they may take the examination *free of charge*. If any of these, after trying the examination and finding their knowledge more complete, or the questions easier than they had anticipated, decide to have their papers examined, they may hand them to the examiner, with the fee of fifty cents, and he will forward them to the Principal of Schools with the papers of his group. Should these papers reach the required standard certificates will be awarded with the others of the group.

It is possible by this change to interest in the work many outsiders, and possibly induce them to take the regular examination next year.

Is it too much to hope that before many years every Bible student, (and that term should include all classes of people), shall feel it a necessary part of his work to take one of these examinations every year? The Institute believes that it is *not* too much, and confidently expects this result.

Current Old Testament Literature.

Current Old Testament Literature.

American and Foreign Publications.

208. *La meilleure version est-ce Ostervald, Segond ou Lausanne?* By J. Vuilleumier. Bâle, Société internationale de traités, 1890.

209. *Einleitung in das alte Testament.* By E. Riehm. Bearb u. hrsg. v. A. Brandt. 11—13. (Schluss-) Lfg. Halle. Strien, 1890.

210. *Names and places in the Old and New Testament and Apocrypha, with their modern identifications.* Compiled by G. Armstrong, and revised by Ch. W. Wilson and Major Conder. London: Watt. 3s. 6d.

211. *Biblical History and Geography.* By H. S. Osborn, LL. D. New York: American Tract Society. $1.25.

212. *The Writers of Genesis and Related Topics. Illustrating Divine Revelation.* By Rev. E. Cowley, D. D. New York: Thomas Whittaker. 1.00.

213. *Die Psalmen, aus dem Hebräischen metrisch ins Deutsche übersetzt u. erläutert.* By Watterich. Baden-Baden: Sommermeyer. 4. —.

214. *The Voices of the Psalms.* By W. Pakenham Walsh, D. D. New York: Thomas Whittaker. 1.50.

215. *Die asaphitische Psalmengruppe in Beziehung auf mackabäische Lieder untersucht.* By W. Kessler. Inaug.-Diss. v. Halle. Halle: Buchdr. des Waisenhauses.

216. *Étude critique sur l'état du texte du livre des proverbes d'après les principales traductions anciennes.* By A. J. Baumgartner. Thèse pour le doctorat. Leipzig. $3.00.

217. *Die Profetie Joel's unter besonderer Rücksicht der Zeitfrage. Inaug.-Diss. v. Halle.* By G. Preuss. Halle.

218. *De Aramaismis libri Ezechielis.* Inaug.-Diss v. Halle. By F. Selle.

219. *Die christliche Eschatologie in den Stadien ihrer Offenbarung im Alten u. Neuen Testamente. Mit besond. Berucksicht. d. Jüd. Eschatologie im Zeitalter Christi.* By L. Atzberger. Freiburg. $1.85.

220. *Le Juif de l'histoire et le Juif de la légende.* By I. Loeb. Versailles: imp. Cerf et fils. 1 fr.

221. *Essai sur origines de la philosophie Judeo—Alexandrine.* By H. Bois. Paris: libr. Fischbacher. 6 fr.

Articles and Reviews.

222. *The Egypticity of the Pentateuch.* By A. H. Kellogg, D. D., in Pres. and Ref. Rev. Oct. 1890.

223. *The Rescue of Lot.* By A. H. Sayce, in Newb. House Mag. Oct. 1890.

224. *Recherches bibliques. XX. La correspondance d' Amènophis IV. et la Bible.* By J. Halévy in Revue des études juiers, avril-juin. 1890.

225. *Defence of the Gutter* [*Tzinnor*]. *2 Sam. v. 8.* By W. F. Birch. in Palestine Exploration Fund, July, 1890.

226. *The Pool that was made.* [*Nehemiah iii. 15, 16*]. By W. F. Birch, in Palestine Exploration Fund, July 1890.

227. *Studies in the Psalter. 22. Psalm 55.* By T. W. Chambers, D. D., in Homiletic Review, Oct. 1890.

228. *The Tsinnor* [*Ps. xlii. 7.*] By E. A. Finn, in Palestine Exploration Fund, July 1890.

229. *Dillmann's Jesaja.* Review by Siegfried, in Theol. Lztg. Sept. 6, 1890.

230. *Hunter's After the Exile.* Critical Notice by C. G. Montefiore, in Jew. Quar. Rev. Oct, 1890.

231. *Holtzmann's Das Ende des jüdischen Staatswesens u. s. w.* Critique by Weizsäcker in Theol. Lztg. Sept. 6, 1890.

232. *The Doctrine of Divine Retribution in the Old Testament, the New Testament and the Rabbinical Literature.* By C. G. Montefiore, J. E. Odgers, and S. Schechter, in Jew. Quar. Rev., Oct. 1890.

233. *Mosaic and Embroidery in the Old Testament.* By E. A. Finn, in Palestine Exploration Fund, July 1890.

234. *Le rosaire dans l'Islam.* By I. Goldziher, in Revue de l'hist. des religions, mai, Juin, 1890.

Current New Testament Literature.

American and Foreign Publications.

235. *A full account and collation of the Greek Cursive Codex Evangelium 604 (with two facsimiles).* By H. C. Hoskier. Together with ten appendices containing (A) The collation of a manuscript in his own possession. (B) A reprint with corrections of Scrivener's list of differences between the editions of Stephens 1550 and Elzevir 1624, etc. London: David Nutt, 1890. 21 s.

236. *Kritische Beiträge zum Leben Jesu u. zur neutest. Topographie Palätinas. Beilage; Neue Forschungen über die Felsenkuppel in Jerusalem.* Von J. u. B. Sepp. München: Lindauer, 1890. 3.

237. *Histore de Jésus-Christ d'après les évangiles et la tradition, expliquée à l'aide des monuments, de la description des lieux et de commentaires des écrivains ecclésiastiques.* By J. J. Bourassé. Tours; lib. Mame et fils, 1890.

238. *Come Forth.* [*Times of Christ.*] By Elizabeth Stuart Phelps and Herbert D. Ward. Boston and New York: Houghton, Mifflin and Co. $1.25.

239. *Biblisch-theologische Untersuchungen, I. Hft. Die Versuchg. Unseres Herrn Jesu Christi.* By J. Bernhard. Lübeck: Dittmer, 1.50.

240. *Juvenci, Evangeliorum libri IV.* Recensuit et commentario critico instruxit J. Hurmer. Wien. 7.20.

241. *Das Lukasevangelium u. die Apostelgeschichte.* By J. Friedrich. Halle: Kaemmerer. 2.40.

242. *Modern Criticism. Considered in its Relation to the Fourth Gospel.* By Henry William Watkins, M. A., D.D., New York. E. P. Dutton & Co. 5.00.

243. *Die Komposition der Paulinischen Hauptbriefe. I. Der Römer- und Galaterbrief.* By D. Völter, Tübingen. $0.90.

244. *Word Studies in the New Testament. The Epistles of Paul—Romans, Corinthians, Ephesians, Philippians, Colossians,* *and Philemon* By M. R. Vincent. Scribner. 4 00.

245. *Der Brief d. Apostels Paulus an die Christen zu Ephesus, f. die Gemeinde ausgelegt.* By C. Ernst Herborn. 1.70.

246. *Prayer as a theory and a fact.* By D. W. Faunce, D. D. American Tract Society. $1.

Articles and Reviews.

247. *The Historic Origin of the New Testament Scriptures* By T. G. Apple, D. D., in Ref. Quar. Rev. Oct. 1890.

248. *Die Stellung des evangelischen Christen zur heiligen Schrift.* By E. Haupt, in Der christl. Welt. 25-32, 1890.

249. *A Few Exegetical Notes.* [Mark 11:22; 2 Tim. 2:26; Luke 13:24; Acts 2:22.] By Howard Crosby, in Hom. Rev. Oct. 1890.

250. *Ueber Johannis den Taufer.* By D. Belser, in Theol. Qrtlsch. 3, 1890.

251. *John the Forerunner.* By A. Bierbower, in Unit. Rev., Oct. 1890.

252. *Le Sermon sur la Montagne et les idées sociales de Jésus-Christ,* By T. Doumergue, in Revue du christianisme pratique III. 17. 1890. 443.

253. *L'nseignement de Jésus sur son retour II.* By C. Bruston, in Revue de théol. et de philos. 4, 1890.

254. *English Theology and the fourth gospel.* By J. A. Cross in The Westminster Review, Aug. 1890.

255. *The Resurrection of Christ.* By G. M. Harmon, in Univ. Quar., Oct. 1890.

256. *Christ and His Miracles.* By F. L. Ferguson, in Pres. Mar., Oct. 1890.

257. *The Christianity of Christ.* By Edw. L. Houghton, in Univ. Quar., Oct. 1890.

258. *Die Johannes-Apokalypse u. die neueste Forschung.* By A. Hilgenfeld, in Ztschr. f. wiss. Theol. XXXIII. 4, 1890.

259. *Prayers and Miracles.* By J. Lellyett, in Christ. Thought, Oct. 1890.

THE

Old and New Testament Student

VOL. XI.	DECEMBER, 1890.	No. 6.

IT IS not uncommon to regret the mischances which have befallen the writings of the classical authors in their transmission from the ancient world. The tragedian Æschylus is supposed to have suffered greatly both in the loss of certain of his works and in the corrupt state of the text in others. That was an unfortunate author whose writings by some mishap were bound up with those of another writer and thus failed to preserve and glorify his own name. But has it ever been recognized as clearly as it ought to be that, of all unfortunate books in the history of literature, in all respects the most unfortunate is the Bible? A volume would be required to do the facts in the case justice. Let it be hoped that a paragraph or so will furnish food for thought on the point.

A PRIMARY misfortune of the Bible is the way in which it has been arranged and organized by its editors. The compilatory method of making up its several books is, indeed, no detriment. That method has marked advantages. The order of the books is to be deplored. What have not the Minor Prophets suffered—to take a single instance—from being bunched together without regard to chronological order at the end of the Old Testament? There is the Book of Psalms which as it stands is the despair of the commentator, being organized on a principle the discovery of which is vital and yet has never been satisfactorily made. In the New Testament the case is the same. There are two arrangements of its several books neither of which has anything of reasonableness in its

21

favor and both of which are misleading.   What shall be said
of that well-meaning but exceedingly disastrous achievement
of Stephens when on that fatal journey he divided the Grcek
Testament into verses, guided, it is said, in making many of
his verses by the jolts which his horse gave him?

ANOTHER misfortune from which the Bible has materially
suffered has arisen from its transmission.   With what a
holy sense of right did those Hebrew scribes, as many
think, destroy all manuscripts of the Old Testament
except the one that they had carefully corrected, so
that now our oldest manuscript dates from the tenth
century A. D.; and every other is substantially like it.
What blows has not the Bible received from its translators.   They have added to it, torn from it, twisted false
meanings out of its particles, wound its tenses into knots,
bound its poetry down or made it walk in step with prose.
They have turned its sublimest sentences into nonsense and
given its words meanings that would have made their writers
gasp.   What a debt have not translators to pay to this much
enduring Book?

BUT THIS is little compared with the unfortunate experiences that have assailed the Bible at the hands of its interpreters.   If translators have twisted sentences, interpreters
have torn them in sunder.   If the former have bound the
Scripture, the latter have cast it into the inner prison.   Cal-
vinist and Arminian, Chiliast and Erastian, Ritualist and
Puritan, have pulled and pounded this Word, and last of all
flung it at the hard heads of their antagonists.   Alas! Is the
Bible still alive?   But it must be subjected to yet one more
misfortune, the darkest and saddest of all.   It has been
betrayed by its friends.   It has called for righteousness and
behold oppression, for purity and behold all kinds of malice
and deceit.   The worst fate that can befall it has befallen it
—men have professed its teachings without obeying them,
have used its arguments without yielding to its claims.

HAVE, then, any books had their misfortunes? Much more so, the Bible. Have these survived all? Much more has the Bible prevailed over all its accumulated disasters. What a testimony to the vital power of the Truth. What an evidence of Divine Inspiration that in spite of the unwisdom of its editors, the ignorance of its translators, the mistaken zeal of its theological friends and the frequent betrayal on the part of its professed followers, the Bible is to-day the light and life of the world.

ATTENTION was called, in a recent number of THE STUDENT, to two striking peculiarities of the Old Testament historical and prophetical books, viz., the lack, in many cases, of a chronological arrangement of the material, and the absence, in many cases, of any sufficient indications of the time of a given event. These were pointed out as facts which must be carefully considered in any true estimate of the material. There are other characteristics which are equally striking and important. One of them is the incompleteness, the fragmentary character of the narratives. We do not mean by this "brevity of statement." It is rather the omission in a given story of many of the points which would seem to us to be important. It is now conceded that we have no record of the first ten or fifteen years of Saul's reign (*cf.* I Sam. 13: 1–3). This throws a new light on Saul's life, for we see that he did not come into conflict immediately after his appointment, as is generally supposed. We are not a little disappointed at having received so meagre an account of Shishak's capture of Jerusalem (1 Kgs. 14: 25, 26). The story of the lives of David and Solomon as told in Samuel is exceedingly incomplete, omitting as it does so many facts, knowledge of which is essential to any just comprehension of the history of religious worship in their times (which are found in Chronicles, *cf.* I Chron. 13: 1–5; 15, 16, 22, 24–27, 28, 29); the story of the same lives is even more fragmentary and incomplete in Chronicles, omitting as it does the account of David's adultery and punishment (2 Sam. 11, 12), Absalom's vengeance upon his brother and his rebellion (2 Sam. 13–20), besides other matter of less importance.

Has the reader of the book of Jonah not asked himself many questions for which, naturally, he might have expected an answer, for example, (1) the location of Jonah's abode, (2) the spot where he was vomited up, (3) an account of his long, wearisome Journey to Nineveh, (4) the name of the Assyrian King, (5) his fate after his rebuke by God, (6) his subsequent relation to Nineveh? Here are but a few of the omissions ; and one must confess that they occasion us more or less confusion. We know very well that a book which covers so much ground must be condensed and fragmentary ; and yet we cannot close our eyes to that other fact, not so often noted, that the Old Testament, brief and condensed as it is, contains a large number of what, at first glance, may *seem* to be wholly unnecessary repetitions; for example, (1) the account of the tabernacle in Exodus, (2) the laws in Exodus, Leviticus, Numbers and Deuteronomy, (3) the history of David, and other kings in Samuel and Kings, and again in Chronicles, (4) David's thanksgiving (2 Sam. 22 ; Ps. 18), (5) the historical portions of Isaiah (Isaiah 36–39; 2 Kings 18–20). Now who can really be blamed for expressing the wish, looking at the matter from a strictly historical standpoint, that the space occupied with these repetitions, might have been employed in giving additional information concerning some of the subjects treated so incompletely? Is it not true, that he who would explain the origin of the present form of the Bible, must have a theory which will account, on the one hand, for this incompleteness, and on the other, for these repetitions? We shall recur to this matter again.

ANOTHER still more difficult fact to explain, and yet one which *must be explained*, is the emphasis laid upon certain special matters which have been selected from what must have been a large number, the remainder being touched upon lightly, or altogether passed over. There is room here only to notice a few cases:* (1) In Judges, a book containing 21 chapters and covering 300 years, three-fourths of the space is given to five subjects, viz., Gideon and his son, Samson,

* For a fuller statement see an article by the Editor in *The Sunday School Times*, July 20th, 1889.

Jephthah, Micah, and the outrage at Gibeah. (2) In 1 Sam. the story of the Witch of Endor takes 25 verses, the plunder of Ziklag by David, 31; while the battle of Gilboa, including the account of the defeat of the army, the death of Saul and Jonathan, the treatment of their bodies, the heroic rescue and burial by the men of Jabesh Gilead, receives only 13 verses. (3) Of the 25 Samuel-chapters (1 Sam 31, and 2 Sam. 1–24), about nine (counting roughly) are found in 1 Chron. 10–29, which covers the same ground; of the 19 chapters of Chronicles, about eight are found in Samuel. In other words, two writers preparing a history of the same period, employing for the most part the same sources, using in many passages, the same language, differ so much from each other that the matter possessed in common amounts, in one case, to a little more than one-third of his material, in the other, to a little less than one-half. (4) Of the 47 chapters of Kings which cover the period 1015–562 B. C., about 450 years, nearly one-fourth is given to the first 40 years (the reign of Solomon): about one-fifth is given to the narratives of Elijah and Elisha; the division of the Kingdom, the most important event in Israelitish history after the Exodus, is treated in 24 verses, the story of the man of God in 32; the history of 25 kings and queens, from Athaliah to Zedekiah, and from Jehu to Joash, including the account of the destruction of both kingdoms, the history of two nations for 322 years—is given 14 chapters,—only one-half more than the number of chapters given to Elijah and Elisha, one-fourth more than the number given to Solomon. Again we say, these *facts* and the multitude like them, must be explained. The sacred histories evidently do not maintain proportion in the treatment of different subjects, at least the proportion which would be observed by a modern historian. *Can* this be explained? Of course it can; yet *not* by the plan, or in accordance with the theory, most commonly presented. All this, together with that which was referred to in the previous editorial will be considered from still another point of view at a later time.

THE prophet was God's messenger and speaks to us as to the men of his time with the Divine authority. His message is freighted with the thought of the Eternal and the Holy God. But what is his message? Is it merely the words, the ideas which are clothed in human language? This is in fact only a portion of the truth which he brings to us. Behind the words is the man; behind the message or rather in it, is the messenger. It may not, indeed, be so important for us to know the man as it is to know the message. Yet, after all, can we really grasp the one without the other? Can one be said to apprehend in its fullness the word of the prophet Isaiah, until he becomes familiar with him whose tongue was touched with celestial flame,—apt symbol of the divine enthusiasm in which his whole being was enfolded. The teaching of Elijah—what a large feature of it was the deed and the life of the man himself. Do we speak of the voice, the word, that the prophet *possesses?* Let us also learn to know and appreciate the voice, the word, that the prophet *is.* Only then can the general course of his teaching be appreciated in its directness and force. From such a point can the clearest light be thrown upon difficult or obscure passages in his writings. The highest interest thus gathers about the study of the prophet himself as the object of the Divine inspiration and thereby the source of an authoritative Divine message to mankind.

DOES the teacher of this Scripture bear in mind that God thus speaks in the inspired man as well as in his word? Does he keep before him also the consequent fact, the great general principle of God's method of teaching, namely, that everywhere He conveys his message to men as well by the teacher himself as by the truth that the teacher would impress by means of language? The voice that the teacher *is* —it, too often, is forgotten in the pursuit after eloquent or attractive speech. The clothing of the thought is more often sought after than the incarnation of the thought in the life of the speaker. But the living of it is in truth the first thing. The communicating of it is only secondary and dependant. The word that the teacher utters is the word that the teacher incarnates. The voice with which the teacher speaks is the voice that the teacher *is.*

THE CAVE OF MACHPELAH.

By Selah Merrill, D. D., LL. D.,

Andover, Mass.

These words, by which we mean the burial place of Abraham, are really a quotation from Gen. 23: 9, and it is in this way that the spot in question is first introduced in Bible history. The word "Machpelah" occurs six times, all of them being in the book of Genesis. Abraham wished to purchase "the cave of Machpelah," "which belonged to Ephron," and which was situated "in the end of his field." The line separating Ephron's field from others ran close to the cave where Sarah was to be buried. It does not follow, however, that this line was also the boundary of Machpelah for the word is used with the article always, and refers to a then well known tract (*sadeh*) of land which had more than one owner. A farmer now would speak of "the pasture" or "the meadows," meaning to him and to all connected with him, a certain well known portion of his farm which was thus distinguished from every other portion. The use in English of the terms "the fells," or "the downs" are a pretty good illustration of the use of "the Machpelah" by the people in and about what we now know as Hebron.* How large the tract of land known as "The Machpelah" was we do not know, but evidently it was large rather than small. A portion of it was owned by Ephron and was known as "his field." At one extremity of his land was located the cave which Abraham was to purchase.

Time is here taken to explain this matter for to many readers of the Bible the terms "field of Ephron," "cave of Machpelah," "field of Ephron in Machpelah," "cave of the field of Machpelah," "cave in the field," "end of the field,"

---

* I do not know any authority for making "Machpelah" mean *double*. The root nâphal, to which it is sometimes referred, means *to double* in the sense of *folding*. The Hebrew language was capable of expressing a dual object without such a makeshift as that.

not to mention "trees of the field," etc., are not a little puzzling.

The statement in Gen. 23: 17, is fuller and more extended in details,—"the field of Ephron, which is in The Machpelah, . . . the field, and the cave which is in it, and all the trees that are in the field inclosed within its entire bound= aries,"—all this passed into the hands of Abraham. Instead of being a puzzle, the statement is very clear;—there was a tract known as "The Machpelah." In it Ephron owned a field, and in one end of his field there was a cave.

We are sometimes annoyed by the lack of definiteness which we think we discover in Hebrew writers. In not a few cases, however, there is an apparent effort to give such specific and minute details that there can be no possible mis- apprehension as to the facts. Of this the transaction between Abraham and Ephron is a good illustration. The following particulars are mentioned which I will enumerate at the risk of slight repetitions:—(1) Ephron was a Hittite living among Hittites. (2) He was the son of Zohar also a Hittite. (3) He had a field in the tract called "The Machpelah," and in the extreme end of his field there was a cave. (4) In every case but one where Machpelah is mentioned it is described as "before or facing Mamre." (5) Pains are taken to state that it was in the land of Canaan. (6) Abraham bought "the cave with the field" (49: 30; 50: 13). (7) He bought also "all the trees that were within the boundary line of Ephron's land." (8) The price asked and paid was four hundred shek- els of silver that was current with the merchant. (9) All this was done in the presence of many witnesses. (10) More- over when the book of Genesis received its final touches, Mamre is explained, for the benefit of later readers, as being then called Hebron (23: 19). Certainly the details here are ample.

The words "before or facing Mamre" are interesting, be- cause Abraham was living in an oak grove on land belonging to a great man named Mamre. In the ten times that this word occurs it is used as the name of a place eight times and as the name of a man twice. Caves and tombs were nearly always in the side of a hill, and "facing Mamre" may imply that the cave that Abraham wanted was within his sight on the opposite side of the valley from where he was.

Two expressions deserve notice:—Abraham bought "the cave with the field," and also "all the trees that were within the boundary line of Ephron's land." Had there been no specification of the kind, Ephron might have said to Abraham "you bought the land but you did not buy the cave or the trees that are on it." In that country it is necessary in transferring land to specify the trees, even a single tree if there be but one, or a spring of water, or whatever else might be of advantage to the owner. I knew a remarkable case of this kind at Jerusalem, a case that was in the courts for two or more years, where the trees on the land were not specified in the deed of it, and the purchaser (a foreigner residing in the country) claimed them as his; the man of whom he bought the land also claimed them, and the courts decided in favor of the latter. If in some matters Hebrew statements are vague, this case of Abraham and Ephron shows that they can be scrupulously definite. The Jews are noted for being poor in topography, but in money transactions they are surprisingly specific.

Time is a far greater destroyer of ancient landmarks than a wicked neighbor (Deut. 27: 17), and after the lapse of thirty-six centuries it would be a marvel if we were still able to point to any spot in or about Hebron and say this was "The Machpelah," this was Ephron's field, this was the cave which Abraham bought for a burial place. This we are not able to do. At the same time with regard to the cave of Machpelah there are very strong reasons for supposing that the precise locality has been preserved. The place pointed out to-day has been handed down from the beginning of our era. In all that time there has been no change. Josephus says that the tombs were marked by beautiful monuments,— as if the nation had taken pride in the preservation,—and gives no hint that their identity had ever been questioned. For the period preceding the birth of Christ the conditions of the country were such that a tradition of this kind would be much more creditable than it could possibly be since that event. But since that event there is no reason for doubt;

the most skeptical yield assent. Hence in the preceding period there ought to be absolute certainty. In this instance there is perfect agreement between Jewish, Mohammedan, and Christian traditions. The case cannot be made stronger than it is by the quotation of the views of few or many scholars, still the judgment of Dr. Robinson may be given as a sample, who says,—" We may rest with confidence in the view that the remarkable external structure of the haram is indeed the work of Jewish hands, erected long before the destruction of the nation, around the sepulchre of their revered progenitors, " The friend of God and his descendants." (2 : 78).

The remark of Robinson should be confined to the certainty of the identification, since as to the age of the structure a question has arisen in recent years, which a few writers consider to be yet an open one. All are agreed that it could not possibly have been erected since the time of Herod the Great. Scholars are divided as to whether the date of its construction should be placed during the reign of Herod or at a much earlier period. Any person acquainted with both would say that the work at Hebron resembles in general the massive stone work in the substructures at Jerusalem, a portion of which has been demonstrated to be the work of Herod. Were this a complete statement of the facts, the case would be ended. A careful examination of the two, however, reveals differences which must be taken into our account: (1) The faces of the stones at Jerusalem are very rough while those at Hebron are smooth. (2) The sunk border on the edge of the stones, the marginal draft popularly called " bevellings," is not so deep on the Hebron stones as on those at Jerusalem. We have also another important fact, that in the ruins of Hyrcanus's palace at Arak El Emir, east of the Jordan, which dates from 180 B. C., there are great stones of Jewish origin nearly or quite identical as to the character of the work upon them with the stones at Hebron. Here are far better means of comparison for the matter of dates than the Jerusalem Herodian work.

Besides the facts now mentioned there are other considerations which make it very improbable that the structure at

Hebron belongs to the time of Herod the Great. (1) Hebron belonged to Idumea and Herod with all his building did not do much in that part of his dominions. (2) A special effort apparently was made by Josephus to specify all the important works of Herod and the structure at Hebron is not among them. (3) Had this structure been a small affair there would be a reason for its omission, but it was one of the finest in the land, and the probability that it would be mentioned, supposing its builder was Herod, increases with the magnificence of the work. (4) The name of the builder is omitted, and the probability of its being omitted increases as the date of its erection recedes from the time of Herod the Great. (5) On the supposition that the Hebron monuments were built by Herod, it is contrary to all that we know of Josephus for him to have spoken of them as he does. He says,—"The monuments of Abraham and his sons are still shown at Hebron, of the most beautiful marble and of exquisite workmanship" (Wars. iv. 9, 7). The inference is that they had not been erected in his day nor during the reign of Herod, but that they had been in existence as a national memorial for a long period.

But if the claim that they are Herodian work is not a valid one, to what period can their erection be assigned? The fact must be borne in mind that two hundred years before our era the Jews at Arak El Emir erected precisely similar work. The Hebron monuments could have been built after the return from the captivity; but to this view the impoverished state of the nation would, as Dean Stanley suggests, be a serious objection, and he is inclined to refer them to the period of the kings and "to none so likely as the sovereigns to whom they are ascribed by Jewish and Mohammedan tradition,—David or Solomon" (Jewish church, 2. 537). Unless indubitable proof can be brought forward to show that they are of the Herodian age, a thing it seems to me impossible, we have a right to ascribe them to an early period as the only date appropriate to Josephus's words, and to consider that generation after generation previous to the birth of Christ had preserved and guarded them with pious care.

VISITORS TO THE MOSK.

Several private persons claim to have entered the Mosk, but the evidence for their having done so is very meagre. If one or two of these have actually seen the inside of the building, they have added nothing to our knowledge of it. The list of those who have been allowed to enter the sacred enclosure is a small one, comprising six different parties. The first was the Prince of Wales in 1862; after him, in order, James Fergusson in 1864; the Marquis of Bute in 1866; the Crown Prince of Prussia, since known as Emperor Frederick III. in 1868; two sons, Albert and George, of the Prince of Wales, in April 1882; and General Lew Wallace in November 1882. With each of these persons, except Mr. Fergusson who entered alone, there was a small party of friends, so that the place has been pretty thoroughly examined.

The first plan made of the Mosk was that in A. P. Stanley's "Sermons in the East," (8vo. Lond. 1863); given also in James Fergusson's "The Holy Sepulchre and the Temple at Jerusalem," (Lond. 1865); and it is found in the appendix to Stanley's "Lectures on the History of the Jewish Church," first series, (American edition, p. 542). A later plan is found in the Quarterly Statement of the Palestine Exploration Fund, October 1882, from notes and measurements made during the visit of the Princes Albert and George in April of that year. Both plans are good and reliable, but the one in Stanley's works (as indicated) gives a clearer idea of the arrangement of the entrance, rooms, and tombs, than that found in the Quarterly Statement.

The interior of the Mosk is considered so sacred by the Mohammedans that a special order from the Sultan is necessary for Christians to enter it. I scarcely need to add that such permission is seldom granted and only on the rarest occasions. The circumstances were all favorable to our visiting the place unmolested as we had an escort of twenty-six soldiers besides the Consular guard. The Governor of Jerusalem and Palestine accompanied us. There were in the party two ladies, Mrs. J. M. Lane of Crawfordsville, Indiana, and the wife of the present writer, and these are the only

Christian women that have entered the Mosk for many centuries.   Not only were our persons protected from harm but
every facility for carefully examining the interior was afforded us.   The custodian was exceedingly dignified and almost
solemn in his look and manner, still he was attentive and
formally courteous.

The Mosk, when one is actually within it, does not appear
large and there is nothing about it that is imposing.   In fact
an air of dilapidation is apparent, as for instance in the orna-
mentation on the walls and the inclosures of the several
tombs.   On the contrary the Oriental rugs with which the
floor is covered are some of the richest that I have ever seen.
The impression of great size is lost perhaps by the fact that
the interior is divided into separate rooms as I will explain.
The building is entered from the southwest corner and the
first few steps from the street are those which travelers are
allowed to touch or stand upon.   The flight ascends to the
extreme southeast corner, turns then a right angle and goes
north up to the level of the floor of the Mosk.   This passage
is lined all the way by massive stones of Jewish workmanship.   The inclosing walls, I have not yet mentioned, are
200 by 115 feet (later measurements make them 197 by 111
feet), and the inclosed space is divided cross-ways into four
sections, one of which is an open court, and the largest which
occupies about one-third of the entire space, was originally a
church.   From the head of the stairs where the floor of the
Mosk is reached, we pass first into the open court, turn directly to the left, that is to the south, and immediately enter
the porch of the church.   Counting the open space as one
section, this porch will be the second of the four mentioned.
Here in small rooms are the tombs of Abraham on the right
and of Sarah on the left.   With our faces still to the south
we enter the church (the third cross section), where, also in
separate rooms, are the tombs of Isaac on the right and that
of Rebecca on the left.   In the north cross section, north of
the open court, are the tombs of Jacob and Leah;—Jacob's
tomb being on the same side of the Mosk as those of Abraham and Isaac.   The tomb of Joseph is in a room by itself
on the west side beyond the old Jewish wall, and evidently a
much later addition.

The reader is asked to remember that the six tombs are arranged on the floor of the Mosk in the form of a parallelogram at equal distances from each other. They are protected by rooms, as I have said, having doors or barred iron gates, so that one, if permitted to do so, can enter and walk around the tomb. I speak of "tombs" because that is the common word; each tomb, however, is a cenotaph four feet wide, eight feet long, and nearly eight feet high, with rounded tops. They are covered with beautiful and costly pieces of oriental silk richly embroidered with gold, those on the men's tombs being green, and those on the women's bright rose color. These are the gifts of different Sultans or other wealthy devotees of the Moslem faith.

These modern conventional cenotaphs, it hardly need be said, have no connection with the actual places of burial of the patriarchs. They with their wives were buried in a cave in the rock which is beneath the floor of the Mosk. To this cave there are in what we call the church, two entrances, one near its south wall and the other near its north wall about where that joins Abraham's tomb. Over the former is a heavy stone slab clamped down with iron bands which are worn smooth by the treading of feet upon them, showing that they have not been removed for generations. The Governor said that he could order the stone removed but the consequences to himself would be disastrous, meaning of course from the government at Constantinople. The entrance near Abraham's tomb was open. The hole was about eighteen inches in diameter and in it a light was suspended so that by getting down on our hands and knees we could see the chamber below. The floor was of earth covered with small loose stones, the walls were the native rock, and in one side of the chamber there were openings to a cave. This rock wall with a rough opening to a cave within it, is in no way unlike hundreds of similar places in Palestine.

What I have now described is all that any visitor has seen of the cave of Machpelah. I find the impression prevailing in some minds that Dean Stanley actually entered the cave. On the contrary he saw no more than we did.

The rooms in which the different tombs stand can be entered by doors or gates as I have explained.   Previous to our visit the gates to Sarah's tomb had not been opened; but by a little pressure we were allowed to enter even that most sacred inclosure.

It has been my aim to make the account of my visit to this interesting spot as brief as possible.   Many more details could be given, but the main facts are now before the reader. In reply to questions that are frequently asked I will say. (1) That some day these caves will be entered and their secrets so long kept from the world will be fully made known. (2) Whatever else may be found in them I am almost certain that they contain no mummies.   The limestone hills of Judea are wholly different from the hot dry sands of Egypt.   The rock is not firm and moisture percolates and penetrates every-where so that wood, iron, or human bodies however carefully prepared, cannot resist decay.   This fact I have often urged whenever I have found persons who were over sanguine as to the revelations to be expected from the opening of these se-cret chambers beneath the Mosk at Hebron.

THE PROPHECY CONCERNING THE CHILD OF

THE FOUR NAMES: ISAIAH IX., 6, 7.

By Professor EDWARD L. CURTIS,

McCormick Theological Seminary, Chicago.

These verses form the climax of a remarkable series of prophecies, belonging to the reign of Ahaz, found in Is. 7: 1–9: 7. The one concerning Immanuel we have already considered.* That was followed by the prophecy of Maher-shalal-hash-baz, declaring the speedy advance of the Assyrian and the downfall of Damascus and Samaria (8: 1–4). The king of Assyria also would not confine himself to the northern kingdom. Like a mighty river he would sweep onward over that country into Judah, not, however, completely subduing the latter; the waters would reach to the neck: a remnant would be saved. The land was Immanuel's (8: 5–8). The assurance couched in that name was exultantly expressed in a grand pæan of defiance toward hostile foes (8: 9f.). The true people of God were also distinguished. Not all of the inhabitants of Judah were to find refuge through Jehovah. Only a remnant, those that feared him rather than foreign ·confederacies. While to the others Jehovah himself would be an instrument of destruction (vs. 12–15). This doctrine concerning the remnant and its indestructibility, the prophet placed on record, sealed among his disciples and then announced his intention of calmly awaiting the impending judgment and promised redemption (vs. 16–18).

Much of Isaiah's prediction was fulfilled. Tiglath-Pileser conquered Syria and ravaged the northern kingdom, carrying into captivity the inhabitants of its eastern provinces (2 Ki. 15: 29; 16: 9). And while Judah at this time, did not then suffer as might have been expected from the prophet's words, from a combined invasion of Assyrian and Egyptian armies,

* See O. N. T. S., November, 1890, pp. 276–280.

(7: 18f.), still its condition was wretched and miserable. The intervention of the Assyrians had indeed removed the danger from the confederate enemies Pekah and Rezin; but this assistance had been obtained at a grievous cost. Heavy tribute had been paid; the treasures, both of the temple and the king's house, and doubtless much treasure also wrung by severe taxation from the people. So impoverished was the land that it is recorded in Chronicles that Judah was ''low'' and that Ahaz had been ''distressed'' and ''not strengthened'' by his alliance with the Assyrian king (2 Chron. 28: 19f.).

Although addressing the people of Judah, Isaiah had regard also to the northern kingdom. He had included its inhabitants in his threat of impending judgment (8: 14). So likewise he extended toward them his pity and assurance of deliverance; and so, when he warned his hearers against consulting wizards and necromancers, and bade them turn to his testimony and doctrine, he gave as a warning of impending punishment a scene of wretchedness and despair, which may have been taken from the experience of unhappy captives from the ravaged districts of Galilee: ''And they shall pass through it [i. e. the land] hardly bestead and hungry; and it shall come to pass when they shall be hungry, they shall fret themselves, and curse their king and their God, and turn their faces upward; and they shall look unto the earth, and behold, distress and darkness, the gloom of anguish,—and into thick darkness they shall be driven away '' (8: 21f.).

To this scene of woe the prophet joined his announcement of the future redemption. Upon these very districts that had so suffered, and were so exposed to danger the light of salvation would, perhaps first shine.* There would be joy like that of the harvest. The yoke of the oppressor would be broken. A victory like that of Gideon over Midian would be gained. The accoutrements of warriors would be destroyed (9: 1–5).

'' For unto us a child is born, unto us a son is given; and · the government shall be upon his shoulder: and his name shall be called Wonderful, Counsellor, Mighty God, Everlasting Father, Prince of Peace. Of the increase of his

* The prophetic intimation was fulfilled to the letter.   Matt. 4: 16.

government and of peace there shall be no end upon the throne of David, and upon his kingdom to establish it, and to uphold it with judgment and with righteousness from henceforth even forever.   The zeal of the Lord of hosts shall perform this " (9: 6f.).

Taking now these verses in connection with those immediately preceding, Isaiah then looked forward to the oppression of the Northern and Southern kingdoms by a foreign power, or regarded this condition already reached through the Assyrian, and expected that the land would be released from its thraldom through a ruler who should manifest the attributes of the fourfold name, and who should establish on the Davidic throne a peaceful, just, and righteous rule of continually extending dominion, which should last forever.   This is the plain and simple meaning of his words.   Thus he sets forth the same elements that are found in the Immanuel prophecy, only the judgment here is left further in the background, while to the front in greater fulness is brought that of the indestructibility and ultimate triumph of Jehovah's people. The indefinite Immanuel here assumes distinctness, and Isaiah gives the first direct definite prophecy of the personal Messianic king.*   This thought, however, was not a new one. In substance it was in the promise made to David of the close relationship to exist between Jehovah and his seed, and of the perpetuity of his house and kingdom (2 Sam. 7: 12–16).   Men must have seen that this promise in its fulness had not been realized in Solomon, although he had built the house for Jehovah: neither could any subsequent king lay any claim to its realization.   The thought of such a future king was close at hand also in the previous prophecies of the triumph of Israel over its enemies and the restoration of the Davidic glory and power (Amos 9: 11f.; Hos. 1: 7, 11; 3: 5).   A kingdom must have a king, and so in the minds of the people there must have been earnest expectation and longing for this ruler.   The distress brought by the weak and impious Ahaz must also have urged the need of a highly endowed monarch.   It was an opportune moment then to declare the Messiah's advent.   The prophet gave him four

* Unless Ps. 110 is to be excepted.

names.* The first is Wonderful-Counselor, or more exactly a Wonder of a Counselor, one who in his statesmanship is a marvel. How the wretched failure of Ahaz in this particular would emphasize the need of this attribute in the Messiah.

The second name Mighty God, (El gibbor), God a hero, has occasioned much discussion. The question raised is whether Isaiah meant by this title directly to teach that the child would be an incarnation of Jehovah. Probably not. Otherwise we cannot explain why he never further unfolded and made central this thought. It was also not foreign to Hebrew usage to apply divine names to men of exalted position. Thus we have the term Elohim, God or gods, given to judges (Ex. 21 : 6) and rulers of Israel (Ps. 82 : 6). This same expression, *el-gibbor*, is found in the plural used of men in Ezk. 32 : 21, and *el* also of Nebuchadnezar in Ezk. 31 : 11. The child, moreover, is not said to be *el gibbor*, but is only thus named, and very frequent was it to give a Hebrew child a name of which *el* was a compound. And hence although this expression stands for Jehovah in 10 : 21, we cannot find that the prophet taught here directly the incarnation of deity. Such a fact however may be regarded *indicated*, awaiting subsequent revelation for its discernment. "If," says Delitzsch, "we look at the spirit of prophecy, the mystery of the incarnation of God is unquestionably indicated in such statements as these. But if we look at the consciousness of the prophet himself nothing further was involved than this, that the Messiah would be the image of God as no other man ever had been (cf. *el.* Ps. 82 ; 1), and that he would have God dwelling within him (cf. Jer. 33 : 16). . . . . The expression did not preclude the fact that the Messiah would be God and man in one person, but it did not penetrate to this depth so far as the Old Testament consciousness was concerned." This child then as a hero, a mighty man of valor or war would be as one divine (cf. Zech. 12 : 6–8).

The next name Everlasting Father, we explain in refer-

* The separation of the first name into two, Wonderful and Counselor as in A. V. and R. V. Text, is plainly wrong. There is nothing distinguishing in the term Counselor. Any king could bear that title. The other names consist of a pair of words ; and hence most likely this one also. The true reading is given in the margin of the R. V.

ence to the fatherhood by Gen. 45 : 8, where Joseph is called a father to Pharaoh, and by Isaiah 22 : 21, where it is said that Eliakim will be a father to the inhabitants of Jerusalem and the house of Judah.   The future king will *perpetually* provide in a fatherly manner for his people.   Did this imply that he would be immortal, or is the word everlasting to be explained as complimentary, of the nature of the salutation, "Let the king live forever," or after the analogy of oriental titles of homage, as Rameses II. of Egypt, for example, was called "endowed with life, eternal and forever."   We cannot, however, so minimize the force of this term.   An immortality certainly was promised.   Was it however of the king himself or of such beneficent rule?   The prophet does not directly decide.   Probably he had no theory about it.   Of the future salvation, peace, righteous government, and wide dominion of the faithful remnant, he was sure.   Of *this* there would be no end.   But exactly *how* God would accomplish this he does not tell us.   In the light of 25 : 8 we should think of immortality belonging both to the king and his subjects; in that of 65 : 20 not immortality but patriarchal longevity, and thus there would be a succession of rulers rather than one only.   Doubtless however the former view of individual immortality is nearer the conception of the prophet than the latter.   We are apt to trouble ourselves far more over the *how* of the future purposes of God than did the Hebrew prophets.   They had the firm assurance of the realization of certain great ends demanded by the divine character, but of the times and ways they appear usually little concerned.*

The name Prince of Peace explains itself.   He would be the victorious author of this peaceful era, and also the security for its continuance.

Such then is our explanation of this passage.   The prophet stands here again as a seer.   The black cloud of Assyrian oppression overhangs his people.   Beyond that is the bright dawn of Immanuel's kingdom.   Isaiah

---

* Another rendering of the words translated everlasting father, or father of eternity, is worthy of notice.   It is, father of booty, distributor of spoils.   This translation is perfectly admissible.   Whether it is to be preferred to the usual one must be decided by the context and thought of the passage.   Dr. Briggs in his *Messianic Prophecy*, page 200, very strongly argues for its adoption.

may have expected this within his own life time, or he may not. His picture of the Messiah here as he looked forward was far different from ours. There was little of the spiritual in his. It served for little more than a type, just as was the old warrior King David. Isaiah saw one perfectly fulfilling the ordinary duties of an earthly monarch, and for this crowned and exalted with his four names. Isaiah saw salvation wrought in deliverance from temporal foes. His vision was circumscribed. Only in the ethical and eternal character of the Messiah's kingdom is it identical with ours. He stood upon Old Testament ground. He had not entered into the promises.

THE EXTERNAL FORM OF THE QURAN.

By Rev. Professor CHARLES HORSWELL,

Evanston, Ill.

In size the Quran is much larger than the New Testament, but it contains only about four-fifths as much material. The ordinary edition presents a very striking and beautiful page; a distinctness of type that is exquisite. As one opens the book for the first time, there seems to be reflected from it something of that mystic reverence with which it has been hallowed by the Muslims. On the title page we read "The Quran; and it leads in the right way and teaches discrimination." The book is divided into 114 chapters, called *suras*. These suras are of very unequal length, some containing twenty-five words, others twenty-five pages. Chapters two to nine, inclusive, contain one-third of the book. The chapters are again divided into verses of unequal length. There is another division by which the Quran is apportioned for public reading, either into sixty or thirty equal parts, each part assigned to a reader, so that the whole book may be read through every day. These last divisions are marked in small type on the margin.

The superscription of each sura consists of three parts. First, the title proper; second, the statement as to where it was revealed, i. e. at Mecca or Medina, with the number of the verses; third, the "Bismillah."

The title proper, which is the first line of the superscription, represents a particular matter treated of, or person mentioned—very often some prominent word. The matter referred to in this title may be in the beginning of the sura, or near the middle, or at the end. In the shorter suras the subject-matter clusters readily enough about some important word or phrase; also in the longer suras, if there is unity of thought or a connected story. But there are many cases where the title stands for the merest fragment of the sura, and has not the remotest connection with the rest of it. For example, the title of the second sura refers to about four verses out of 285. Sura ten, called "Jonah," might as well have received half a dozen other titles, for not more than a fifth of its material—and that the very last in the sura—has any connection whatever with Jonah.

To read, in succession, these so-called titles, gives little or no idea of what the chapters contain—"The Cow, The Table, The Spider, Abraham, The Night-Journey, The Greeks, The Striking, The Creator, The Resurrection, The Wrapped-Up, Abu Laheb, The Afternoon, The Elephant, Declaration of God's Unity."

What evidence is there that these titles were the work of Muhammed? *First*—The editorial work of the Quran furnishes manifold proof of the superstitious reverence of the compilers. There is little probability that *they* added them. *Second*—In the MSS. copies neither the chapters nor the verses are numbered. As the constant use of the suras in public worship required some means of reference, there must have been some way of distinguishing them. *Third*—Some of the suras Muhammed mentions by their titles—e. g., at the battle of Honein he addressed a company of his followers as "The men of the sura Bacr."

The second line of the superscription states whether the sura was revealed at Mecca or Medina. In some cases we find part of it belonging to Mecca and part to Medina. If this matter be in dispute, it is so stated. In the MSS., verses are not numbered. The reason for this is evident. The chief disagreement between the several editions of the Quran consists in the division and number of the verses. Some editions have only 6,000 verses, one as high as 6,236.

The third line of the superscription, found everywhere, except in the ninth sura, is the "Bismillah"—"In the Name of the Most Merciful God." This is a peculiar mark, used everywhere as the distinguishing characteristic of their religion, it being counted a sort of impiety to omit it.

Prefixed to twenty-nine chapters of the Quran are certain letters of the alphabet, sometimes one letter, sometimes two, sometimes three, and in one case five. A. L. M. is the most common combination. Many ingenious conjectures have been made as to their import: (1) That they stand for the words "*Amar li Muhammed*," meaning "At the command of Muhammed;" (2) for Allah, Gabriel and Muhammed; (3) numerically, the letters represent seventy-one. Some drew from this the conclusion that in seventy-one years the Muslim faith would be universal. There is one observation of more special note, that, in cases where these letters occur, there is reference, in the opening lines of the sura, to the "revelation" or "handing down." Only two suras that have the letters begin differently, and only four suras that begin in this way lack the letters. Muhammed may have meant these letters as a mystic reference to the original text, in heaven. (Commentators generally agree that no one but God knows their meaning.)

The suras are placed in the Quran to-day just as they were arranged by Zeid in his first collection. There is an utter lack of sequence, logical or chronological. The initial or opening prayer stands first. After this there seems to be an effort to arrange the suras according to their length; the longest first. But even this is not strictly adhered to. We can scarcely think that the present arrangement received any sanction from Muhammed. On the other hand, there is every evidence to prove that if there had been any fixed order for the material while the prophet lived, the compilers would have scrupulously followed it. The present disorder must be attributed to the condition of the material from which the collection was made, and to the false zeal of the compiler, which left the Quran a chaotic jumble. We find in it a portion produced at Medina immediately preceding a passage revealed long before at Mecca; a command placed directly after a later one which cancels or modifies it; an argument suddenly disturbed by the introduction of a sentence foreign to its purport. The fact that some of the suras are so short, naturally suggests that the longer ones may be compilations, especially since short passages were often given out in driblets, and even single verses, as occasion required. There is a tradition to the effect that Muhammed used to direct his amanuensis to enter *this material* in the sura which treated of such and such a subject.

To show that these statements as to arrangement are not exaggerations, and that we may appreciate the painstaking patience by which critics have obtained their results in the last twenty-five years, let me quote from an earnest advocate of Muhammed, writing in 1840. Abuse of Muhammed put Carlyle in the mood to defend the prophet's character. In doing this he was necessarily led to say something about the book. There is no doubt about Carlyle's intentions. He distinctly asserts, "I mean to say all the good of him I justly can," but "I must say the Quran is as toilsome reading as I ever undertook. A wearisome, confused jumble, crude, incondite, endless iterations, long-windedness, entanglement, *most* crude, incondite. Insupportable stupidity in short. Nothing but a sense of duty could carry any European through the Quran. We read in it—as we might in the state paper-office—unreadable masses of lumber, that perhaps we may get some glimpses of a remarkable man."

Since the Quran is the chief source of information, both for Muhammed and the Muslim religion, and only as we read it aright can we interpret the life of Muhammed and the faith of his followers, it is clear that the importance of a critical arrangement cannot be over-estimated. The problem is not a simple one, and the results obtained vary. Three methods have been employed. First, the Muslim compiler, with Pharisaic reverence, "performing his ablutions every time he approached his task, daring only to put the sacred fragments in juxtaposition; leaving legend, doctrine, prophecy in one interminable mass, told over and over again with little verbal variation;" not venturing to select from repeated versions of the same incident, nor to reconcile differences, nor to connect abrupt transitions of context by the alteration of a single letter. This is the form of the Quran as it comes to the English reader in the ordinary translation. Over against this method of dealing with the material, is the school of criticism that regards the *entire* Quran as a piece of patchwork, that overlooks the characteristics of the Semitic mind and attempts to square the book by standards foreign to the literature. Nöldeke confesses that he has carried this style of criticism too far, and Wellhausen thinks Sprenger has done the same.

Between these extreme views is another that is satisfied with drawing a somewhat distinct line between the Mecca and Medina Suras, corresponding to the radical change experienced in the life of the author. Since the Medina suras are colored by events fairly well known, the dates of the separate suras are obtained with some degree of accuracy. The Mecca suras present greater difficulties. Prof. Weil has classified them into three groups. The short suras are the oldest. They are farthest removed in style from the Medina passages, and form a distinct group. It is not difficult to form another cluster of the *later* Meccan suras, that show marked affinity with those of Medina. Between these two groups stand a number of suras which bear the marks of transition from the first to the third. These groups cannot be separated by sharp lines, and within any group it is altogether impossible to determine even a probable chronological order.

We have only to speak of style so far as it affects the *form*. Muhammed declined to be rated as a poet. No one of the fifty-five titles of the Quran indicate that it is poetry. The variety of the material demanded a similar variety in the method of treatment. A prose style would well suit much of the matter in the Quran. But Muhammed adopted a rhymed prose, which could well express the more poetic sections, but imposes on the Quran, as a whole, a very burdensome yoke. There is a persistent effort to give to the terminations of verses similar sounds. In the second sura, which is the longest, the majority of verses end with the syllable " *un* " or " *in*." In sura thirty-five there is the same effort to use the letter " *r* " at the close. The combination may differ, and the uniformity with which it is carried out, but the effort is quite generally manifest. This has made the style stiff and unnatural, since it has dominated both the order and the choice of words. It has also caused abruptness by the introduction of irrelevant matter and led to endless repetition of familiar phrases, such as " the powerful, " the wise," "the merciful," "the compassionate." It has also given different forms to the same word. In sura 69, verse 17, there can' be little doubt but that the choice of the numeral eight is determined by sound and not by fact. As the number refers to the angels that bear the throne of God, it manifests the extreme influence of the rhyme. In some cases we find not only a recurring syllable, but a recurring sentence. In sura 55 the words, "Which, therefore, of your Lord's benefits will ye ungratefully deny," are repeated thirty-one times. The facts, too, that so many sentences begin with "On a day when," where the connection is invisible; that in sura 18 the words "till that" occur eight times as a conjunction in close succession; go to prove that Muhammed was not a master of style.

A comparative study of the external forms of the Quran and the Bible suggests some parallels that are of interest.

(1) In the Quran God is represented as speaking in a more direct form, if possible, than in the Bible. It is dominated from first to last by a " Thus saith the Lord."

(2) The text of the Quran has been preserved with the greatest care. To countenance a various reading is by a Muslim regarded as an offense against the state. " No other work " (says Muir) " has remained for twelve centuries with so pure a text."

(3) Not only have the words and letters of the Quran been counted, but pains have been taken to compute the number of times each letter of the alphabet occurs.

(4) On the matter of vowel points it is worthy of notice that the texts were pointed about the same time, and for the same purpose, i. e. to preserve a standard text. In each case they were soon regarded by many as an original element of the book. In each case there has been a fierce and prolonged contest as to the origin of every minutia of the text. By the Muslims the question of whether the Quran was uncreated and eternal was controverted with so much heat "that it occasioned many calamities under some of the Caliphs," making necessary a public edict, declaring the Quran to be created, and that those who held the contrary opinion should be whipped, imprisoned and put to death. On the other hand, Christian theologians in Switzerland in 1678 enacted a law that no person should be licensed to preach unless he publicly declared that he believed in the divinity of the Hebrew vowel points and accents.

(5) Under the head of superscriptions there is first in the case of the Quran and the Bible the question of their genuineness; second their relation to the subject-matter. What has been said in regard to the inaptness of the titles of the Quran has its parallel in the bere'shith of Genesis, the shemôth of Exodus, the wayyiqra' of Leviticus, the bemidhbar of Numbers, and the debharim of Deuteronomy. The title "Samuel," as applied to the first two books of the Kings and the fanciful divisions of the cxix. Psalm, are further examples.

(6) With the mysterious letters of the Quran may be compared the Majuscular and Minuscular letters of the Massorites. Concerning their interpretation it is interesting to know that a Mr. W. H. Black, F. S. A., in a paper read before the Chronological Society of London, October 4th, 1864, propounded the theory that the sum total of the Majuscular letters is designed to give the date of the Pentateuch.

(7) Aside from the parallel divisions of chapter and verse, the Quran and the Bible are divided for systematic reading in public service.

(8) Attention has been called to the lack of arrangement

in the Quran. There is abundant evidence that some of the material now combined existed at an earlier time in separate form. This suggests at once the question of the analysis of the Pentateuch, and of a first and second Isaiah.

(9) Several fragments of the Quran are preserved as genuine that are not in the text, so that the question of the *canon* finds its parallel.

(10) The necessity of a careful study of the historic background is ever present in the Quran, as in the Bible, in the scientific interpretation of the material.

(11) The absence of historical data, in both books, is most worthy of notice. Muhammed's name occurs but five times in the Quran, and only two contemporaries are mentioned. If we put beside this the statement from the lips of Ali, "There is not a verse in the Quran of which I do not know the matter, the parties to whom it refers, and the place and time of its revelation, whether by night or by day, whether in the plains or upon the mountain," and keep in mind at the same time the immense activity and the many personal encounters of the prophet's life, we are led to wonder at the suppression of historic detail, as we wonder at a similar absence of historical data in the songs of Deborah and Hannah, in the Psalter and the book of Job.

PSALM XLV.

By Rev. Professor THOS. HILL RICH,

Cobb Divinity School, Lewiston, Me.

I. AN INTERPRETATION OF THE PSALM.

There are those who see in this psalm, only the epithalamium of an earthly king. But if a secular song, why should it be entrusted to the leader of Temple music? and if it were such, then neither its composition, nor its execution would befit Korahites, whose singing was consecrated to the worship of Jehovah. Besides "Maskil" tells of *pious consideration;* and the "delights" which the song rehearses, are by the original stamped with holiness.

Its extended heading suggests that the song is of deep import.

That it has a place among the psalms, that tradition refers it to Messiah, that proof of Messiah's dignity is hence derived by the epistle to the Hebrews, and that expressions in the song, if addressed to a mortal king, would be gross flattery —all point to him, whose coronation, and priesthood, and all-prevailing dominion, David celebrates in psalms 2 and 110.

Here is sung, by one familiar with the doings and splendor of Solomon's court, the marriage of the peerless king Messiah—"*the holy and divine union of Christ with the Church !*"

The following is the sacred singer's course of thought.

Verse 1. He says, that like water from a fountain, there wells from his heart matter for rich discourse; and as he fashions it, his constant thought is: " My work (my creation) is in honor of a great king! " That he may give expression to his full heart, he asks that words may flow from his tongue —freely, as from the reed of a skillful scribe.

Verse 2. The beauty of this king he extols, as beyond human comparison! his speech as having surpassing sweetness! [Corporeal beauty cannot be here in mind, for that is perishable; but *spiritual* beauty, and gracious lips (compare Luke 4: 23.) tell of God's enduring blessing—perceived to be upon this king.]

Verses 3 and 4. To this king so fair and gracious, there also belongs prowess; by reason of which the poet invokes him to take to himself his sword—his irresistible glory, and thus equipped to go forth to victory in behalf of sincere men, suffering wrongfully. He predicts that in such expedition, the king's right hand will be sure to perform—will as it were, *guide him to*—stupendous deeds!

Verse 5. To the seer, his petition has even now fulfilment; for to his eye the king is present, with sharpened arrows, (ready for immediate use). But before the seer has well noted, they have sped—yonder *whole nations* are falling, are prostrate beneath the conqueror's chariot! for lo, those fatal arrows have pierced their heart!

The king's enemies slain, the time is fit to speak of the stability of his throne, and the seer honoring him as Divine declares,

Verse 6, that the king's rule is—everlasting! Not only are there now none from without to disturb his rule, but *within* it is strong, by reason of his care for the lowly, by his incorruptible dealing with the proud oppressor, by his *uniform* justice—all implied in his *sceptre* of *equity* (compare Is. 11: 4).

Verse 7. Even all along in the past the king has cleaved to the·right, and consequently abhorred that which is evil. (The past tense of the Revision is in accord with the LXX., the Vulgate, and English versions before 1611.)

This steadfast doing implies effort, self-denial—merit, to which has now come reward and a festal day, whereon the king receives from his God an anointing, that bestows upon him unparalleled felicity!

Verse 8. Anointing calls to mind the "precious ointment" used for that purpose. It has run down to the king's robes (compare Ps. 133,) and so filled them with fragrance, that its spices seem to be their very warp and woof. [Perfumes are greatly esteemed by the orientals.]

Glad in heart, and in glad raiment, the king comes to

splendid palaces (the plural of grandeur) where only gladness greets him.

Verse 9. Princesses here do him honor; and lo! one in array so dazzling, that it seems of simple, purest gold, has place at the king's right hand—the place of queen!

Verses 10, 11, 12, Of this bride, come to such exaltation, the seer implores an earnest hearing; and with allusion to the law of marriage (Gen. 2 : 24), and to the calling of Abraham (Gen. 12 : 1), he exhorts her to entire devotion to the king, lest otherwise she repel his ardent affection for her. That he is *lord* tells of superior worth, and right to be honored and loved; and she should therefore give him loving reverence. If she does so, honor will come to her, and the mightiest and richest will bow before her face.

Verse 13. And now, a time having elapsed since her betrothal, this daughter of a king, in gorgeous apparel, awaits in her father's palace the coming of the king, her bridegroom, to take her for his wife, and to the home that he has prepared for her.

Verse 14. The bridegroom approaches. (1. Maccabees 9 : 37–40, shows that the bridegroom did not always come all the way, but that the bridal party went out to meet him.) With pomp they lead forth the bride to meet him, spreading tapestries in the way for her to tread upon. The princesses spoken of above, are her associates, and follow in her train. They like her are brought unto the king. (That is, to be his brides. Which shows that the language is figurative. For while Solomon and other kings married many wives, they married them one by one.)

Verse 15. The procession moves on with glad music and demonstrations of joy, until at length it enters the palace of the royal bridegroom, and the marriage feast begins. (Compare Rev. 19; 7–9.)

Verse 16. The seer addressing the bridegroom, predicts from this marriage a glorious offspring, to become princes over the king's world-wide domain!

Verse 17. The seer is determined to celebrate this king in all the generations to come! (Perhaps he sees that his inspired song will live, even as it has done. Or perhaps he

speaks as a member of the living church of God.)   The seer
is confident that the excellencies of king Messiah, being declared, men will confess his worth, and give thanks to him
for his benefits—forevermore!

II.   A Free Rendering of the Psalm.

To the Chief Musician.   Set to (the melody) "Lilies."   By the Sons of
Korah.   A Maskil.   A Song of Delights.

My heart is overflowing with a goodly theme!
    Unto myself I say:
    " My work respects—a king!"
My tongue, be pen of writer apt.

    Far fairer thou than sons of men!
    Grace into thy lips is poured—
Token that God has blessed thee evermore!

Gird thy sword upon thy thigh, O Mighty One!—
    Thy splendor and thy majesty;
    Yea, with thy majesty girt round,
      Ride prosperously forth,
    For sake of truth, and right oppressed;
And deeds that awe, let thy right hand point out to thee!
    Thine arrows, they are sharp—
    Lo! peoples underneath thee fall—
    In heart of them who hate the king.

    Thy throne, O God! forever and forever stands;
    Sceptre of equity, the sceptre of thy realm!
    Thou hast loved right, and hated wickedness;
    For this, has God, thy God, anointed thee
With oil of gladness—on thy fellows not bestowed!
    Myrrh, and aloes, cassia—thy garments all;
From ivory palaces sweet strains sound out to welcome thee;
    King's daughters to thy state belong;
    At thy right hand, lo! stands a queen,
      Shining in Ophir gold!

Hear, daughter, and perceive, and bow thine ear;
Forget thy people, and thy father's house;
That so thy beauty may delight the king!
For he is thy lord, and thou shouldest worship him!
Then the daughter of Tyre with gifts—shall sue to thee
Even they who are richest in all the earth!

All glorious the royal maiden in the palace sits:
Her raiment—textures wrought with gold.
On gay embroidery is she conducted to the king;
Her virgin companions in her train are brought to thee—
Conducted all with joyfulness and exultation!
    They enter now the palace of—a king!

    Where thy fathers stood, shall be thy sons,
    Whom thou mayest princes make in all the earth.
O, let me celebrate thy name in every age!
    So peoples will give thanks to thee,
    Forever and forevermore!

III. NOTES ON PSALM 45.

Verse 6. The Hebrew uses great conciseness. "Joshua" = Jehovah's salvation, stands for: "He to whom Jehovah gives salvation;" "Zedekiah" = Jehovah's righteousness, stands for: "He by whom Jehovah deals righteousness;" and when Jer. 33, designates Messiah as: "Jehovah our righteousness," it teaches, that by Messiah Jehovah secures for us righteousness. In the prophets, "David" often stands for: "son of David." So we need not be altogether surprised, that he who has already been called the Son of God, by way of eminence (Ps. 2.) and bidden to take his seat on the throne of God (Ps. 110.), should here be called—"God." There was no Hebrew adjective corresponding to one "divine," "godlike," that would have served the poet had he cared to express himself less strongly. The "thy God" of the next verse shows a limitation of the language here.

Verse 8. The "*honorable* women" of our versions, signifies, such as *confer honor.* Literally: "King's daughters are among the precious ones (or, things); that is, they enter into

23

the constituents of the king's rare estate.   Luther renders here: "In deinem Schmuck gehen der Könige Töchter" (in thy set of jewels kings' daughters have a place).

These princesses represent the gentile nations, now converted.   They are the queens (little princesses) of Is. 49: 23, who there give the marrow of their life to the people of God.

The queen who appears at the king's right hand, is Israel turned from her idolatry, and we have here the re-betrothal of Hosea 2: 20.

With the Jews, betrothal bound as marriage does with us. Its formalities would occur at the home of the bride—in her father's house; and the address of verses 10, 11, 12, was suited to such occasion.

An interval, longer or shorter, occurred between betrothal and the marriage, whose essential ceremony, was the *taking* of the bride from her father's house.

Verse 11. The union of God and his people, of Christ to his church is elsewhere compared to the marriage relation (see Is. 62: 5, and Ephes. 5: 22).

THE LIFE AND TIMES OF THE CHRIST,

BASED ON LUKE.

By William R. Harper and George S. Goodspeed,

Yale University.

(Copyrighted, 1890.)

STUDIES XLIX. AND L.—THE BURIAL, RESURRECTION AND ASCEN-SION. LUKE 23 : 50–24 : 53.

Remark.—It is desirable that in beginning each " study " the entire passage assigned be read over rapidly and the main divisions of the narrative noted.

I. EXAMINATION OF THE MATERIAL.

[It will be noted that the following order is observed invariably in this work; (1) the verse or section is read and its contents stated in a general way; (2) important or difficult words and phrases are studied; (3) a complete statement of the contents of the verse or section is formed in view of the work already done; (4) the religious teaching is sought.]

§ 1.   Chapter 23 : 50–56.

1. Read and note a subject: *The Burial of Jesus.*
2. Among other important words and phrases note (1) *councillor* (23 : 50), i. e. member of the Sanhedrim ; (2) *had not consented* (23 : 51), had he objected ? (3) *city of the Jews,* why is this statement made ? (4) *was looking,* etc., not meaning necessarily a disciple of Jesus, cf. John 19 : 38 ; (5) *tomb,* etc. (23 : 53), significance of the two descriptive clauses following ? (6) *preparation* (23 : 54), for what ? (7) *prepared spices,* etc. (23 : 56), with what design ? (8) *on the Sabbath they rested,* etc., peculiar to Luke, why ?
3. The thought of the passage may be worked out into the student's own statement.
4. A practical thought is found in the fact that the death of Jesus brought Joseph to a decision openly to minister to him.   His character is proved by the crisis.

§ 2.   Chapter 24 : 1–12.

1. A suggested subject is : *Jesus risen.*
2. Words and phrases of special interest are : (1) *the stone* (24 : 2), cf. Mt. 27 : 60; (2) *entered in and found not* (24 : 3), significance of this ? (3) *two men stood* (24 : 4), compare Mk. 16 : 5 and explain ; (4) *he spake unto you,* etc. (24 : 6), when was this ? (5) *all the rest* (24 : 9), who are meant ? (6) *Mary, the mother of James* (24 : 10), cf. Mk. 15 : 40; (7) *they disbelieved* (24 : 11), why mention this ? (8) *but Peter,* etc. (24 : 12), recall his last appearance ; (9) *cloths by themselves,* what could this mean ?

3. The student may work out his own condensation of the passage.
4. Consider how those who are seeking in this extremity to do what they can for their Lord are rewarded with the first knowledge of his resurrection.

§ 3. Chapter 24 : 13-35.

1. The student may read the passage and name a subject.
2. The student may study the following special points: (1) *two of them* (24 : 13), not apostles but disciples; (2) *questioned* (24 : 15), as though they could not agree on any explanation; (3) *Jesus drew near,* etc., why should he have sought these somewhat inferior disciples? (4) *were holden* (24 : 16), (a) because of absorption in their thoughts, or (b) supernaturally? (5) *named Cleopas* (24 : 18), light on Luke's informant? (6) a *prophet* (24 : 19), how explain this conception? (7) *chief priests* (24 : 20), note where they place the cause of Jesus' death; (8) *hoped* (24 : 21), what light on the general feeling among Jesus' followers at this time? (9) *slow of heart to believe* (24 : 25), meaning? (10) *and to enter,* etc. (24 : 26), i. e. and *thus* to enter; (11) *he made as though,* etc. (24 : 28), i. e. to test them; (12) *eyes were opened,* etc. (24 : 31), supernaturally? (13) *to Simon* (24 : 24), significance of this?
3. The statement of the thought may be prepared by the student.
4. The thought of the sympathy of Jesus with the difficulties of his disciples and the skilful way he deals with them, is full of interest.

§ 4. Chapter 24 : 36-43.

1. Consider the following subject: *Jesus' Appearance to the Company of Disciples.*
2. (1) *As they spake* (24 : 36), i. e. on the evening of that day; (2) *reasonings* (24 : 38), light upon their state of mind; (3) *see my hands,* etc. (24 : 39), i. e. that they are those of the crucified Jesus; (4) *handle,* another proof; (5) *did eat,* (24 : 43), the third proof.
3. The thought may be expressed by the student in his own words.
4. The student may decide on the religious teaching.

§ 5. Chapter 24 : 44-49.

1. The student may make his own statement of the subject.
2. Important words and phrases are: (1) *and he said,* etc. (24 : 44), at this time? cf. Mt. 28 : 16; (2) *how that all things,* etc., why remind them of this? (3) *then opened he,* etc. (24 : 45), how (a) supernaturally? or (b) by repeated interviews and explanations as to the way to study the O. T.? (4) *should be preached* (24 : 47), (a) emphatic, (b) why now? (c) how is this "written?" (5) *witnesses* (24 : 48), in what sense? (6) *the promise of my Father* (24 : 49), (a) i. e. I give you the Holy Spirit which my Father promised, (b) when was this promised?
3. The condensed statement may be made by the student.
4. Consider as a religious thought the emphasis laid by Jesus on the Old Testament Scriptures, and our duty to study them.

§ 6. Chapter 24 : 50-53.

1. After reading, consider a subject: *The Ascension of Jesus.*
2. (1) *Led them out* (24 : 50), (a) at this same time? (b) whom? (2) *he was parted* (24 : 51); (3) *into heaven;* (4) *worshiped him* (24 : 52); (5) *great joy,* why at this time? (6) *continually in the temple* (24 : 53).
3. The student may work out the thought.
4. The religious teaching of the Ascension—what is it?

II. CLASSIFICATION OF THE MATERIAL.

1. Contents and Summary.

1) **The Contents.** The following table of contents is to be mastered.

THE BURIAL, RESURRECTION AND ASCENSION.

§ 1. THE BURIAL OF JESUS.
§ 2. JESUS RISEN.
§ 3. JESUS AND THE TWO DISCIPLES.
§ 4. JESUS' APPEARANCE TO THE COMPANY OF DISCIPLES.
§ 5. THE LAST INSTRUCTIONS.
§ 6. THE ASCENSION OF JESUS.

2) **The Summary.** The student may study carefully, and criticize the following summary statement of the thought, reducing it to smaller dimensions as far as possible :
Joseph, a councillor, but friendly to Jesus' work, gets Pilate's permission to take Jesus' body, and just before Sabbath he puts it in a new rock-tomb, the women friends of Jesus looking on. Duly resting on the Sabbath, they bring spices 'at dawn, but find the tomb open, the body gone, and two angels there who remind them, startled, of what Jesus said about his rising the third day. The women are not believed when they tell the disciples of this, though Peter runs to the tomb and wonders at the sight. Two disciples walk to Emmaus, and sadly discussing the affair, are met by Jesus, whom they do not recognize. He shows them how the Scripture is fulfilled in his dying, reveals himself at supper and vanishes. They go to tell the disciples who have heard that Simon has seen him. Suddenly Jesus stands there, calms their fear by showing them that he is no ghost, and makes them understand clearly the Scripture testimony to the gospel for the world in his death and resurrection. This they are to preach after they have received power. Leaving them outside the city, he blesses them, and ascends into heaven. They worship Him, and, returning to Jerusalem, praise God.

2. Observations upon the Material.

308) 23 : 50, 51. Jesus had some men of high position among his followers.

309) 23 : 53, 56. Some burial customs are alluded to. *

310) 23 : 54. The question is whether (1) this was the day on which "preparation" was made merely for the Sabbath, or (2) this was the Preparation both for the Sabbath and for the Passover, which came on the Sabbath that year, cf. John 19 : 14. †

311) 23 : 53-55. There seems to be no doubt of the fact that Jesus really died. ‡

312) 23 : 56. Mark seems to imply (16 : 16), that these spices were bought when the Sabbath was over. §

* See Stapfer, *Palestine in the time of Christ*, pp. 165-171.

† See Gardiner, *Harmony*, p. 220 ; *Edersheim*, II., pp. 567, 568.

‡ The certainty of the death of Jesus before his burial is raised above every rational doubt, and partially attested by the manner of His burial. *Van O.*, p. 384.

§ Possibly, we have two groups of women—the two Maries and Joanna, and the others (ch. 24: 10)—taking part in the same work; possibly, what they did on the Friday afternoon or evening was not enough, and it was necessary to buy more spices as soon as the shops were open on Saturday evening. *Plumptre*, p. 393.

It would be better to assume, as Luke makes no mention of the hour, that he had put that item of his narrative out of its proper order. *Bliss*, p. 343.

313) 23 : 55, 56. The interest taken by these women is very striking. They certainly do not expect his resurrection. *

314) 24 : 2. Luke refers to an incident of which, however, he makes no previous mention.

315) 24 : 3, 4. The expectations and perplexity of the women are indirect proofs of the death of Jesus, and therefore of the reality of the resurrection.

316) 24 : 11. The disbelief of the apostles shows their idea about the death of Jesus and his resurrection.

317) 24 : 12. This verse about which there is some doubt links Luke's narrative with that of John.

318) 24 : 1-12. A comparison of Luke's account with those of the other Gospels shows many divergencies and much confusion.†

319) 24 : 13-35. This narrative is peculiar to Luke, and one of the two disciples was probably his informant. ‡

320) 24 : 18. This inquiry shows the excitement that prevailed in Jerusalem during these days.

321) 24 : 30, 31. Jesus acted as the host, and it seems that the familiar action and manner disclosed the truth to them. §

322) 24 : 16, 31, 37. Jesus does not seem to have the same appearance as before his death. (Cf. Mk. 16 : 12.)∥

323) 24 : 37. The terror is the occasion for a more thorough and convincing proof of his resurrection. ¶

324) 24 : 25, 26, 44. Jesus makes great use of

---

* And so the very spices the women prepare for the embalming are a silent but a fragrant testimony to the reality of the Resurrection. They show the drift of the disciples' thought. Burton, *Gospel of St. Luke*, p. 401.

† The arranging of them all into a clearly consistent history is, confessedly, a perplexing task, as would be the same in the case of any exciting fact, presenting many phases to many interested persons. *Bliss*, p. 344.

Each, though presenting different details, indicates a movement from doubt to certainty, from fear to hope and joy. These phenomena in the written records effectually dispose of all the theories which seek to set aside the Resurrection of our Lord as a historical fact. Such narratives could not be utter falsehoods ; had they been the invention of later times, the divergencies would not have appeared. *Riddle*, p. 351.

To the different narrators, the central point of interest lay in one or the other aspect of the circumstances connected with the Resurrection. Not only St. Matthew, but also St. Luke, so compresses the narrative that the distinction of points of time is almost effaced. St. Luke seems to crowd into the Easter Evening what himself tells us occupied forty days. His is, so to speak, the pre-eminently Jerusalem account of the evidence of the Resurrection ; that of St. Matthew, the pre-eminently Galilean account of it. *Edersheim*, II., 621, 622.

‡ The particularity of detail, and the fact that the whole chapter seems to give the impressions of one of the two who walked to Emmaus, have led some to the opinion that Luke was himself the companion of Cleopas. But Luke was probably a Gentile. It is most likely that Luke derived his information from Cleopas or his companion. *Riddle*, p. 356.

§ This taking the bread, and blessing it, and breaking it, and then giving it to them, was no ordinary act of courtesy, or welcome, or friendship, which, from a master, or teacher, might be shown to his disciples. It resembles too closely the great sacramental act in the upper room, when Jesus was alone with his apostles, for us to mistake its solemn sacramental character. *Pulp. Com.*, II., p. 272.

As the two disciples had not been present at the institution of the Lord's Supper, they could not be reminded of that. It was rather in the way of his usual custom of praising God for His goodness, at the beginning of a meal. *Bliss*, p. 350.

∥ It is vain to give any simply natural explanation of the failure of the disciples to recognize Christ. After the Resurrection he was known as he pleased, and not necessarily at once. . . . Till they who gazed on him were placed in something of a spiritual harmony with the Lord, they could not recognize him. Westcott, quoted in *Pulp. Com.*, II., p. 270.

[On 24 : 15, 16.] They were discussing with each other the possible reconciliation of difficulties and clearing up of their perplexity. This absorption in the theme of their discourse might itself have hindered their noticing particularly the man. *Bliss*, p. 348. Natural causes probably aided in preventing the recognition. A quiet, vigorous, dignified traveler, such as He appeared to be, would not be readily recognized as the One so lately languid in death on the cross. *Riddle*, p. 357.

¶ All perceived the resemblance between the object in view and Jesus, but they could not be persuaded of the identity, so utterly unprepared were they for seeing the dead one alive again; and their theory at first was just that of Strauss, that what they saw was a ghost or spectre. And the very fact that they entertained that theory makes it impossible for us to entertain it. Bruce, *Training*, etc., p. 432.

the Old Testament in proving the necessity of his death. *

375) 24 : 50-53. In this Gospel is the most em-

phasis put on the Ascension, and much is
omitted relating to the events of these
forty days. †

3. Topics for Study.

1) **The Resurrection.** [Obs. 311, 313, 315, 316, 318, 321-324] : (1) Investigate and
develop the following considerations in their bearing upon the reality of the
resurrection, ‡ (a) the death and burial of Jesus, (b) the empty tomb on the
first day of the week, (c) the collapse of the disciples after the death of Jesus,
their temporary disbelief and the contrast presented in their courage, faith and
energy after being persuaded of his resurrection, § (d) the belief of his family
after their previous unbelief, ‖ (e) the testimony of St. Paul, 1 Cor. 15 : 1-8, (f)
the testimony of the early church, (g) the spirit of the early church. (2) Apply
the above considerations to (a) the " deception" theory, (b) the " delusion"
theory; (c) the " inward vision " theory. (3) The significance of the resurrection of Jesus, in relation to (a) the gospel history, (b) the apostles, ¶ (c) Jesus
himself.

2) **The Chronology.** ** [Obs. 310] : (1) Note the common testimony of the Gospels
(as well as of tradition) that Jesus rose on the first day of the week (Sunday),
cf. Lk. 24 : 1 ; Mt. 28 : 1 ; John 20 : 1. (2) From this point trace back the
events of (a) Saturday, (Lk. 23 : 56), (b) Friday, Lk. 23 : 44 ; 22 : 66, (c)
Thursday, Lk. 22 : 34, 14, 7, (d) Wednesday, Mk. 14 : 1-11, (e) Tuesday,
Lk. 20 : 1, 2, Mk. 11 : 20, 27 ; (f) Monday, Lk. 19 : 45, 46, Mk. 11 : 12 ; (g)

---

* They who consult the teaching of Jesus and his apostles, with respect to the prophecies concerning the Messiah, need not grope in uncertainty, but should, nevertheless, remember that the
Lord probably directed the attention of the disciples . . . . less to isolated Scriptures than to the
whole tenor of the Old Testament, in its typical and symbolical character. *Van O.*, p. 392, cf.
also p. 394

[On 24 : 45.] This was doubtless the work of repeated interviews. *Riddle*, p. 366.

† He evidently lays great stress upon the importance of this last scene, both as a piece of evidence, and as a theme of teaching ; for he not only concludes his Gospel with it, but commences
his book of the Acts with the same recital. *Pulp. Com.*, p. 275.

Was it altogether undesigned that our Evangelist, omitting other appearances of the forty days,
yet throws such a wealth of interest and of coloring into that first Easter day, filling it up from its
early dawn to its late evening ? We think not. He is writing to and for the Gentiles, whose
Sabbaths are not on the last but on the first day of the week, and he stays to picture for us the
first Lord's day, the day chosen by the Lord of the Sabbath for this high consecration. Burton,
Gospel of St. Luke, p. 415.

‡ See a strong but discriminating discussion in Weiss' *Life of Christ*, III. pp. 383 *seq.*

§ Their despair after their Lord's crucifixion gives great weight to the testimony borne by them
to the *fact* of His resurrection. Men in such a mood were not likely to believe in the latter event
except because it could not reasonably be disbelieved. . . . The evangelists have carefully
chronicled these doubts that we might have no doubt. Bruce, *Training*, etc. pp. 492, 495. The
alleged resurrection of Christ was accompanied by the indisputable resurrection of Christianity,
and how is the latter to be accounted for except by the former? . . . As Christ rose from the
dead in a transfigured body, so did Christianity. It had put off its carnality. What effected this
change ? They say it was the resurrection. . . . But their testimony is not proof that He rose
The incontestable proof is the change itself—the fact that suddenly they had become courageous,
hopeful, etc. Stalker, *Life of Christ*, p. 148.

‖ This point is impressively brought out in Stalker, *Imago Christi*, pp. 52-54.

¶ See Bruce. *Kingdom of God*, p. 305.

** See *Plumptre*, Excursus, p. 414.

Sunday, Mk. 11 : 11. (3) Endeavor to determine on which day the Passover fell, whether (a) Thursday-Friday, or (b) Friday-Saturday.

3) The Risen Jesus.* [Obs. 322] : (1) Study the Scripture statements as to the life and person of Jesus during this period; cf. Lk. 24 : 15, 16, 30, 31, 36, 37, 39, 43; Mk. 16 : 9, 12, 14; Mt. 28 : 9, 17; John 20 : 15, 17, 19, 27; 21 : 4, 13, 15; Acts 1 : 3. (2) Observe that from Acts 1 : 3 this period is called "the great forty days." (3) Decide, if possible, from the above passages between the following views; (a) Jesus rose with his perfected "resurrection body," in which he manifests himself to the disciples, (b) Jesus rose with his earthly body, which at the time of his ascension was transformed into the "resurrection body," (c) he rose with his earthly body, which was, during this period, gradually being transformed, etc., (d) he adopted an earthly body for these appearances, the glorified body with which he rose being suited only for the heavenly life. (4) Suggest some reasons why Jesus appeared so seldom and to the disciples only. (5) Note some results of this forty days' period, (a) certainty of the resurrection, (b) restoration of Peter, John 21 : 15-17, (c) instruction as to the future, cf. Acts 1 : 3-8, (d) organization of the new community. Mt. 28 : 18-20.

4) The Ascension. [Obs. 325] : (1) Study the Scripture statements, Lk. 24 : 51; Mk. 16 : 19; Acts 1 : 9. (2) Compare also Lk. 9 : 51; John 14 : 2, 12; 16 : 5, 28; 17 : 11; 20 : 17; Eph. 4 : 10. (3) Note the relation between the resurrection and the ascension.† (4) The bearing of these statements and considerations in (1) (2) (3) upon the objective reality of the ascension. (5) Some reasons why no direct statements are given in Matthew and John. (6) Significance of the ascension, (a) its naturalness in the life of Jesus, (b) as the means to his exaltation, (c) its bearing on the locality of heaven, ‡ (d) in the life of the church and the individual believer. Mk. 16 : 20; John 16 : 7.

4. Religious Teaching.

The important thought to be considered in its religious and practical bearings is, *The Gospel of the Resurrection :* (1) The resurrection of Jesus in its bearing upon the personal life of the believer, (a) the assurance of acceptance with God, Rom. 4 : 24, 25; 8 : 34, (b) the incentive to a new life and the power of attaining it, 2 Cor. 5 : 14, 15; Rom. 5 : 10; 6 : 4, 5; Col. 3 : 1-4; Phil. 3 : 10, etc., (c) the certainty of personal resurrection of the whole man, 1 Cor. 15 : 20; John 6 : 39, 40; 1 Thess. 4 : 14. (2) The resurrection of Jesus in its bearing upon the relations and conditions of the resurrection life and society, (a) "we shall know each other there ; " (b) a perfected fellowship with the divine-human Jesus Christ, Phil. 1 : 23.

---

* A note on the subject is found in *Riddle*, p. 365.

† In trying to show that this was a miracle distinct from that of the resurrection, it is useless to appeal to the apostolic announcement. For even when it evidently speaks of an ascension to heaven (1 Pet. 3 : 22; Eph. 4 : 8-10) it only thinks of the exaltation as being in connection with the Resurrection. As certainly as Jesus rose in the body, i. e. in a glorified body, so certainly was He raised to heaven in that body. . . . In this sense Jesus' corporeal ascension is of course produced by His resurrection and with this it stands or falls. *Weiss*, III, p. 409.

‡ The change which Christ revealed by the ascension was not a change of place but a change of state ; not local but spiritual. Westcott, *Gospel of the Resurrection.*

STUDIES LI. AND LII.—THE LIFE AND WORK OF JESUS THE CHRIST
IN THE GOSPEL OF LUKE.

Remarks. 1. In bringing to a close these studies of Luke's gospel it will be found
helpful to review the fifty " studies " somewhat carefully, and to obtain a complete view of the whole Gospel.

2. The aim will be to gain general conceptions, and time should not be spent
on particular points, except where the student feels a special deficiency.

3. Such a general view will have its most important benefit in organizing and
fixing the results of previous " Studies," and will supply the standpoint from
which the interpretation of particular passages can be made. No verse or
section can fully be understood apart from this general relation to the whole
material.

4. It will be found profitable to read in connection with these " studies " one of
the smaller lives of Jesus Christ. Stalker's *Life of Christ* * or Vallings' *Jesus
Christ the Divine Man* † are excellent for this purpose and either one can be
read through in two or three hours. A larger book is the abridged edition of
Edersheim's *Life and Times of Jesus the Messiah.* ‡

5. It is believed that the student will recognize the great importance of *mas-
tering* the material and will give the necessary time and study to accomplish
this result.

I. EXAMINATION OF THE MATERIAL.

1. Let the student, with paper and pencil in hand, write down in order and carefully,
one under the other the subjects and " contents " of " studies " I.-L. (omitting
of course " studies " XIX. and XX.)

> REMARK.—This may seem to be a formidable undertaking, but let it be remembered (1) that
> these headings number in all only about 175 titles, (2) that only by such a complete table can
> one gain an idea of the contents of Luke as a whole, (3) that writing fixes one's knowledge
> as nothing else can, (4) that having done this, you have what is practically a " Table of
> Contents to the Gospel of Luke," (5) that therefore it should be undertaken with fidelity
> and confidence in the results.

2. With this list completed the student will read the whole Gospel of Luke through
at one sitting, comparing the separate headings of the " Table of Contents "
and noting as the reading proceeds the progress made in working through the
" Table."

3. As a third step the student will again read slowly and thoughtfully the " Table of
Contents " which has been prepared, (1) recalling, as best he can, in the course
of reading the separate headings, the contents of the passage indicated by each
heading (i. e. thinking through the scripture passage), and (2) checking off
those headings, the material suggested by which is not familiar or fails to be
easily recalled.

4. A second and a third reading of the " Table of Contents " after this fashion will be
found increasingly profitable but is not insisted upon.

---

* New York and Chicago : F. H. Revell, pp. 166, price 60 cts.   † New York: Randolph, pp. 226,
price $1.00.   ‡ New York: Randolph, pp. 645, price $2.00.

5. The student is now given the largest freedom in the selection of methods by which to fix the material of the Gospel in the mind. This division of the work should not be given over until there is a reasonable confidence in one's familiarity with the general course and contents of the Gospel.

II. CLASSIFICATION OF THE MATERIAL.

1. Contents and Summary.

1) **The Contents.** An organized outline of the Life of Jesus the Christ as given in Luke is here suggested. It is desired that the student fill in the chapters and verses of the Gospel included under each heading e. g. § 3 *The Forerunner and his Work. Luke* 3 : 1-22.

THE LIFE OF JESUS THE CHRIST.

§ 1. THE INTRODUCTION.

§ 2. THE STORIES OF THE INFANCY AND YOUTH.

§ 3. THE FORERUNNER AND HIS WORK.

§ 4. THE GALILEAN MINISTRY.
　　1) The Introduction.
　　2) The Beginning.
　　3) The Opposition.
　　4) The Central Period of Activity.
　　5) The Close.

§ 5. THE PEREAN MINISTRY.
　　1) The First Stage—Evangelization and Opposition.
　　2) The Second Stage—Condemnation and Extension.
　　3) The Third Stage—The Close.

§ 6. THE JERUSALEM MINISTRY.
　　1) The Opening.
　　2) The Controversies.
　　3) The Work with the Twelve.
　　4) The End.

2) **The Summary.** The student may prepare as careful a summary of the whole Gospel of Luke as the time will allow.

2. Topics for Study.

The following " topics for study " are suggested and partially worked out. References to the literature of the subject are added.

1) **The Gospel of Luke.*** (1) The author.† (2) The peculiar characteristics, ‡ (a)

---

* In connection with this general topic the Introductions to the Commentaries may be consulted, e. g. those of *Farrar, Lindsay, Plumptre, Pulpit,* etc.

† The best account is in *Plumptre.*

‡ On this point *Farrar* is the best, and his *Messages of the Books,* pp. 70-93 is full and interesting on all the topics ; see *Lindsay,* p. 18.

style, (b) contents, (c) form, (d) theology. *   (3) The purpose. †   (4) Those
for whom it was written. ‡   (5) Relation to other Gospels. §

2) Jesus the Christ, as set forth in this Gospel. || (1) His life in outline.   (2)
His personality as revealed (a) iu his early years, (b) in the Temptation, (c) in
the Galilean ministry, (d) in the Perean ministry, (e) in the Jerusalem ministry,
(f) in the last scenes.   (3) The argument of the Gospel (a) for his humanity,
(b) for his divinity, (c) for the recognition of both elements.   (4) Special characteristics of Jesus as brought out in this Gospel.

3. Religious Teaching.

The student may turn to Luke 1 : 4 and consider the *Practical purpose of this Gospel ;* ¶
(1) the need for the realization of this purpose in the disciple (a) intellectually,
(b) spiritually :   (2) how this purpose was realized in this Gospel for the
disciples to whom it was written :   (3) how it may be realized for the disciples
of the present day ;   (4) what has been attained by us in this study.

---

* See *Pulpit Com.*, Introduction III. " The Especial Teaching of St. Luke," and also Westcott, *Introduction to the Gospels*, pp. 372-381.

† *Westcott*, pp. 189-192.   ‡ *Plumptre*, Intro. IV.   § *Lindsay*, Intro. p. 16 ; *Plumptre*, VI.

|| On this topic and on the general subject, special attention is called to *The Gospel of St.
Luke*, by Rev. Henry Burton, New York ; Armstrongs. This is a recent issue of the " Expositor's Bible," and well worth reading as a summing up of the whole review.

¶ A most helpful outline with suggestive remarks on these points is found in the *Pulpit Commentary, Luke*, vol. I. pp. 27-29.

REPORT OF THE PRINCIPAL OF SCHOOLS
OF THE
AMERICAN INSTITUTE OF SACRED LITERATURE.

[At the annual meeting, held at the Diocesan House, 29 Lafayette Place, New York City, October 25th, 1890.]

To the Directors of the American Institute of Sacred Literature :—

The Principal of Schools herewith submits his first Annual Report. The Report will include (1) a brief statement of the work of the Institute during the year which has closed, and (2) recommendations concerning the work for the future. At the meeting of the organization, held in New York City, October 12th, a work was reorganized which had been in progress nine years. During four of these nine years it had been conducted as a personal undertaking, and during the remaining five under the auspices of the American Institute of Hebrew. By the action of the American Institute of Hebrew, taken at a meeting held in New Haven in May, 1889, the work of the Institute of Hebrew terminated December 1, 1889. The five years' work of the Institute of Hebrew, confined exclusively to Hebrew and the cognate languages, formed, therefore, the basis on which the new work of the Institute of Sacred Literature was to be built. There was really no dividing line between the two. On December 1st, the work, which had before that date been done under the name of one organization, went on without change or interruption under the new organization. Additional departments had, meanwhile, been organized, and were in operation. By a vote of the Institute of Sacred Literature, at its meeting in April, 1890, the Institute agreed to assume the responsibilities of the Institute of Hebrew as soon as the fifth Annual Report of the Institute of Hebrew should have been acted upon. At a meeting held this morning at nine o'clock, the Reports of the Principal of Schools and of the Treasurer were received by a quorum of the old Institute of Hebrew. This action makes the connection between the two organizations complete, and binds them together as one.

The history of the year's work is a most significant and interesting one. More than eight hundred students have been enrolled during the year in its correspondence courses, more than one thousand students received instruction during the summer in the various schools held under its auspices, and a thousand special examiners in every State and many foreign countries are to-day preparing groups of men and women for the special examination which is to be offered by the Institute December 30th on the Life of the Christ. The year beginning October 1, 1889, has not been a complete year. The first prospectus was not ready until late in November. Work in the several departments was not opened until January 1 ; yet, in spite of delays and difficulties, the work has developed in a manner which is exceedingly gratifying. In the detailed history of the year the Report will consider in order (1) the work of the Correspondence Schools, the Institute Clubs, and the Examination Clubs conducted directly by the Institute itself, (2) the work of the Institute accomplished through its Local Boards, and (3) the work accomplished in connection with outside organizations.

I. THE HEBREW CORRESPONDENCE SCHOOLS.

MEMBERSHIP SEPT. 30, 1890.

Course.	Hebrew.	Greek.	E. N. T.	E. O. T.	Arab.	Total.
I.	296	49	(Luke) 103	(Sam.) 8	15	
II.	154	12	————	———	—	
III.	82					
IV.	48					
	——	—				——
	580	61				766

STATISTICS CONCERNING WORK OF SCHOOLS.

	Hebrew.	Greek.	E. N. T.	E. O. T.	Arab.	Total.
New members enrolled,	194	61	103	8	5	371
Students retired,	96	—	——	—	2	98
Net gain,	98	61	103	8	3	273
Graduated in various courses,	81	—	——	—	1	
Denominations represented,	31	12				
States and countries repr'd :—						
In United States and Canada,	51					
" other lands,	12					
No. of women,	28	15	44	1		
" " men outside ministry :—						
Teachers,	60 ⎫					
Students,	35 ⎬ 135	10	34	2	8	
Other occupations,	40 ⎭					

EXAMINATION PAPERS CORRECTED.

Course.	Hebrew.	Greek.	E. N. T.	E. O. T.	Ar.	Total.
I.	1902	226	456	19	48	
II.	1452	12	——	—	—	
III.	809					
IV.	106					
	——	——				
Total,	4269	238				

Letters written with papers and in general work of the School, - 1257

REMARKS UPON THE STATISTICS.

1) During 1886 the number of examination papers corrected in Hebrew was 4,313; during 1887, a year of only eleven months, 3,950; during 1888, 4,504; during 1889, 5,045; during 1890, calculating from October 1, 1889, to October 1, 1890, about 5,300.

2) During the first six years of the School there were completed 219 courses, during the seventh year 79, during the eighth year 79, during the ninth year 107, during the tenth year 81.

3) As has been stated, the arrangements for correspondence work in Greek and the English Bible were not completed until after January 1st; the report of these departments, therefore, covers the period of practically eight months instead of twelve. The number of members, as well as recitations, is rapidly increasing.

4) Not a few members, who had hitherto been working in Hebrew, have been transferred to one of the English or Greek courses. The number of those who have stopped work during the year is about the same as in preceding years. The number of new students is less in proportion, because, during the months October to December, 1889—the best months in the year for receiving students—no aggressive effort was made, and because of uncertainty of the plans which might be adopted by the new Institute.

5) The reasons for discontinuance may be classified as follows : (*a*) entrance upon seminary studies, (*b*) failure, (*c*) death, (*d*) over-pressure of regular

duties, (*e*) permanent appointment to some denominational work, (*f*) discouragment, (*g*) insufficient education.

Assistants in the Correspondence Work.—In the work of the year the Principal has been assisted by Mr. C. E. Crandall, to whom has been entrusted much of the detail relating to the Hebrew correspondence work. Mr. Crandall has been connected with this work for eight years. His work demands the most painstaking accuracy, as well as a large amount of patience. In both of these qualities he excels. Mr. George S. Goodspeed has taken charge of the papers in the Greek correspondence work, and has assisted in the preparation of the printed lesson-sheets of that department. Mr. F. K. Sanders, besides assisting in the work of correcting Hebrew papers, has prepared the lesson-papers, corrected the examination papers in the English Bible Department, and also assisted in the general aggressive work of the Institute. Mr. Daniel Shepardson, Jr., has, since August 1st, assisted in correcting Hebrew and Arabic papers. The work of the Examination Department has been conducted during the early part of the year by Mr. A. M. Wilson, and during the latter part by Mr. Shepardson and Miss G. L. Chamberlain. Assistance of a most valuable character in all departments has been rendered by the stenographers, Miss H. J. Bassett and Miss J. R. Cobb.

2. INSTITUTE BIBLE CLUBS.

1) *The general attitude toward them.*—There is evidence of a clear and satisfactory nature that *many people* are looking for the work done in this department, viz., a systematic Bible study furnishing definite results. There are scores of inquiries in reference to it. As soon as a feasible scheme has been presented we may confidently expect a ready acceptance.

2) *The work of the year.*—During the past year this part of the work has not received the share of attention which it deserved. There has been some definite correspondence with clubs, and a large number are now ready to begin work. It is not possible, however, to report any considerable amount of work on the part of clubs during the past year. Special mention may be made of the club at New Bedford, Mass., which has done earnest and faithful work throughout the year—work, too, which has shown most marked improvement from week to week. The other departments of the Institute demanded so much attention that little has been done to push the work of this department. The announcements made in the general circular were hardly definite enough, and there was a confusion between corresponding clubs and non-corresponding clubs ; and this indefiniteness has prevented our realizing the results otherwise attainable.

3) *New plans.*—As an outcome of the experience of the year, we have been able to formulate a plan which will reduce the burden on the office, and consequently the expense. A pamphlet has been prepared indicating clearly the object, method, courses, cost, etc., of a Bible club. Various Young Peoples' Societies are manifesting a decided interest in Bible study. Advanced classes in Sunday-schools and in Y. M. C. A.'s are ready to take it up. The different factors in the case are now clearly presented, and it is only necessary that we move forward to enroll, at a small calculation, 500–1000 clubs during the coming year. Clubs will be, as heretofore, of two kinds, corresponding and non-corresponding. A corresponding club will choose a secretary and leader, pay a fee of $5.00, with an additional 50 cents for each member of the club, be enrolled under the name of its leader, with whom correspondence will be

conducted, carry out its work regularly according to a carefully prepared direction-sheet which is sent to each member of the club, report its work every two weeks (at the same time sending in (*a*) the results of the topical work done on the studies, (*b*) answers to the questions of an examination-paper furnished for each lesson, (*c*) questions on the paper which may be asked by members of the class), and receive an examination at the close of its work. The fee of $5.00 will pay for the correspondence instruction of the leader. This insures the maintenance of a high standard of work, and the proper use by the leader of the material.   The leader will keep several weeks ahead of his class.   *Non-corresponding clubs* will be enrolled for a fee of 50 cents for each member.   Over these clubs the Institute will exercise control in regard to the instructor, reserving the right to reject him.   It will furnish to each member of the club a direction-sheet for study, and will give each member of the club an examination at the close.

3. THE EXAMINATION DEPARTMENT.

1) *The plan.*—For the general plan of the proposed examination on the Life of the Christ you are referred to the accompanying circular, which announces the grades of the examination, the required preparation, the time and places, the work of the Special Examiners, the character of the enrollment, method of conducting the examination, the certificates to be granted, and the fee, with specimen examination-papers.   In addition to the material contained in this circular, we have granted permission to Special Examiners to use their own discretion in inviting to join their groups in the examination, without charge, those who, through timidity or for other sufficient reason, do not wish to have their papers examined or to try for the certificate of the Institute.   If these persons, after trying the examination and finding their knowledge more complete, decide to have their papers examined, they are to be forwarded with other papers of the group, with the examination-fee of 50 cents.

2) *The work which has been done.*—(1) There have been distributed 30,000 announcements and 20,000 direction-sheets, besides a large amount of other printed matter ; (2) the plan has been presented at ten summer schools, in both the religious and secular press, especially in *The Sunday-School Times* and THE OLD AND NEW TESTAMENT STUDENT ; (3) it has been presented and discussed at many Sunday-school conventions and conventions of Young Peoples' Societies ; (4) the work, however, has been accomplished chiefly through Special Examiners (5,000 persons, ministers and Christian workers, whose names have been gathered from every possible source, have been solicited to act as Examiners) ; (5) careful attention has been given to those who have made inquiry for information, and through these many groups for examination have been obtained ; (6) in several large cities the plan has been presented at the meetings of ministers' associations.

3) *The present situation.*—There are enrolled as examiners 1,000 names, as is shown by the accompanying lists.   In the list are represented 44 States and Territories, 9 Provinces of Canada, Mexico, England, Ireland, Japan, China, Syria and India.   From reports received we may be confident that at least 600 of these examiners are conducting Bible-classes of from 5 to 50 members, each of which is studying the Gospel of Luke with a view to this examination.   Many examiners, who are Sunday-school superintendents, are presenting the matter to their entire schools, and through an arrangement of different grades of questions, are trying to stimulate the study of the Sunday-school lessons of the entire school by the aid of the examination.

4) *Difficulties.*—In prosecuting the plan many difficulties have presented themselves ; as (1) that of securing the attention of the persons addressed. Of the 5,000 people with whom communication have been entered into, 1,000 have accepted and less than 700 have refused.   3,000, however, have given no heed to the request.   This is probably due to the fact that printed letters have been sent them.   In future, printed letters will be used as little as possible, and personal letters substituted for them. (2) That of securing examiners. Of the 700 who have refused to act, the prevailing reason assigned is lack of time.   Ministers with large parishes are too busy.   In some cases the work has been delegated to assistants with good results.   It would be better to try to reach Sunday-school superintendents and Bible-teachers directly, but there is great difficulty in obtaining the names of such persons.   Besides, it is not safe to ask persons of whom we know nothing but the name.   There is great danger all the time of appointing the wrong person.   There is, therefore, need of extreme caution in this regard, and while some mistakes have been made, it is believed that in general only the best persons have been selected.   (3) Experience also is necessary before the work could be properly organized. The novelty of the undertaking has been an obstacle in its way.   People are not accustomed to think of the responsibility of preparation in Sunday-school Bible study, nor are they willing to give the time necessary.   (4) The majority of people dread an examination upon a subject upon which they should be, but are not, familiar.   (5) At the first announcement the expense was too great. It was an experiment.   If few took the examination, the few must be charged enough to cover the expense.   As soon as it was seen that the plan was an acceptable one, the fee was made 50 cents for every person taking the examination, whether singly or in groups.

5) *The outlook.*—It is clearly evident that the plan has received a most cordial reception wherever it has been presented.   Conventions of Young People's Societies are advocating it in many cases, although unsolicited by us. New Hampshire is undergoing systematic canvassing by the Christian Endeavor Society.   The same has also been inaugurated in Wisconsin, Iowa and other States.   From these States there are reports of enthusiastic clubs. Hundreds of letters received from every quarter asking for information concerning the plan show that there is a field, and need of some such incentive. Scarcely a single letter has been received disapproving of the plan.   Many examiners, who have been unable for various reasons to form clubs this year, write that they will take hold next year ; and that they have no doubt of their ability to secure groups for the examination in '91, in which case there will be more time for preparation and canvassing of the field.   The broadening of the plan by allowing examiners to invite, at their discretion, others to take part who do not wish to send their papers to the Institute, will, without doubt, help to take away the fear of the examination. and will make it possible for it to be taken by a much larger number.   With systematic care and proper aggressive work in the lines already inaugurated, it seems practically certain that at least 10,000 people may take the examination this year, and double that number the following year.

4.   THE INSTITUTE LOCAL BOARDS.

1) *The Philadelphia Local Board* of the American Institute of Sacred Literature had its real beginning in a meeting held at the Protestant Episcopal Divinity School, June 24, 1889.   At that meeting a committee was

appointed to get together, at a later time, a number of gentlemen who would be interested in the proposed organization. That committee was composed of the Rev. Drs. Bartlett, Beckley, Dana, Hilprecht and Trumbull, and the Rev. Mr. Batten. This committee gave a dinner at the Hotel Stratford, October 31, 1889. At that dinner the Principal explained, in detail, the proposed work of the American Institute and of the Local Boards. A Board of Directors, as named below, was selected.

Directors—Rev. Dr. George D. Baker, Rev. L. W. Batten, Rev. Dr. Edward T. Bartlett, Rev. Dr. John T. Beckley, Rev. Dr. C. W. Buoy, Rev. Dr. George Dana Boardman, Mr. George H. Crozer, Rev. Dr. S. W. Dana, Rev. Dr. Charles A. Dickey, Prof. W. R. Harper, Prof. J. Rendel Harris, Mr. Charles C. Harrison, Prof. H. V. Hilprecht, Rev. Dr. Henry E. Jacobs. Major W. H. Lambert, Rev. Dr. W. J. Mann, Rev. Dr. S. D. McConnell, Rev. Dr. W. N. McVickar, Mr. Robert C. Ogden, Hon. Robert E Pattison, Dr. William Pepper, Rev. Dr. J. DeWolfe Perry, Rev. Dr. Henry G. Weston.

Officers—President, Rev. Dr. S. W. Dana ; Treasurer, Major W. H. Lambert ; Secretary, Rev. L. W. Batten.

Executive Committee—Rev. Dr. E. T. Bartlett, Rev. Dr. John T. Beckley, Rev. Dr. Henry E. Jacobs, Rev. L. W. Batten, Secretary ; Rev. Dr. S. W. Dana.

Finance Committee—Rev. Dr. C. W. Buoy, Mr. George H. Crozer, Major W. H. Lambert, Treas. ; Rev. Dr. W. J. Mann, Rev. Dr. W. N. McVickar.

The Constitution of the Society has been filed with the Principal of Schools, and is in accordance with the general Constitution of the Institute of Sacred Literature. Under the direction of the Philadelphia Local Board there have been conducted (1) a winter course of ten lectures on the earlier Old Testament Prophets, with an examination, and (2) a summer school of three weeks (June 12th to July 2d), for the details of which you are referred to the accompanying circulars and the Annual Report of the Philadelphia Local Board. The plans of the Philadelphia Local Board for the coming winter are more comprehensive than those of last winter, it being proposed to offer instruction not only in the Old Testament, but likewise in the New Testament, and, still further, in the biblical languages. The Board is considering the question, and perhaps at this date has decided it, whether it will not be better to conduct a winter school on a larger scale and give up the summer school. The intense heat of Philadelphia, and the early season at which the school is held, prevent a large attendance. On the other hand, the local interest is very great, and no locality presents a more encouraging field for the work of the Institute.

2) *The New Haven Local Board* of the American Institute of Sacred Literature was organized in November, 1889. The following Board of Directors was selected.

Members of the Local Board—L. O. Baird, Charles L. Baldwin, J. B. Baldwin, Lester Bradner, Sr., Rev. Dr. M. B. Chapman, Rev. E. A. Cleaveland, Rev. James A. Coote, A. W. Holmes, C. H. Howland, S. C. Johnson, Rev. E. S. Lines, Rev. F. R. Luckey, Rev. W. F. Markwick, Rev. John H. Mason, Rev. Dr. S. McChesney, J. Y. McDermott, Solomon Mead, Rev. D. Means, E. E. Mix, Rev. Dr. T. T. Munger, Rev. H. P. Nichols, Frank W. Pardee, Rev. E. M. Poteat, F. C. Sherman, Rev. Dr. Newman Smyth, W. L. Squires, John W. Townsend, J. B. Underwood, Pierce N. Welch.

The following officers were appointed :—Prof. George B. Stevens, D. D., President ; Rev. M. B. Chapman, D. D., Vice-President ; Samuel C. Johnson, Secretary ; Lester Bradner, Sr., Treasurer ; William R. Harper, Principal of Schools.

The Constitution of the Board has been filed with the Principal of Schools, and is in accordance with the Constitution of the Institute. Under the direction of the Board there have been conducted (1) a Winter School, furnishing instruction in the English Bible—Old and New Testament—and beginning Greek ; (2) a Summer School (May 22d to June 11th), for the details of which you are referred to the circulars of announcement and the Report of the New Haven Local Board.

3) *The Chicago Local Board* was organized in January, 1890. The following gentlemen were selected as the officers of the Board :—W. C. Roberts, D. D., LL. D., President ; S. I. Curtiss, D. D., Vice-President ; Charles Horswell, B. D., Secretary ; J. H. Houghteling, Treasurer.

The following were the committees appointed :—

Committee of Instruction—Prof. E. L. Curtis, Rev. W. H. Vibbert, Rev. A. K. Parker, Messrs. A. G. Lane and R. E. Jenkins.

Committee of Finance—Messrs. J. L. Houghteling, J. B. Hobbs, C. F. Gates, O. S. Lyford, and Rev. M. W. Stryker, all of Chicago.

Under the direction of this Board there was conducted a Summer School at Lake Bluff, Ill. (Aug. 14-Sept. 3). Instruction was given in the English Bible, Hebrew, New Testament Greek and Arabic. The School was under the joint management of the Chicago Local Board and the Lake Bluff Assembly, the latter contributing one thousand dollars toward the expenses of the school. For the details of the work you are referred to the circular of announcement and the Report of the Secretary of the Chicago Local Board.

4) *The Boston Local Board* was organized in May, 1890. The following are the officers and directors selected :—

Officers—President, Prof. C. R. Brown, Newton Centre, Mass. ; Vice-President, Dean William E. Huntington; 12 Somerset St., Boston ; Secretary, Edward H. Chandler, Room 30, Congregational House, Boston ; Treasurer, A. G. Lawson, D. D., 41 Temple Place, Boston ; Auditor, Hon. E. M. McPherson, 5 Tremont St., Boston ; Directors (*ex-officio*), Prof. W. R. Harper, Prof. J. H. Thayer, Prof. C. R. Brown, Prof. M. D. Buell. *Term expires in 1891*—Prof. E. D. Burton, Newton Centre ; Rev. Francis E. Clark, Auburndale ; Rev. A. J. Gordon, Boston ; Rev. J. W. Hamilton, East Boston ; Prof. H. S. Nash, Cambridge ; Prof. W. H. Ryder, Andover ; Rev. J. L. Scott, Jamaica Plain ; Mr. F. P. Shumway, Jr., Melrose ; Rev. R. Cotton Smith, Boston ; Mr. A. R. Weed, Newton. *Term expires in 1892*—Prof. D. W. Abercrombie, Worcester ; Rev. D. N. Beach, Cambridge ; Mr. J. L. Gordon, Boston ; Rev. W. E. Griffis, Boston ; Rev. W. I. Haven, Boston ; Rev. G. E, Horr, Charlestown ; Prof. Max Kellner, Cambridge ; Rev. F. H. Knight, Jamaica Plain ; Rev. Charles Parkhurst, Boston ; Rev. F. W. Ryder, East Boston. *Term expires in 1893*—Mr. Howard A. Bridgman, Boston ; Rev. Phillips Brooks, Boston ; Mr. Edward H. Chandler, Boston ; Mr. M. F. Dickinson, Jr., Boston ; Dr. Samuel Eliot, Boston ; Dean W. E. Huntington, Boston ; Rev. Albert G. Lawson, Roxbury ; Hon. E. M. McPherson, Boston ; Rev. W. D. Roberts, Boston.

The season was so far advanced that it was decided not to arrange for summer work. An active interest has been shown, and a liberal programme for winter instruction has been prepared, including lecture courses, with examinations, on Old Testament Prophecy of the Assyrian period, the Closing Events of our Lord's Life, and class-room instruction in Hebrew and New Testament Greek both for beginners and advanced students. For the details you are referred to the circular of announcement.

5. WORK IN CONNECTION WITH OUTSIDE ORGANIZATIONS.

1) *Chautauqua Work.*—In accordance with the policy adopted by the Directors, schools were held at Chautauqua, N. Y., under the joint management of the Institute of Sacred Literature and the Chautauqua Assembly. These schools were :—

(1)   A Christian Endeavor School of the English Bible (July 5–July 18), with which the authorities of the Y. P. S. C. E. were officially connected. The students who made application for this school numbered about 45. It was found practicable to join the classes of this school with those of the General School of the English Bible conducted at the same time at Chautauqua. Pres. F. E. Clark of the Christian Endeavor was present at the opening of the school and delivered the preliminary address.

(2)   College Students' School of the English Bible (July 19–Aug. 1), in the management of which the International Committee of the Y. M. C. A. also shared.   Instruction was given in the English Bible—Old and New Testament —by Professors Broadus, Ballantine and Harper.   Special lectures on the College Y. M. C. A. work were given by Messrs. C. K. Ober and J. R. Mott, the secretaries of the International Committee. The attendance in this school varied in different classes ; the maximum reached in any class was 69.

(3)   The Bible Teachers' School of the English Bible (Aug. 2–15), in which instruction was given in the English Bible—Old and New Testament—by Professors Ballantine, Horswell and Harper. The maximum attendance in any one class was 45.

(4)   Three General Schools of the English Bible (July 5–Aug. 15), in which instruction was given in the English Bible—Old and New Testament—by Professors Burnham, McClenahan, Horswell, Weidner, Ballantine, Broadus, Batten and Harper. The maximum attendance in any one class was 145.

(5)   Two schools of Hebrew, three weeks each, beginning respectively July 5th, July 26th, in which instruction was given in Hebrew, Arabic and Assyrian by Professors McClenahan, Harper, Horswell, Ballantine, Burnham, Batten, and by Dr. Robert F. Harper ; the number of students enrolled, 54.

(6)   Two schools of New Testament Greek, beginning respectively July 5th, July 26th, in which courses for beginners and more advanced students were provided and instructed by Professors Weidner and Horswell. The work of the school included also special lectures on topics connected with Oriental and Biblical History and Literature, and special Bible studies on the Minor Prophets and Psalms. These lectures were attended by 200–3000 people. In order to show the constituency of the schools, the following statistics may be of interest :—

The following educational institutions were represented by members of faculty, who took work in the School of Sacred Literature :—

Clark University, Ga. ; Knoxville College, Tenn. ; Cotner University, Neb. ; Trinity University, Texas ; Columbia Theological Seminary, S. C. ; Caldwell University, Ky. ; McMaster University, Canada ; Bishop Ridley College, Ontário ; Danville Theological Seminary, Ky. ; Hiram College, Ohio ; Washburn College, Kansas ; Healdsburg College, California ; Bethany College, W. Va. ; Indiana University, Indiana ; Rio Grande College, Ohio ; Fisk University, Tenn. ; Chicago Central Bible School ; Wheaton College, Ill. ; Brethren's Normal College, Pa. ; Slavic Bible Readers' School, Ohio ; Bucknell University, Pa. ; Lehigh University, Pa. ; Hillsdale College, Mich. ; University of Vermont ; Centre College, Ky. ; Battle Creek College, Mich. ; Oxford Female College, O. ; Ohio Wesleyan University ; Millersburg Female College, Ky. ; Mt. Morris College, Ill. ; Oberlin, O. ; Gammon Theological Seminary, Ga.

The following educational institutions were represented by students :—

Rollins College, Florida ; University of Michigan ; Garrett Biblical Institute ; Adelbert College ; Rochester Theological Seminary ; Union College, New York ; Chicago Theological Seminary ; University of Wooster, O. ; Yale ; Virginia Theological Seminary ; Cornell ; Crozer Seminary ; Episcopal

Theological Seminary, Mass. ; Harvard ; Amherst ; Westminister, Pa. ; Normal College, Pa. ; Westminister Theological Seminary, Ind. ; Washington and Jefferson, Pa. ; University of Rochester, N. Y. ; Buchtel College, O. ; Hamilton College, N. Y. ; Bucknell University, Pa. ; Oberlin ; Princeton ; De Pauw University, Ind. ; General Theological Seminary, N. Y. ; Alma College, Ont. ; University of Minnesota ; Mt. Holyoke College, Mass. ; Colgate University, N. Y. ; Syracuse University, N. Y. ; Denison University, O. ; Battle Creek College, Mich. ; Swathmore College, Pa. ; Tufts Divinity School, Mass. ; Woman's Medical College, Pa.

States represented by members of School of Sacred Literature : New York 64, Pennsylvania 50, Ohio 50, Illinois, 20, Michigan 17, Connecticut 15, Massachusetts 11, Kentucky 10, Georgia 6, New Jersey 6, Iowa 6, Indiana 6, Texas 5, Virginia 5, Minnesota 5, Canada 5, Tennessee 4, Nebraska 3, Rhode Island 3, West Virginia 2, Vermont 2, South Carolina 2, Maryland 2, Missouri 2, Colorado 2, California 2, Florida 1, District of Columbia 1, Mississippi 1, Kansas 1, North Carolina 1, Wisconsin 1, Prince Edward Island 1.

Denominations of students in School of Sacred Literature :—

Presbyterian 84, Methodist Episcopal 64, Congregational 37, Baptist 30, Protestant Episcopal 20, United Presbyterian 18, Seven Day Adventists 8, Disciples 7, Friends 5, German Baptist 5, Cumberland Presbyterian 4, Free Baptist 4, Unitarian 4, Reformed 3, Reformed Presbyterian 2, United Brethren 2, Universalist 2, Lutheran 2, Church of Christ 1, Evangelical Lutheran 1, Dutch Reformed 1, Evangelical Association 1, Methodist Protestant 1, M. E. South 1.

Occupations of students in School of Sacred Literature :—

Ministers 50, college students 44, college professors 27, preparatory school students 21, theological students 20, home duties 19, public school teachers 15, teachers (grade not given) 12, teachers in academy 7, teachers in high schools 5, teachers in theological seminaries 4, Y. M. C. A. secretaries 3, college presidents 2, teachers in seminary 2, teachers in normal schools 2, teachers of music 2, medical missionary 2, superintendent of Sunday-school work 1, lumber dealer 1, carpenter 1, Bible school teacher 1, editor 1, normal college teacher 1, dressmaker 1, dentist 1, travelling salesman 1, evangelist 1, merchant 1, city missionary 1, patent lawyer 1, elocutionist 1, medical student 1, law student 1, miller 1, banker 1, clerk 1, fruit grower 1, builder 1, principal of schools 1.

Degrees received by Members of School of Sacred Literature :—

A. B. 66, A. M. 27, B. S. 8, B. D. 7, B. Ph. 2, Ph. D. 1, D. D. 3, LL. B. 2, M. D. 2, B. Let. 2, M. E. D. 2, B. E. D. 1, M. Ph. 1, C. E. 1, B. P. 1, M. S. 1. Members of C. L. S. C. 75. Members of Correspondence College 19.

2) *Other Assembly work.*—Besides the work done in connection with the Chautauqua Assembly, the following special courses and Assembly work were carried on under the auspices of the Institute :—

(1) The Utah School (July 8–30). The work of this school included Hebrew and the English New Testament, under the charge of Prof. E. L. Curtis, McCormick Theological Seminary, and the Rev. Thomas F. Day. Forty-nine students were in attendance, for the most part ministers and teachers. The work is reported as having been most enthusiastic. Of the 49, 4 carried on the study of Hebrew during the three weeks, 45 made a special study of the Gospel of Luke, devoting to it 30 hours of class-room work in six days.

(2) The Silver Lake School, conducted by Rev. W. C. Wilbor, Ph. D. (July 14–Aug. 7). In this school 12 students made a careful study of the Gospel of Luke in English. No classes in Greek and Hebrew were organized, though instruction in these subjects was offered by Rev. J. A. Smith and the Rev. J. L. Davies.

(3) The Bay View School (July 25–Aug. 15). In this school 57 persons were enrolled, 17 in recitation class and 40 in the lectures, all paying fees. The

instructors were Dr. F. K. Sanders in Hebrew and the Old Testament, Prof. W. J. Phelps in Greek and the New Testament, and Dr. Duryea general lecturer.   There were given two hours a day of Hebrew instruction, two of New Testament Greek, two of English Bible, Old Testament History and the Gospel of Luke and one course of lectures.   It is of interest to know that 10 correspondence students have already been received from this school.

(4)   Sayler Springs School (July 27–Aug. 10).   Instruction was offered in Greek, Hebrew and the English Bible.   No Greek class was organized, and beginning Hebrew was organized under Prof. Ira M. Price, and the class in the English Bible under Prof. A. A. Kendrick.   The interest in the school was not great.

(5)   Framingham Assembly (July).   No fees were charged at this assembly. Mr. Clyde H. Votaw conducted work under the direction of the Institute in the English New Testament and in New Testament Greek.   The success of the work was marked, 65 students being enrolled in the Greek class, and 100 in the course in Luke.   This beginning work was so successful as to occasion a request by those in charge of the Assembly for a regularly organized school next summer.

Correspondence is already in progress with a large number of the Assemblies for a union of effort in the work of next season.

6.   THE   SUMMER   SCHOOLS.

1)   SCHOOLS—DATES—PLACES.

1. New England School, May 22 (9 a. m.)—June 11 (6 p. m.), Yale Divinity School, New Haven, Conn.   2. Philadelphia School, June 12 (9 a. m.)—July 2 (6 p. m.), University of Pennsylvania, Philadelphia, Pa.   3. First Chautauqua School, July 5 (9 a. m.)—July 25 (6 p. m.), Chautauqua, N. Y.   4. Second Chautauqua School, July 26 (9 a. m.)—Aug. 14 (6 p. m.), Chautauqua, N. Y. 5. Chicago School, Aug. 14 (9 a. m.)—Sept. 3 (6 p. m.), Lake Bluff (near Chicago), Illinois.

2)   INSTRUCTORS.

Prof. W. G. Ballantine, Rev. L. W. Batten, Pres. John A. Broadus, Prof. C. R. Brown, Prof. S. Burnham, Prof. A. S. Carrier, Prof. James A. Craig, C. E. Crandall, Prof. E. L. Curtis, Prof. George H. Gilbert, George S. Goodspeed, Prof. E. P. Gould, Robert Francis Harper, Prof. W. R. Harper, Prof. H. V. Hilprecht, Prof. Charles Horswell, Prof. Morris Jastrow, Prof. Wallace W. Lovejoy, Prof. D. A. McClenahan, Prof. F. W. Phelps, Frank C. Porter, Prof. R. W. Rogers, Prof. John R. Sampey, F. K. Sanders, Prof. George B. Stevens, Prof. J. M. Stifler, Prof. Barnard C. Taylor, W. C. Wilbor, Bishop John H. Vincent, Prof. Revere F. Weidner, A. M. Wilson.

3)   The membership was as follows :—

New England School		251
Philadelphia	"	101
Chautauqua	"	334
Chicago	"	91
Bay View	"	57
Utah		49
Silver Lake	"	12
Framingham	"	165
Total,		1060

4)   For the details of the work in each school, you are referred to what has already been said in the special reports which accompany this general report.

7. GENERAL AFFILIATION WITH OTHER INSTITUTIONS.

1) *Affiliation with the Theological Union of Victoria College.*—At the annual business meeting of the Theological Union of Victoria College, the Secretary, on behalf of the Committee on Correspondence School, reported a scheme of affiliation with "The American Institute of Sacred Literature," by which the present F. T. L. course of the Theological Union should be supplanted by a course selected from the Correspondence School Department of the A. I. S. L., to be selected from the courses in Biblical Hebrew, New Testament Greek and the English Bible ; the reading and examination to be done through the instructors of the Institute, and the degree of "Fellow in Theological Literature" to be granted by the Union when certificates of having passed the studies required by the curriculum are received from the Principal of Institute schools. Revs. N. Burwash, S. T. D. ; G. C. Workman, Ph. D. ; F. H. Wallace, B. D. ; D. G. Sutherland, D. D. ; and A. M. Phillips, B. D., were appointed a committee to prepare a curriculum and perfect arrangements with the Institute for the F. T. L. course.

The committee selected *nine courses*, three in Hebrew, three in Greek, and three in the English Bible. The plan of affiliation provides that (1) the regular fee shall be paid, (2) that an allowance of $1.00 per student be given to the Secretary of the Union, to be employed in advertising and circularizing, (3) to give certificates only to those who do work of a high order of merit. Already many of their ministers have been enrolled in the school, and are taking an active part in the club and examination work of the Institute.

2) *The Christian Endeavor and other societies.*—Besides the action which has been taken by several Christian Endeavor State Conventions, viz., New Hampshire, Iowa, Wisconsin, and others, the President and General Secretary of the Christian Endeavor Society, together with the Board of Trustees, are considering the question of making Bible study an important feature henceforth of that organization. The question has also been asked whether the work of the Society may be conducted through the American Institute of Sacred Literature if the Directors of the Institute will consent to an arrangement looking to that end. It is proposed that in each Christian Endeavor Local Society there shall be appointed a Bible committee, whose business it shall be to organize, so far as possible, Bible work in connection with that Society. Through this Bible committee, and through the combined Bible committees of Christian Endeavor Unions, an effort will be made (1) to induce members of the society to attend the summer schools held under the auspices of the Institute, and, if necessary, to organize in connection with the Institute new summer schools, (2) to organize winter schools and courses of instruction, (3) to induce those capable of so doing to enter the correspondence courses of the Institute, (4) to organize, where possible, corresponding clubs, and (5) where none of the plans may be introduced, to organize clubs for the Institute's examinations. The plan provides that all communications shall be sent to the Institute direct, that all fees shall be paid the Institute, and that the Institute shall assume the responsibility for all instruction. The definite plan is now under consideration. No one can doubt that this is a most significant movement. The only question that suggests itself is, how the Institute can provide for such an enormous increase in its work. But for the thorough organization thus far effected, such an affiliation would be impracticable.

3) *The College Y. M. C. A's.*—One of the most fruitful fields for work is the American college. If there are any men who ought to be induced to study

the Bible, it is college men. The active religious work of the College Y. M. C. A's should be supplemented by the rigorous intellectual study of the Bible. With this end in view, plans are being prepared looking toward an arrangement by which college men shall be induced (1) to attend the summer schools of the Institute ; (2) take up individually the correspondence work ; (3) to organize Bible Institutes of three and four days' duration ; (4) to take examinations on special courses of study. These arrangements have already been completed in several institutions—e. g., Yale, Vassar, Colgate, Wellesley and others. The International Committee is somewhat slow to join hands in the work, but decided progress has been made within the past 60 days.

8. THE WORK IN GENERAL.

1) *The Principal.*—The Principal was employed by the Local Boards in the Summer Schools held at New Haven, Philadelphia, Chautauqua and Chicago. His work in the office has been about the same in amount and character in former years. The labor involved is severe and taxing. But for the valuable aid rendered by assistants, especially Mr. Sanders and Mr. Crandall, it would have been impossible for the work to have been carried through. Mr. Sanders has aided especially in the external or aggressive work, Mr. Crandall in the internal work, that is, the work with those enrolled as students. For the work of the year in connection with the Institute, the Principal desires to receive no salary.

2) *The general aggressive work.*—During the nine months beginning January 1st personal correspondence has been conducted with 191 persons in Hebrew and Cognates, 157 concerning Greek, 569 concerning English Bible, 42 concerning Bible clubs, 170 concerning Summer Schools, 208 concerning matters of a general nature, more than 2,000 concerning examinations. The total number of letters sent out includes 1,327 to inquirers, 284 to names sent in by friends of the work, special letters sent to individuals whose names were in our files 4,999, general letters 7,267, dictated letters 4,350, examination letters (estimated) 9000, total 27,227. This estimate, except in two particulars, is by actual count. About 4,000 General Prospectuses, 15,000 Summer Prospectuses, and 25,000 smaller circulars have been distributed.

3) *Subscriptions.*—Only $1,631 has been received from subscriptions, over against 5,413 in 1887, 4,881 in '86, 3,356 in 1888, 2,252 in 1889. The fact is that no particular effort was made to secure funds until toward the close of the year. An earlier effort would have been made but for two reasons, (1) a hesitation to solicit funds in quarters in which the solicitation might interfere with the work of Local Boards, (2) a hope that, after all, the receipts might balance the expenditures. The contributions to Local Boards has amounted to about $560 to the New Haven Board, $1,100 to the Philadelphia Board, $1,000 to the Chicago Board, the aggregate being larger than in any previous year of the work.

MEASURES ADOPTED BY THE DIRECTORS AT THE ANNUAL MEETING.

1) *Whereas*, at a meeting of this Institute, held in New York, April 7, 1890, it was voted, "that the Institute of Sacred Literature take the affairs of the Institute of Hebrew, when the latter has, by vote, passed them over to it," and

Whereas, this Institute is now officially informed that the Institute of Hebrew, at a meeting held in New York, October 25, 1890, has passed the following vote, viz., "that the work and assets of the Institute of Hebrew be passed over to the American Institute of Sacred Literature, on condition that said Institute assume the debts and obligations of the Institute of Hebrew, the date of the transfer to be Dec. 1, 1889," therefore,

Resolved, that this Institute does now accept the work and assets of the Institute of Hebrew, and also assumes the debts and obligations of the said Institute of Hebrew, as said work, assets, debts and obligations stood Dec. 1, 1889. And,

Whereas, this Institute has received a request from the Institute of Hebrew, that a statement of the general and financial situation of the Institute of Hebrew, at the date of transfer, and the reasons for this transfer, to be prepared by the Principal of Schools and Treasurer of that Institute, be spread upon the minutes of the American Institute of Sacred Literature, therefore,

Resolved, that the Secretary be instructed to spread such a statement upon the minutes, when a copy of it shall be furnished him by the Principal of Schools and Treasurer of the Institute of Hebrew.

2) That the Secretary be instructed to give notice to the Directors, before the next annual meeting, of the following proposed changes in the constitution, whereby the number of its Directors shall be increased by three, and whereby the time of its annual meeting shall be changed from October to November, viz. :—

(1) to amend Article 5 by striking out the word *fifteen* and substituting the word *eighteen*, and by striking out the word *five*, thrice occurring, and substituting the word *six;*

(2) to amend Article 8 by striking out the word *October* and substituting the word *November*.

3) That the plan submitted by the Principal for state organization be approved, with the understanding that it be limited to Illinois and Kansas, for the present year, and that details be referred to the Executive Committee.

4) That the Institute give special attention to the organization of Local Institutes along the lines of university extension.

5) That a meeting be arranged for, in which papers shall be read upon some important Biblical theme by eminent men, said papers to be subsequently published in book form.

6) That the Institute offer the following special examinations, with prizes, viz. :—

(1) To Seniors and Juniors in College, an examination on some book of the English Bible or some Biblical topic, about the first week in May, 1891 ;

(2) To Seniors and Juniors in College, an examination in the elements of Hebrew, about the first week in June, 1891 ;

(3) To men entering the Divinity School, an examination in the elements of Hebrew, about the first week in October, 1891 ;

(4) To men who have studied Hebrew one year in the Divinity School, an examination, about the first week in October, 1891.

7) That an examination be offered Dec. 31, 1891, on the Life of the Christ, and also one on the Gospel of John.

8) That the Secretary be requested to correspond with Schools, Colleges and Universities in the United States and Canada, with a view to a formulated statement concerning the amount and character of the instruction given in Hebrew, New Testament Greek, and the English Bible.

REPORT OF THE TREASURER

OF THE

AMERICAN INSTITUTE OF SACRED LITERATURE

For the Year Ending October 1, 1890.

RECEIPTS.	DISBURSEMENTS.
CORRESPONDENCE SCHOOL.	**CORRESPONDENCE SCHOOL.**
Tuition Fees:	Hebrew Department:
Hebrew department...$1,074.50	Salaries.....................$721.50
Greek " ... 290.40	Postage.... .. ..,........ 187.75
English " ... 524.82	Printing and stationery.. 150.97
Cognate " ... 89.24	——— $1,060.22
——— $1,978.96	Greek Department:
Examination........................ 99.40	Salaries 656.00
SUMMER SCHOOLS:	Postage.... .. . . 178.29
10 per cent. of receipts.............. 162.50	Printing and stationery.. 150.97
Endowments.. .... 1,631.00	——— $985.26
Loans.............. .... 674.72	English Department:
	Salaries.... .... 639.48
	Postage 173.21
	Printing and stationery.. 150.97
	——— $963.66
	Cognate Department:
	Salaries.................. 205.38
	Postage.................. 111.37
	——— $316.75
	Examination Department:
	Salaries...... .... 504.33
	Postage.... ....,........ 214.50
	Printing and stationery.. 2,53.01
	——— $951.84
	Rent, 1 year...................... 81.25
	General office expenses............ 187.60
Total.......................... $4,546.58	Total.. ... . $4,546.58

ASSETS.	LIABILITIES.
Tuition arrears (estimated)......... $216.00	Accounts payable (printing and
Advertising...................... ..... 106.00	stationery)...................... $610.36
Summer Schools' arrears........... 370.00	Salaries... .... 231.70
Office furniture...................... 70.00	Advertising......................... 35.00
Excess of liabilities................... 789.88	Loans 674.72
$1,551.88	$1,551.88

I have examined the above accounts and found them correct.

GEORGE B. STEVENS, Auditor.

October 24, 1890.

DONORS TO ENDOWMENT FUND.

Charles L. Colby	$ 10.00
Morris K. Jessup	50.00
S. W. McWilliams	100.00
T. J. Salsman	1.00
J. D. Rockefeller	400.00
F. N. Bartlett	2.00
D. Stuart Dodge	200.00
Miss Olivin Hoadley	20.00
Dr. W. W. Keen	10.00
Rev. Allen Lewis	15.00
W. E. Dodge	100.00
Rev. W. M. Taylor	3.00
E. L. Corthell	100.00
J. B. Thresher	20.00
Rev. A. Brooks	50.00
J. M. Denison	50.00
W. R. Harper	250.00
James McCormick	250.00
	———$1,631.00

𝕭𝖎𝖇𝖑𝖎𝖈𝖆𝖑 𝕹𝖔𝖙𝖊𝖘.

The Old Testament and Nature. In Watson's vigorous book of exposition on Judges and Ruth is a statement concerning the view of nature which appears in the song of Deborah. The picture which rose before the imagination of the prophetess was that of a great thunder-storm which is an echo of that which resounds through Sinai's peaks. Sinai once flowed down in volcanic glow and rush. The insight of the seer revealed God in these present and past phenomena of the physical world. As Ewald says: "Forbidden to recognize, and, as it were, grasp the God of heaven in any material form, or to adore even in the heavens themselves any constant symbols of His being and His power, yet yearning more in spirit for manifestations of His invisible existence, Israel's mind was ever on the stretch for any hint in nature of the unseen Celestial Being, for any glimpse of His mysterious ways, and its courage rose to a far higher pitch when Divine encouragement and impulse seemed to come from the material world." The origin, causes, and growth of the Hebrew idea of nature is a most interesting topic and one not yet fully worked out.

The Gospel of John. Dr. Watkins in his recent lectures on the relation of modern criticism to the Gospel of John declares that the key of the book lies in "translation, or if this term has acquired too narrow a meaning, transmutation, re-formation, growth; nor need we shrink from the true sense of the terms, development and evolution." He believes that this thought explains all the peculiarities of it as compared with the other New Testament writings. This applies in reference to the changes in language, from Aramaic to Greek; in time, of half a century from youth to age; in place, from Palestine to Ephesus; in outward moulds of thought, from the simplicity of Jewish fishermen or the ritual of Pharisees, to the great meeting ground of sects and creeds in Asia Minor. View this development in the right light and you have swept away the foundations of all the reasonable criticisms of negative thinkers.

The Vocabulary of the Gospel. He has an interesting presentation, in the same volume, of the peculiar vocabulary of John. Put it in the light of the age. Men were trying to grasp God. The Gnostics talked of *Arche*, and *Propator*, and *Zoe* and *Monogenes* and *Anthropos* and *Logos*; of *Grace*, and *Glory* and *Truth*, and the rest by which men made successive links to reach from earth to heaven. John spoke to such men with such thoughts and what did he say? "In *Arche* was the *Logos* and the *Logos* was face to face with God, yea, the *Logos* was God. The same was in *Arche* face to face with God. . . . . That which hath been made was *Zoe*, in him; and the *Zoe* was the *Phos* of the *Anthropoi*," etc. How reasonable is the conclusion that John could have spoken with power to men with these thoughts in no other way than that in which the Gospel does speak. How attractive and convincing is the view which Watkins styles "translation" or development.

The Site of Lachish. In the STUDENT for November, some information was given in regard to the supposed identification of the biblical Lachish in the ruins of Tell Hesy where Mr. Petrie is excavating. In the *Bibliotheca Sacra* of Oct. 1890 appears a note from Prof. J. A. Paine in which he maintains that Tell Hesy is not Lachish for the following reasons among others: (1) It cannot satisfy the conditions which are demanded by the statements of Eusebius and Jerome concerning Lachish, e. g., Lachish was inhabited in the days of these fathers while Tell Hesy ceased to be inhabited seven centuries before ; nor is it in the proper position relative to other sites as indicated by them. (2) Lachish, so far as we know, never suffered at the hands of Nebuchadnezzar, but Tell Hesy did. (3) Lachish was besieged by Sennacherib but the pictures of the reign made by the Assyrians themselves do not tally with the conditions present at Tell Hesy. These and some other considerations are insurmountable. Tell Hesy cannot be Lachish. What can it be then? It is a very old site. Prof. Paine suggests Gath and gives a number of arguments in favor of this identification. Students will look with interest on the further discussion of this question which certainly seems to be open to debate in view of the considerations urged by Professor Paine.

The Spirits in Prison: 1 Peter 3: 18–20. Interest in this obscure text and the possible inferences from it seem to be perennial. Rev. Dr. Witherspoon offers in the *Homiletic Review* for Nov. 1890 a new interpretation. The original element in his exegesis he regards as the view taken of the phrases *in flesh* and *in spirit*. The one designates the fleshly organism in which alone Christ could be put to death. What then must the other phrase denote if not that organism which could receive quickening? But the only adequate and satisfactory object of this quickening could be the spiritual body, the human soul entering the transformed body and quickening it to life. Hence the activity which Christ undertook was undertaken after his resurrection when he entered the spiritual body. As to the question of this activity, the work that Jesus did in his "preaching" was proclamation of his victory over sin and death, a proclamation made to the universe and heard to its remotest bounds by those antediluvians who might be supposed on account of their great guilt to inhabit this outer circle of darkness. The purpose of the apostle in the whole passage, which was to encourage the persecuted saints, would be strongly effected by the teaching of these particular verses thus interpreted. The interpretation if correct removes this passage from the realm of teaching regarding probation and brings it into harmony with the context. It is interesting but still not convincing especially in its central idea, the explanation of "in spirit."

Luke 7: 37 and Mary Magdalene. In reply to a question as to the ground for identifying the woman that was a sinner with Mary of Magdala, Professor A. B. Bruce replies, in the *Expository Times* as follows: "Nothing is known. The Fathers of the Western Church who first, hesitatingly, favored the identification (Ambrose, Jerome, Augustine) knew nothing more than we know. The universal currency of the opinion that the two women were one and the same person, during the Middle Ages, was due to the authority of Gregory the Great. The adoption of the view by the translators of the Authorized Version, as shown in the heading of Luke vii., 'Mary Magdalene anointeth Christ's feet,' only exemplifies the tenacity with which opinion holds

its place in the human mind after it has been fairly rooted. The great majority of modern commentators entirely discard it. The chief source of the long
prevalent idea is the same as that which has given rise to many other legends,
the desire to know as much as possible concerning persons whose names are
surrounded with a halo of religious interest. Who was the woman that was a
sinner? Who was Mary called Magdalene? Can the two have been one?
There is just one fact in the gospel narrative that suggests and gives a slight
plausibility to the conjecture. Immediately after relating the story of the
anointing in the house of Simon the Pharisee, Luke goes on to tell of certain
women who followed Jesus on His itinerant ministry, and ministered unto
Him of their substance (Luke viii. 1–3). The first named is ' Mary called
Magdalene, out of whom went seven devils.' Evidently there was some link
of connection between the two narratives in the Evangelist's mind. What was
it? Did he know that the woman that was a sinner was one of the women
who followed Jesus—say, the Magdalene? Or was the link of connection
simply the general thought: following Jesus and ministering to His wants
was the frequent result of benefit received from Him ; penitents forgiven, demoniacs healed thus went into peace and found deep rest for their souls? The
latter hypothesis sufficiently explains the order of the narrative, but the former
attracts by its greater definiteness. It has been regarded as a point in its
favor that Mary of Magdala had been possessed of seven devils. The seven
devils are interpreted to mean a very sinful life. But the notion that the
demoniacs were specially great sinners has no foundation in the gospel history."

Jewish Philosophy. It was the opinion of the late Professor Munk, according to a writer in the *Jewish Messenger*, that the Hebrews did not excel in
philosophy. Philosophy, left to itself, must end in pantheism ; the religion of
Israel bridged the chasm of human reasoning by the assertion of faith. But
this opinion has been opposed and the opposite view asserted by Spiegler who
has written what he calls the History of Jewish Philosophy. The writer above
alluded to does not commend Spiegler's work. He criticizes it both in form
and matter, calling it " a medley of undigested reading and bombastic phraseology" "the product of an undisciplined mind" and totally denying its
fundamental position that the true philosophy of Judaism is pantheism.
Spinoza is Spiegler's hero, "the emancipator of philosophy from the yoke of
religion." The historian of Jewish Philosophy who holds that Moses taught
pantheistic monotheism in mystic language to an initiated circle, who ignores
the biblical material and exalts the Kabbala, has not by any means added
largely to our stock of sound learning on this subject. The truth seems to be
with Professor Munk. Israel's chief note is religion not philosophy. There is
philosophy in the Bible, the philosophy of God but it is in the forms of life, in
the language of religion. Wherever Jews have been philosophers they have
received the impulse from without, they have yielded to a mode of thought
which was not native and therefore have not been great except in their aberra-
tions. Of this course of things Spinoza is the best example.

Contributed Notes.

Philippians III. 7. (1) *The translation*; "But whatever things were gain to me, these I have reckoned as loss by reason of Christ."

(2) *Notes*; (a) "whatever things," i. e., things of such a character as those just named in the verses preceding; (b) "to me," dativus commodi; (c) "gain," this is a pecuniary metaphor, signifying wealth in possession, that which had been gained. The "things" just mentioned *were* wealth from the old Jewish standpoint; (d) "I have reckoned," it is a deliberate estimate, made in the past and still firmly held; (e) "loss," the idea here is not of ' damage," " detriment." The idea which appeared in the use of the word ' gain"' is continued here. The word *Zemia* in classical Greek signifies ' penalty" or " fine," something with which a man is forced to part. Here the thought is of a "loss," a "deprivation." As if a brick (supposedly) of gold should turn out base metal, Paul's Jewish position ("gain") has turned out to be (not a "damage"—his whole teaching is opposed to this) but *worthless* in respect of salvation, and hence he had suffered (as regards that position) *loss;* (f) "by reason of Christ,' i. e, Christ is the cause of this change in valuation. This new "reckoning" is not "for Christ's sake," or "in exchange for Christ"—but "by reason of Christ," because he had seen Christ in His true majesty.

(3) *Thought*; the great thought of the passage therefore, is—*The change in spiritual valuation resulting from the vision of Christ.*   F.

Matthew XVI. 18. (1) *The translation.* "Thou art a stone and upon (such stone as) this stone I will build my church."

(2) *Notes*; (a) "a stone" (*Petros*), this must mean "a piece of rock." Never in the New Testament or in classical Greek does it mean "rock" in the generic or abstract sense. Note the word *petrodes* which means "stony" as applied to soil, not "rocky;" (b) "this stone" (*petra*), this word on the other hand never means a "piece of rock" but is abstract, generic, signifying "rock." Liddell and Scott show clearly that in classical Greek it never can be used for a single stone. Hence in this passage, *petra* is not equivalent to *petros*,—the latter is a single piece or specimen of the former; accordingly, "on this *petra*" must signify "on this sort of stone" i. e., "on this material." To illustrate the distinction which is made here;—I might pick up a bar of iron and say: This is *iron* and on this *iron* depends all the industry and development of modern civilization. Here are the two senses of "iron," the specific and the generic. Civilization does not depend on this (piece of) iron but on this (sort of) iron.

(3) *Conclusion:* The church is built not on Peter's confession, nor on Peter as an individual. It is built on Petrine material, on such material as this petrine specimen. Peter is then *sample* and *part of* the eternal foundation.

                F.

Correspondence.

To the Editor of THE OLD AND NEW TESTAMENT STUDENT :

The Rev. Canon Driver in a note to the undersigned writes as follows : "I do not for a moment imagine that Isaiah 53 and 61 : 1–3 refer to Cyrus. In *Isaiah, His Life and Times*, pp. 177–180 I considered them to be fulfilled by Christ. As regards 61 : 1–3 the only question is whether the prophet is to be supposed to be speaking, or the "servant of the Lord ;" I prefer the latter alternative. Nor do I suppose that any part of ch. 40 relates to Cyrus. I only suppose Cyrus to be referred to where he is named, or obviously alluded to, as 41 : 2, 25 ; 44 : 28 ; 45 : 1–5, 13 ; 46 : 11.

As this *differs* from what some of his readers supposed to be the actual meaning of the Regius Professor of Hebrew at Oxford and is in itself a contribution to the exegesis of the prophet, I send it at once to the STUDENT ; and also because I included the learned Canon among those who interpret "historically" the latter portions of Isaiah. See that chapter in *The Writers of Genesis*, pp. 115–138, and compare the first twenty lines of p. 279 of OLD AND NEW TESTAMENT STUDENT for November, 1890. E. COWLEY.

New York City.

General Notes and Notices.

One of the most influential and well known scholars in the line of Old Testament work is Professor C. A. Briggs, D. D., of Union Theological Seminary. He has recently been transferred from the chair of Hebrew and Old Testament exegesis to that of Biblical Theology in the same institution. This new department has just been endowed through the liberality of Charles Butler, Esq., and is called in honor of Dr. Edward Robinson, the Robinson Professorship of Biblical Theology. The peculiar gifts of Professor Briggs will have ample scope in this field of investigation where he has already won large success.

Among forthcoming publications of the winter are the following works of interest to the student of the Scriptures : A Concordance to the Septuagint, prepared by the late Dr. E. Hatch ; in the Cambridge Bible for Schools Series, The Psalms by Professor Kirkpatrick, the Epistle to the Galatians by Professor Perowne, the Epistles to the Thessalonians by Professor Findlay, the Epistles to Timothy and Titus by Rev. A. E. Humphreys, the Revelation by the late Mr. Simcox ; the Psalms of the Pharisees, called also the Psalms of Solomon, by Professors Ryle and James of Cambridge ; The Old Testament in Greek, Vol. II, 1 Chronicles to Ecclesiasticus ; the Peshitto Version of the Gospels, by Rev. Mr. Gwilliam ; The Historic Origin and Religious Ideas of the Psalter, the Bampton Lectures of Canon Cheyne ; the volumes on Romans, Proverbs and Ezekiel in the Pulpit Commentary ; The Gospel according to St. Luke, the Greek text of Westcott and Hort, with notes by Rev. John Bond.

Synopses of Important Articles.

The Historic Origin of the New Testament Scriptures.* The historic origin of the Scriptures is something apart from the question of their inspiration which belongs to their ideal origin. The apostles had at first little thought of writing down their recollections of Jesus' life. They expected Christ to come in their generation. Their constant preaching tended to preserve and keep in a more or less fixed form the tradition of His life. This became one source of our Gospels. But there were written sources too and some have conjectured an original written source on which the three Synoptics built. This was the Hebrew Matthew. Thus the written Gospels we have grew up as naturally and humanly as was the earthly origin and development of the Incarnate Word. There was no thought of their being Sacred Scriptures alongside of the Old Testament Scriptures until a much later period. They were written like the epistles for temporary needs to satisfy the wants of their generation. But whatever difficulties may exist as regards the exact historic facts concerning their authorship, their historic origin cannot be questioned. The difficulty lies in the question of their credibility. Consider four remarks, (1) we must distinguish between the witness to facts and the inferences as to the meaning and ground of these facts. The apostles were certainly competent witnesses to the facts connected with the resurrection. Whether they rightly interpreted the facts is another question. (2) The objection is made that the bias of the apostles in favor of miracles makes their testimony for them of no value. The reply is that their bias was rather against the character that Christ displayed and, as the writings themselves show, they were forced against their prejudices to accept His ideal and character; (3) these disciples were competent to give their own experience growing out of their faith in Christ. This testimony was to the Messiahship and salvation of Jesus Christ. Still this testimony, while strong, is subjective; (4) the strongest objective argument is the merely historical representation of Christ given in the Gospels
An earnest and well-reasoned argument.

The Egypticity of the Pentateuch, an argument for its traditional authorship.† Believing in the Mosaic editorship of the Pentateuch the author seeks to find evidence from Egyptian sources in favor of this view:—(1) The Hebrew designation of Egypt is not "Kham" the monumental term, but "Mizraim" a dual Hebrew form. This use of the dual of an Egyptian word ("Mzaru," fortress, fortified) reveals the presence of an editor who was, like Moses, an Egyptian; for the idea of duality pervades the whole of Egypt's history and literature. The editor must have been familiar with the details of Egyptian thought, since he has described it not as "Kham," but as the two

* By Thos. G. Apple, D. D., LL. D., in *Reformed Quarterly Review*, Oct. 1890, pp. 429-448.

† By Rev. Alfred H. Kellogg, D. D., in *The Presbyterian and Reformed Review*, October, 1890, pp. 533-555.

" M-zars," just as every king was designated "lord of the two lands." (2) The Hebrew and Egyptian traditions as to the origin of the Egyptians and their ethnic and linguistic affinities. It is tested by the latest scientific research. The Egyptians, with the Cushites and Canaanites were descendants of Ham and, as the Pentateuch represents them, lived before dispersion at their home in the cradle of the race in Asia. The Hebrew tradition on this point is strictly Egyptian in its conception and expression and shows an Egyptian editor. (3) The Hebrew cosmogony shows familiarity with Egyptian, rather than with Babylonian sources. The very expression, e. g., "in beginning," "morning and evening" are Egyptian; the "chaos" and the word for God "Elohim" as contrasted with Jehovah Elohim in chap. 2, are suggestive. Ex. 6: 2, 3 is to be taken literally, that "Jehovah" was first used by Moses; but how are we to explain the frequent use of the name "Jehovah" in the book of Genesis, unless as an undesigned coincidence reflecting the editorship of the very man who in reality first used it? The idea of "Jehovah" as the "being" or "becoming," "the self-existent one" pervades all Egyptian literature. The idea is suggested by the "ankh" or cross borne in the hand of every Egyptian God. (4) The story of the Hebrews and their relations with Egypt furnishes the culminating argument for the Mosaic editorship. The editor knew all about Egypt. He made no mistake. His accuracy is seen in the most minute particulars. No Hebrew living after Moses had the degree of familiarity required. In short, "no prophet or scribe of Israel, subsequent to Moses' era, can be mentioned, who, as a Redactor, would have edited the Pentateuch in so Egyptian a way."

Acute, interesting, definite and sturdy; but sometimes also far-fetched, illogical, dogmatic, and assumptive.

John the Forerunner.* John the Baptist and Paul have had scarcely less influence than Jesus upon Christianity. John was properly the founder of the ecclesiastical features of Christianity. He was an agitator but would have had only transitory influence but for the fact that Jesus took up his work. He stirred men to act but Jesus taught and stirred them to think. The word "repent" and the rite of baptism are his contribution to Christianity. He did not prepare the people to receive Jesus or prepare Jesus for his work. He simply aroused men. Hillel was the one who most influenced Jesus and the thought of Christianity. John was one of those prophets so characteristic of the Hebrew nation. What contributed to his success was the political and religious hopes of his nation and time. But his success was greater than he expected. He had roused a revolution. The whole nation was ready for war. He might have been Messiah himself. But he did not see his way ahead and turned the thoughts and expectations of the people to another leader, Jesus. These two leaders kept working together for some time. Each appeared equally the founder of a religion and it may well have been doubted then which was to be greater. But Jesus had ideas and John had not. So the influence of the latter gradually fell off. Jesus aroused the people to think. John's disciples gradually went over to Jesus. By this act Christianity was made a composite religion. The disciples of John demanded baptism and repentance. Thus the simplicity and directness of Christ's religion were

* By Austin Bierbower, in *Unitarian Review*, Oct. 1890, pp. 302-318.

early modified.   John has always been held in high esteem by the Orientals. He stands at the head of the Zoroastrian Gnostic system.   Several Christian sects took him as their patron saint.   It is claimed that our Gospels studiously repress the activity and influence of John.   Many believe that John the Baptist instead of Jesus or Buddha is to be the " Light of Asia."

An article which contains much crude theorizing and reveals not a little ignorance.   It calls attention, however, in an exaggerated way, to the position and influence of John the Baptist in the beginnings of Christianity.   We have too much neglected this inquiry and it demands careful investigation.

***

Doctrine of Divine Retribution in the Old Testament.*   In the Old Testament retribution belongs to Time and not to Eternity.   It takes the form of "judgments," appearing in calamities.   The responsibility for sin was joint and several and these judgments might fall upon the subject for the sin of the king, on the son for the sin of the father, on the nation for the sin of the individual.   When the consciousness of the individual began to be felt, situations arose in which this theory would not hold good and attempts at reconciliation follow.   The earlier ideas regarded God as watching over the tribe or nation as a whole and punishing crimes against social morality upon the wrong doer or his family.   Later it is sins against himself that he punishes.   He is God of the tribe and hence favors Israel against its enemies.   He is strictly just in bringing punishment on the community or family for the sin of one but his mercy is shown in letting the consequences of virtue extend through more generations than those of sin.   His punishments are purely material.   The eighth century prophets hold substantially the same views.   Ezekiel first discusses the difficulties of the doctrine of social solidarity.   Exiled Jews fancied that they were suffering from their fathers' sins and that there was no escape. Ezekiel himself had told them that they must be punished.   But now he tells them that only the guilty shall suffer, the righteous shall live.   But this does not turn out to be entirely satisfactory.   Hence come the perplexities of Job and Ecclesiastes.   Suffering is regarded as disciplinary in the case of the righteous, or the "suffering Servant" endures his ills for the well-being of his people.   The historical books filled with the national idea regard the history of Isarel as a holy history in which God interferes directly to punish sin by adversity and calamity.   But that theory would not apply to the present and hence came difficulty.   The thought of the nation clung to the theory that misfortune implied sin and the higher thought of the second part of Isaiah was not accepted.   The Psalter reveals the bliss of spiritual communion with God in spite of external circumstances.   The law, however, fixed the mind on an ideal of holiness and thus promoted escape from the material theory of retribution, in proclaiming that the love and service of God is its own reward.

An informing article, which, on the basis of the Wellhausen view of the order of the Old Testament books, builds up an interesting theory of the development of this doctrine.

*By C. G. Montefiore, in the *Jewish Quarterly Review*, Oct. 1890, pp. 1-12.

𝕭𝖔𝖔𝖐 𝕹𝖔𝖙𝖎𝖈𝖊𝖘.

Judges and Ruth.

Judges and Ruth. By Rev. Robert A. Watson, M. A. " The Expositor's Bible." New York : A. C. Armstrong and Son. Price $1.50.

This recent issue of the Expositor's Bible Series has many points of interest and merit. In a very marked degree the writer has entered into the spirit of the time and scenes with which he is engaged. His style is clear and vivid. His knowledge of recent works on these books is fairly up to the times. Three points call for special remarks, (1) The conservative attitude is maintained throughout. The mosaic legislation in its completeness is regarded as having preceded this period and the silence of the literature regarding it, as well as the absence of all signs of its observance, is regarded in the light of a lapse. Some original views are offered e. g. the absence of Judah from Gideon's army is explained from the later supremacy of Judah in religious affairs. Such a supremacy demands a long period of preparation. Therefore at this time she was absorbed in ecclesiastical matters, and " while the northern tribes were suffering and fighting, Judah went her own way enjoying peace and organizing worship" (p 167). The book of Ruth is regarded as having been written in Solomon's time. (2) The fertility of the writer in applications of the material of these two Scriptures to modern life is extraordinary. Some of this work is remarkably well done. Much must be regarded as extravagant and false. The "shibboleth" episode furnishes the occasion for a fierce onslaught upon those popular writers of the present day who lead the very elect to say " sibboleth" along with them, and the author promises before long a "new and resolute sifting at the fords." Manoah and his wife are blamed because nothing is said of their ever having instructed the young Samson in righteousness, purity and mercifulness; they "made the mistake of thinking that moral education and discipline would come naturally." The lion experience of Samson seems specially to have caught the expositor's fancy. The fact that Samson, is said to have kept silence about this little feat points the moral that we talk too much about temptations and their awful power. " We encourage moral weakness and unfaithfulness to duty by exaggerating the force of evil influences." But Samson a little later gets some honey out of the same lion and the Bible states that while he distributed the honey he said nothing about the source whence it came. What deep lesson there lies in this silence the expositor fails to tell us. There is no lesson for us in either statement. The application suggested in the first is merely fanciful. Another equally unusual exposition is the lesson drawn from the circumstance that Boaz permitted Ruth to keep gleaning in his fields and did not amply supply her wants. This significant fact rebukes our modern fashion of helping (a) the poor in this world's goods by lavishing on them our benevolence, and (b) those who would study the Scriptures by pouring into them so much information and spiritual food without their working for it. These lessons may all be good and necessary but it is nonsense to find them in this passage. (3) The author is a rigid puritan and, if we read rightly between the lines, an English nonconformist or a low churchman. He enjoys a sly dig at the Established Church and its errors. He believes that charity, amiability and catholicity are good, yes, admirable, of course, but too often truth, the truth for which our fathers fought, is sacrificed to these purely emotional virtues. We must stand for truth, for doctrine and let these others go. Too many are ready nowadays, to yield to the spirit of the times and ally themselves to the Philistines. This is the time for the resolute stroke like that of Samson, that divides party from party. Our age needs a new divider. We are on altogether too good terms with those Philistines. A writer of our day, with these strong, stern conceptions, finds the Book of Judges, in its pictures both of the the apostasies and the crude revivals which characterized the Israelites of the period, a writing after his own heart. He has produced a useful if, in some respects, an overdrawn and slightly hysterical exposition.

Martineau's Authority in Religion.

The Seat of Authority in Religion. By James Martineau, D. D., LL. D., etc. London and New York: Longmans, Green and Co. Price $4.50.

This book of Dr. Martineau is a disappointment to the most of those who open its pages. Its style is characterized by all of the author's grace and fervor. But its views are either those with which readers of his previous volumes have become familiar, or those which by their negative character as related to Christianity surprise and disturb those who are accustomed to Dr. Martineau's positive attitude toward religious questions. The work is divided into five books, (1) Authority implied in Religion, where the positions of his " Ethical Theory" and " Study of Religion" are practically synoptized ; (2) Authority artificially misplaced, where he attacks the trustworthiness of the Scriptures, especially the Gospels ; (3) Divine Authority intermixed with Human Theory, where he discusses natural and revealed religion ; (4) Severance of undivine Elements from Christendom, in which the evangelical views of Jesus and his word are opposed ; (5) The Divine in the Human, a summing up and statement of the sole authority in Religion, the personal realization of God in the human soul.

Unevangelical writers are laughing openly at orthodox thinkers who have been hailing Dr. Martineau as an ally of evangelical Christianity and taking him to their hearts only to find that he was fundamentally hostile to their dearest ideas. Yet these heterodox writers themselves are constrained to allow that in entering on the work of literary criticism of the Gospels, their champion has left the field in which all acknowledge him a master and has not in all respects succeeded in maintaining his reputation there. The judgment of Dr. Sanday upon this feature of the book, given in a recent issue of an English periodical, is worthy of careful consideration. " To sum up briefly my opinion of Dr. Martineau's book. From the critical side, from which alone I have dealt with it, I honestly do not think it an important book. It is not a book that need be read. To speak quite frankly, it is in my opinion a book which is better left unread. It is what I should call a dangerous book—not at all in the sense that it contains heretical doctrine, for that one is, of course, prepared—but because the attractiveness of its style is out of all proportion to the solidity of its substructure. Dr. Martineau is not only a very skillful writer, but he is also a very confident one ; and confidence is apt to be catching. To the student who brings with him a large grain of salt, and who will test each proposition as it arises, and ask what is the ground for the dogmatic assertions which are made so repeatedly as to what is, and what is not, an anachronism at any given time, the book will do no harm : the criticism of it may, in fact, be a good intellectual exercise ; though, so far as positive results are concerned, I suspect that he would be much better employed in reading *Types*

l Th a or A Stud a Religion. But the eneral reader who

comes to the book with only a smattering of knowledge, and has not the time or the opportunity to test what is put before him, will be apt to be carried away by the glow and enthusiasm of an eloquent pen into positions at which he would never arrive by sound and circumspect reasoning."

The Pulpit Commentary: Isaiah.

The Book of the Prophet Isaiah. Exposition and Homiletics by Rev. George Rawlinson, M. A.   Homilies by various authors. New York : A. D. F. Randolph and Co. 2 volumes.

In taking up a new Commentary on the Book of Isaiah we naturally inquire what is the position assumed by the writer, whether he treats the book as a unit or as a composite structure, whether he has availed himself of the material furnished by the Inscriptions, whether he has attempted to give the historical setting of the separate prophecies, and what his views are in regard to the Messianic idea.

As to the position of the author of this Commentary there is no doubt.   To him the book is a unit and the "Great Unknown" is nothing else than an imaginary personage. The literature of the Monuments has been made to contribute its part to the elucidation of the text. Thus the historical conditions have been recognized to some extent. The Messianic expectations are regarded as centering in a personal Redeemer, who was no other than Jesus Christ.

The Introduction tells us that the first thirty-five chapters are prophetic, the word prophetic being here used in the sense of didactic, admonitory and hortatory in contradistinction to narrative. The next four chapters (36–39) are historical, containing a plain and simple narrative of certain events that took place in the reign of Hezekiah. In the rest of the book (40–66) Isaiah throws himself into the period of the captivity with a faith, a fervor, and a power of realization which are all his own, and aims to comfort the people in their affliction.

The general arrangement of these three main divisions is chronological, but there are indications of a lack of chronological order in the make up of the first, and possibly the last of these divisions.

This is natural, since the prophecies were not committed to writing before, or as soon as, they were delivered. In their earliest written form they were a number of separate documents. These documents were put together from time to time. The compiler grouped together the prophecies that were similar in character without any regard to chronological order. Rawlinson, however, does not tell us whether the gradual accretion of the book is to be ascribed to the action of the prophet himself or to that of later editors. According to the author the vision recorded in chap. 6, does not constitute the original call of Isaiah. It was a new designation to introduce more solemnly a general declaration of God's dispensations in regard to his people and the fates of the nations. In a supplementary note to chap. 7, the different views of the Immanuel prophecy are presented. The view adopted sees in it a double bearing and a double fulfilment. It is held to be so worded as to have a further meaning than the obvious and literal, a meaning which was even the original design and principal intention of the prophet, viz., the Messianic one.

The expository portion is worthy of attention on the part of those who aim to understand the Book of Isaiah, but the Homiletic material furnished by Canon Rawlinson's associates in the work, is not of such a character as to advance the real value of the Commentary.

THE EXAMINATION ON LUKE
OF THE AMERICAN INSTITUTE OF SACRED
LITERATURE.

The Time for the Examination on Luke is rapidly approaching and reports from all parts of the world are coming in.

A class of special interest writes from Guntur, India. It is composed of three missionaries, one sub-pastor, one school-mistress, and three Brahmans, one of whom is a school-master, one a writer.

A number of examiners have been added to the list since the last issue of the STUDENT. Their names appear below.

An Interesting Feature of the reports from groups for the examination on Luke is the formation of preparatory classes taught by the special examiners.

Many wide-awake Bible classes have sprung into existence, we hope, to stay. An Institution which aims to promote Bible Study must be ready to adjust its methods to every need, accordingly a plan has been devised for meeting the future want of these new Bible classes and for young peoples' societies, church classes, Christian Associations, and all organizations for Bible study.

This plan is given in detail in a pamphlet issued by the Institute, which will be sent to any one on application.

By this method the most careful and systematic study of the Bible may be pursued under competent leaders, and it will soon become an established fact that an interesting method of work is all that is needed to make Bible study as popular and as thorough as that of any other subject.

SPECIAL EXAMINERS ENROLLED SINCE OCT. 18.

Rev. E. A. Stone, Champaign, Ill.
Rev. J. B. Fleming, Rochelle, Ill.
Rev. R. I. Fleming, Batavia, Ill.
Rev. W. S. Hooper, Mattoon, Ill.
Mr. R. H. Harper, Chicago, Ill.
Mr. W. S. Roney, Terre Haute, Ind.
Rev. J. H. Hackley, Knoxville, Iowa.
Rev. W. F. Matthews, Cottonwood Falls, Kan.
Mr. Joseph F. Fielden, Winchester, Mass.
Rev. Harvey S. Jordan, Lansing, Mich.
Rev. E. R. Pope, Rochester, Minn.
Rev. F. M. Rule, Mankato, Minn.
Mr. A. W. Shaw, Lincoln, Neb.
Mr. H. P. Dewey, Concord, N. H.
Rev. Herbert S. Brown, Lockport, N. Y.
Rev. Arthur Thompson, Warwick, N. Y.

Rev. W. L. Burdett, Adamsville, Ohio.
Mr. C. R. Marsh, Eugene, Oregon.
Rev. C. C. Paling, Lafayette, Oregon.
Rev. Geo. W. Black, Grant's Pass, Oregon.
Mr. C. D. Fay, Portland, Oregon.
Rev. R. S. Jones, Scranton, Pa.
Rev. Chas. Wood, D.D., Germantown, Pa.
Rev. John Barry, Richmond, Ark.
Rev. Chas. Winbigler, Riverside, Cal.
Rev. H. A. Davenport, Bridgeport, Conn.
Rev. Azel W. Hazen, Middletown, Conn.
Rev. G. R. White, Yarmouth, N. S.
Rev. John Scringer, Montreal, Canada.
Rev. C. A. Bowker, Dallas, Oregon.
Rev. Walter Scott, Suffield, Conn.

Current Old Testament Literature.

American and Foreign Publications.

260. *Notes et documents sur la Bible poly-glotte de Paris.* By L. Dorez.

261. *Recherches Bibliques.* By J. Halévy, 10 fasc. Versailles ; imp. Cerf et fils.

262. *Les Livres saints et la critique rationaliste.* Histoire et refutation des objections des incrédules contre les saintes Écritures. By F. Vigouroux. Paris : Roger et Chernoviz.

263. *Das mosaisch-talmudisch Erbrecht.* By M. Block. Budapest. 2—.

264. *Der Richter Simson. Ein historisch-mythologischer Versuch.* By Rich. Sonntag. Duisburg : Ewlch.

265. *L'Héroïne du Cantique de Cantiques.* By Ch. Trillon de la Bigottière. Paris : Palmé.

266. *Der Mensch in Stande der Schuld nach dem Buche Jesaja.* Exegetisch herausgestellt u. zusammenfassend dargelegt. By M. Gerlach. Leipzig : Faber. 3.60.

267. *Atlas géographique de la Bible, d'apres les documents anciens et les meilleures sources francaises, anglaises et allemandes contemporaines.* By C. L. Fillion et H. Nicole. Paris et Lyon : libr. Delhomme et Briguet.

Articles and Reviews.

268. *The Impregnable Rock of Holy Scripture.* By Rt. Hon. W. E. Gladstone, in S. S. Times, Nov. 1, 1890.

269. *Beitrage zur Entstehungsgeschichte des Pentateuchs. I. Der Grundfehler aller heutigen Pentateuchkritik.* By Klostermann, in Neue kirchl. Ztschr. I. g, 1890.

270. *Die Uroffenbarung nach biblischer Lehre u. nach heidnischer Irrlehre. II.* [*Gen. VI.-XI.*] By O. Naumann, in Der Beweis des Glaubens, Aug. 1890.

271. *Die Geschichte Josephs u. die ägyptischen Denkmäler.* By O. Zöckler, in Der Beweis des Glaubens, Aug. 1890.

272. *Cara's Gli Hyksos.* Review by Sayce, in Academy, Sept. 20, 1890.

273. *Rodwell's Mosaic Sacrifices in Lev. 1.-8.* Review by T. Tyler, in Acad., Sept. 20, 1890.

274. *Driver's Samuel.* Review in S. S.

Times, Nov. 8, 1890.

275. *Die Geschichte Davids im Lichte protestantischer Bibelkritik und Geschichtschreibung.* By J. Selbst, in Der Katholik, Juni, Juli, Aug. 1890.

276. *Nehemie et Esdras.—Une nouvelle hypothèse ur la chronologie d l'epoque de la restauration.* By A. Van Hoonacker, in Le Muséon 4, 1890.

277. *Ezra the Scribe.* By Prof. A. B. Hyde, in Meth. Rev., Nov. Dec. 1890.

278. *Gilbert's Poetry of Job.* Review by W. W. Moore, in Pres. Quar., Oct. 1890.

279. *Die Dichtung im Buche Hiob.* By M. Fischer, in Prot. Kirchztg. 30, 1890.

280. *Le Faust de Goethe et le livre de Job.* By M. Aguiléra, in Revue chrétienne, avril, mai 1890.

281. *La littérature des Pauvres dàns la Bible. I. Les Psaumes.* By I. Loeb, in Revue des Études Juives, avril-juin 1890.

282. *Studies in the Psalter. 23. The Thirty-Third Psalm.* By Dr. T. W. Chambers in Hom. Rev. Nov. 1, 1890.

283. *The Prophecy of Amos.* By Prof M. S. Terry, in Meth. Rev., Nov.-Dec., 1890.

284. *Der Gebrauch des Gottesnamens Jehowah Tsebaoth.* By K. Schulz, in Jahrbücher f. prot, Theol. xvi. 3, 1890.

285. *The Figurative Element in Bible Language.* By Canon Farrar, in S. S. Times, Oct. 11, 1890.

286. *Wellhausen's History of Israel.* By R. T. Polk, in Univ. Quar., Oct. 1890.

287. *Sur ce que Tacite dit des Juifs.* By C. Thiancourt, in Revue des Études Juives avril-juin 1890.

288. *Preservation of Sacred Texts before Moses' Day.* By Rev. Prof. H. Osgood, in S. S. Times, Nov. 8, 1890.

289. *Conder's Palestine.* Review in S. S. Times, Oct. 25, 1890.

290. *Critical Note. Not Lachish but Gath.* By Prof. J. A. Paine, in Bib. Sacra, Oct. 1890.

291. *Geology and Sacred Chronology.* By C. W. Gallagher, in Meth. Rev. Nov. Dec. 1890.

192. *De velis Iudaicis.* By Th. Birt, in Rhein. Museum f. Philol. 45, 3, 1890.

293. *Recent Explorations in Egypt.* By J. N. Fradenburgh, in Meth. Rev., Nov.-Dec. 1890.

Current New Testament Literature.

American and Foreign Publications.

294. *Geschichte d. neutestamentlichen Kanons.* By Th. Zahn. 2. Bd. Urkunden u. Belege zum 1. u. 3. Bd. 1. Halfte. Leipzig ; Deichert Nachf. 10.50.

295. *Some Central Points of Our Lord's Ministry.* By Dr. Henry Wace. London. 6s.

296. *Die Lehre Jesu.* 2. Thl. Der Inhalt der Lehre Jesu. By H. H. Wendt. Göttingen: Vandenhoeck and Ruprecht's Verl. 12. —

297. *Beiträge zur Aushellung der Geschichte u. der Briefe d. Apostels Paulus.* By M. Krenkel. Braunschweig, Schwetschke and Sohn. 9. —

298. *The Spiritual Development of St. Paul.* By Rev. George Matheson. Edinburgh: Blackwood. 5s.

299. *Gemeinschaftspflege u. Evangelisation iu ihrem Verhältniss zu einander. — 1. Petri 5. 5—7.* By Koch. Referat erstattet v. H. Neviandt. Bron: Schergens. 20.

300. *Die Offenbarung St. Johannis, f. das Verständnis der Gemeinde ausgelegt.* By E. Kratzenstein. 2 Aufl. Halle : Fricke's Verl. 3. —

Articles and Reviews.

301. *Simcox, Language of the New Testament.* Review in Bib. Sacra, Oct. 1890.

302. *The Leading Problems of New Testament Discussion.* By Prof. G. H. Schodde, in Hom. Rev., Nov. 1890.

303. *Christ and His Miracles.* By F. L. Ferguson, in Pres. Quar. Oct. 1890.

304. *The Miracles of our Lord. 23. The Feeding of the Four Thousand.* By W. J. Deane, in Hom. Mag. Oct. 1890.

305. *La critique et l'histoire dans une vie de Jésus-Christ.* By F. H. Didon, in Revue deu deux mondes Oct. 1, 1890.

306. *Die Unerfindbarkeit des Lebensbildes Jesu.* By Borchert, in Der Beweis des Glaubens, April 1890.

307. *Jésus socialiste : étude exégétique. I. Jésus et le prêt à intérêt.* By P. Minault, in Revue du christianisme pratique III. 17, juillet 1890.

308. *The Humor of our Lord.* By Rev. A. B. Grosart, in The Expos. Times, Nov. 1890.

309. *Zur Kritik der Apostelgeschichte.* By A. Jacobsen, in Ztschr. f. Wiss. Theol. XXXIII. 4, 1890.

310. *All or none? The Epistles of Paul. IV.* By J. M Robertson, in The Scots Magazine, Aug. 1890.

311. *The Epistles of St. Paul in the fires of modern criticism.* By Th. Zahn, [From Luthardt's Zeitschrift für kirchliche Wissenschaft. 1889, Oct. transl, by H. E. Jacobs], in The Lutheran Church Review, July, 1890.

312. *Quelques réflexions sur le thème de l'Epître aux Romains, à propos du commentaire de M. Godet.* By A. Gretillat, in Revue de theol., et de philos., 4, 1890.

313. *2 Cor. vi. 14—vii. 1.* By W. Sanday, in The Classical Review, 8, 1890.

314. *Phil. 3. 13, 14,* By Jehle, in Theol. Studien aus Württemberg, 4, 1889.

315. *Christ Preaching to the Spirits in Prison.* By Rev. T. D. Witherspoon, in Hom. Rev. Nov. 1890.

316. *Oriental myths and Christian parallels.* By F. Layard, in The Scottish Review, July 1890.

GENERAL INDEX

GENERAL INDEX.

Lightning Source UK Ltd.
Milton Keynes UK
UKHW011619160119
335572UK00012B/1053/P